Praise for
The Great Reset

"Marc Morano's *The Great Reset* exposes the well-coordinated effort to crush human freedom under the guise of fighting COVID, climate change, and 'misinformation.' The book takes a deep dive into the global organizations and billionaires who are pushing for a leveling of human freedom under the guise of fighting permanent crises. Morano reveals how climate activists are eager to transition from COVID lockdowns into climate lockdowns and silence anyone who questions them. This book also lays out a vision for freedom-loving citizens to halt this dystopian vision of our future. A must-read for those who want to understand and fight back against rule by unelected 'experts' and bureaucrats."

> **—Mark Levin,** bestselling author and host of *The Mark Levin Show* and *Life, Liberty, and Levin*

"Whether you agree or disagree with Marc Morano, his book is one worth reading. Filled with extensive research, *The Great Reset* includes facts and information you can't find anywhere else. Marc takes a deep dive and unpacks the questions surrounding our economy, the pandemic, and the effort to make a global society no matter the cost."

> **—Sean Hannity,** host of *Hannity* on Fox News and of the nationally syndicated radio program *The Sean Hannity Show*

"We have been sleepwalking into a dystopia. Those who would be our overlords haven't even tried to hide their plans, yet most people have been weirdly quiescent. Marc Morano has written the *Common Sense* of our time. May it, like its eighteenth-century counterpart, awaken a spirit of resistance that overthrows tyrants and changes the world."

> **—Thomas Woods,** *New York Times*–bestselling author and winner of the Hayek Lifetime Achievement Award

"Marc Morano unpacks the lie that the U.S. government and its agencies and globalizing interests are interested in improving the health and welfare of the citizens that they control. He shows that the 'covid' and 'climate change' campaigns are glaring examples of actuating an improper agenda to control us more completely and to deprive us of expression, democratic influence, and resources."

> —**Denis Rancourt,** physicist, former professor and environmental science researcher at the University of Ottawa

"They really are coming to reset us. They want to remake the world in the image of their merciless god of Science. There will be no area of life that will not fall under their god's sway. This sounds absurd—until you read Morano's *Great Reset* book and see that this is what they openly, loudly, and stridently, desire."

> —**William M. Briggs,** statistician, former professor at the Cornell Medical School, and coauthor of *The Price of Panic: How the Tyranny of Experts Turned a Pandemic into a Catastrophe*

"At least when George Orwell wrote about dystopian society, it was fiction. But as Marc Morano makes clear in his brilliantly detailed *Great Reset*, there are those working actively today to bring about a real world where only the select few rule at the top and the rest exist to serve. Read Marc Morano's *The Great Reset* to see the full breathtaking scope of the Left's global battlefield so as to fight effectively for individual rights and, hopefully, win."

> —**Cheryl Chumley,** online opinion editor at the *Washington Times* and bestselling author of *Lockdown: The Socialist Plan to Take Away Your Freedom*

"Across the wide world, Marc Morano knows more than anyone the plans of the powerful who subscribe to the globalist and climate cults. The reader learns of a dystopian coup in the making before it turns from a forbidden conspiracy theory into an irreversible system combining the evils of old communism (into which I was born), can-cel culture, and Covid-type lockdowns. This transformation can be prevented if enough readers become familiar with the key scientific facts as well as the pseudo-scientific hysterical attack on them and on prosperity and freedom."

> **—Luboš Motl,** physicist and former faculty member at Harvard University

"Morano exposes how the Davos crowd wants to impose perma-nent lockdowns on the unwashed masses—that's you and me—and how they are maneuvering to transition COVID lockdowns into cli-mate lockdowns. Morano reveals how doctors are now diagnosing patients with 'climate change' and adding 'climate change' as a cause of death on death certificates. This book will be your go-to source on how the global agenda is not about controlling viruses or the climate but about controlling you. Help keep George Orwell fiction, read this book and fight back!"

> **—James Delingpole,** host of the legendary *Delingpod* pod-cast and author of *Watermelons: How Environmentalists Are Killing the Planet, Destroying the Economy and Stealing Your Children's Future*

"For years Marc Morano has been my 'go-to' source when I want information that counters the politicized science of 'climate change.' In his new book, he shows us how bureaucrats and elites are impos-ing their worldview without our permission and even knowledge. It's another warning sign that if we don't fight back against this subtle evil we will be forced to submit to it."

> **—Cal Thomas,** nationally syndicated columnist

THE GREAT RESET

THE GREAT RESET

Global Elites and the Permanent Lockdown

MARC MORANO

To Susan & Stanford,

[signature]

Regnery Publishing
WASHINGTON, D.C.

Regnery® is a registered trademark and its colophon is a trademark of Salem Communications Holding Corporation

Cataloging-in-Publication data on file with the Library of Congress

ISBN: 978-1-68451-238-6
eISBN: 978-1-68451-276-8

Library of Congress Control Number: 2022941097

Published in the United States by
Regnery Publishing,
A Division of Salem Media Group
Washington, D.C.
www.Regnery.com

Manufactured in the United States of America

10 9 8 7 6 5 4 3 2 1

Books are available in quantity for promotional or premium use. For information on discounts and terms, please visit our website: www.Regnery.com.

This book is dedicated to those who refused to comply and asserted their universal human yearning for freedom from government oppression. Kudos to the parent resistance that welled up in local school districts against mask mandates, to the mass resistance to lockdowns, to the rejection of censorship, to the open defiance of vaccine passports, and to those who refused to acquiesce to the "new normal" being imposed upon the world without the consent of the governed.

CONTENTS

You walk into this room at your own risk because it leads to the future, not a future that will be but one that might be. This is not a new world, it is simply an extension of what began in the old one. It has patterned itself after every dictator who has ever planted the ripping imprint of a boot on the pages of history since the beginning of time. It has refinements, technological advances, and a more sophisticated approach to the destruction of human freedom. But like every one of the super-states that preceded it, it has one iron rule: logic is an enemy and truth is a menace.

—Rod Serling, *The Twilight Zone*

Foreword by Sebastian Gorka

I can remember it now. It was a chilly November night. I was nineteen years old. And my parents and I watched the old-school cathode-ray tube TV transfixed. We were watching the fall of the Iron Curtain. Live.

"Fall" is not the right word, however. The wall that had been built by the brutal East German Communist regime to keep its "citizens" from escaping to freedom didn't collapse in some passive sense like a rotten, punked-out tree in a humid bayou swamp. It was being dismantled piece by piece by the captive people of East Berlin. Using hand tools.

November 9, 1989, was all the more significant for our family given that my parents were living in exile, political refugees from Communism themselves. My father had been liberated from a political prison where he was serving a life sentence for resisting the Hungarian dictatorship as a young Christian university student. My mother, the daughter of another political prisoner, was seventeen years old when she escaped to the West, holding the hand of my father, her future husband, as they crossed the minefield into neutral Austria, as Soviet troops were crushing the Hungarian Revolution back in Budapest.

They had made a new life in England, where I was born and raised, and they were convinced that they would die in exile, with their family members still trapped behind the Iron Curtain. And here we were watching formerly enslaved people liberate themselves as the border guard troops of an ossified and utterly morally bankrupt regime just watched in stupefaction.

To give credit where credit is due, it was actually the Hungarians who had inflicted the first chink in the armor of the Communist system and the Warsaw Pact. Two months earlier, the "reform" Communist regime in Budapest had allowed East German tourists to leave Hungary into Austria, without the acquiescence of Honecker's Communist government in East Berlin. The mass exodus of funny little Trabant cars from East to West was the beginning of the end for Karl Marx's "workers' paradise." In the months and years to come, barbed-wire border regimes would be cut, the Berlin Wall would be breached, and free elections would be held in state after state until, finally, on Christmas Day 1991, the Soviet Union, which had enslaved millions and murdered millions, dissolved itself, and the Cold War was won. It was the greatest Christmas gift the Gorka family had ever received.

But did we actually win?

Recent events have sadly reaffirmed that the spirit of Marx is less of a ghost and more of an implacable and insatiable zombie that simply will not stop in its genocidal mission.

There are, of course, the remaining Communist regimes. From Cuba, to North Korea, to China with its forced-labor camps, state-sanctioned organ harvesting, and COVID "research" facilities, more than one and a half billion souls live under a red flag, trapped by a truly demonic ideology that has taken the lives of more than 100 million human beings since the Winter Palace was stormed in 1917. Communism is very much still alive for those living in these prison states. Then there is what we should call the "new Communism," or what my wife and muse, Katie Gorka, has labelled the "Next-Gen Marxists."

The end of the Cold War should have assigned Socialism to the "ash heap of history" in the West. Instead it has transmogrified and metastasized. Thanks to the invidious influence of Foucault's apostles, the Frankfurt School, the New Left, the Alinsky-ites, and the likes of Zinn, Chomsky, and Moore, the ideas of Marx are more popular in the West than they ever have been before. How is this possible? Well the answer to that question is lengthy and multifaceted, deserving of its own book. (Please don't tell our publisher, Regnery, I said that!) But one critical element of that answer is the core of the book you are now holding, and that is the repackaging and cloaking of Marxist ideology using the politically correct terms "social justice," "equity," "diversity," and "inclusivity." All this done in the service of a "Great Reset" driven by an unelected elite of billionaires and pseudo-experts.

I will forever owe a debt of gratitude to Marc Morano for his service in providing me the intellectual ammunition to puncture the propaganda of the Climate Change extremists. I had grown up listening to one after another of the catastrophic Cassandras lecturing free people on the coming Ice Age, neo-Malthusian overpopulation, Ozone Depletion, Acid Rain, and "Climate Change," but it was Marc's seminal book *The Politically Incorrect Guide to Climate Change* that became my intellectual armory of actual science and real data on how carbon dioxide is not a pollutant but actually the fuel for life and how the world is NOT going to end in twelve years (sorry AOC, it's not).

But the old watermelon of environmentalist cultism—green on the outside, deep Commie red on the inside—is old news. With the rise of anti-democratic institutions like the World Economic Forum and the radical activism of unaccountable billionaires like Bill Gates and George Soros, allied to the insatiable greed for power of COVID lockdown–drunk politicians, we are facing a new Devil's brew, a concatenation of forces who want to control all aspects of your life, from what you are allowed to eat, to what mode of transport you are allowed to use, and even the words you are permitted to utter. The Great Reset is real. The Great Reset is the greatest threat to your liberty since that wall fell over thirty years ago. You need to understand what its propagators intend for you and your family, and you need to get engaged and stop them. Now read on!

Sebastian Gorka, Ph.D.

host of America First and former Strategist to the President

CHAPTER 1

The Great Reset

What is the Great Reset? A true dystopian nightmare where every aspect of your existence is observed and regulated by unseen bureaucrats—all for your own good. The Great Reset is the long-planned reorganization of the world imposed by technocratic global elites.

With COVID-19, the Great Reset is becoming a reality.

The World Economic Forum (WEF) has called for "a Great Reset of capitalism" in response to COVID—and to help fight climate change. The World Economic Forum is very blunt about its utopian Great Reset vision.

"The pandemic represents a rare but narrow window of opportunity to reflect, reimagine, and reset our world to create a healthier, more equitable, and more prosperous future," WEF founding chairman Klaus Schwab wrote in June 2020. "Populations have overwhelmingly shown a willingness to make sacrifices."

"The changes we have already seen in response to COVID-19 prove that a reset of our economic and social foundations is possible.... The world must act jointly and swiftly to revamp all aspects of our societies and economies, from education to social contracts and working conditions," Schwab explained. "Every country, from the United States to China, must participate, and every industry, from oil and gas to tech, must be transformed. In short, we need a 'Great Reset' of capitalism."[1]

Maurice Newman, a former advisor to Australian prime minister Tony Abbott, explained what this really means: "Stripped of the propaganda, the Great Reset is not new. It's another fascist experiment being pushed by controlling elitists. Economic growth and social mobility must be subordinate to the collective.... Think inequality, serfdom and misery."[2]

The unprecedented suspension of liberties in response to the COVID-19 pandemic has emboldened the forces behind the Great Reset to achieve their centrally planned vision: monitoring, planning, censoring, crushing dissent, controlling the lives of the masses for our "safety"—all in the name of "The Science." The very real threat of oppressive rule by unelected experts in government is now threatening to engulf the world in the wake of the COVID lockdowns, "phased re-openings," vaccine passports, contact tracing, mask mandates, capacity limits, bans on church services and social gatherings, stay-at-home orders, and travel restrictions. Citizens of once-free Western democracies faced limits on where and when they could go out—subject to the whims of government bureaucrats. These drastic limits on our liberties were put in place largely without legislative votes or public hearings. In addition, climate-inspired energy regulations, massive government spending, supply chain issues, food shortages, debt, out-of-control crime in major cities, spiraling inflation, wars, and economic "degrowth" all helped create the perfect pandemonium to empower the forces of the Great Reset.

"You'll own nothing. And you'll be happy." That is the utopian vision of the WEF and its founder Klaus Schwab. "Whatever you want you'll rent and it'll be delivered by drone." Meat will be "an occasional treat," the WEF prognosticated in a 2016 video (which has since been deleted from their website).[3]

The WEF chose the year 2030 as the date by which their vision will be imposed on the world. "Welcome to 2030. I own nothing, have no privacy, and life has never been better," said a 2017 tweet from the WEF.

Stills captured from "8 Predictions for the World in 2030," a 2016 World Economic Forum video, which has been removed from the WEF website. *Rebel News*[4]

World Economic Forum ✔ @wef · Nov 10, 2017   ...
Welcome to 2030. I own nothing, have no privacy, and life has never been better wef.ch/2yP0008 #gfc17

💬 104   🔁 389   ❤️ 166   ⬆️

Tweet from the World Economic Forum. *Screenshot by the author*[5]

"Flu d'État"

COVID-19 gave the world a chance to see the never-let-a-crisis-go-to-waste strategy in action.

As healthcare journalist Peter Barry Chowka observed at the American Thinker, "There's been what I've called a flu d'état—a takeover of our supposedly democratic political process by unelected and unaccountable administrative state medical bureaucrats who are deeply and permanently

"I'm Selfish?"

"You force others to inject themselves with dangerous substances
so YOU can feel safe.

"You force others to cover their
source of oxygen for months so
YOU can feel safe.

"You force others to lose their
jobs and retirements so YOU can
feel safe.

"You force others to stay home
so YOU can feel safe."

—meme circulating the internet
in 2020[7]

embedded in the system of modern medicine—a collection of businesses that now consumes about twenty percent of the Gross National Product."[6]

According to Chowka, "Overnight, our society is doing what radical leftist Rep. Alexandria Ocasio-Cortez (D-NY) and her fellow Green New Deal fanatics have demanded: An almost total end to air travel; personal automobile travel down to a trickle; promises of free health care for all quickly becoming the new status quo; and the ability of people to sit at home without working and receive a paycheck from the government. The Democrats want that to continue indefinitely."

COVID-19 "is being politically weaponized, including as part of a much larger agenda that fast tracks a global system of surveillance, medical mandates, and control," Chowka added. "Will the Covid-19 PsyOp succeed?" he asked.

American life was transformed after COVID came on the scene. Citizens of America and other countries across the globe were suddenly told they had to stay at home. The public health bureaucracies mandated that people could leave their homes only for approved "essential services," and Americans saw the imposition of government curfews. We were banned from attending weddings and funerals and barred from hosting backyard barbeques. If you dared rebel, your neighbors—in a practice borrowed from the now defunct Eastern European communist nations—could snitch on you to the government, and they would get rewarded, while you could have public utilities like water and electricity cut off for your disobedience.[8]

A Dystopian Future

"The year is 2043. Covid variant phi beta epsilon is ravaging 0.0026% of the population, you go outside for your government mandated 30 minute exercise, it's 1 a.m. not the best time, but they alternate your schedule so eventually everyone does get some sunlight. You quadruple mask and put on your plastic helmet. You gaze longingly at the sky. A man riding his bicycle points his flashlight at you 'Why aren't you doing your stretches and cardio?' He asks, you recognize him as your neighbor (maybe, it's been some time since you last saw anyone). 'It's because of people like you not obeying that the lockdowns have been extended another 4 years.' He mumbles through his layers of masks. He reports you to Alphabet-Google and your social credit score drops 5 points, good luck buying bread this week." —internet meme circulating in 2021[9]

Children were confined to their homes as schools closed around the globe. If you were allowed out of your house at all, you had the mask yourself. (Double, triple, and even quadruple masks were recommended as "safety first" became the motto.) Masking was mandatory, even outdoors at parks. Governments, allegedly concerned with our health, closed jogging trails and gyms, and even kids were told to stay inside to avoid virus exposure. The medical health bureaucracies mandated everyone stay at home, where people were reduced to staring at screens, ordering fast-food takeout, and isolating themselves. They had to defer medical appointments indefinitely and stay out of the sunshine. Thus "two weeks to flatten the curve" turned into a new dystopian normal.[10]

The forces pushing the Great Reset were ecstatic at the transformation of the world, as long-held rights vanished overnight.

Even in the most open democracies, citizens saw:

- Everyone stripped of their basic civil rights
- Trillions of dollars' worth of wealth transferred from the poor and middle class to the ruling class

- Small businesses decimated as woke corporate chains thrived
- International travel and domestic travel stopped or severely restricted
- Extreme pressure to get jabbed for COVID, including a push for vaccine "passports"
- Citizens conditioned to systematic dehumanization and depersonalization as part of a massive psyop that instilled viral fears on an unprecedented level
- Societies repressed for months on end, causing a pent-up rage that fueled mass riots
- Climate campaigners seeking to expand the "global warming" agenda that—not surprisingly—features more of everything else on this list

"They want to dictate it, control, regulate, mastermind from above." That's how former Czech Republic president Václav Klaus described the climate agenda. "It's just the quantitative increasing of all the ways of how to block free human activity."[11] That's exactly what the authorities were able to achieve with the COVID-19 lockdowns—and now the technocrats want to impose a permanent version.

Conveniently, all of these impositions and impacts were straight out of the playbook of the Great Reset agenda. Well before the pandemic came along, the Great Reset already included the goals of global governance, carbon taxes, empowering unelected bureaucrats, and heavy regulations on nearly every aspect of human endeavor. The virus provided the perfect opportunity to accelerate the transition of Western democracies toward something much more like a Chinese-style one-party state, with unelected public health officials acting as the new authoritarians. With COVID-19 the public could be kept in fear, and that fear could enable the public health bureaucracy to exert the kind of control elites and government experts have sought for decades—a kind of control far more extreme than anything that had previously been implemented to solve the alleged climate "emergency."

On March 23, 2020, President Donald Trump explained in all caps on Twitter, "WE CANNOT LET THE CURE BE WORSE THAN THE PROBLEM ITSELF. AT THE END OF THE 15 DAY PERIOD, WE WILL MAKE A DECISION AS TO WHICH WAY WE WANT TO GO!"[12]

The "15 days to slow the spread" morphed into endless days, and the "cure" was far "worse than the problem itself." The "15 days to flatten the curve" saw a collapse of global freedoms. Democrat governors and the unelected health bureaucracy were emboldened to commandeer the Constitution and impose a medical tyranny, all on the model of the Chinese Communist Party's lockdown.

A more accurate slogan would have been "15 days to begin your conditioning to accept a new level of tyranny."

The U.S. and global economies ground to a standstill. America was transformed, seemingly overnight, by one of the most liberty-robbing policies ever instituted. The "two weeks" to flatten the curve of the virus ended up flattening America's Constitution, freedoms, common sense, science, and public health. To justify all of this, the science was bastard-ized, and unelected public health bureaucrats were endowed with dictator-like powers virtually overnight in what had been free nations.

The level of authoritarian control imposed on once-free societies was staggering. But the media and the medical-health bureaucracy praised the lockdowns, despite the destroyed livelihoods, economic ruin, delayed cancer treatments, and higher drug-addiction and suicide rates. Politicians told us, "We're all in this together," but in reality they—along with government bureaucrats, media cheerleaders, and academics—all got their full salaries during the lockdowns while "inessential" blue-collar workers were laid off. Amazon had record profits, while mom-and-pop shops went out of business. We were NOT "all in this together."

Dr. Vinay Prasad, a hematologist-oncologist and associate professor of medicine at the University of California San Francisco, declared these public health measures a total failure. "When the history books are written about the use of non-pharmacologic measures during this pandemic, we will look as pre-historic and barbaric and tribal as our ancestors during

> **"Torment Us without End"**
> "Of all tyrannies a tyranny sincerely exercised for the good of its victims may be the most oppressive. It may be better to live under robber barons than under omnipotent moral busybodies. The robber baron's cruelty may sometimes sleep, his cupidity may at some point be satiated; but those who torment us for our own good will torment us without end for they do so with the approval of their own conscience." —C. S. Lewis[14]

the plagues of the middle ages," Prasad wrote.[13]

"The WEF envisions a future where we the people own nothing, and we all live in a 'citizen-centered welfare state' while governments and 'stakeholders' own and control the means of production," technology journalist Tim Hinchliffe explained on The Sociable in 2020.

"The Great Reset agenda calls for a complete restructuring of society under a new form of stakeholder capitalism, where ownership is obsolete and privacy is non-existent thanks to invasive technologies coming out of the Fourth Industrial Revolution that will lead us to, in [WEF chairman Klaus] Schwab's words, 'a fusion of our physical, our digital, and our biological identities,'" according to Hinchliffe.[15]

In 2016 the WEF website summed up the organization's vision of the year 2030:

> Welcome to the year 2030. Welcome to my city—or should I say, "our city." I don't own anything. I don't own a car. I don't own a house. I don't own any appliances or any clothes.
> It might seem odd to you, but it makes perfect sense for us in this city. Everything you considered a product, has now become a service. We have access to transportation, accommodation, food and all the things we need in our daily lives. One by one all these things became free, so it ended up not making sense for us to own much....
> Once in a while I get annoyed about the fact that I have no real privacy. Nowhere I can go and not be registered. I

know that, somewhere, everything I do, think and dream of is recorded. I just hope that nobody will use it against me.[16]

"There isn't much talk of freedom in the WEF's great reset discussions," Hinchliffe pointed out. "Instead, they offer a utopia of more equity, inclusivity, and prosperity by sacrificing personal ownership, privacy, and liberty—the very foundations of constitutional republics."[17]

As German economics professor Antony P. Mueller explained in 2020, "The lockdown and its consequences have brought a foretaste of what is to come: a permanent state of fear, strict behavioral control, massive loss of jobs, and growing dependence on the state."

According to Mueller, "This coming technocracy involves close cooperation between the heads of the digital industry and of governments. With programs such as guaranteed minimum income and healthcare for all, the new kind of governance combines strict societal control with the promise of comprehensive social justice."

Mueller detailed, "Earlier totalitarian regimes needed mass executions and concentration camps to maintain their power. Now, with the help of new technologies, it is believed, dissenters can easily be identified and marginalized. The nonconformists

"Weapons of Obedience"

"Many people argue that this pandemic . . . was planned from the outset, that it's part of a sinister scheme. I can't tell you the answer to that. I don't have enough evidence," Robert F. Kennedy Jr. said during a speech at an anti-lockdown protest in Berlin in 2020. Kennedy is the chair of the Children's Health Defense, a nonprofit concerned with the effects of lockdowns, mask mandates and vaccinations.

"I will tell you this, if you create these mechanisms for control, they become weapons of obedience for authoritarian regimes no matter how beneficial or innocent the people who created them," Kennedy said.

"Once you create them, they will be abused. A hundred percent guarantee that they will be abused," he added.[18]

will be silenced by disqualifying divergent opinions as morally despicable."

He added, "Under the order envisioned by the Great Reset, the advancement of technology is not meant to serve the improvement of the conditions of the people but to submit the individual to the tyranny of a technocratic state. 'The experts know better' is the justification."[19]

According to Chapman University professor Joel Kotkin, author of *The Coming of Neo-Feudalism*, "America's elite has adopted the fascist dream of a corporate oligarchy" that was espoused by Italy's former dictator Benito Mussolini.

"Indeed, Mussolini's idea of an economy controlled from above, with generous benefits but dominated by large business interests, is gradually supplanting the old liberal capitalist model. In the West, for example, the 'Great Reset,' introduced by the World Economic Forum's Klaus Schwab, proposes an expanded welfare state and an economy that transcends the market for the greater goal of serving racial and gender 'equity,' as well as saving the planet," Kotkin wrote.

"Even today, China, in many aspects the model fascist state of our times, follows Il Duce's model of cementing the corporate elite into the power structure. Since 2000, a hundred billionaires sit in the country's Communist legislation, a development that Mao would never have countenanced," according to Kotkin.

"Today's oligarchs are particularly keen on the progressive non-profit sector, which provides important support for their political and social advocacy—a means for them to make politically correct statements about climate change, gender and race, while still obtaining enormous profit margins and unprecedented wealth," Kotkin noted. "A handful of giant tech corporations now account for nearly 40% of the value of the Standard and Poor Index, a level of concentration unprecedented in modern history."[20]

"The tech oligarchs are creating something similar to what Aldous Huxley called in *Brave New World Revisited* a 'scientific caste system.' There is 'no good reason,' Huxley wrote in the 1958, that 'a thoroughly scientific dictatorship should ever be overthrown.' It will condition its subjects from the womb so that they 'grow up to love their servitude' and 'never dream of revolution,'" Kotkin noted.[21]

Huxley's chilling speech to the California Media School in 1961 prefigured today's headlines:

> There will be, in the next generation or so, a pharmacological method of making people love their servitude, and producing dictatorship without tears, so to speak, producing a kind of painless concentration camp for entire societies, so that people will in fact have their liberties taken away from them, but will rather enjoy it, because they will be distracted from any desire to rebel by propaganda or brainwashing, or brainwashing enhanced by pharmacological methods. And this seems to be the final revolution.[22]

Kotkin points out how prescient Huxley was: "The fusion of government with large oligopolistic companies, and the technologically-enhanced collection of private information, allow the new autocracies to monitor our lives in ways that Mao, Stalin or Hitler would have envied."[23]

Kotkin added: "And these woke oligarchs, like their fascist counterparts before them, see little use for democracy.[24]

> **"Imposing Authoritarian Government"**
>
> "This grand social experiment in locking up healthy people is a test run for impositng authoritarian government, and it won't end well. People will push back—because *they have to.*" —author Michael Fumento on the COVID-19 lockdowns[25]

"Abuse of Emergency Powers"

In 2021 the BBC featured an analysis examining "when governments abuse emergency powers." Luke Kemp, a research associate at the Centre for the Study of Existential Risk at the University of Cambridge, observed how "history shows that during times of crisis, politicians tend to reach for more power."

"The Roman dictator was one of the earliest and most famous examples of state-sanctioned emergency powers.... Emergency powers have come a long way since Rome. They have become global and regular," Kemp wrote. He further explained:

> The entire Third Reich occurred during a state of emergency that lasted 12 years. It began in 1933 after Hitler invoked Article 48 of the Weimar Republic, allowing for the use of emergency decrees without parliamentary approval.
>   Such a despotic drift is not uncommon. The abuse of emergency powers also marked the descent from Republic to Empire in Rome, the centralisation of political power in the Middle Ages, and the entrenchment of previously oppressive regimes in countries such as Chile and apartheid South Africa.[26]

"The 2001 USA Patriot Act allowed the US Congress itself to expand surveillance powers," Kemp wrote. "Emergency powers tend to only go one way: top-down. During an emergency, the knee-jerk reaction is always to stomp-down, to reinforce those atop hierarchies in the state and significantly curtail the freedoms, voice and agency of citizens, often in a draconian fashion."[27]

Today's politicians have used the coronavirus, terrorism, climate change, "misinformation," "gun violence," and so forth to justify government "emergency" declarations. Many government leaders pounced on the declared COVID emergency and became virtual dictators overnight.

In 2022 the Department of Homeland Security even issued a "National Terrorism Advisory System Bulletin" warning that anyone who "undermine[s] public trust in government institutions" is now considered a terrorist threat.[28]

Attorney Michael P. Senger, author of "China's Global Lockdown Propaganda Campaign," pointed out, "As a rule of thumb, if you find yourself supporting a two year state of emergency, censorship, suspension of the rights of broad swathes of the population, and permanent changes to the way human beings interact, you're probably on the wrong side of history."[29]

Justin Haskins, the director of the Heartland Institute's Stopping Socialism Project, summed up the Great Reset this way: "In June 2020, the World Economic Forum—working alongside officials from large corporations, banks, financial institutions and activist groups—launched a far-reaching initiative that aims to push the 'reset' button on the global economy. They ominously called it the 'Great Reset,' and since its creation, it has received a massive amount of support from leaders of the ruling class, both here in the United States and around the world."[30]

Dr. Anne McCloskey, a practicing physician who also works with the Ireland-based Freedom Alliance, published an editorial in the *British Medical Journal* complaining about the article "Covid-19: Social Murder, They Wrote—Elected, Unaccountable, and Unrepentant."[31] She also pointed out, in a video detailing what had happened to the world under the lockdowns, "Viruses don't make laws, governments do."

"Across the world," McCloskey said, "there are millions of people who are awakening to the understanding that this current health crisis, this so-called pandemic, is a Trojan horse, which has been used to

"Voiceless Submissives"

"In the name of Covid, the State has already thrust itself into every corner of our existence. It has come between husbands and wives at the ends of their lives. It has forbidden the old to embrace their grandchildren. It has denied us funerals and weddings, locked the churches, silenced the ancient monastic music of cathedral choirs and prevented the free worship of God for the first time in 800 years, and banned us (unless we are Left-wing) from holding or attending public meetings. It has ordered us to stay at home, scolded or fined us for sunbathing, going on country rambles or even entering our front gardens." –Peter Hitchens, "Face Masks Turn Us into Voiceless Submissives—and It's Not Science Forcing Us to Wear Them, It's Politics."[32]

introduce a new era for humanity—the Great Reset, the Fourth Industrial Revolution, Building Back Better—whatever catchy, chirpy name the bankers and billionaires are calling it, it's not good for you and me, for the ordinary people."

The Real Coup

"In less than 12 months they closed our businesses, forced us to wear muzzles, kept us from our families, killed off our sports, burned down our cities, forcibly seized power, and shut down our speech. Then they accused *us* of the coup." –Raheem Kassam, former chief advisor to UK Independence Party (UKIP) leader Nigel Farage[33]

According to McCloskey, "Relationships between individuals, families, communities, governments, and nations will change fundamentally. They're coming for you, your family, your job, your savings, your home, your pension, your culture, your traditions, your freedom, your very way of life—unless we unite to resist. We do not consent. This is not a conspiracy theory but the outworking of a scheme written by people who hate the human race. Agenda 21 has been implemented now and will come to pass unless we unite to resist." McCloskey continued by describing the measures already experienced:

> What we did see…was removal of our most basic and inalienable rights to work, to air, to move, to associate, to kiss, to hug, to go to church, to bury our dead with dignity, to live our lives as we see fit. We saw the removal of our right to speak, to protest, to object to this tyranny. We saw censorship, character assassination, and banishment of scientists and professors who dared to offer an alternative narrative. We saw our children and young people locked up, denied their education, the right to play outside, to live their precious young lives however they and their parents saw fit. We've seen millions of the poorest and most marginalized people on the

planet pushed to starvation and death because of the economic fallout, because poverty kills. I've worked as a GP
[general practitioner] throughout this past year and I've not
seen people gasping for breath from COVID, but people
utterly abandoned by their health system. People in despair
from loneliness, from isolation, from fear—people who
haven't seen their families and loved ones for months and
whose lives are infinitely poorer as a result. I've seen delayed
cancer diagnoses, people having treatments canceled just
willy-nilly, people dying waiting for elective procedures,
people in pain who can't get help.

McCloskey concluded, "If we take away the psychological abuse
of populations across this planet, using applied behavioral psychology designed to keep them in terror; if we take away the signage, the
arrows, the one-way systems, 'walk,' 'don't walk,' the yellow notices
on every flat surface, the sanitization, the masks, all the parapher-
nalia of this neuro-linguistic program and mental abuse, which tells
us that we are the biohazards, we are a danger to our families and

---

"Health Dictatorship"

"The purpose of the Great Reset is the imposition of a health dictatorship
aiming at the imposition of liberticidal measures, hidden behind tempting
promises of ensuring a universal income and cancelling individual debt.
The price of these concessions from the International Monetary Fund
will be the renunciation of private property. . . . Beyond the enormous
economic interests that motivate the promoters of the Great Reset, the
imposition of the vaccination will be accompanied by the requirement of
a health passport and a digital ID, with the consequent contact tracing
of the population of the entire world." —Archbishop Carlo Maria Viganò,
former apostolic nuncio to the United States, in an open letter to President
Trump in 2020[34]

friends; if we take all this away, there is nothing to see—the emperor has no clothes."[35]

As citizens suffered, politicians, government leaders, and the ruling classes saw nothing but the promise of a brighter future—for expanding, massive, government control.

"One of the Least Deadly Pandemics in the Last 2000 Years"

In their 2020 book *COVID-19: The Great Reset*, WEF founder Klaus Schwab and Thierry Malleret actually admit that the virus was not the threat many claimed. In fact, they go so far as to call it "one of the least deadly pandemics...over the last 2000 years" and state openly:

> There is no denying that the COVID-19 virus has more often than not been a personal catastrophe for the millions affected by it, and for their families and communities. However, at a global level, if viewed in terms of the percentage of the global population affected, the corona crisis is (so far) one of the least deadly pandemics the world has experienced over the last 2000 years. In all likelihood, unless the pandemic evolves in an unforeseen way, the consequences of COVID-19 in terms of health and mortality will be mild compared to previous pandemics. At the end of June 2020...COVID-19 has killed less than 0.006% of the world population. To put this low figure into context in terms of lethality, the Spanish flu killed 2.7% of the world's population and HIV/AIDS 0.6%.[36]

Left unexplained by Schwab and Malleret is how this reality never quite made it to the public health bureaucracies, academia, the media, and our government officials.

But one Dutch politician, Thierry Baudet, got it. Baudet, a member of the House of Representatives of the Netherlands, gave perhaps the best summation during a speech on what he termed the "collective psychosis" of the COVID-19 mandates.

"I hope that there will be a moment that we wake up, that we realize this is a collective psychosis. That locking down the entire country, half of the world for 1.5 years because of a flu variety is insane. That walking around with those silly, useless masks is insanity. That we conform ourselves to these completely senseless distancing rules. That we see that our businesses, our social lives have been destroyed," Baudet said during a speech to the House.

"I hope that we realize that with the hysteria about this Chinese flu as the pretext, an entire infrastructure has been built. An infrastructure that can be used again at any moment due to any occurrence. Lockdowns, mass social distancing, no more traveling, no handshakes, ridiculous experimental jabs," Baudet continued.

"The COVID phase has been a practice to train obedience. Our parliament and the [Dutch prime minister Mark] Rutte regime have passed this training with grace. Congratulations, Klaus Schwab will be proud of you. The globalist plans can be carried out and the next step towards mass surveillance and total control can be taken," he concluded.[37]

"Exaggerating the Risks"

"In March [2020], governors and health officials took our freedom by exaggerating the risks of #SarsCov2. Now they want to trade it back for masks and contact tracing and made-up rules. No. Never."—former *New York Times* reporter Alex Berenson, author of *Pandemia: How Coronavirus Hysteria Took Over Our Government, Rights, and Lives*[38]

"Re-Imagine Economic Systems"

But most world leaders followed the WEF-WHO-CDC-China–COVID-lockdown Reset narrative. "This pandemic has provided an opportunity for a Reset. This is our chance to accelerate our pre-pandemic efforts to re-imagine economic systems that actually address global challenges like extreme poverty, inequality, and climate change," Canadian prime minister Justin Trudeau said at a September 2020 UN conference.[39]

Trudeau appeared eager to embrace the radical transformation that Schwab had outlined in *COVID-19: The Great Reset*.[40] Trudeau is a product of Schwab's Forum of Young Global Leaders.[41]

"Radical changes of such consequence are coming that some pundits have referred to a 'before coronavirus' (BC) and 'after coronavirus' (AC) era. We will continue to be surprised by both the rapidity and unexpected nature of these changes—as they conflate with each other, they will provoke second-, third-, fourth- and more-order consequences, cascading effects and unforeseen outcomes," the Canadian prime minister said.[42]

For Trudeau, governing by emergency declaration was the realization of his years-long jealousy of Communist China's one-party state. "There is a level of admiration I actually have for China because, you know, their basic dictatorship is allowing them to actually turn their economy around on a dime and say we need to go green...we need to start, you know, investing in solar," Trudeau revealed in 2013. "There is a flexibility that I know [Prime Minister] Stephen Harper must dream about: having a dictatorship that he could do everything he wanted."[43]

President Biden also found governing with expanded government powers interesting. "We're at an inflection point, I believe, in the world economy, not just the world economy, the world, that occurs

> ### "Globally Coordinated Assaults on Liberty"
> "Build Back Better is the code phrase for one of the most terrifying and dangerous, globally co-ordinated assaults on liberty and prosperity in the history of mankind.... Build Back Better means totalitarian rule by a global, technocratic elite—as constrictive and immiserating as life under fascism or communism. This hideous New World Order is the Great Reset. It sounds like a conspiracy theory but the people behind it are perfectly open about it."—Breitbart columnist James Delingpole[44]

every three or four generations," Biden said. "Now is the time when things are shifting and there's going to be a New World Order out there."[45]

President Joe Biden's climate envoy John Kerry was also on board. "Yes, [the Great Reset] will happen. And I think it will happen with greater speed and with greater intensity than a lot of people might imagine," former secretary of state Kerry said in December of 2020.[46]

"The recovery from the coronavirus crisis represents an opportunity to reset the global economy and prioritize sustainable development without further damaging the planet, Prince Charles said at the opening of a World Economic Forum (WEF) virtual meeting," reported *The Guardian* in June 2020. "We have a unique but rapidly shrinking window of opportunity to learn lessons and reset ourselves on a more sustainable path," the Prince of Wales opined.[47]

The World Economic Forum, the driving force behind the Great Reset, was waiting for just the right opportunity to see their vision become reality. In *COVID-19: The Great Reset*, "Schwab and Malleret place Covid-19 in a long tradition of events which have facilitated sudden and significant changes to our societies," noted Paul Cudenec, who works on the No Deal For Nature campaign opposing attempts by the WEF to financialize nature on a global scale.

"Obsessive Fanatics"

"There are few more obsessive fanatics than the technocrat who is convinced that he is reordering an imperfect world for its own good."—former UK Supreme Court judge Jonathan Sumption[48]

"They also join many contemporary 'conspiracy theorists' in making a direct comparison between Covid-19 and 9/11," Cudenec explained, pointing to this passage from Schwab and Malleret's *Great Reset* book:

This is what happened after the terrorist attacks of 11 September 2001. All around the world, new security measures like employing widespread cameras, requiring electronic ID cards and logging employees or visitors in and out became the norm. At that time, these measures were deemed extreme, but today they are used everywhere and considered "normal."[49]

"The Greatest Threats to Liberty"

"Over the past two centuries, the greatest threats to liberty have come from governments, both foreign and domestic. And from the beaches of Normandy to the civil rights movement of the 1960s, Americans have repeatedly conquered the challenges placed before them by those seeking to extinguish or limit individual rights.

"However, over the past few years, a new, potentially catastrophic danger has emerged, but not primarily from the halls of Congress or state capitols. This threat to freedom has largely emanated from the boardrooms of the world's wealthiest, most powerful corporations, large financial institutions, central banks, and international organizations like the United Nations and World Economic Forum." —talk show host Glenn Beck's sample 2021 "Letter to Congress" for concerned Americans to send to their representatives[50]

Justin Haskins of the Heartland Institute explained how the Reset is structured. "The Great Reset has two primary components. The first is an expansion of government programs, taxes and regulations, which together affect virtually every industry in the world, from oil and gas to healthcare and technology.

"The second, arguably much more important part of the Reset is the complete alteration of the way most of the world's largest businesses are evaluated.... Rather than try to improve markets by ridding them of corruption, Great Reset supporters want to double down on cronyism by giving the ruling class—including central banks, academics, government officials, union leaders and corporate titans—greater control over markets," Haskins wrote.

"The way they plan to do this is through something called environmental, social and governance (ESG) standards, which are also sometimes referred to as 'sustainable investment,' 'inclusive capitalism' or 'stakeholder capitalism,'" he added.

But ESG is far from "inclusive." Haskins detailed how "investors and financial institutions have repeatedly said in recent months that they will phase out their business relationships with those who don't support some or all ESG goals."

"With ESG measures in place, businesses are evaluated based on the racial and gender composition of their staff, their carbon footprint, the size of their buildings, how committed they are to fighting climate change and a bunch of other social justice concerns. After being evaluated, companies are then given (or they self-report) ESG scores that are meant to help investors, regulators and governments have a better understanding of who the 'bad' and 'good' companies are," Haskins wrote.[51]

An integral part of the Great Reset is central-bank control of digital currency that will give governments the power to turn off your personal banking on a whim. "So what are Central Bank Digital Currencies? Well, in a way, it's like turning all money into food stamps. It can allow for all sorts of constraints to be placed on currency, including where, when, by whom, and on what it can be spent," explained Alexandros Marinos, the CEO of the technology company Balena Inc.[52] "How far are we from a world where a pandemic is declared, and within a few months everyone is mandated to accept a medical procedure or lose access to their assets, or even the ability to buy food until they comply?" Marinos asked.[53]

Tracking Your Life

"Picture your life in a place where everything you do: What you buy, how you behave, is tracked. The government gives you a score, and the score is a measure of how trustworthy you are as a citizen. It sounds like that [UK television] show *Black Mirror*, but it's actually happening in China." —introduction to 2021 Edward Snowden video, "Will It Be Mandatory? It Is Happening Now!!"[54]

Klaus Schwab's book on the Great Reset makes it clear that whatever life you may have enjoyed before COVID was based on a broken system that will not be returning.

In fact, Schwab and coauthor Thierry Malleret almost make it seem like you should be happy that COVID-19 and the lockdowns happened because the "crisis" will enable the vision of the Great Reset to move forward unabated. COVID-19 has been the great accelerant for the Great Reset.

The Great Narrative, Schwab and Malleret's 253-page sequel to *The Great Reset*, came out in 2022. This follow-up book "encapsulates the Davos Vision, and explores how we can shape a constructive, common narrative for the future," the WEF announced. *The Great Narrative* delves more heavily into the role climate change will play in pushing the WEF's narrative forward.[55]

In June of 2020, Schwab wasted no time in inserting the Great Reset into COVID-19.

Lockdown or Else!

In June 2020 Belarussian president Aleksandr Lukashenko described how the World Bank and the International Monetary Fund (IMF) tried to coerce and bribe his nation to follow the lemming nations and lock down for COVID-19.

"It is ready to fund us ten times more than it offered initially as a token of commendation for our efficient fight against this virus. The World Bank has even asked the Healthcare Ministry to share the experience. Meanwhile, the IMF continues to demand from us quarantine measures, isolation, a curfew. This is nonsense. We will not dance to anyone's tune," said the president.[56]

"We must build entirely new foundations for our economic and social systems.... In fact, one silver lining of the pandemic is that it has shown how quickly we can make radical changes to our lifestyles. Almost instantly, the crisis forced businesses and individuals to abandon practices long claimed to be essential, from frequent air travel to working in an office.... A Great Reset agenda would ensure that investments advance shared goals, such as equality and sustainability."[57]

Breitbart columnist James Delingpole commented, "This might all seem pie in the sky—the demented ravings of a German so sinister-looking and sounding that he would have made an excellent Blofeld in the Bond movies—were it not for one major problem: lots of world leaders, billionaire businessmen and other masters of the universe are totally onboard with the project"—including Biden.

Delingpole explained, "It all sounds like something out of a dystopian novel in the manner of *Nineteen Eighty-Four*, many people are under the illusion that the Great Reset is a conspiracy theory they can safely ignore. But as a commenter at Lockdown Sceptics puts it, 'It's not a conspiracy when they tell you what they are doing.'"[58]

Or to put it another way: With the COVID lockdowns, 2020 became the year that conspiracy realities outnumbered conspiracy theories.

> ### "All Simply Euphemisms for 'Police State'"
> "Lockdowns, mandates, curfews, closures, states of emergency, government quarantine, medical misinformation, tracking, tracing, restrictions, and freedom passes are all simply euphemisms for 'police state.'"
> —attorney Michael P. Senger, author of "China's Global Lockdown Propaganda Campaign"[59]

Make no mistake, the Great Reset is well documented. Schwab has written quite openly about that plan—including the idea that the opportunity for implementing key features of it would be "emergency circumstances (such as a pandemic)."

In his 2018 book, *Shaping the Future of the Fourth Industrial Revolution*, Schwab revealed how easy it would be to "overcome" the "limits" of data privacy. He proposed "public-private data-sharing agreements that 'break glass in case of emergency.' These come into play only under pre-agreed emergency circumstances (such as a pandemic) and can help reduce delays and improve the coordination of first responders, temporarily allowing data sharing that would be illegal under normal circumstances."[60]

The WEF's "Global Risks Report 2019" also acknowledged that a surveillance state can be manipulated by tyrannical rulers. "Authoritarianism is easier in a world of total visibility and traceability, while democracy may turn out to be more difficult," the WEF report stated.[61]

So, in a pandemic "emergency," all privacy safeguards would be abolished. Schwab's book was published in 2018, just two years before coronavirus "emergency" was declared.

WEF even cohosted a conference in October 2019—"Event 201"— which modeled a fictional pandemic complete with lockdowns, masks, and massive suppression of free speech. That WEF conference harked back to an eerily similar 2010 Rockefeller Foundation future-scenario event. (See chapters 2, 6, 7, and 8 below for more on these events and for the 2018 pandemic simulation "Clade X," on which the WEP partnered up with the Johns Hopkins Center for Health Security.)

"Policy Goals That Pre-Date COVID"

"'Great Reset' and the 'New Normal' are policy goals that pre-date Covid, and are far more important than any of the tools used to pursue them.... They've shown us their hand. They've told us—upfront and out loud—what they want to achieve. Total economic control, marked depreciation of living standards, removal of national sovereignty and radical erosion of individual liberties. That's the endgame here. They said so."—Kit Knightly, OffGuardian[62]

"The Great Reset is the latest and greatest pet project of the World Economic Forum, the United Nations, the Council on Foreign Relations, the Royal Institute for International Affairs, and other globalist organizations," wrote William F. Jasper, the senior editor of the *New American*.

"Here we have the Deep State globalist elites of the WEF—Wall Street bankers, megacorp CEOs, princes, prime ministers, presidents, and mass-murdering communist dictators—clinking champagne glasses and supping on caviar while posing as social-justice warriors. These are the folks whose luxury Learjets and grandiose Gulf Streams clog the skies over Europe every January as the world's billionaires, along with their kept politicians and NGO activists, flock to Davos, Switzerland, for another virtue-signaling, world-government–promoting extravaganza," Jasper explained.

"It is obvious from the hundreds of pages dedicated to The Great Reset on the WEF website, and its many conferences, webinars, studies, and reports on this project, that it didn't begin with the Wuhan outbreak," he added.

"What then is the most immediate, concrete goal for The Great Reset? The most obvious is the WEF's insistence on enactment and implementation of the UN Agenda 2030 and its Sustainable Development Goals, the massive 17-point plan for regimentation of the entire planet—and everyone on it," Jasper concluded.[64]

> **"Bought Academia, Bought Politicians, Bought the Press"**
>
> "A few rich billionaires bought academia, bought politicians, bought the press, bought social media, bought the government health agencies—and here we are." —researcher Tony Heller of Real Climate Science[63]

Ivan Wecke, a journalist from Open Democracy rejected "conspiracy theories" about the Great Reset, but nevertheless revealed what he considered to be the dark motives behind it. "At the heart of conspiracy theories are supposed secret agendas and malicious intent. While these may be absent from the WEF's Great Reset initiative, what I found was something almost as sinister hiding in plain sight. In fact, more sinister because it's real and it's happening now. And it involves things as fundamental as our food, our data and our vaccines," Wecke wrote.

"The WEF, best known for its annual meeting of high-net-worth individuals in Davos, Switzerland, describes itself as an international organization for public-private cooperation. WEF partners include some of the biggest companies in oil (Saudi Aramco, Shell, Chevron, BP), food (Unilever, The Coca-Cola Company, Nestlé), technology (Facebook, Google, Amazon, Microsoft, Apple) and pharmaceuticals (AstraZeneca, Pfizer, Moderna)," Wecke reported.[65]

"Who Runs the World? BlackRock and Vanguard"

In an essay on the Great Reset at the anti-state, anti-war, pro-market LewRockwell.com website, Bill Sardi revealed, "The stock of the world's largest corporations are owned by the same institutional investors. They all own each other. This means that 'competing' brands, like Coke and Pepsi aren't really competitors, at all, since their stock is owned by exactly the same investment companies, investment funds, insurance companies, banks and in some cases, governments." In his essay titled "Who Runs the World? BlackRock and Vanguard," Sardi noted that "Bloomberg calls BlackRock 'The fourth branch of government,' because it's the only private agency that closely works with the central banks."

Sardi added, "Two investment companies, Vanguard and BlackRock hold a monopoly in all industries in the world and they, in turn, are owned by the richest families in the world, some of whom are royalty and who have been very rich since before the Industrial Revolution. Why doesn't everybody know this? Why aren't there movies and documentaries about this? Why isn't it in the news? Because 90% of the international media is owned by nine media conglomerates."[66]

"Permanent Renters"

"If You Sell a House These Days, the Buyer Might Be a Pension Fund," blared a *Wall Street Journal* headline in 2021. "Yield-chasing investors are snapping up single-family homes, competing with ordinary Americans and driving up prices," the article explained.

The *Journal* quoted real-estate consultant John Burns, who estimated that in the top U.S. housing markets about one in every five houses sold is purchased by an owner who never moves in. BlackRock is merely one hundreds of "companies and investment firms" purchasing thousands of homes and, in some cases, "entire neighborhoods."[67]

According to Mike Danes of OilPrice, BlackRock is the world's largest asset manager and a key supporter of the Great Reset, while "fueling a $120 trillion transformation on Wall St."[68]

As CulturalHusbandry pointed out on Twitter, "Now, your potential lower to middle class home owner is positioned to be a permanent renter. . . .

This is wealth redistribution, and it ain't rich people's wealth that's getting redistributed. It's normal American middle class, salt of the earth wealth heading into the hands of the world's most powerful entities and individuals." The thread was a detailed analysis of the *Wall Street Journal* report. "This is a fundamental reorganization of society," the tweet stated. "As permanent, guaranteed renters you're pissing away a lifetime of equity and the chance for mobility. You just become a peasant. The Great Reset is real. It is happening. This will be the greatest transfer of wealth, and greatest consolidation of power in the history of mankind," the analysis explained.

"This is warfare. Make no doubt about it. Lloyds bank in London is doing it, as is every great financial institute across the world. . . . BlackRock, Vanguard, and State Street control 20 trillion dollars worth of assets. BlackRock alone has a 10 billion a year surplus. . . . They may accomplish feudalism in 15 years."[69]

The Great Food Reset

America's food security is being threatened by the forces of the Great Reset. "Biden Says to Expect 'Real' Food Shortages Due to Ukraine War," blared a headline from Bloomberg News in 2022. "It's going to be real," Biden asserted.[70]

A food crisis is just the ticket for even more chaos that the WEF can exploit for their Reset agenda. "Over the last decade" China has been "snapping up farmland and purchasing major agribusinesses," according to a 2021 report by *POLITICO*. "By the start of 2020, Chinese owners controlled about 192,000 agricultural acres in the U.S., worth $1.9 billion, including land used for farming, ranching and forestry, according to the Agriculture Department."

During a House Appropriations Committee hearing, Republican representative Dan Newhouse of Washington State noted that "the current trend in the U.S. is leading us toward the creation of a Chinese-owned agricultural land monopoly."[71]

At the same time, Bill Gates is now "the nation's largest farmland owner" and is turning farmers into "renters," according to NBC News.[72] Gates's fake-meat agenda could transform American farming. "All rich

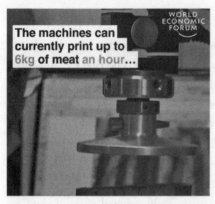

The machines can currently print up to 6kg of meat an hour...

WORLD ECONOMIC FORUM

Meat-printing machine. *World Economic Forum*[74]

countries should move to 100% synthetic beef," Gates has urged.[73] The World Economic Forum is so eager to promote synthetic "meat" that they are touting numerous ways to print up to 6 kilograms of the fake meat an hour.

As part of this new coerced Great Diet Reset, the WEF has been advocating eating bugs to save the planet. The Davos-based group has explained, "Why we might be eating insects soon."[75]

In an essay titled "The Medical Objectification of the Human Person," Robert Freudenthal, a psychiatrist in the London National Health Service, wrote, "The last twenty months have seen an unprecedented transfer of wealth from poor to rich, and from small independent businesses to large corporations." In part this is due to "the stranglehold of large corporations forming monopolies as smaller competitors have been forcibly closed."

Freudenthal explained, "This process, which has led to an expansion of wealth of the billionaire class, is built on a societal shift in which we have all become primarily medical objects, rather than citizens living in and sharing in society together. Rather than be 'in partnership' with medical decision makers, we have become objects—objects to be masked, vaccinated, tracked and traced. As objects we become a resource for financial exploitation, from which profit can be made."[76]

"Billionaires Lecture Millionaires"

"What's unusual about this global communist takeover plan is that it originates not from some meeting of hair-shirt sociology students at Berkeley but from the World Economic Forum, which hosts the annual meeting at Davos where billionaires lecture millionaires on how ordinary people live."—James Delingpole[77]

Robert F. Kennedy Jr. warned that the oppressive COVID mandates are leading humanity into a new dark age: "I think this is an historical jeopardy to humanity that we've never seen before. The Black Plague and World War Two are arguably rivals for it. But I would argue that this is the worst thing that's ever happened to humanity because the essential ambition of the totalitarian state is to control," Kennedy said in an interview about his book *The Real Anthony Fauci: Bill Gates, Big Pharma, and the Global War on Democracy and Public Health.*

"For the first time in history, because of the technological revolution, the capacity for totalitarian forces to literally control every aspect of human expression and even human thought is now unprecedented," Kennedy explained. "Bill Gates brags that he's going to be able to watch, with his sixty thousand satellites, every square inch of the Earth twenty-four hours a day. At least in other parts of history, you could run, you could hide, and you could collect forces and begin opposition and we can't do that anymore.... In Hitler's time, you could run for a border; there were ways that a certain number of people were going to escape and were going to regroup."[78]

At a November 12 press conference in Switerland, Kennedy explained the motivations for the seemingly endless COVID restrictions and the limitations on free speech. "This pandemic has impoverished the world and created five hundred new billionaires, and those are the people who are strip-mining our economies and making themselves rich. Is it a coincidence that these are the same people who are censoring criticism of the government policies that are bringing them trillions of dollars? People aren't stupid. We can see what's happening. We can ask the question,

> **"Spend the Holidays Alone"**
> "What does the Great Reset look like? This is what it looks like: The people in charge doing whatever they want because they're in charge. There will be no live music in the Great Reset. Choirs will be illegal unless they are singing the praises of Kamala Harris. Christmas will be banned. 'Sorry, put on your mask and spend the holidays alone. Good luck.'" –Tucker Carlson[79]

'Cui bono?' And the answer is the people who are benefiting are the people who are squeezing away our constitutional rights and engineering the destruction of democracy worldwide," Kennedy explained.[80]

UK House of Lords member Daniel Hannan warned that the new normal may never go away. "Are we in danger of permanently tilting the balance so that we have preemptive stay-at-home orders, or other restrictions, on the off-chance—every time there is something that may turn out or may not to be a severe public health risk?" Hannan asked. "The thing that has most alarmed me over the last eighteen months has been a reversal in the burden of proof. When we are proposing to take away people's elemental freedoms, the onus must be on the proponents of change to prove their case."

Hannan continued: "How are we not opening the door to the same reasoning every time in future, so that we have a see-saw of constant lockdowns or other bans and restrictions every time something happens—just to be on the safe side? And, my Lords, that would be a fundamental alteration in the relationship between state and citizen."[81]

Democracies were tested by the government response to COVID-19. "We believed that we had a Constitution that protected us, we thought it was there for us. We can read the Bill of Rights and see that we have freedom of speech and freedom of religion," explained Jeffrey A. Tucker, editorial director for the American Institute for Economic Research and the author of *Liberty or Lockdown*. "Then truly it seems like we woke up practically overnight to a different world in which we're managed from the top by a tiny elite that's determining whether I can go to church, how many people I can have in my home, whether I can grab a beer, whether I can open my business, whether I can get my teeth cleaned. I mean, every aspect of life came to be managed and controlled practically overnight. As I'm describing this, it sounds like a dystopian nightmare, and it was."[82]

As Tucker Carlson pointed out, "Essentially, they were willing to dismantle everything we called civilization in the name of bludgeoning one pathogen without regard to the consequences."[83]

There is a movement afoot to ensure the "new normal" of COVID-style restrictions will never end. "The Scottish Government wants its emergency coronavirus powers to become permanent—including the ability to order schools to close, impose lockdowns and operate virtual courts," the *National* newspaper in Scotland reported. The politicians are eager to have their powers extended "for any future outbreak of an infectious disease, so long as they believe" that there is a threat of "significant harm to human health."[84]

"You're the Nazi"

"There was a lesson to learn from the Holocaust. . . . And the lesson is you're the Nazi. That's the lesson. . . . I've been teaching my students since 1993—it's like, 'If you were there, that would have been you.' You think well, *I'd be Oscar Schindler. I'd be rescuing the Jews.* It's like, 'No, I'm afraid not. You'd at least not be saying anything, and you might also be actively participating. You might also enjoy it. You never know.'"
—University of Toronto psychology professor and author Jordan Peterson[85]

Sesame Street Is "Here to Help"

The Great Reset has even infected *Sesame Street*. PBS partnered with the World Economic Forum to promote a "reset in education." Sesame Workshop's Sherrie Westin joined the Forum's Great Reset podcast in October 2020 and told the audience, "COVID is both an opportunity and an alarm bell. That to say, if we don't invest in education, it will be at our peril."[86] But *Sesame Street* did even more, with the beloved Muppet Grover starring in an episode titled "Resetting Education with Sesame Street."

"Hello, everybody, it is I, your cute and adorable pal, Grover, with a message for listeners of the Great Reset," he announced. "You are in luck because I know a thing or two about resetting. Mm-hmm, mm-hmm. I reset my alarm clock every morning. Ha, ha, ha. But you are talking about resetting the entire world. Now that is a very big job. Well, my friend Miss Sherrie Westin and I are here to help."[87]

If the World Economic Forum and the rest of the Davos crowd were looking for a global environment in which to enact their central planning vision of a Great Reset, it would be hard to imagine a better one, or a time more conducive to their agenda than the chaotic post–COVID-19–lockdown world.

The vision of transforming the world so that unelected bureaucrats take even more control of our everyday life now has what it needs to push it along. The last several years have seen endless emergency declarations, wars, massive government spending, debt, runaway inflation, supply chain issues, increases in crime, food shortages, no privacy from Big Brother–style government and corporate snooping, skyrocketing energy prices that chip away at car and homeownership, threats of climate lockdowns, oppressive censorship, crushing of dissent, and limits on freedom of travel and physical autonomy.

All of this chaos is music to the ears of those who don't like the messiness of human freedom. The WEF's vision is to crowd us all into urban areas. They want us to own nothing. They want to regulate literally every aspect of our lives. Bedlam is a useful way to collapse the current system and install a Great Reset. It is all part of the plan: destroy the old order and make the population so desperate that you can impose policies that make them weaker and more dependent on the government.

As author Joel Kotkin noted, "The oligarchs and their allies in the clerisy want to impose a Universal Basic Income, to keep the peasants from suffering too much and possibly rebelling."[88]

The Great Reset adherents will always claim that any "crisis" that emerges is "proof" that the world needs to consolidate even more power in the hands of fewer and fewer people.

The merging of government and corporate power has proven to be the greatest threat to individual liberty. It is driven in part by the ideology that holds that citizens can't be left to their own devices or they will ruin the Earth, create inequity, become white supremacists, not know how to raise their kids, destroy the climate, and generally make poor decisions. The adherents of the bureaucratic state believe that people must have their lives essentially planned and boxed: the masses need credentialed experts to lay out their lives. And remember, the credentialed bureaucratic-expert class is committed to supporting the goals and methods of the regime in power.

This book lays out the facts about the Great Reset, including its origins, its funding, and who the players are—from Anthony Fauci to Bill Gates to the World Health Organization (WHO) to George Soros—and it reveals how COVID-19 enabled a global acceleration toward the Great Reset. We follow the evidence and reveal how lockdowns—a "solution" worse than the disease—kill, and how they also have accomplished one of the greatest transfers of wealth in history, a transfer to the billionaire class.

This book will expose how "The Science" was manipulated by politicians and an unelected public health cabal to implement previously planned tyrannical policies that greatly benefited those in power.

This book will detail the crushing of dissent and free speech and delve into how Big Tech tyranny does the bidding of the Great Reset. This book will also reveal how prominent left-wing figures such as feminist Naomi Wolf and environmental activist Robert F. Kennedy Jr. became heroes of the Reset resistance.

Two chapters are devoted to uncovering the COVID-climate connection and demonstrating how COVID lockdowns are morphing into climate lockdowns in plain sight. The final chapter will lay out what is at stake—and how a Great Reject is necessary to fight the Great Reset.

Unless the Great Reset is challenged, exposed, debunked, and defeated, the world is facing a permanent lockdown, enforced with a mix of viral fears and climate alarm—bringing George Orwell's *Nineteen Eighty-Four* dystopian vision into reality.

CHAPTER 2

The Origins of the Great Reset

The forces behind the Great Reset have been moving incrementally for decades, and for decades they were poised to move rapidly at the first opportunity of any real or perceived crisis. The impulse of some human beings to control other human beings is as old as the human race. Restricted liberty has been the norm, from feudal serfdom to the eugenics movement in Progressive-era America, and from totalitarianism in Italy, Germany, the Soviet Union, and China in the twentieth and twenty-first centuries, to the rise of the technocratic biosecurity state.

As economist Milton Friedman noted, freedom has been fleeting in human history. "Free societies of the kind we've been lucky enough to experience for the last 100, 150 years—are a very rare exception in human history. Most people, most of history...have lived in tyranny and misery," Friedman said in 1999.[1]

There is nothing like a "crisis" to advance expansion of state power. Just as gun-control advocates pounce whenever there is a mass shooting, the Great Reset promoters moved in instantly when the COVID-19 arrived. The administrative state that was envisioned by President Woodrow Wilson, who became president in 1913, was "a government structure where politics and administration could operate separately from one another," according to Ballotpedia. "Under this structure, government administration could be managed by neutral experts."[2] But, as will become apparent, "neutral experts" are very hard to come by in the realm of government since bureaucrats always default to measures that increase the power of the state.

As statistician William M. Briggs noted, "James Burnham wrote *The Managerial Revolution: What Is Happening in the World* in 1941 to argue that capitalism was waning and being replaced everywhere by

"Executive Arm Growing"

Socialist economist Stuart Chase's 1932 book *A New Deal* was the inspiration for President Franklin Delano Roosevelt's New Deal. Chase was a member of FDR's "kitchen cabinet."[3] He promoted the "managerial revolution," which he referred to as "System X" in his 1942 book, *When the War Ends: The Road We Are Traveling 1914-1942*.

Chase's vision of the world sounds an awful lot like the WEF's Great Reset. In *When the War Ends*, Chase outlined the key components of transforming "Free Enterprise into 'X'":

> A strong, centralized government.
> An executive arm growing at the expense of the legislative and judicial arms. . . .
> The control of banking, credit and security exchanges by the government. . . .
> The abandonment of gold in favor of managed currencies. . . .
> The control of energy sources—hydroelectric power, coal, petroleum, natural gas.
> The control of transportation—railway, highway, airway, waterway.
> The control of agricultural production. . . .
> Not much "taking over" of property or industries in the old socialistic sense. The formula appears to be control without ownership . . .
> The state control of communications and propaganda.[4]

Chase loved the idea of managing all aspects of society. As he asked at the end of *A New Deal*, "Why should the Soviets have all the fun remaking the world?"[5]

managerialism. He was right." He added, "The term *managerialism*, though Burnham had good reason to use it, does not sing to us, and is not now as accurate, as we'll see. I propose instead *Expertocracy*, the rule of credentialed Experts." As Briggs explained, "*Socialism* now roughly translates to Burnham's *managerial economy*."[6]

The 1990s saw the rise of the "New World Order" under President George H. W. Bush. But despite the very real expansion of the powers of the state by the Patriot Act and the war on terror, liberty-loving Americans' fears of the "New World Order" under Bush seem positively quaint in the post-COVID-19–lockdown world of today. The COVID lockdowns have shown that the threat of a radically expanded New World Order in the guise of the Great Reset has teeth.

Journalist Neil Clark explained how the war on terror paved the way for the COVID response. "Twenty years on from 9/11, the 'War on Terror' has morphed into a 'war' against the West's own populations," Clark wrote. "Consider the way that the countries which invaded Afghanistan—and took part in the other wars mentioned above, under the banner of 'Freedom and Democracy,' have morphed into authoritarian police states since March 2020, with hard lockdown Australia being the most shocking example," Clark noted.

"The bombs may not have been falling on Western populations, as they did on Afghans, Libyans and Iraqis, but nevertheless I don't think it's hyperbolic at all to describe what's been going on these last 18 months as a kind of war. There's certainly been relentless psychological warfare, designed to wear us down physically and mentally, with lockdowns and threat of further lockdowns being a key component in the new 'Project Fear,'" Clark explained.

"Afghanistan may have been important in 2001, as the gateway to a series of post 9-11 wars, but in 2021, there's an even bigger operation being undertaken. Namely, implementing the Davos set's 'Great Reset' and all that it entails," he added.[7]

Maurice Newman, a former advisor to Australian prime minister Tony Abbott, detailed just who is behind the Great Reset. "The World

Economic Forum, a Geneva-based non-profit foundation whose ranks include Prince Charles and other climate change crusaders like Al Gore and Greta Thunberg, together with the secretary-general of the United Nations, the president of the European Central Bank, the secretary-general of the OECD, the managing director of the IMF, George Soros, world trade union leaders, chief executives of Big Tech and representatives of NGOs like Greenpeace and WWF, believes climate action must be top of the global agenda as we emerge from Covid-19," Newman wrote. Other organizations and individuals who are involved in setting the global agenda include the Council on Foreign Relations, the Bilderberg Group, the Trilateral Commission, and Bill Gates, to name a few.

"Much of the WEF's agenda can be found in America's radical Left's Green New Deal, which addresses climate change and economic inequality," Newman added.[8]

Klaus Schwab, founder of the World Economic Forum in Davos, Switzerland, first uttered the phrase "Great Reset" back in 2014. Schwab founded the World Economic Forum, originally named the European Management Forum, in 1971.

"It took Schwab and the Davos elite about six years to watch their great reset ideology grow from a tiny Swiss seed in 2014 to a European super-flower pollinating the entire globe in 2020," Tim Hinchliffe, the editor of The Sociable wrote.[9]

From Citizens to "Stakeholders"

As chapter 1 revealed, Schwab promoted the ideology of "stakeholder" capitalism in which corporations merge into closer cooperation with the government. He demands global governance in order to achieve it.

Also in 1971, Schwab laid out his vision in his book *Moderne Unternehmensführung im Maschinenbau* (*Modern Company Management in Mechanical Engineering*).[10] No Deal for Nature campaigner Paul Cudenec explained at the website Winter Oak that Schwab "effectively redefined human beings not as citizens, free individuals or members of communities, but as secondary participants in a massive commercial enterprise."

Cudenec added, "The 'partnerships' which the WEF creates are aimed at replacing democracy with a global leadership of hand-picked and unelected individuals whose duty is not to serve the public, but to impose the rule of the 1% on that public with as little interference from the rest of us as possible."[11]

"It's the Right Thing to Do"

In 2020 *Time* magazine reported that "Walmart CEO Doug McMillon says it's time to reinvent capitalism post-coronavirus." McMillon is all in on the Great Reset. "I think the growing interest in stakeholder capitalism stems from companies genuinely invested in doing good for our world, because it's the right thing to do and because businesses who take this approach are stronger. We simply won't be here if we don't take care of the very things that allow us to exist: our associates, customers, suppliers and the planet. That's not up for debate," McMillon explained.[12]

As the *Hindustan Times* reported, Schwab is on a "first-name basis" with Bill Gates and many world leaders.[13]

Vanity Fair magazine featured Schwab in 2022 in a profile titled "'He Has an Incredible Knack to Smell the Next Fad': How Klaus Schwab Built a Billionaire Circus at Davos."

"Klaus Schwab, the ringmaster of festivities at the World Economic Forum in Davos, has been known to tell underlings that he anticipates one day receiving a Nobel Peace Prize. In a surprise to no one else, Oslo has yet to ring," wrote Peter S. Goodman for *Vanity Fair*.

"On his travels, he demands the privileges of a visiting head of state, complete with welcoming delegations at the airport," Goodman revealed. "When a Forum employee who was late for a meeting once pulled into Schwab's spot in the parking lot, aware that the boss was overseas, he caught wind of it, and insisted that she be fired, relenting only after senior staff intervened to save her."

"Schwab has constructed a refuge for the outlandishly wealthy, an exclusive zone where they are free to pursue deals and sundry shenanigans while enjoying the cover of participating in a virtuous undertaking. Their mere presence in Davos at the Forum signals their empathy and sensitivity," Goodman wrote of the three thousand yearly attendees of the Davos forum.

Goodman authored the book *Davos Man: How the Billionaires Devoured the World*. As Goodman explained in the *Vanity Fair* article, "In truth, Davos Man has pillaged the global economy, exploiting workers, plundering housing and health care, and dismantling government programs while transferring the bounty to his personal bank accounts tucked in jurisdictions beyond the reach of any pain-in-the-ass tax collector."

He added, "Top executives can fly in and meet a dozen heads of state in the course of four or five days, sitting across tables in soundproof rooms, beyond the purview of securities regulators, journalists, and other hindrances."[14]

"Schwab is a great fan of Greta Thunberg, of course, who had barely stood up from the pavement after her one-girl protest in Stockholm before being whisked off to address the WEF at Davos," Cudenec explained.

The WEF Founder is "a supporter of the proposed global New Deal for Nature, particularly via Voice for the Planet, which was launched at the WEF in Davos in 2019 by the Global Shapers, a youth-grooming organisation created by Schwab in 2011 and aptly described by investigative journalist Cory Morningstar as 'a grotesque display of corporate malfeasance disguised as good,'" Cudenec wrote.

"The original fascist project, in Italy and Germany, was all about a merger of state and business. While communism envisages the take-over of business and industry by the government, which—theoretically!—acts in the interests of the people, fascism was all about using the state to protect and advance the interests of the wealthy elite," wrote Cudenec.[15]

The World Economic Forum and the United Nations are collaborating on the Great Reset vision. The UN Development Program partnered up with the WEF to produce a "2030Vision" of "sustainable development."[16]

Just how influential is the World Economic Forum? In 2017, Schwab told former U.S. presidential advisor David Gergen at the Harvard Kennedy School's Institute of Politics just how the WEF has "penetrated" governments around the world.

> **"Audition for the Role of James Bond Supervillain"**
>
> "The personage of Schwab represents the aims, ideologies, and political connections of the ruling technocracy better than any other figure.... In a seeming audition for the role of James Bond supervillain Blofeld, head of the criminal organization SPECTRE which is bent on world domination, Schwab proclaims the coming of a worldwide 'Great Reset' during the summer of 2020."
> —Raelle Kaia, "Why Are They Doing This?"[17]

"And I have to say, when I mention our names, like [former German chancellor] Mrs. [Angela] Merkel, even [Russian President] Vladimir Putin and so on—they all have been young global leaders of the World Economic Forum," Schwab explained to Gergen.

"But what we are very proud of now is the young generation like [Canadian] Prime Minister Trudeau, president of Argentina and so on. So we penetrate the cabinets. So, yesterday, I was at a reception for Prime Minister Trudeau and I would know that half of this cabinet, or even more than half of this cabinet, are from our actually young global leaders of the World Economic Forum," Schwab bragged.

"It's true in Argentina and it's true in France now, I mean with the president [Emmanuel Macron] a young global leader," he added.[18]

Schwab's 2018 book *Shaping the Future of the Fourth Industrial Revolution* revealed a frightening ideology of merging man and machine: "Today's external devices—from wearable computers to virtual reality headsets—will almost certainly become implantable in our bodies and brains. Exoskeletons and prosthetics will increase our physical power, while advances in neurotechnology enhance our cognitive abilities. We will become better able to manipulate our own genes, and those of our children. These developments raise profound questions: Where do we draw the line between human and machine? What does it mean to be human?"[19]

"We'll All Have Brain Implants"

Klaus Schwab and Google cofounder Sergey Brin mused about our possible transhumanist future during a World Economic Forum meeting in 2017.

Schwab asked Brin, "Can you imagine that in 10 years when we are sitting here we have an implant in our brains and I can immediately feel, because you all will have implants, I can—and we measure you, all your brainwaves—and I can immediately tell you how the people react, or I can feel how the people react to your answers? Is it imaginable?"

"I think that is imaginable," Brin replied.

The WEF calls this technology the "Fourth Industrial Revolution," which, as their website explains, "is characterized by a range of new technologies that are fusing the physical, digital and biological worlds, impacting all disciplines, economies and industries, and even challenging ideas about what it means to be human."[20]

Cudenec explained: "A whole section of [Schwab's] book is devoted to the theme 'Altering the Human Being.' Here he drools over 'the ability of new technologies to literally become part of us' and invokes a cyborg future involving 'curious mixes of digital-and-analog life that will redefine our very natures.'"[21]

As Schwab explained in a WEF video, "The Fourth Industrial Revolution will impact our lives completely. It will not only change how we communicate, how we produce, how we consume. It will change, actually, our own identity."[22]

China Is the Model

Economist Sanjeev Sabhlok resigned from his job in the Department of Treasury and Finance in Victoria, Australia, in September 2020 "to protest the outrageous violations of liberty" of the COVID lockdowns.[23] Sabhlok was appalled that the formerly free world was taking its cues from China—where viral videos showed people apparently dropping dead in the streets and Chinese officials literally sealing people in their homes.

"Politicians across the world have thoroughly enjoyed the power that lockdowns and mandatory mask policies have given them," Sabhlok wrote. "They love public health—a gift that keeps giving. They will not return liberty to the people anytime soon. Instead, they will follow [China's general secretary Xi] Jinping's orders through his mouthpiece, the WHO (or the Imperial College or one of the many other 'experts' across the West who owe their primary allegiance to China)."[25]

Partnering with George Soros for "Reputable Media"

In its 2018–2019 *Annual Report*, the World Economic Forum touted its "joint venture" with United for News, a "multistakeholder coalition of industry, media and civil society," including George Soros' Open Society Foundations, "with a shared mission of supporting and sustaining reputable media in the digital age."

As the WEF announced, "The coalition significantly increased the number of members, adding Edelman, GroupM, AppNexus, World Association of Newspapers and News Publishers, the BBC's 50:50 project, Sembra Media, News Gain and Open Society Foundations, and now counts 17 collaborating organizations."[24]

As Sabhlok asked, "So how did the world get it so wrong? The answer, hiding in plain sight, is: China. While the Great Hysteria was going on, Donald Trump went from an unlosable situation to fighting for his career. And the entire world went backward but China will likely end up with GDP growth, becoming stronger than ever before."[26]

Patrick Wood, author of *Technocracy Rising: The Trojan Horse of Global Transformation*, has explained, "China intends to conquer the world with authoritarian Technocracy rather than guns and missiles. Thus far, they are excelling and the rest of the world is regressing. There is no give and take in China; it's their way or the highway. The rest of the world is just starting to figure this out."[27]

J. Brooks Spector, a former American diplomat in Africa and East Asia who has taught at the University of the Witwatersrand, points out that China "actually appropriates much from modern, Western-style capitalism, as well as from the technocracy movement that was popular in the 1930s."

Spector says we are seeing "the rise of Chinese technocratic authoritarianism and the erosion of Western democracy." The 1930s "social movement essentially advocated replacing all those confusing, bickering politicians and selfish businesspeople with scientists and engineers who had the technical expertise to appropriately manage the economy best, with the best of all possible solutions to problems. By now, of course, there is very little being drawn from the Marxism that

Clueless on China

Dr. Anthony Fauci of the Centers for Disease Control, who became the face of the public health response to the coronavirus in the United States, apparently cannot conceive that China would ever harm its own citizens: "The idea, I think, is quite far-fetched that the Chinese deliberately engineered something so that they could kill themselves, as well as other people. I think that's a bit far out," Fauci said in 2021 in a CNN interview.[28]

"Far-fetched" for China's government to kill their own people? Does Dr. Fauci read the *Washington Post*? In 2016, the *Post* crowned China's chairman Mao Zedong, the founding father of the People's Republic of China, "the biggest mass murderer in the history of the world," noting that "both Hitler and Stalin were outdone by Mao Zedong. From 1958 to 1962, his Great Leap Forward policy led to the deaths of up to 45 million people—easily making it the biggest episode of mass murder ever recorded."[29]

Talk show host Derek Hunter, the author of *Outrage, Inc.: How the Liberal Mob Ruined Science, Journalism, and Hollywood*, ridiculed Fauci's comments. "Yes, a communist regime currently committing genocide and known for enslaving its citizens for fun and profit would never, ever consider incurring some losses in population to damage the economies of the rest of the world thinking they'd come out ahead in the deal," Hunter quipped.[30]

their technocratic-authoritarian state's leaders ostensibly say it is firmly grounded in," Spector explains.

"For the Chinese and their acolytes elsewhere, this technocratic authoritarianism is *the* wave of the future. Moreover, promoting it has become a hallmark of a new, increasingly assertive, self-assured Chinese diplomacy—something very different from the behaviour of the old China on the world stage."[31]

Chinese Puppet?

World Health Organization director general Tedros Ghebreyesus is closely aligned with the Chinese communist government. "Tedros's [2017] candidacy was mired in several scandals. Ethiopians and concerned global citizens pleaded with the countries voting in the election to reject Tedros because he was a representative of a repressive political regime who had helped to build and maintain a surveillance state with a total lack of government transparency," Stacey Rudin observed in an article at the American Institute for Economic Research in which she discussed "the China-paved path to WHO director-general."

"Critics pointed out that Tedros was 'comfortable with the secrecy of autocratic states'—a characteristic that could wreak havoc on the world if he assumed a position of power within the WHO," Rudin explained.

"Tedros's strongest and most important backer," according to Rudin, "was not an individual, but a government: China."[32]

Abhijit Iyer-Mitra of the Institute of Peace and Conflict Studies was even more blunt: "China propped Tedros." Iyer-Mitra wrote, "As commentator Chitra Subramaniam describes it, China started a scheme for global health colonisation and won because America didn't think it was important enough."

Iyer-Mitra added, "The Chinese leveraged their investments across Africa to force the African Union to back Tedr[os], [and] also got Pakistan to withdraw its candidate who was opposing him," Iyer-Mitra noted. As Iyer-Mitra pointed out, "One reason that Tedros has gotten away with so much brazen cronyism is that America pays little to no attention to global public health, save pouring in money as a sugar daddy."[33]

And Tedros repaid the favor to China. "As I have said repeatedly since my return from Beijing, the Chinese government is to be congratulated for the extraordinary measures it has taken to contain the outbreak, despite the severe social and economic impact those measures are having on the Chinese people," Tedros declared in January 2020 as COVID-19 was spreading.

"In many ways, China is actually setting a new standard for outbreak response. It's not an exaggeration," Tedros concluded.[35]

"Suppression Is the Only Viable Strategy"

Unfortunately, Tedros wasn't the only one looking to China as a model.

Attorney Michael P. Senger, author of "China's Global Lockdown Propaganda Campaign," has explained how the WHO, the Centers for Disease Control (CDC), and almost all public health institutions followed the lead of China. "By corrupting global institutions, promoting hysterical data, publishing fraudulent science, and deploying propaganda on an unprecedented scale, Beijing transformed the snake oil of lockdowns into 'science,' the greatest crime of the 21st century to date," Senger wrote.[36] "COVID lockdowns aren't science, they're CCP propaganda," as Senger said on his Twitter profile.[37]

Senger pointed out, "In March 2020, liberal democracy ground to a sudden stop. Like the Reichstag Fire of 1933, historians may never know how SARS-CoV-2 came about. For scientists, exploring its origins would be a rewarding endeavor if it weren't precluded by the jackboot of Xi's CCP. But while intelligence agencies spent months investigating the virus's origins, the world employed an unprecedented response that proved far more devastating than the virus itself: mass quarantines modeled on those imposed in China, commonly referred to as 'lockdowns.'"

Senger explained, "It was the greatest geopolitical catastrophe since the Second World War. And it was all for nothing. Lockdowns had never been about science. They'd sprung into global policy on the order of the CCP princeling who was now the most influential member of the Baby Boom generation."[38]

"A Quasi-Military Agency"

Robert F. Kennedy Jr. explains the origins of the Centers for Disease Control, the federal agency that led the public health response to the coronavirus in the United States: "The CDC's legacy as the public health service . . . was as a quasi-military agency—and at the time the vaccine system, the vaccine program, was launched—the purpose was a national-defense purpose. And they wanted to make sure that vaccines could be quickly formulated and deployed in order to derail attacks by foreign countries."[39]

Neil Ferguson, who was on the Imperial College COVID-19 Response Team and the UK's Scientific Emergency Group for Emergencies (SAGE)—until he was caught violating COVID–social-distancing measures—revealed how China inspired the global lockdowns.

"[China is] a communist one-party state, we said. We couldn't get away with it in Europe, we thought...and then Italy did it. And we realized we could," Ferguson told the *Times* of London.

"If China had not done it," Ferguson said, "the year would have been very different."

As Ferguson explained, "I think people's sense of what is possible in terms of control changed quite dramatically between January and March" of 2020.[40]

So the lockdowns were based on the example set by Communist China—and on flimsy and ever-evolving science. As Michael Fumento charged in early April of 2020, the Imperial College model, which provided the scientific impetus for the lockdowns, had already been "abandoned" by its "chief researcher"—who was...Neil Ferguson.

> ### China Rules
>
> "In the U.K. Government's official Coronavirus Action Plan from March 3, 2020, discussing social distancing, school closures, and rapid COVID test and vaccine development, nearly every source the U.K. government cited was from China. All the measures outlined in New Zealand's official COVID-19 Elimination Strategy document—'physical distancing' 'widespread testing' 'surveillance'—were adopted from China based on the reported success of the CCP's Wuhan lockdown.... One after another, world leaders tipped over like dominoes, their national bureaucracies falling in line to cease all social and economic activity for the first time in history.... Based on WHO guidance, citing Chinese journal articles, doctors around the world began putting patients on ventilators en masse, killing thousands before a grassroots campaign stopped the practice."—attorney Michael P. Senger, author of "China's Global Lockdown Propaganda Campaign"[41]

As Fumento pointed out, "Neil Ferguson, the chief researcher of that model, dropped 510,000 to 20,000. He just abandoned his model—threw it in the trash can. Yet that model has driven California, New York, and all these other states to institute lockdowns."

Fumento is a journalist and author who has investigated health issues and epidemics and debunked dubious scientific claims "for the past thirty-five years." He wrote books on *The Myth of Heterosexual AIDS: How a Tragedy Has Been Distorted by the Media and Partisan Politics* and *BioEvolution: How Biotechnology is Changing Our World*. "Many responded to the AIDS outbreak saying, 'Everybody's going to get it now.' I called BS and was right," Fumento observed. He pointed out that the public health experts have a woeful track record on predictions of disease outbreaks from AIDS through "SARS, Ebola I, Ebola II, Creutzfeldt-Jakob (aka 'mad cow') disease, avian flu, and the Zika virus."

"Every single time, I called it right, and by some great coincidence, the public-health people always called it wrong," Fumento said.

And they wildly overhyped COVID-19 as well. As Fumento explained in early April, "Imperial College—which did more than any other institution to drive these lockdowns—has just abandoned their model. It predicted that if we did nothing, up to 2.2 million people would die in the United States from COVID-19, and at best—with a lockdown—1.1 million people would die. That was best case scenario: 1.1 million people. Really? But they also said that 510,000 Brits would die without a lockdown."[42] That was the number Ferguson and the Imperial College suddenly dropped down to 20,000.

Ferguson abandoned his own model, but the global damage was done. Ferguson's frightening modeling had driven the United States of America straight into lockdowns: Deborah Birx, the head of the Trump administration's Coronavirus Response team, credited Ferguson's speculative modeling study with changing the CDC's advice to recommending working from home and avoiding gatherings of ten or more people. "We had new information coming out from a model, and what had the biggest impact in the model is social distancing, small groups, not going in public in large groups," Birx said.

Ferguson was sure that society-wide lockdowns, enforced by governments, were the only option. In March of 2020, when Ferguson presented UK prime minister Boris Johnson with his viral-modeling scare-scenario claiming a massive death toll unless lockdowns were embraced, the modeling paper urged, "Suppression is the only viable strategy."

Ferguson explained, "We will have to maintain some level of social distancing, a significant level of social distancing, probably indefinitely until we have a vaccine available."[43]

Locking down had gained public acceptance quickly. Britain and New York locked down hard in March (and by the first week of April even Florida had jumped onto the bandwagon).[45] That was only a couple of months after Dr. Fauci had seemed to think that lockdowns were not even a remote option in the United States. In January of 2020, Fauci had opined that the authoritarian clampdown in China—which, he noted, "shut out the traffic out of Wuhan, planes, trucks, buses, ferries, rail"— was not going to happen here. "There's no chance in the world that we could do that to Chicago or to New York or to San Francisco, but they're doing it," Fauci said, referring to China. "So, let's see what happens."[46]

We saw. And unfortunately what we saw was very different from "no chance in the world" that we would follow China into lockdown. It turned out to be a horrifying reality.

Failed Models

But Ferguson's position of influence is undeserved according to long-time public health observers like Fumento: "During the mad cow scare he 'modeled' 50 to 50,000 cases. What kind of a model is that? Of what value is it? It serves the same purpose as all of these models: to scare people and get in the news. He knows how this plays out in the news:

'Imperial College Model predicts as many as 50,000 deaths from mad cow disease!' Final total number: 176. Hey, it was within the range!" Fumento explained.

Fumento then described "Farr's Law...[which] was first promulgated in 1840, which is, importantly, eight years before the first public health organization anywhere in the world. It says that all epidemics—meaning *all* epidemics—follow a more or less bell-shaped curve. They start out with a very steep incline. And then over time they slope and they slope, and then they eventually flatten and go down. That may seem obvious even to those who don't know about the law. Yet we hear with each new epidemic, 'If the virus continues to spread at the current rate...,' and the answer is always the same: Viruses never continue to spread at the current rate—never, ever, ever."[47]

Business Insider noted, "In 2009, one of Ferguson's models predicted 65,000 people could die from the Swine Flu outbreak in the UK—the final figure was below 500."

"I much prefer to be accused of overreacting than under-reacting," Ferguson revealed in February 2020. He also admitted, "We don't have a crystal ball."[48]

Fumento objects to the high regard in which Ferguson is held by policy makers. "Such people should be held accountable. Instead they're given a pass to repeat it all over again—and cause the next hysteria," Fumento said. Fumento asked why the United States was lured into "following the Chinese model" of lockdowns. "When did the Chinese government begin to set an example for the free world?"

But don't expect calls for more lockdowns with future viruses to abate. As Fumento noted, the proponents of more lockdowns "all have secure jobs." He pointed out, "If you work for the World Health Organization or the CDC, COVID is not going to put you out of a job; it probably will get you more money. If you're a tenured professor at Imperial College, or anywhere, you're not going to lose your job to COVID-19. If anything, you have a lot more free time on your hands because the universities are closed or have moved classes online. By and large, the people making the projections that have led to these measures have nothing to lose."[49]

Follow the Money

The United Kingdom's Imperial College is part of Bill Gates's vast funding empire. "Imperial College London has announced a $14.5 million grant from the Bill & Melinda Gates Foundation in support of efforts to improve and expand access to health care in developing countries," announced Philanthropy News Digest on December 13, 2018.[50]

In July 2020, the Gates Foundation gave another million-dollar–plus grant to Imperial College to "to evaluate the potential efficacy of a Ribonucleic acid (RNA) vaccine against COVID-19."[51]

Ferguson cofounded the MRC Centre for Global Infectious Disease Analysis, based at Imperial College, in 2008. The center advises governments about pathogen outbreaks and receives tens of millions of dollars in annual funding from the Bill & Melinda Gates Foundation.

Ferguson's center also works with the UK National Health Service and the U.S. Centers for Disease Prevention and Control, and it provides

---

Big Pharma

"The pharmaceutical companies had not only corrupted our politicians with huge amounts of lobbying money, they had captured the agencies that are supposed to protect Americans from public health threats . . . the CDC, the FDA, the HHS. . . .

"Congress had been corrupted, the regulatory agencies were captured, they had become sock puppets for the industry they were supposed to regulate. The press had been sidelined and worst of all, they had passed a law in our country in 1986 that gave pharmaceutical companies complete immunity from liability. . . .

"Pharmaceutical companies [are] the most powerful, more powerful than oil, more powerful than the chemical industry. . . . The pharmaceutical industry is operating and capturing politicians and running governments in every nation on the globe." —Robert F. Kennedy Jr.[52]

the World Health Organization with "rapid analysis of urgent infectious disease problems."[53]

> ### "To Acclimate the Public"
> "The purpose of lockdowns prior to vaccination was to acclimate the public to lockdowns after vaccination." —Michael P. Senger, author of "China's Global Lockdown Propaganda Campaign"[54]

Inflating the Risks—and His Reputation

Fumento has been a longtime observer of Dr. Anthony Fauci, the director of the National Institute of Allergy and Infectious Diseases (NIAID).[55] Fauci is the highest-paid federal employee and oversees an annual budget of $6 billion.[56]

Fauci "was sole author of a 1983 piece in the prestigious JAMA in which he declared the disease [AIDS] might be transmissible by 'routine close contact, as within a family household,'" Fumento wrote. Fauci "shortly thereafter ascended to the position he holds to this day. Long after it was established that AIDS was actually extremely hard to transmit, Fauci nonetheless continued to raise hue and cry. In 1987, columnist George Will asserted on national TV that the threat to heterosexuals was overstated. 'That's not correct,' Fauci protested, followed by a prediction that the percentage of AIDS cases contracted via heterosexual transmission (then at 4%) would rise to 10% by 1991. No, it never rose above 4%," Fumento pointed out.[57]

In 2021, an old video surfaced of Fauci speculating about how AIDS was transmitted. Fauci explained in the video: "If the close contact of a child is a household contact, perhaps there will be a certain number of cases of individuals who are just living with and in close contact with someone with AIDS, or at risk of AIDS, who does not necessarily have to have intimate sexual contact or share a needle, but just the ordinary close contact that one sees in normal interpersonal relations."[58]

Investigative journalist Justin Hart commented on Fauci's claims in the video. "Look at how confident he is in spouting this nonsense. Fauci never changes. He goes full throttle into fearmongering only to be proven wrong. No wonder we were so frightened of AIDS," Hart wrote.[59]

Fumento explained that Fauci "repeated the pattern during successive disease panics, such as when he declared 16 years ago that we're 'due' for 'massive person-to-person' spread of Avian flu A/H5N1. How massive? While Fauci didn't define the term, according to one estimate by a CDC modeler 'even in the best-case scenarios' worldwide it would 'cause 2 to 7 million deaths.'" But Fumento's research found that "as it turned out, the disease killed 440 worldwide." In another example, "Fauci sounded alarm over the threat of the Zika virus, demanding billions more in taxpayer funds. It barely touched two U.S. states before burning out on its own."[60]

No HIV Lockdowns

"When HIV was a horrible epidemic people died very tragic deaths. But we didn't lock people up even when people demanded that anyone with HIV should be. No one locked up healthy people. . . . I keep thinking about how the AIDS epidemic was managed. That was managed back when we were still a free society. Many people died, it is absolutely tragic, but the state did not lock up everyone." —Naomi Wolf in 2021[61]

Fumento was incensed when Fauci "falsely" made a "Spanish flu" comparison to COVID-19. "The comparison to the 1918–19 flu was always ludicrous, based not on science but primal fear," Fumento wrote.

"We already know that COVID-19 has a far lower mortality rate than even lesser 20th-century flu pandemics. The CDC's 'best estimate' is around 0.26 percent. That compares to about 0.67 percent for the 'Asian flu' of 1957–58, which in turn was vastly milder than Spanish flu," Fumento explained.

"Further, even a virus far more deadly than that of the Spanish flu would not pose a similar threat because of tremendously different conditions then and now," he added. "In 1918, the world was at war. In part because of that, people were in far poorer general health than we are today, with malnourishment commonplace. We know malnourishment is a powerful factor in infectious disease severity," Fumento pointed out.

And Fauci should know better. "This is rather important: There were no antibiotics in 1918–19, and, as one medical journal paper put it, 'The majority of deaths in the 1918–1919 influenza pandemic likely resulted directly from secondary bacterial pneumonia caused by common upper respiratory-tract bacteria.' The chief researcher for that paper? Dr. Anthony Fauci."[62]

Fauci has built up his reputation "by saying what the MSM wants to hear, be it with AIDS, avian flu, Zika, or COVID-19," Fumento wrote. Fauci has a reputation as a prodigious researcher and published scientist. "In a 2019 analysis of Google Scholar citations, Dr. Fauci ranked as the 41st most highly cited researcher of all time," according to Fauci's official NIAID bio. And "according to the Web of Science, he ranked 8th out of more than 2.2 million authors in the field of immunology by total citation count between 1980 and January 2019." Fauci's bio states he is the "author, coauthor, or editor of more than 1,300 scientific publications, including several textbooks."

Fumento is not buying it. "Actually, he's just a bit too incredible," Fumento said. "Even back then [in the 1980s], his CV listing all the papers on which he was lead or co-researcher was so heavy it practically required a forklift."

"This would be extremely impressive," Fumento explained, "but remember we're talking about someone who for the past 36 years was supposed to be working full-time as an *administrator* when he's not throwing first pitches, not doing individual research." As Fumento pointed out, "There are simply too many papers listing Fauci on too many disparate subjects, and too often as lead researcher."

Fumento offered what may be the true explanation for Fauci's mile-high stack of scientific publications. "There's always steep competition to get in the top-ranked journals and it would appear that the true researchers are putting Fauci's name on their papers to push them up the ladder in exchange for which he gets yet one more academic publication attributed to him, as noted usually with him as lead researcher. It's a shame he's not part of Marvel's Avengers," Fumento wrote.[63]

Robert F. Kennedy Jr.'s 2021 book *The Real Anthony Fauci* revealed a side of Fauci not seen in the media. Kennedy labeled Fauci "the J. Edgar Hoover of public health." The book reveals how Fauci engaged in "the subversion of democracy by a drug industry that manipulates regulators like sock puppets." RFK Jr. claims Fauci "exercises dictatorial control over the army of 'knowledge-and-innovation' leaders who appear nightly on TV to parrot his orthodoxies and 'debunk' his opponents." The book also reports that Fauci "repeatedly concocted and weaponized fraudulent pandemics, including bird flu (2005), swine flu (2009) and Zika (2015–2016), in order to sell novel vaccines" and that he "partnered with the Pentagon and intelligence agencies to conduct 'gain-of-function' experiments to breed pandemic superbugs."[64]

"Control over the Fates of Billions"

Fauci has many close ties to both Bill Gates and the WHO, including funding and joint projects. Fauci was chosen to be part of the Leadership Council of the Gates-founded "Decade of Vaccines" project. "The World Health Organization (WHO), UNICEF, the National Institute of Allergy and Infectious Diseases (NIAID) and the Bill & Melinda Gates Foundation have announced a collaboration to increase coordination across the international vaccine community and create a Global Vaccine Action Plan," read the 2010 WHO press release.[65] Gates committed $10 billion to the project.

And in October 2019 it was announced: "NIH, Bill and Melinda Gates Foundation collaborate to develop gene-based HIV treatment." The Gates Foundation pledged to contribute $100 million to the National Institute of Health to support Fauci's National Institute of Allergy and Infectious Diseases research into HIV.[66]

Gates is a key player in the Great Reset. Klaus Schwab praised Gates in 2008 at the Davos annual meeting: "If in the twenty-second century a book will be written about the entrepreneur of the twenty-first century.... I'm sure that the person who will foremost come to the mind of those historians is certainly Bill Gates."[67]

"Gates' unimaginable wealth has been used to gain control over every corner of the fields of public health, medical research and vaccine development. And now that we are presented with the very problem that Gates has been talking about for years, we will soon find that this software developer with no medical training is going to leverage that wealth into control over the fates of billions of people," investigative journalist James Corbett explained.[68]

The World Health Organization, also a key player in the Great Reset, utilized COVID-19 to promote lockdowns and advance the goals of the World Economic Forum.

WHO Done It

The World Health Organization has a long track record of attempting to use viral fears to essentially reset the global economy.

As Michael Fumento reported in *Forbes*, "In a September [2009] speech WHO Director-General Chan said 'ministers of health' should take advantage of the 'devastating impact' swine flu will have on poorer nations to get out the message that 'changes in the functioning of the global economy' are needed to 'distribute wealth on the basis of' values 'like community, solidarity, equity and social justice.' She further declared it should be used as a weapon against 'international policies and systems that govern financial markets, economies, commerce, trade and foreign affairs.'"[69]

The World Health Organization's second largest donor, behind the United States government, is (drumroll, please) . . . the Bill & Melinda Gates Foundation. According to the 2018 WHO financial report, while the U.S. government's contribution was in the amount of more than $281 million, the Gates Foundation came in at over $228 million—out of the total $2.2 billion that made up the WHO annual budget. (Gates gave over $324 million to WHO in 2017.) The Gates Foundation contributed more to the WHO than many developed nations.[70]

Vaccination versus Population?

In 2010 Bill Gates explained, "The world today has 6.8 billion people. That's headed up to about 9 billion. Now, if we do a really great job on new vaccines, health care, reproductive health services, we could lower that by perhaps 10 or 15 percent."[71]

Gates clarified the statement in 2018, explaining, "What we found out is that as health improves, families choose to have less children.... The population growth goes down as we improve health."[72]

Nevertheless, many people not on board with the hope to shrink the number of human beings in the world continue to be wary of a link between vaccines and population control. While their fear may give birth to conspiracy theories, their distrust of Gates and other global elites is not without foundation.

Gates played a key role in the COVID-19 lockdowns, mandates, and vaccines. "Bars and restaurants in most of the country will be closed as we go into this wave. And I think, sadly, that's appropriate," Gates told CNN in December 2020.[73]

Gates helped push massive coronavirus hysteria and lockdowns as the only solution. In August of 2020, Gates praised China for its strict lockdowns. Gates said that the Chinese "in their typical fairly authoritarian way, they did a very good job of suppressing the virus. There may have been a lot of individual rights that were violated there, but the overall macro effect that they achieved is kind of amazing." He added that China "kept the virus numbers to very low levels compared to most countries."

Gates also personally praised the most authoritarian COVID lockdowns anywhere on the planet. He lauded Australia's militarization response as the model for the United States to follow. Gates called for a "very different regimen so all countries can get on top of cases very quickly and be more like Australia than Europe or the U.S. ended up being." Gates said this in August 2021, as Victoria in Australia moved into its sixth lockdown after just eight cases of COVID were reported.[74]

"Bill Gates is no public health expert. He is not a doctor, an epidemiologist or an infectious disease researcher. Yet somehow he has become a central figure in the lives of billions of people, presuming to dictate the medical actions that will be required for the world to go 'back to normal," Corbett stated.

How did Gates go from a computer geek peddling a mediocre operating system to dictating international public health policy to the adulation of the media? Money, money, money.

"Gates has surpassed Rockefeller's legacy with the Bill & Melinda Gates Foundation long having eclipsed The Rockefeller Foundation as the largest private foundation in the world, with $46.8 billion of assets on its books that it wields in its stated program areas of global health and development, global growth, and global policy advocacy," Corbett reported.[75]

Reprogramming the Human Race

"[Bill Gates] was perhaps the primary figure responsible for planting the seed in the American (and perhaps global) consciousness, as early as March 2020, that the world would have to stay in lockdown until a vaccine was developed and administered to the vast majority of the world's population. One might wonder what gives Gates the authority to declare what the world must do. One might also wonder whether the man has a conflict of interest in such recommendations, given the fact that vaccines are currently his primary business concern. . . . Pharmaceuticals (particularly vaccines) are analogous to software when seen through the mechanized eyes of technocracy. Human beings are analogous to the computer systems this software is designed to modify." —Raelle Kaia, "Why Are They Doing This?"[76]

The Bill & Melinda Gates Foundation pumps out tens of millions of dollars annually to pay for positive media. Media partnerships and sponsorships essentially buy slick public relations for Gates and his foundations.

Gates influences coverage of global health and development issues as a "top 10 donor" to BBC's Media Action organization.[77] In the United Kingdom, he also funds *The Guardian*'s Global Development website.[78]

And Gates funds NPR's global-health coverage.[79]

He also provides funding to the key "Our World in Data" website that bills itself as providing "daily updated research and data" on the "coronavirus pandemic."[80]

Gates funds world-health coverage on ABC News—with cash grants. Even the *New York Times* was taken aback by Gates paying ABC News. "ABC News has entered into an unusual financial agreement with the Bill and Melinda Gates Foundation to back a yearlong project investigating global health problems and their potential solutions," the *Times* reported in 2010. The paper quoted ABC News admitting that the network "had never accepted a cash grant before."[81]

When the *PBS NewsHour with Jim Lehrer* was given a $3.5 million Gates Foundation grant to set up a special reporting division "to expand global health coverage," the funding essentially brought Gates's vision and philosophy to the reporting. "*NewsHour* correspondents will travel worldwide to produce forty to fifty documentary-style reports on global health issues" reported Philanthropy News Digest in 2008.

Gates's money did not just buy coverage, it turned "reporters" for PBS into paid lobbyists for Gates's global-health mission. "The *NewsHour* will also launch an outreach effort to put the coverage in front of policymakers, scientists, medical professionals, and others in the global health community."[82]

During the height of COVID-19 fears, Gates appeared regularly on *NewsHour* and could always count on softball questions from his paid crew at PBS. An April 2020 "news-segment" interview with Gates by anchor Judy Woodruff revealed the extent of the journalistic rot at the Gates-funded show.

Woodruff opened the interview with Gates by gushing, "One of the best-informed voices is that of businessman and philanthropist Bill Gates. The cofounder of Microsoft has spent the last few decades focused through the Bill and Melinda Gates Foundation on improving global health, including reducing the spread of infectious diseases."

She said, "You were one of the prescient few years ago who said that an infectious disease outbreak was coming that could kill millions of people"—neglecting to mention that warning cries of the possibility of another Spanish flu hitting someday had been ubiquitous in global health since the time of the original Spanish flu.

But Woodruff was not finished performing for Gates's bought-and-paid-for PR. "Well, Bill Gates, we thank you very much for spending the time with us, for talking with us today. Thank you and we wish you and what you are doing at the Foundation the very best," Woodruff concluded.[83]

In response to concerns that the journalistic integrity of PBS *NewsHour* was being compromised by the millions in Gates funding, communications chief Rob Flynn defended the show by suggesting that "there are not a heck of a lot of things you could touch in global health these days that would not have some kind of Gates tentacle."[84]

"The Final Solution"

Bill Gates appeared on *The Late Show with Stephen Colbert* in April 2020 to discuss the "return to normal" from COVID-19.

Gates: And then the final solution—which is a year to two years off—is the vaccine. So we've got to go full-speed ahead on all three fronts.

Colbert: Just to head off the conspiracy theorists, maybe we shouldn't call the vaccine "the final solution."

Gates: Good point.

Colbert: Maybe just "the best solution."

Gates: (laughing) Yeah, the return-to-normal solution.[85]

Investigative journalist James Corbett has explained the stranglehold Gates has on public health. "It comes as no surprise, then, that—far beyond the $250 million that the Gates Foundation has pledged to the 'fight' against coronavirus—every aspect of the current coronavirus pandemic involves organizations, groups and individuals with direct ties to Gates funding," Corbett reported.[86]

The Lancet expressed serious concerns about the Gates Foundation's influence on public health. "Apart from questions over its investments, the Gates Foundation has received little external scrutiny," *The Lancet* said in a May 2009 editorial noting Gates's $3 billion annual spending at the time. The medical journal reported:

> Last year, Devi Sridhar and Rajaie Batniji reported that the Foundation gave most of its grants to organizations in high-income countries....
>
> Their study shows even more robustly that the grants made by the Foundation do not reflect the burden of disease endured by those in deepest poverty. In an accompanying Comment, Robert Black and colleagues discuss the alarmingly poor correlation between the Foundation's funding and childhood disease priorities.
>
> The concern expressed to us by many scientists who have long worked in low-income settings is that important health programs are being distorted by large grants from the Gates Foundation....
>
> There is also a serious anxiety about the transparency of the Foundation's operation.... The first guiding principle of the Foundation is that it is "driven by the interests and passions of the Gates family." An annual letter from Bill Gates summarizes those passions, referring to newspaper articles, books, and chance events that have shaped the Foundation's strategy. For such a large and influential investor in global health, is such a whimsical governance principle good enough?[87]

Gates quite literally rules media, academia, government officials around the world, and the WHO.

How Did They Know?

A May 2010 future-scenario planning report on pandemics from the Rockefeller Foundation is chilling reading post–COVID-19. You would almost get the idea that the response to COVID-19 was foreseen ahead of time. More than ten years in advance of the actual pandemic, this report laid out an almost-exact blueprint of how governments would react, with details including the impacts of viral lockdowns and mask mandates.

The 2010 Rockefeller document was titled *Scenarios for the Future of Technology and International Development,* and the section on future pandemics was headed "Lock Step." It laid out the following hypothetical scenario: "In 2012, the pandemic that the world had been anticipating for years finally hit. Unlike 2009's H1N1, this new influenza strain—originating from wild geese—was extremely virulent and deadly."

The 2010 Rockefeller report envisioned "a world of tighter top-down government control and more authoritarian leadership, with limited innovation and growing citizen pushback."[88]

The Rockefeller Foundation and the Global Business Network produced the 2010 scenarios report to "to consider the roles of philanthropy and technology in future scenarios," according to television station WUSA 9 in Washington, D.C.[89]

According to the hypothetical scenario in the Rockefeller report, "The pandemic also had a deadly effect on economies: international mobility of both people and goods screeched to a halt, debilitating industries like tourism and breaking global supply chains. Even locally, normally bustling shops and office buildings sat empty for months, devoid of both employees and customers."

The report's authors presciently forecasted that "during the pandemic, national leaders around the world flexed their authority and imposed airtight rules and restrictions, from the mandatory wearing of face masks to body-temperature checks at the entries to communal spaces like train stations and supermarkets. Even after the pandemic faded, this more authoritarian control and oversight of citizens and their activities stuck and even intensified. In order to protect themselves from the spread of increasingly global problems—from pandemics and transnational terrorism to environmental crises and rising poverty—leaders around the world took a firmer grip on power."

The 2010 Rockefeller report accurately foresaw the battle over civil liberties from the COVID lockdowns. It also accurately noted that "the presence of so many top-down rules and norms greatly inhibited entrepreneurial activity."

The Rockefeller report even predicted how readily large sections of the population would submit to being locked down. "Citizens willingly gave up some of their sovereignty—and their privacy—to more paternalistic states in exchange for greater safety and stability. Citizens were more tolerant, and even eager, for top-down direction and oversight, and national leaders had more latitude to impose order in the ways they saw fit. In developed countries, this heightened oversight took many forms: biometric IDs for all citizens, for example, and tighter regulation of key industries whose stability was deemed vital to national interests," the 2010 report noted.

The Rockefeller Foundation's planning report also noted how China would be lauded for flexing authoritarian government viral policies: "A few countries did fare better—China in particular. The Chinese government's quick imposition and enforcement of mandatory quarantine for all citizens, as well as its instant and near-hermetic sealing off of all borders, saved millions of lives, stopping the spread of the virus far earlier than in other countries and enabling a swifter post-pandemic recovery."

The report criticized the U.S. response to the hypothetical virus as weak and ineffective in comparison. "The United States's initial policy of 'strongly discouraging' citizens from flying proved deadly in its leniency, accelerating the spread of the virus not just within the U.S. but across borders," it stated.

The planning report also predicted "technology trends" familiar to us: "Scanners using advanced functional magnetic resonance imaging (fMRI) technology [will] become the norm at airports and other public areas to detect abnormal behavior that may indicate 'antisocial intent.'"[90]

In July of 2020, *USA Today* noted that the 2010 Rockefeller report included parts "eerily reminiscent of the ongoing novel coronavirus pandemic."[91] But the media worked overtime to downplay the Rockefeller future-scenario report.

Fearing how lockdown opponents might utilize the Rockefeller report, WUSA 9 pleaded that "the document showcases what could possibly happen as a result of a pandemic. However, it's not some kind of plan, or even necessarily a prediction, for the current pandemic." The WUSA 9 report did admit that the 2010 Rockefeller "scenario does describe events that play out similarly to what we've seen in the real world."[92]

More Pandemic Scenarios

In the case of the World Economic Forum, the idea of exploiting any real or imagined crisis to impose their ideological vision on the world goes back at least to 2014.

As technology journalist Tim Hinchliffe reported at The Sociable, "Between 2014 and 2017, the WEF called to reshape, restart, reboot, and reset the global order every single year, each aimed at solving various 'crises.'"

Hinchliffe lays out the timeline:

- 2014: WEF publishes meeting agenda entitled "The Reshaping of the World: Consequences for Society, Politics and Business."
- 2015: WEF publishes article in collaboration with VOX EU called "We need to press restart on the global economy."
- 2016: WEF holds panel called "How to reboot the global economy."

- 2017: WEF publishes article saying, "Our world needs a reset in how we operate."[93]

In 2018, the World Economic Forum and the Johns Hopkins Center for Health Security engaged in a pandemic exercise similar to the 2010 Rockefeller event.

On May 15, 2018, just two years before the world was plunged into COVID-19 lockdowns, the Johns Hopkins Center for Health Security and the WEF hosted the "Clade X" pandemic event.[94] The Clade X exercise simulated a real-time virus outbreak, complete with mock video newscasts of anchors warning of the theoretical pandemic.

The Clade X event featured panels with government officials who warned that the world was not prepared to deal with the simulated global pandemic.

At the close of the Clade X simulation, the WEF concluded, "In the end, the outcome was tragic: the most catastrophic pandemic in history with hundreds of millions of deaths, economic collapse and societal upheaval."[95]

In addition, a third major pandemic exercise, "Event 201," which took place in October 2019, was conducted as part of a joint effort sponsored by the World Economic Forum, the Bill & Melinda Gates Foundation, and the Johns Hopkins Center for Health Security just before COVID-19 began to spread in Wuhan China. Event 201 portrayed a hypothetical coronavirus pandemic that would kill 65 million people, necessitating a global coordinated response between governments, international organizations, and global business concerns.[96]

CHAPTER 3

How the COVID-19 Response Accelerated the Great Reset

"One of the great lessons of the past five centuries in Europe and America is this: acute crises contribute to boosting the power of the state. It's always been the case and there is no reason why it should be different with the COVID-19 pandemic." That quotation is from Klaus Schwab and Thierry Malleret's book *COVID-19: The Great Reset*, published in 2020.[1]

That was the year that governments worldwide invented new ways to punish their citizens with tyrannical lockdowns, curfews, shelter-in-place orders, mask regulations, vaccination passports, and other mandates that were not even in the playbook of the public health bureaucracy before COVID. A global viral pandemic was just the ticket to end the old order of things and bring about a "new normal." When the pandemic hit, the forces behind the Great Reset were poised to never let a crisis go to waste, and these forces were in place to accelerate the radical transformation of society they had long sought.

"Waiting for Just the Right Moment to Pounce"

"I am not one for melodramatic comparisons, but in seriousness, in what kind of country do people wake up and find that in the middle of the night a minister passed a law, without warning or Parliamentary approval, that bans them going to the pub with people they don't live with?" asked human rights lawyer Adam Wagner.[2]

The answer to that question? A country and a world in which a Great Reset was planned and waiting for just the right moment to pounce. COVID-19 lockdowns and fear moved the Great Reset a long way toward its planners' goal.

Waking Up to the Great Reset

COVID-19 lockdowns happened almost overnight and remained in place for months, with constantly moving goalposts for when they could be lifted. It was nothing short of the suspension of democracy. In place of government by elected legislators, it was a complete deferral to the expertise of a credentialed class to formulate far-reaching policies at a whim.

Public health bureaucrats, whose names no one had even known before, were now wielding massive state powers to enforce quarantine, isolation, and mask mandates; restrictions on weddings, funerals, barbeques, and playgrounds; and even rules for how long you were permitted to leave your house, and for what purpose.

And what if you violated any of the edicts of these unelected health bureaucrats? Your friends, neighbors, or even family members could turn you into the authorities. Los Angeles mayor Eric Garcetti, in fact, encouraged citizens to report violators of the COVID stay-at-home orders with the slogan, "Snitches get rewards."[3]

Progressive activist Robert F. Kennedy Jr. sounded the alarm over how coronavirus restrictions were being manipulated to transform the world into tyranny. "Governments love pandemics the same way that they love wars because it gives them power, it gives them, it gives them control, and it gives them the capacity to impose obedience on human beings; and today we have an inflection of new technologies that give governments the capacity to impose controls on populations that have never been imagined before in human history!" Kennedy said. "The biosecurity agenda that people like Bill Gates and Anthony Fauci and Davos and all of these people who are running now the

> **Never Let a "Crisis Go to Waste"**
>
> "You never want a serious crisis to go to waste. And what I mean by that—it's an opportunity to do things that you think you could not do before." —Rahm Emanuel, Barack Obama's chief of staff in 2008[4]

global economy—they have understood for years that they have a power that no totalitarian government has ever had available to it, which is the biosecurity [state]," Kennedy explained.[5] Recall that the annual meeting at Davos, which is attended by the leaders of the world's most powerful countries, is a meeting of the World Economic Forum, founded in 1971 by Klaus Schwab, author of *The Great Reset*.

"Letting Lab Coats Run the World"

The United States is entering into a new phase where "The Danger of Letting Lab Coats Run the World" is palpable. That was the headline of a piece by Bill Dunne at American Thinker. "It should be clear by now that most of the world's leaders were stampeded over the lockdown cliff like so many lemmings. What caused the stampede is even more remarkable: a tiny coterie of obscure, soft-spoken epidemiologists in white lab coats playing with numbers.... The aim was to cause panic," he wrote. "We were plunged into the grandest of experiments in authoritarian paternalism, whereby we plebeians—i.e., those without government jobs—are deemed incompetent to judge if it's safe to take a dip in the ocean or a walk in the woods. We can, though, crowd into a Walmart or the local supermarket."[6]

French president Emmanuel Macron warned citizens to stay confined to their homes and urged, "We must all limit the number of people with who[m] we're in contact with every single day. Scientists say so."[7]

Scientists say so. As C. S. Lewis warned, "I dread government in the name of science. That is how tyrannies come in."[8] And tyrannies came in—fast—with COVID.

The World Economic Forum went full throttle on the Great Reset. They didn't want to let a crisis go to waste. UN leaders, globalists, power-hungry public health bureaucrats, and blue-state governors saw the greatest opportunity in a lifetime to expand the power of the state.

Ending Freedom

"In the sweep of history, intellectuals have specialized in conjuring rationales for why freedom needs to be ended in favor of top-state statist forms of social planning. There were religious reasons, genetic reasons, end-of-history reasons, security reasons, and a hundred more.

"Every age has generated some fashionable and overriding reason why people cannot be free. Public health is the reason of the moment."
—Jeffrey A. Tucker of the Brownstone Institute, author of *Liberty or Lockdown*[9]

In fact, as COVID-19 came on the scene and the world copied China, tried-and-true public health guidelines for pandemics were jettisoned. Renowned epidemiologist Donald Henderson, who oversaw the ten-year international effort to rid the world of smallpox and is credited with launching global childhood-vaccination programs, wrote in 2006 on the best way to deal with a viral pandemic. Henderson was awarded the Presidential Medal of Freedom in 2002.[10]

"Experience has shown that communities faced with epidemics or other adverse events respond best and with the least anxiety when the normal social functioning of the community is least disrupted," Henderson wrote in a 2006 *Biosecurity and Bioterrorism* paper titled "Disease Mitigation Measures in the Control of Pandemic Influenza.[11]

But the world wholly ignored that experience. World leaders, public health bureaucracies, governors, mayors, academia, and the media fell all over themselves during COVID-19 to instill the maximum anxiety and fear possible with dire scare scenarios of mass deaths.

"The New Western Normal"

"The pandemic state of emergency did indeed shatter the consensus about individual freedom. Across the developed world, the liberal privileging of individual freedom has been replaced by a *de facto* acceptance that state power absolutely must be ordered to the common good, up to and including coercive measures where necessary. . . . The new Western normal is one of authoritarian regimes now visibly reluctant to relinquish their grip on a state of emergency." —Mary Harrington, editor at the British magazine UnHerd [12]

With hysterical virus models peddling Spanish flu–scale doom on the world and videos out of China purporting to show people dropping dead in the street, the forces of statism moved quickly to frighten people everywhere and shut down the world.

"In early 2020, the public turned to the advice of scientific authorities when confronted with an apparent viral outbreak. Soon after, most nations followed the advice of prominent scientists and implemented restrictions commonly referred to as 'lockdowns,'" attorney Michael P. Senger, writing about "China's Global Lockdown Propaganda Campaign" for the Tablet, explained. [13]

Made in China

"While the policies varied by jurisdiction, in general they involved restrictions on gatherings and movements and the closure of schools, businesses, and public places, inspired by those imposed by the Chinese Communist Party (CCP) in Hubei Province," Senger wrote. [14]

"In February 2020, a team from Imperial College London led by physicist Neil Ferguson ran a computer model that played an outsized role in justifying lockdowns in most countries. Imperial forecast that by Oct 2020, 2.2 million people in the U.S. would die as a result of COVID, and recommended months of lockdowns. The model predicted the United States could incur up to one million deaths even with 'enhanced social distancing.'" [15]

"I Forget to Be Scared"

"Masks are very simply symbolic. All they are is a sign: 'You are in a dangerous time, you need to listen to us.' If I don't see people wearing masks, I forget to be scared. And that's why they want people wearing masks, and it just could not be clearer." —Alex Berenson on *Tucker Carlson Tonight*, July 16, 2021[16]

Senger noted that enacting lockdowns for a virus was unheard of. "Indeed, to our knowledge, no scientist ever publicly supported imposing lockdowns until Xi Jinping, General Secretary of the Chinese Communist Party, personally authorized the 'unprecedented lockdown of Wuhan and other cities beginning on Jan. 23, [2020],'" Senger wrote.[17]

An editorial the *British Medical Journal* published in March 2021 echoed Senger's analysis. "In March [2020], at a time when the behavior and lethality of this infection was largely unknown, and in the justifiable panic following camera footage of people falling dead in the streets of Wuhan, the WHO's pandemic response plan, updated as recently as October 2019 was torn up," wrote Dr. Anne McCloskey.

"Fifty years of scientific and epidemiological research was dismissed, and instead Britain and Ireland, along with most of the developed world adopted the model espoused by the Chinese Communist Party," explained McCloskey, a practicing physician who also works with the Ireland-based Freedom Alliance.

The world we once knew or thought we knew was transformed, seemingly overnight. "The entire healthy population was locked up, elderly people were taken from hospital beds without expectation of further medical care, and legislation was passed, without parliamentary debate, removing fundamental human and constitutional rights—to movement, to association, to earn a living, to an education, to engage in public worship, and to access the range of medical services to which people were hitherto entitled," McCloskey wrote.[18]

Klaus Schwab, the World Economic Forum, China, the WHO, Gates, and the other forces behind the Great Reset had to be pleased as everyday liberties of citizens around the world were vaporized in favor of the collective good, with rule by an unelected expert class.

"Governments were advised in this course of action by scientists and medics whose identity, qualifications and aptitude for this work [were] largely hidden from public scrutiny. Even now, the conflicts of interest of these people on whose advice our futures depend are not publicly available," McCloskey explained.[19]

On September 14, 2020, federal district judge William S. Stickman IV issued an opinion on the legality of COVID-19 lockdowns in a case involving Butler County, Pennsylvania.

"While, unquestionably, states and local governments restricted certain activities for a limited period of time to mitigate the Spanish Flu, there is no record of any imposition of a population lockdown in response to that disease or any other in our history," Judge Stickman explained in *County of Butler v. Thomas W. Wolf*:

> The fact is that the lockdowns imposed across the United States in early 2020 in response to the COVID-19 pandemic are unprecedented in the history of our Commonwealth and our Country. They have never been used in response to any other disease in our history. They were not recommendations made by the CDC. They were unheard of by the people [of] this nation until just this year. It appears as though the imposition of lockdowns in Wuhan and other areas of China—a nation unconstrained by concern for civil liberties and constitutional norms—started a domino effect where one country, and state, after another imposed draconian and hitherto untried measures on their citizens. The lockdowns are, therefore, truly unprecedented from a legal perspective.[20]

In January 2020 the World Health Organization went into full propaganda mode for China when the Chinese locked down Wuhan and the Hubei province. "China's decision to lock down Wuhan, a city of 11

Throwing Out the Rulebook

"During the 1918–1919 flu pandemic, some American cities closed schools, churches and theaters, banned large gatherings and funerals and restricted store hours. But none imposed stay-at-home orders or closed all nonessential businesses. No such measures were imposed during the 1957 flu pandemic, the next-deadliest one; even schools stayed open.

"Lockdowns weren't part of the contemporary playbook, either. Canada's pandemic guidelines concluded that restrictions on movement were 'impractical, if not impossible.' The U.S. Centers for Disease Control and Prevention, in its 2017 community mitigation guidelines for pandemic flu, didn't recommend stay-at-home orders or closing nonessential businesses even for a flu as severe as the one a century ago." —Greg Ip in the *Wall Street Journal*, August of 2020[21]

million people, shows how committed the authorities are to contain[ing] a viral outbreak that emerged in a seafood market there, a World Health Organization representative in Beijing said," noted a January 23, 2020, report by Reuters.

World Health Organization official Gauden Galea "told Reuters the move, also now replicated in nearby Huanggang, was beyond WHO guidelines," the news agency reported. According to Galea, "the lockdown of 11 million people is unprecedented in public health history, so it is certainly not a recommendation the WHO has made." Locking down Wuhan was "a very important indication of the commitment to contain the epidemic in the place where it is most concentrated," Galea stated, adding that the public health community had to wait and see if the lockdown would work to stop the spread of the virus.[22]

By just one week later, on January 30, 2020, the WHO had apparently decided not to wait for any results but instead simply declared that China was doing an awesome job with their unprecedented lockdowns.[23]

The Virtue of Cowardice

"Socrates made clear in Plato's *Republic* that he did not want doctors to rule. Philosophers or even poets would be better governors of society, because they at least attempt to understand political and social life in its entirety and minister to the human soul. Doctors, by contrast, tend to disregard the soul: it is the nature of their art to focus on the body in lieu of higher concerns. . . . But rule by public health officials, under which we increasingly live today, encourages excessive risk-aversion and almost transforms cowardice into a virtue." –Jeffrey H. Anderson, director of the Bureau of Justice Statistics at the U.S. Department of Justice from 2017 to 2021[24]

WHO Loves Authoritarianism?

WHO director general Tedros Adhanom Ghebreyesus, who, as we have seen, owes his position to Communist China, had praise for his Chinese paymasters. "As I have said repeatedly since my return from Beijing, the Chinese government is to be congratulated for the extraordinary measures it has taken to contain the outbreak, despite the severe social and economic impact those measures are having on the Chinese people," Tedros gushed.

Tedros continued his campaigning for China's actions. "The speed with which China detected the outbreak, isolated the virus, sequenced the genome and shared it with WHO and the world are [sic] very impressive, and beyond words. So is China's commitment to transparency and to supporting other countries," he said.[25]

Tedros also said that he was personally "very impressed and encouraged by the [Chinese] president's detailed knowledge of the outbreak."[26] He claimed that "in many ways, China is actually setting a new standard for outbreak response. It's not an exaggeration."[27]

Ruling by Ridicule

"Hundreds of thousands of social media posts later traced to China praised the lockdown, and criticized and ridiculed world leaders who failed to follow suit." –Stacey Rudin at the American Institute for Economic Research[28]

The WHO's Emergency Committee also issued similar praise for China's show of authoritarianism. "The measures China has taken are good not only for that country but also for the rest of the world," the WHO dutifully reported. "The Committee welcomed the leadership and political commitment of the very highest levels of Chinese government, their commitment to transparency, and the efforts made to investigate and contain the current outbreak."[29]

Human rights activists, on the other hand, were horrified by the authoritarian lockdown that China was imposing on their citizens—and by the praise it was garnering from the World Health Organization.

"That the Chinese government can lock millions of people into cities with almost no advance notice should not be considered anything other than terrifying," said Frances Eve, the deputy director of research at Chinese Human Rights Defenders. "Human rights should not be a casualty to the coronavirus crisis.... The WHO is ignoring Chinese government suppression of human rights regarding the outbreak, including severe restrictions on freedom of expression," Eve wrote in *The Guardian*.

"The Measures Themselves Sow the Fear"

"[Lockdowns] thus create a feedback loop in which the measures themselves sow the fear that makes citizens . . . believe their risk of dying from COVID-19 is hundreds of times greater than it really is, which in turn causes them to support more lockdown measures."—attorney Michael P. Senger, author of "China's Global Lockdown Propaganda Campaign"[30]

"China's response to the outbreak included a month-long government cover-up in Wuhan, the centre of the outbreak, that led to the rapid spread of the coronavirus," Eve pointed out.

Eve ridiculed the WHO for touting China's "transparency." As she wrote, "Despite early evidence of human-to-human transmission when medical staff became infected, this information was not relayed to the public for weeks. Hardly a 'commitment to transparency.'"

In addition, "Chinese police punished frontline doctors for 'spreading rumors' for trying to warn the public in late December [2019]. Police are still engaged in a campaign to detain Chinese netizens for spreading so-called 'rumours,'" Eve wrote in February 2020. "Activists have been threatened with jail if they share foreign news articles or post on social media about the coronavirus outbreak."

"A Subjugated Population of Undifferentiated Automatons"

Masks "work to signal political obedience and ferret out enemies of the state who do not go along. If government wants a subjugated population of undifferentiated automatons, universal mask mandates take a solid step in that direction. What they are after is not public health. . . . The longer the mask mandates exist, the more money government raises and the less incentive authorities have to relax them or allow them to go unenforced." –Jeffrey A. Tucker of the Brownstone Institute, author of *Liberty or Lockdown*[31]

As Eve pointed out, the World Health Organization had betrayed its own principles: "The WHO declares that core principles of human rights and health includes accountability, equality and non-discrimination and participation. It even acknowledges that 'participation is important to accountability as it provides…checks and balances which do not allow unitary leadership to exercise power in an arbitrary manner.'" In contrast to the principles espoused by the WHO, "China is not a democracy and the people cannot remove their leaders from power for governance failures related to the coronavirus outbreak. People expressing discontent online can go to prison. There is no free press and journalists trying to report on the frontline are obstructed, detained, and their stories deleted from the internet. Medical staff are gagged. Civil society organisations decimated by Xi's crackdowns on human rights cannot work on the frontlines to support hospitals and communities. Frightened netizens are labelled 'rumour-mongers.'"

In conclusion, Eve urged, "This should not be the new standard for outbreak response. The WHO should abide by its own human rights principles and demand the Chinese government end its censorship and police suppression surrounding the coronavirus outbreak.[32]

The February 2020 "Report of the WHO-China Joint Mission on Coronavirus Disease 2019 (COVID-19)" included lavish praise for China's lockdowns. "China's uncompromising and rigorous use of non-pharmaceutical measures to contain transmission of the COVID-19 virus in multiple settings provides vital lessons for the global response," the report proclaimed.[33]

Bruce Aylward—the former assistant director general of the WHO and senior advisor to WHO director general Tedros—headed up the WHO "Mission" to China and had nothing but rave reviews for China's lockdowns. "China has taken one of the most ancient approaches for infectious disease control and rolled out probably the most ambitious, and I would say, agile and aggressive disease containment effort in history," Aylward explained on February 24, 2020,

Na-Na Na-Na Na! I Can't *Hear* You!

According to the Hong Kong Free Press, "World Health Organization advisor Bruce Aylward ended a video call with an RTHK journalist after she asked him about Taiwan's status."

"At first, [Aylward] appeared to pretend not to hear producer Yvonne Tong's question about whether the UN body would reconsider Taiwan's membership. 'I'm sorry, I couldn't hear your question, Yvonne . . . Let's move to another one then,' he said.

"When Tong called him back to ask again about Taiwan and its coronavirus measures, Aylward said: 'Well, we've already talked about China.' He then ended the interview, which was part of RTHK's weekly news show *The Pulse*.

"Taiwan has been ruled by the Republic of China government since 1945, but Beijing insists the island is part of its territory and pressures other countries and international bodies to follow its 'One China' policy. Taiwan is excluded from the WHO," Hong Kong Free Press noted. "Aylward has regularly featured in Chinese state media after he led a WHO mission to the country during the outbreak."[34]

during a "Press Conference of WHO-China Joint Mission on COVID-19."

"What China has demonstrated is, you have to do this. If you do it, you can save lives and prevent thousands of cases of what is a very difficult disease," Aylward urged.[35]

On February 26, 2020, the WHO's Aylward was in campaign mode for China's oppressive lockdown. "Copy China's response to COVID-19," Aylward urged the world in an interview with CGTN—China Global Television Network—in Europe.[36]

As Michael P. Senger pointed out, the World Health Organization was pushing the policy of a totalitarian dictatorship on the entire world with little justification. "The WHO did not even consider other countries' economic circumstances, demographics, or even their number of COVID-19 cases—which were very few in most of the world—before instructing the entire world that 'you have to do this,'" Senger wrote. "Anytime anyone endorses a lockdown for any length of time, even a few minutes, they are endorsing a Xi Jinping policy."[37]

"Society Permanently in Crisis"

"COVID was the best thing to ever happen to these people. The panic over an unknown virus caused too many of us to rush to give up freedoms we once knew to be essential: The right to travel, for example, or the right to eat in a restaurant; the right to protest in public; and in many cases, the right to run a business and take [care] of our families; literally the right to say goodbye to our elders and to bury our dead. . . . We've rolled out the blueprint for a society that is nominally free, but willing to throw freedom away in a crisis. So now, the leadership class has realized there's a lot of value to keeping society permanently in crisis." —Christopher Bedford, senior editor at The Federalist[38]

Jane Fonda was so enthralled with the COVID lockdowns and restrictions that she blurted out an inconvenient truth. "COVID is God's gift to the Left," the actress and activist said—then suddenly realized and admitted, "That's a terrible thing to say." Fonda called COVID an "existential crossroads" for the world. "What a great gift, what a tremendous opportunity, we're just so lucky—we have to use it with every ounce of intelligence and courage and wherewithal we have."[39]

It was a "gift" that not everybody was glad to receive. Oliver Smith, travel correspondent for *The Telegraph*, summed up the global lockdowns this way: "No holidays, no weddings, no family celebrations, no live music, no live sport, no nights out, no cinemas, no theatre, no bustling bars, no buzzing restaurants. No spontaneity, nor any way to plan for the future. No life. Enough is enough."[40]

CHAPTER 4

Following "The Science"— or the Chinese?

In the name of safety, the residents of the formerly free world gave up liberty and allowed "two weeks to flatten the curve" to turn into endless lockdowns, including stay-at-home orders, curfews, church closures, businesses decimated, schools canceled, and "phased reopenings"— which inevitably turned into a seesaw battle of restrictions loosened and tightened. "The lockdown and its consequences have brought a foretaste of what is to come: a permanent state of fear, strict behavioral control, massive loss of jobs, and growing dependence on the state," as German economics professor Antony P. Mueller explained.[1]

A "permanent state of fear" based on dodgy statistics and questionable epidemiology. "The Science" behind the policies does not hold up to scrutiny.

Dr. Deborah Birx, the former White House Coronavirus Response Coordinator under President Donald Trump, revealed that "if someone dies with COVID-19, we are counting that as a COVID-19 death."[2]

That's "with" COVID-19, not "from" COVID-19—a crucial distinction, and one that may not have been reflected in the coronavirus death counts.

Thus Dr. Thomas T. Siler said succinctly, "Let's demand a recount… of COVID deaths." When Siler analyzed the official death count from COVID-19, he found that it came up wanting because of changes made

81

by the CDC to the criteria for determining the deaths—and because of financial incentives Congress had put in place.

The Congressional CARES Act, which authorized more funding for hospitals with COVID patients, also created an incentive to push positive COVID-test results and patient "cases."

"Perhaps done with good intentions, this incentivized financially pushing the COVID-19 diagnosis to the top of the list so that hospitals can pay for the care they give," Siler wrote.[3]

And it wasn't just the death counts and the case counts. As Robert F. Kennedy Jr. pointed out, "They cannot tell you what the case fatality rate for COVID is, that's basic. They cannot give us a PCR test that actually works. They don't have—they have to change the definition of COVID on the death certificates, constantly, to make it look more and more dangerous. The one thing they are good at is pumping up fear."[4]

COVID Deaths...by Gunshot

A Colorado coroner blew the whistle on how "two of their five deaths related to COVID-19 were people who died of gunshot wounds," reported CBS Denver affiliate CBS4.

The coroner, Brenda Bock, says because "they tested positive for COVID-19 within the past 30 days, they were classified as 'deaths among cases.'" She told CBS, "It's absurd that they would even put that on there."

"The state health department says the Centers for Disease Control and Prevention requires them to report people who've died with COVID-19 in their systems because it's crucial for public health surveillance," CBS reported.[5]

Siler noted, "According to the CDC, only 6% of those who died with the COVID-19 infection had no other pre-existing health conditions. The other 94% had an average of four medical conditions already affecting their health."

As he explained, "This does not mean that only 6% of these deaths resulted from COVID-19. But it also does not mean that 100% of the deaths among people with other medical conditions should be counted as death from COVID-19 either. If we counted each death that tested positive for flu or had symptoms of flu as an 'influenza death,' we would also have hundreds of thousands of flu deaths each year."

Siler's analysis found that "applying that same logic to COVID-19 means that conservatively 25–50% of the deaths labeled *from* COVID-19 more likely died *with* COVID-19."

"The CDC also made influenza deaths magically vanish for this flu season. The CDC created a new category of death from pneumonia, influenza, and COVID-19 to lump those causes together. This only created confusion about COVID-19 deaths—and please, don't say that masking and distancing reduced influenza deaths while not reducing COVID-19 deaths," Siler wrote. "The fundamental difference was that, no matter the patient's ultimate cause of death, the new system mandated that COVID-19 must always be the first cause of death, with the other conditions listed as 'contributing factors'—the opposite of the old system."[6]

"Accounting Fraud"

"The WHO's PCR guidance was paired with new international ICD-10 codes for COVID deaths to make COVID-19 quite possibly the deadliest accounting fraud of all time. According to this coding guidance, if a decedent had either tested positive or been in contact with anyone who had, within several weeks prior to their death, then the death should be classified as a COVID-19 death. The result was a terrifying number of supposed 'COVID-19 deaths' that bore little relation to the number of 'excess deaths' in a given year, even in states and countries that employed few lockdown measures." –attorney Michael P. Senger, author of "China's Global Lockdown Propaganda Campaign"[7]

A study in Science, Public Health Policy, & the Law reported that on March 24, 2020, the CDC altered the way deaths were tabulated, and the new method created an inflated death toll from COVID-19. The report found "major problems with the process by which the CDC was able to generate inaccurate data during a crisis."

The report stated:

The CDC has advocated for social isolation, social distancing, and personal protective equipment use as primary mitigation strategies in response to the COVID-19 crisis, while simultaneously refusing to acknowledge the promise of inexpensive pharmaceutical and natural treatments. These mitigation strategies were promoted largely in response to projection model fatality forecasts that have proven to be substantially inaccurate.... Why would the CDC decide against using a system of data collection & reporting they authored, and which has been in use nationwide for 17 years without incident, in favor of an untested & unproven system exclusively for COVID-19 without discussion and peer-review? Did the CDC's decision to abandon a known and proven effective system also breach several federal laws that ensure data accuracy and integrity? Did the CDC knowingly alter rules for reporting cause of death in the presence of comorbidity exclusively for COVID-19? If so, why?[8]

Auditing the Death Count

"In Minnesota in December 2020, lawmakers Mary Farmer and Dr. Scott Jensen conducted a state audit of COVID-19 deaths, eventually sifting through 2,800 death certificates. They found that 800 patients (almost 30%) did not have SARS-COV-2 listed as a cause for death. They have appealed to their state for changes and asked for a national audit of COVID-19 deaths." –Thomas T. Siler at American Thinker[9]

Marty Makary, a Johns Hopkins physician, estimated that the COVID-19 infection fatality rate is 0.23 percent, which is not very different from a bad influenza season. "About 1 in 600 Americans has died of Covid-19, which translates to a population fatality rate of about 0.15%. The Covid-19 infection fatality rate is about 0.23%," Makary wrote in 2021.[10]

Thomas Siler asked the key question at American Thinker: "If the CDC ceases to be a reliable source for health data, some of our state governments manipulate data, and the major media outlets have no interest in investigating and reporting the truth, how long will the American people go along with this medical tyranny of lockdowns, masking, social distancing, and financial ruin?"[11]

Cheryl Chumley, the author of *Police State USA: How Orwell's Nightmare Is Becoming Our Reality*, pointed out the problem with how public health agencies relished their authoritarian role in COVID. "No medical bureaucrat should ever hold so much power in America, a country where individual rights and the individual right to self-determine [are] supposed to reign," Chumley wrote in 2021. "But all in all, the takeaway is this: Health officials employed by the government are there to advise, recommend, guide and provide scientific and medical facts—but not to dictate. Not to demand. Not to order....

"Fauci, on the coronavirus, has been decidedly political. His science has been politicized. His scientific guidance has been weaponized. His ties to China and the Wuhan lab uncomfortably close," Chumley wrote. "It's high time—past time—to take back America from the bureaucrats. They never should have had that much power in the first place."[12]

But Dr. Fauci doesn't see the problem—as became clear when Ohio Congressman Jim Jordan asked Fauci directly about the issue at an April 2021 House Committee hearing:

> **Jordan:** What objective outcome do we have to reach before Americans get their liberties and freedoms back?
> **Fauci:** You know, you're indicating liberty and freedom. I look at it as a public health measure to prevent people from dying and going to the hospital.
> **Jordan:** You don't think Americans' liberties have been threatened the last year, Dr. Fauci? They have been assaulted, their liberties have.

Fauci: I don't look at this as a liberty thing, Congressman Jordan.

Jordan: Well, that's obvious.

Fauci: I look at this as a public health thing. I disagree with you on that completely.

Jordan: Do you think the Constitution is suspended during a virus, during a pandemic? It is certainly not.

Jordan summed up: "Dr. Fauci, over the last year, Americans' First Amendment rights have been completely attacked. Your right to go to church, your right to assemble, your right to petition your government, freedom of the press, freedom of speech—have all have been assaulted."[13]

> ### No Cost-Benefit Analysis
> "Thomas Sowell famously wrote, 'Only in government is any benefit, however small, considered to be worth any cost, however large.' This is essentially where we are in our response to COVID-19."—David Catron in the *American Spectator*[14]

Former UK Supreme Court judge Lord Sumption explained the threat to our liberties. "Do we really want to be the kind of society where basic freedoms are conditional on the decisions of politicians in thrall to scientists and statisticians? Where human beings are just tools of public policy?" Sumption asked.

"To say that life is priceless and nothing else counts is just empty rhetoric.... There is more to life than the avoidance of death," he added. "To say that there are no limits is the stuff of tyrants. Every despot who ever lived thought that he was coercing his subjects for their own good or that of society at large," the judge pointed out.

"A society in which the Government can confine most of the population without controversy is not one in which civilized people would want to live, regardless of their answers to these questions. Is it worth it?"

Sumption asked. "The lockdown is, without doubt, the greatest interference with personal liberty in our history."[15]

Former Harvard University physicist Dr. Luboš Motl wrote early on during the lockdowns that "25 million Americans became unemployed in 5 weeks.... Many people want this insanity to continue. As far as I know, it has never happened in the history of civilizations that the bulk of a large enough nation, let alone the world, was kept at home for several months."

Motl explained, "The precautionary principle has only been promoted as a meme since the 1970s when it appeared as the 'Vorsorgeprinzip' in German discussions about deforestation and sea pollution. The precautionary principle is an extremely dangerous fallacy whose purpose is to make an absolutely irrational assumption—namely that some risks must be considered infinitely more critical than all other risks—sound more intelligent or maybe even scientific.... You are 'obliged' to do even things that actually make the public health conditions worse."[16]

Economist Sanjeev Sabhlok urged Western nations to build in civil-liberty protections against future lockdowns: "This pandemic should lead to the rewriting of all textbooks in epidemiology and should lead to a law (like they have in Sweden) that governments must require court orders for each individual, to restrain them at home for quarantine or lockdown."[17]

"Prisoners in a So-Called Liberal Democracy"

Sky News TV broadcaster Alan Jones deplored the fact that Australians had been made "prisoners in a so-called democracy" in July 2020.

"When will this end? More importantly, what will the end look like? When will someone give us our lives back? We can look after our own health. We're not stupid. We know how to look after ourselves. We have been made prisoners in our so-called liberal democracy," Jones explained.

"Freedoms taken from us, the very freedoms men and women died for. We're creating a dangerous environment here, perpetuating the view that governments have the answers—are you kidding me? Those who created the problem and the disproportionate response, now reckon they have the answer?"[18]

"Australia Traded Away Too Much Liberty" read a headline in *The Atlantic*. The subhead asked, "How Long Can a Democracy Maintain Emergency Restrictions and Still Call Itself a Free Country?" Conor Friedersdorf wrote, "Before 2020, the idea of Australia all but forbidding its citizens from leaving the country, a restriction associated with Communist regimes, was unthinkable. Today, it is a widely accepted policy."

Friedersdorf wondered, "But if a country indefinitely forbids its own citizens from leaving its borders, strands tens of thousands of its citizens abroad, puts strict rules on intrastate travel, prohibits citizens from leaving home without an excuse from an official government list, mandates masks even when people are outdoors and socially distanced, deploys the military to enforce those rules, bans protest, and arrests and fines dissenters, is that country still a liberal democracy?"[19]

As Australia was transformed into an authoritarian dystopia, Bill Gates urged the world to follow the former penal colony's lead. "If every country does what Australia did, then you wouldn't be calling [the next outbreak] a pandemic," Gates declared.[20]

Not to be outdone, Canada tried to keep up with Australia's impressive COVID tyranny. In 2022 Canadian prime minister Justin Trudeau invoked martial law to stop the Canadian truckers' "Freedom Convoy" protest of COVID mandates. Historian Victor Davis Hanson noted how Canada arrested and tried to "financially destroy truckers on the charge that their largely peaceful protests are 'dismantling the Canadian economy' that had already been dismantled for two years under some of the most draconian lockdowns in the world."

The truckers who descended on the Canadian capital of Ottawa played "the role of the proverbial straw that may break the back of a once compliant Canadian citizenry, burdened by over two years of masks, lockdowns, and vaccination mandates," Hanson wrote.[21]

Judge Andrew Napolitano exposed the "government's emergency powers myth," pointing out how autocratic state governors invoked these supposed "powers" to tyrannize their citizens.

"[New Jersey Governor Phil] Murphy quite literally issued executive orders barring folks from doing what the Constitution guarantees them the right to do, and he imposed criminal penalties for violating his orders, and he had folks who defied him arrested and prosecuted. Stated differently, he assumed the powers of the state legislature—which is to write the laws—and he violated his oath to uphold the Constitution," Napolitano explained.

> **"Far Scarier than Any Virus"**
> "This is what the Left wants. They want people stripped of wealth, isolated, and terrified. They want sources of joy—church, sporting events, vacations, large social gatherings—eliminated. This is how they get control. And it's far scarier than any virus."
> —Julie Kelly at American Greatness, March 12, 2020[22]

"If government officials could declare an emergency whenever they wished and thereby be relieved of the obligation to defend the Constitution—and the rights it guarantees—then no liberty is safe," Napolitano wrote.

"During the War Between the States, Abraham Lincoln did more than disparage [natural rights]. He ordered the military to arrest newspaper editors and even public officials in the North and confine them without trial because he disapproved of their criticism of him," the judge wrote.

"In a unanimous decision, cited hundreds of times, the Supreme Court rejected the concept that 'emergency' somehow creates or increases government power. The court condemned 'emergency' as a doctrine the fruits of which none is 'more pernicious.' This condemnation is still the law of the land today, and it applies to the states as well as to the feds," Napolitano explained.

"The Ninth Amendment—which today restrains the feds and the states—is the work of James Madison's genius. Madison, who chaired the House of Representatives committee that wrote the Bill of Rights, wrestled along with his colleagues about the best way to protect unenumerated rights," the judge added. "If the government declares an emergency, can it thereby acquire the lawful power to interfere with constitutionally guaranteed freedoms? In a word: No."[23]

Feminist icon and former Clinton-administration advisor Naomi Wolf spoke out in 2020 as COVID-19 lockdowns persisted long past the "two weeks to flatten the curve."

"We are at step ten of the ten steps needed for fascism to take root in America," Wolf wrote in October 2020. "The onset of the COVID-19 pandemic has given those in power the tool needed to finish the job, which is why it's very important to understand that lockdown is not a quarantine."

Wolf noted that "this long, determined path toward authoritarianism" had been laid out in her bestselling book *The End of America*.

"So we are here at step ten. Let's look now at a massive euphemism that is allowing for the various power grabs we will explore, that the COVID-19 pandemic facilitates.... National leaders are using the term 'quarantine' to refer to acts of closing down economic activity in entire states and even nations, and of restricting all citizens' travel to and from entire states lines or across borders to countries. This 'quarantine' has in turn shut down engines of economic activity," Wolf wrote.

"Our global and nation by nation 'lockdown' really doesn't look much like any disease-related 'quarantines' in history at all. The large-scale forced closure of businesses, and the cordoning off of complete societies, with movements of both healthy and infected citizens restricted by the state, is something other than historical 'quarantine' altogether," she pointed out.

"There seems to be no exit strategy from this crisis, to regain the public spaces and processes in which real democracy takes place," Wolf wrote. "When will it be safe enough? What is that benchmark? Given how great COVID policies are for those who hate democracy and profit from its demise, I am warning that at this point it is unlikely ever to be deemed by our leaders safe enough to resume a full democracy, medical reality, and even a potential full recovery of our collective health from this pandemic, notwithstanding; not unless we do some hard independent thinking about how we make decisions as a community," she added.

"Nationwide restrictions of all citizens, healthy and ill; restrictions of citizens' movements; and suppression of all economic activity, have indeed been used in the past," Wolf wrote. "But these edicts on this scale have not been used in the past to solve the problem of infectious diseases. Rather, they have been used in the past to solve the problem of democracy itself," she pointed out.

"Staying home, sick with well; and state-wide or nationally restricted movement; is not a time-honored medical practice, but a drastic social experiment which has been tried at scale only in closed societies," Wolf wrote.[24]

British columnist Peter Hitchens warned about the lockdowns from the outset. Lockdowns are "the biggest state takeover of life and work ever attempted by non-Communists," Hitchens wrote.[25]

"All the crudest weapons of despotism, the curfew, the presumption of guilt and the power of arbitrary arrest, are taking shape in the midst of what used to be a free country," Hitchens pointed out about the COVID lockdowns, which he called "a frightening series of restrictions on ancient liberties and vast increases in police and state powers."

Hitchens wrote, "Even Vladimir Putin might hesitate before doing anything so blatant." He lamented that citizens of the United Kingdom were so willing to "surrender centuries-old liberties in an afternoon" and "seem to despise our ancient hard-bought freedom and actually want to rush into the warm, firm arms of Big Brother."

"Imagine, police officers forcing you to be screened for a disease, and locking you up for 48 hours if you object. Is this China or Britain?" Hitchens asked. "How long before we need passes to go out in the streets, as in any other banana republic?"[26]

Prisoners of War

The global lockdowns were eerily reminiscent of what prisoners of war have had to endure, as documented in Albert D. Biderman's

September 1957 paper "Communist Attempts to Elicit False Confessions from Air Force Prisoners of War." Biderman, a social-science researcher, wrote the report on the torture and brainwashing techniques used by the Chinese and North Koreans during the Korean War for the Air Force Office for Social Science Programs.[27]

Physicist Denis Rancourt drew the parallel. "COVID = Large-scale application of the Biderman chart of coercion, which is an expert torture method for prisoners of war," Rancourt explained.[28]

Sanjeev Sabhlok agreed. "Indeed—there's a very strong overlap between communist or Nazi propaganda techniques and the techniques being used during this pandemic by allegedly free societies," Sabhlok wrote.[29]

Biderman's work has been used by human rights organizations and anti-abuse groups. The Wheaton, Illinois, Family Shelter Service used Biderman's research to illustrate the warning signs of domestic violence.

"Domestic violence experts believe that batterers use these same techniques," the Family Shelter Service chart handout explained. The chart includes language that literally describes the COVID lockdowns:

Isolation
    Deprives victim of all social support...
    Makes victim dependent upon abuser
Control or Distortion of Perceptions
    ... Eliminates information that is not in agreement with the abuser's message
    Punishes actions or responses that demonstrate independence or resistance...
Humiliation or Degradation:
    ...Heightens feelings of incompetence
    Induces mental and physical exhaustion
Threats
    Creates anxiety and despair...
Demonstrating Omnipotence or Superiority or Power
    Demonstrates to victim that resistance is futile

CHART I.—COMMUNIST COERCIVE METHODS
FOR ELICITING INDIVIDUAL COMPLIANCE

General Method	Effects (Purposes?)	Variants
1. Isolation	Deprives Victim of all Social Support of his Ability to Resist Develops an Intense Concern with Self Makes Victim Dependent on Interrogator	Complete Solitary Confinement Complete Isolation Semi-Isolation Group Isolation
2. Monopolization of Perception	Fixes Attention upon Immediate Predicament; Fosters Introspection Eliminates Stimuli Competing with those Controlled by Captor Frustrates all Actions not Consistent with Compliance	Physical Isolation Darkness or Bright Light Barren Environment Restricted Movement Monotonous Food
3. Induced Debilitation; Exhaustion	Weakens Mental and Physical Ability to Resist	Semi-Starvation Exposure Exploitation of Wounds; Induced Illness Sleep Deprivation Prolonged Constraint Prolonged Interrogation or Forced Writing Over Exertion
4. Threats	Cultivates Anxiety and Despair	Threats of Death Threats of Non-repatriation Threats of Endless Isolation and Interrogation Vague Threats Threats Against Family Mysterious Changes of Treatment
5. Occasional Indulgences	Provides Positive Motivation for Compliance Hinders Adjustment to Deprivation	Occasional Favors Fluctuations of Interrogators' Attitudes Promises Rewards for Partial Compliance Tantalizing
6. Demonstrating "Omnipotence" and "Omniscience"	Suggests Futility of Resistance	Confrontations Pretending Cooperation Taken for Granted Demonstrating Complete Control over Victim's Fate
7. Degradation	Makes Costs of Resistance Appear More Damaging to Self-Esteem than Capitulation Reduces Prisoner to "Animal Level" Concerns	Personal Hygiene Prevented Filthy, Infested Surroundings Demeaning Punishments Insults and Taunts Denial of Privacy
8. Enforcing Trivial Demands	Develops Habit of Compliance	Forced Writing Enforcement of Minute Rules

Biderman's Chart of Coercion, a tool developed to explain the methods used to brainwash prisoners of war and break their will. *Office for Social Science Programs, Air Force Personnel and Training Research Center, Air Research and Development Command*

Enforcing Trivial Demands

Demands are often trivial, contradictory and non-achievable

Reinforces who has power and control…

Occasional Indulgences

Provides positive motivation for conforming to abuser's demands.[30]

Amnesty International has also featured the chart.[31]

Inside Australia's "Covid Internment Camp"

"Hayley Hodgson, 26, moved to Darwin from Melbourne to escape the never-ending lockdowns—only to find herself locked up in a Covid Internment Camp without even having the virus" reported Unherd TV in December 2021.

"It all began when a friend of hers tested positive. She recounts how investigators came to her home shortly afterwards, having run the numberplate of her scooter to identify her as a 'close contact,'" Unherd reported. "So then the police officers blocked my driveway," Hodgson explained. "I walked out and I said, 'What's going on, are you guys testing me for COVID? What's happening?' They said, 'No, you're getting taken away. And you have no choice. . . .' I just said, 'I don't consent to this.'"

Hodgson detailed her fourteen-day internment in the camp: "You literally get put on the back of a golf buggy with your bags. And these people are in hazmat suits and everything. They don't want to come near you because they think you're infectious. And they literally drop you to your room. And they leave you. They don't come and say anything, they don't check up, they don't do anything. You get delivered your meals once a day. And you are just left. . . . You feel like you're in prison. You feel like you've done something wrong, it's inhumane what they're doing. You are so small, they just overpower you. And you're literally nothing. It's like 'You do what we say, or you're in trouble, we'll lock you up for longer.' Yeah, they were even threatening me that if I was to do this again, 'We will extend your time in here.'"[32]

"Pure Psychological Torture"

One furious mother in Brooklyn laid out the prisoner-of-war mentality created by these arbitrary COVID lockdowns.

"It wasn't actually the virus that I was afraid of, but the lockdowns. I was so deeply psychologically damaged from the NYC lockdown in the spring that I lived in perpetual terror of it happening again," explained "NYC Angry Mom" in a series of viral tweets in May 2021.

"[Governor Andrew] Cuomo spent the entire summer and fall threatening and browbeating us for our 'bad behavior' and I deeply internalized this message. I remember screaming at my neighbors and telling them that if they didn't put on a mask, they were going to face my wrath if my kids' school was closed. At one point, Cuomo put us into an arbitrary microcluster and we escaped closed schools by only a few blocks. I spent the entire school year watching every stupid metric and desperately trying to get three steps ahead of Cuomo."

She also said, "To be clear, I never supported the lockdowns. I thought they were an abomination. Pure psychological torture. Masks felt like the compromise to keep us out of lockdown, and I got angry when everyone wouldn't comply to keep us out of lockdown."

"If you go back and watch Cuomo's briefings, the threat of closures (dependent on our behavior!) was a daily phenomenon. And when they happened, they were metric-free, indefinite in nature, arbitrary and capricious. Completely at the whim of one man, and one man only."

She explained how a society was imprisoned:

Lockdowns were something completely out of our control.

We opened the door to something new and nefarious—(inept) governments having 100% power over their citizens' doings, with fear as a powerful motivator for compliance....

It shouldn't need to be explicitly stated that it's not sustainable (or humane) to demand people sacrifice:

- Time with loved ones
- Education
- Livelihood
- Socialization

For months on end, or even YEARS.

Yet, this was/is unapologetically the expectation in many parts of the US.[33]

Stockholm Syndrome

Not everyone living under lockdowns wanted their freedom back. Many people seemed to be suffering from what is known as Stockholm Syndrome, after a phenomenon first noted almost forty years ago.

"When it became clear to Jan-Erik Olsson that he wouldn't be able to flee the bank he was attempting to rob, he decided to take hostages. For six days in August of 1973, the four hostages and their captor got to know each other, and once rescued, the hostages not only refused to testify against Jan-Erik, they actually raised money for his defense," Devin Balkind explained in a June 2020 article at the Gotham Gazette. "This bizarre phenomenon, where 'hostages develop a psychological alliance with their captors' is now known as Stockholm Syndrome."

Balkind observed, "As coronavirus lockdown begins to lift in New York City and residents begin to resume their lives in the 'new normal,' the signs of Stockholm Syndrome are all around us." He pointed out, "Despite overseeing what is objectively the world's least effective response to coronavirus in the entire world, resulting in the deaths of a staggering 0.2% of the city's population, Governor Andrew Cuomo and Mayor Bill de Blasio had, as of May 6 [2020], unfathomably high approval ratings of 81% and 63%, respectively."

As Balkind noted, "During the peak of the crisis in early April [2020], *Rolling Stone* published 'Andrew Cuomo Takes Charge,' a glowing piece of journalistic pomp; a prominent local politics magazine showcased Cuomo as 'the most popular man in America' and 'the nation's most eligible bachelor'; and another publication called him 'America's Governor' while he made friendly interview appearances all over cable news and those stations also carried his daily briefings live for weeks, growing his allure. Trevor Noah and Ellen DeGeneres came out as #CuomoSexual at the same time over 500 New York City residents were dying a day—the most of any city in the world."[34]

Despite this appalling track record, Governor Cuomo's COVID policies had some big fans—including one Dr. Anthony Fauci. "New York got hit worse than any place in the world. And they did it correctly by doing the things that you're talking about," Fauci gushed in July of 2020.[35]

"The Fear of Freedom"

Stockholm Syndrome infected lockdown victims globally. "I'm Loath to Admit It, But Part of Me Is Frightened of Leaving Lockdown," was the headline of a February 24, 2021, column by Simon Kelner for United Kingdom's *i* newsaper.

"Desperate though we all may be for life to open up again, I can't be the only person in England who's pleased that Boris Johnson has opted for a cautious approach towards ending lockdown.

"Not because I'm worried from an epidemiological point of view. It's more that his exit strategy will give me the time to come to terms with this strange and unnerving feeling I have—the fear of freedom," Kelner wrote.

"It's a curious form of Stockholm syndrome. Like captives preparing to emerge into the daylight, we will soon be forced to acclimatize to real life again after being conditioned by lockdown to exist within narrow horizons, and with limited expectations," Kelner explained.

"There is a peculiar comfort in having no freedom of choice," he added.[36]

"A Decade or Longer"

In December 2021, when the omicron variant of COVID-19 arrived, UK public health seemed regenerated by the new scare and declared another five to ten years of mandates to battle the virus. "Covid will be a threat to the NHS for at least the next five years and testing and vaccines may be needed for a decade or longer, the government's scientific advisers have said," *The Times* of London reported. "Ministers have been told that it will take 'at least a further five years for Covid-19 to settle to a predictable endemic state'—where the virus lingers in the background but does not threaten to rapidly overwhelm the health system."[37]

The *Northwich Guardian* newspaper in the United Kingdom echoed these sentiments. In an April 2021 column titled "'Lockdown Stockholm Syndrome' Sets in as Restrictions Ease," a columnist writing under the moniker "The Fly in the Ointment" admitted, "In some ways, I feel that I may be suffering from some kind of coronavirus lockdown Stockholm Syndrome. I've quite liked being locked down and working from home and the idea of opening up society too quickly fills me with a degree of anxiety and more than a little apprehension.

"My real fear is that we have been here before, opening up too quickly with the resultant rise in Covid infections, hospitalizations and subsequent deaths. I can't help but think there have been times during this pandemic the government has put public wealth before public health."

He concluded, "So excuse me if I don't join the wave of lockdown relaxation euphoria and rush out to the shops just yet."[38]

Amy Hobbs, a research associate at the Johns Hopkins Bloomberg School of Public Health explained, "I expect that wearing a mask will become part of my daily life, moving forward, even after a vaccine is deployed."[39]

"Ver Are Your Paperz!"

Statistician William M. Briggs rejected the entire approach to COVID that utilized lockdowns and mask mandates. "Raise your hand if you're tired of hearing from 'experts,'" Briggs wrote.[40] "Stay inside or die!" Briggs mocked, noting, "*Ver are your paperz!* comes to the good ol' USA."[41]

The Resistance

But some people were willing to risk their livelihoods to oppose this new normal.

The old story of individuals standing against tyranny was played out around the country. A New Jersey gym in Bellmawr refused to be shut down, and the owners racked up over $1 million in fines. Ultimately Atilis Gym owners Ian Smith and Frank Trumbetti were arrested and charged with "fourth-degree contempt, obstruction, and violation of a disaster-control act" for staying open and refusing to follow the state's lockdown orders.

"'After Atilis Gym refused to comply with multiple criminal citations and Superior Court orders, including a contempt of court order issued, today law enforcement entered the premises to ensure closure of the gym and to abate the public health risks,' a spokesperson for New Jersey Attorney General Gurbir Grewal said in a statement" on July 27, 2020.

Gym owners Smith and Trumbetti were greeted by flag-waving supporters chanting "U.S.A." for defying New Jersey's lockdown orders on business. "Welcome to America 2020, where feeding your family and standing up for your Constitutional rights is illegal," the gym's Facebook post stated, adding that New Jersey governor Phil Murphy was "flexing his little tyrant muscles finally." A defiant Smith declared, "We will not be backing down under any circumstances," despite the arrests and fines of more than $1.2 million.[42] "Free men don't ask permission. Or for forgiveness," Smith averred.[43]

Matt Strickland, the owner of food-truck-turned-restaurant Gourmeltz in Fredericksburg, Virginia, defied the lockdown orders and mask mandates and faced a blizzard of local, state, and federal coercion to make him comply.

Virginia's attorney general filed an injunction against Strickland and attempted to convince a circuit court judge to force him to shut down. But Strickland made the following argument: "We've been operating this way since June [2020] and there have been zero cases linked back to my restaurant. My employees have never been positive for COVID nor myself.... How I'm a substantial and imminent threat to the community, I'm not so sure."

The circuit court judge ruled in Strickland's favor, allowing his restaurant to stay open.

"I realized all of these mandates and regulations that the governor was putting into place was about something other than our health and safety 'cause they just made—they made no sense. And they were actually stripping my customers, my employees, and my constitutional rights and freedoms from us," Strickland explained.

"So I decided not to be a part of that, and decided to let my, my customers decide for themselves whether or not they wanted to wear a mask and sit at a bar," he said.

"I fought my whole, my whole adult life in Iraq and Afghanistan against things like that—dictatorships, which is what this is kind of starting to be."[44]

"An Inflection Point"

The coronavirus lockdowns and other restrictions played a central role in advancing the Great Reset upon the world. The COVID theater of stay-at-home orders, masks, curfews, and contradictory and ever-changing rules to make us all "safe" hit the public like a giant psyop, moving everyone closer to accepting future public health restrictions without questioning them.

"We are at an inflection point—I believe in human history—the largest and most critical inflection point that human humanity has ever encountered. For many years totalitarian or authoritarian states have used the power of fear to engineer compliance in populations," Robert F. Kennedy Jr. said.

During the Great Depression, Kennedy added, "we were very lucky that we had a leader, Franklin Roosevelt. And he said, 'The only thing we have to fear is fear itself.' He understood that fear would drive us into totalitarianism." In contrast, said Kennedy, "Hitler could point at the

"Totalitarian Inclinations"

"They were able to tap into the deep well of totalitarian inclinations of 'politicians' everywhere and at the same time so clearly demonstrated how they can be led around by the nose. These totalitarians now command the police and armies and they discard and ignore the very laws that founded their countries/states only to introduce personal mandates.

"Hence, they were able to create whole prison nations (Australia and New Zealand being the most notable, but there are many others) and semi-tyrannical despotisms (U.K., Ireland, France, Spain, Italy, and many states as well as the Federal Government in the US, Canada, and others) where none existed before.

"They were able to enlist, very effectively, most major media in most countries as sources of propaganda and brainwashing, and they have profited from it. —Roger W. Koops, a chemist who worked in the pharmaceutical and biotechnology industry for over twenty-five years[45]

Jews and say, 'Those are the big threat, we need to be frightened of them, and you and everybody else needs to obey so that we can fight them off.'"[46]

Naomi Wolf echoed Kennedy's analysis. "North Korea and China have indeed utilized the cordoning off of entire regions and putting them under no-movement rules for everyone. The Chinese Communist Party, long before the COVID pandemic, was among few modern societies to restrict citizens' physical movements nationally and regionally. As dissident escapees from North Korea report, North Korean nationals have also long been unable to move freely around the country without proper documentation, even for family visits," Wolf noted. She then described how Jews in Nazi Germany also lost the freedom of movement:

Europe is not immune to this in the past—it has seen such regional and national "lockdown" too, but that was in countries that suffered from fascist leadership: In 1935–36, the passports of Jews in Germany were restricted. Eventually, restrictions on leaving the country would keep Jewish Germans from escaping altogether.

From 1939 to 1941, laws imposing various increasing restrictions on the movements of Jews put members of the Jewish community into effective "lockdown" as citizens within the larger German society ("infection" was a frequent trope used by anti-Semitic literature about the threat of Jews intermingling with Aryans). These laws prevented Jews from entering certain neighborhoods, and from traveling on buses. Walled Jewish residential areas, called ghettos, were often traditional in European cities; but state-mandated restrictions during the Nazi occupation turned them into residential prisons.

As Wolf explained, "On 16 November 1940, the gates were closed to the Warsaw Ghetto, a community of 400,000, thus making it impossible for the Jewish inhabitants to earn livelihoods; this closure and denial of the power of earning a living was instrumental in the weakening of potential resistance on the parts of victims of this segregation."

She concluded, "But large-scale totalitarian-style restrictions of citizens' movements by the state are new to the postwar democratic West and unheard-of in actual open societies; even past pandemics...have not been excuses in such societies to venture into this drastic territory."[47]

As Kennedy pointed out, the goal of public health restrictions was to "get us to voluntarily give up, relinquish our human rights, our civil rights, and walk like sheep into the abattoir. Now they have a source of fear that is the most pervasive and all-encompassing power that they've ever had, which is the fear of pandemics."

Kennedy explained, "My father told me when I was a child, 'People in authority lie.' And we all, if we are going to continue to live in a democracy, we need to understand that people in authority lie. People in authority will abuse every power that we relinquish to them, and right now we are giving them the power to micromanage every bit of our lives—twenty-four hours a day they're going to know where we are, they're going to know the money that we spend, they're going to have access to our children. They're going to have the right to compel unwanted medical interventions on us."

Australia Returns to Its Prison Colony Roots

"Greater Sydney, Australia extends lockdown and announces stricter measures.

"Exercise now limited to one hour, masked, per day. Curfew after 9pm. And police now authorized to seal entire apartment buildings like the CCP claims to have done in Wuhan." —attorney Michael P. Senger[48]

"Australia

- Army deployed to enforce lockdown.
- Mothers fined $1000 for talking outdoors.
- Police patrolling kids['] playgrounds.
- Building a 'quarantine camp.'

"Don't like it?

"Citizens are banned from leaving country.

"If you protest, police shoot you with RUBBER BULLETS." —Swedish journalist Peter Imanuelsen, editor in chief of the Times of Sweden[49]

According to Kennedy, "The Nazis did that in the camps in World War II. They tested vaccines on gypsies and Jews, and the world was so horrified after the war that we signed the Nuremberg Charter. And we all pledge when we do that, we would never again impose unwanted medical interventions on human beings without informed consent. And yet in two years, all of that conviction has suddenly disappeared, and people are walking around in masks, when the science has not been explained to them," Kennedy said.

"These government agencies are orchestrating obedience. And it is not democratic. It's not the product of democracy. It's the product of a pharmaceutical driven biosecurity agenda that will enslave the entire human race and plunge us into a dystopian nightmare where the apocalyptical forces of ignorance and greed will be running our lives and ruining our children and destroying all the dreams and dignity that we hope to give to our children," Kennedy declared.[50]

HBO's Bill Maher blamed the George Floyd protests against the police on the "reckless experiment" of lockdowns.

"When you coop people up with no hope and no jobs, why not go out in the streets?" Maher said. "I wonder what America will look like. What do police departments look like if they have to fight this all the time? This reckless experiment of closing down an entire country for months at a time is not going to look good in the future."

"We seem to have just focused on this one thing," Maher observed. "It wasn't inevitable that the economy be shut down.... We've had pandemics before."[51]

Maher's reaction against COVID fears and lockdowns extended into a certain lack of respect for the intelligence of young people. "You know the reason why advertisers in this country love the 18 to 34 demographic? Because it's the most gullible," Maher explained.

"Thirty-six percent of millennials think it might be a good idea to try communism, but much of the world did try it. I know, millennials think that doesn't count because they weren't alive when it happened. But it did happen. And there are people around who remember it. Pining for communism? It's like pining for Betamax or Myspace," Maher quipped.

"So when you say you're old, you don't get it. Get what? Abolish the police and the Border Patrol and capitalism and cancel Lincoln? No, I get it. The problem isn't that I don't get what you're saying or that I'm old. The problem is that your ideas are stupid," Maher insisted.

Maher was on a roll. "Twenty percent of Gen Z agree with the statement, 'society would be better off if all property was owned by the public and managed by the government,' and another 29% saying they don't know if that's a good idea. Here's who does know: anyone who wasn't born yesterday," he ranted.[52]

CHAPTER 5

A Solution Worse than the Disease: Lockdowns Kill

G eorge Soros, the billionaire progressive activist, saw COVID-19 as an opportunity to impose previously "inconceivable" alterations on a "scared" society. "I would describe it as a revolutionary moment when the range of possibilities is much greater than in normal times," Soros said in 2020. "What is inconceivable in normal times becomes not only possible but actually happens. People are disoriented and scared."[1]

Soros had previously claimed, in 2019, that "the arc of history doesn't follow its own course. It needs to be bent. I am really engaged in trying to bend it in the right direction."[2]

The forces behind the Great Reset were ready and able to "bend" history when COVID hit; "inconceivable" lockdowns and related restrictions became the new normal.

Deferred treatment for cancer, heart conditions, addiction, and suicidal depression is just one example of why lockdowns have been called "a crime against humanity."[3] COVID-19 lockdowns and mandates also cause poverty, and poverty kills. Locking people up in endless cycles of COVID restrictions, keeping them away from their loved ones, jobs, and routine medical checks—not to mention destroying the economy—had far-reaching impacts.

Economist Sanjeev Sabhlok calls the COVID-19 lockdown stampede "The Great Hysteria."[4]

Sabhlok tweeted, "Comprehensive groupthink and incompetence has prevailed."[5] Scientists and politicians are "panting like a mad monster in the excitement of their total power over the people," he explained.

"Net Harm"

Sabhlok exposed the madness behind the COVID lockdowns: "The science has also always been clear. Even if this virus had been as bad as Spanish flu, lockdowns would not be a remedy. Innumerable scientific studies both before and in 2020 confirm that lockdowns don't work and, instead, cause net harm."[6]

Statistician William M. Briggs, coauthor of the book *The Price of Panic: How the Tyranny of Experts Turned a Pandemic into a Catastrophe*, agreed. "Lockdowns force everybody in tight quarters, just like in fall when we go inside to escape the cold, there to more efficiently spread respiratory and other communicable diseases," Briggs wrote. "All experts knew this before 2020. They pretended to forget it after that."[7]

As Sabhlok explained, "Lockdowns had never been imposed in the past for a respiratory flu-like virus. Not a single scientist prior to 2020 ever recommended such measures. Lockdowns have only been imposed once before, for Ebola, and found to be ineffective."[8]

"A True Killer"

"Covid is a true killer. So far it's killed the flu, cancer, heart disease—it killed the ability to think, logic & common sense. It killed the economy, the working class, & millions of jobs. It killed millions of businesses, human connection, love and compassion." —a Twitter wag posting under the handle Colin's Tweet's #LearnToLiveWithIt (@GovPolicyDoubt)[9]

Dr. Scott Atlas, who was an advisor to President Trump late in the COVID-19 crisis, did not mince words.

"The prolonged lockdowns are a complete disaster. They are a complete disaster for missed healthcare; they are a complete disaster for average working families," Atlas explained, adding that "people have been killed by people who want to have prolonged lockdowns."

Atlas detailed the crushing impacts of lockdowns:

- Forty-six percent of the most common types of cancers were not diagnosed during the lockdown....
- Half of people who had chemotherapy appointments didn't show up; that's 650,000 Americans.
- Half of people who had immunizations for children didn't come in out of the fear instilled by our so-called public health experts....
- We had more than 200,000 cases of child abuse not reported....
- One out of four young, college-age Americans have contemplated killing themselves during the month of June [2020]; that's a CDC report.

Public health experts presided over a policy that is a "complete epic failure," Atlas explained. "History will record the faces of the public health expertise as some of the most sinful, egregious, epic failures in the history of public policy. They have killed people with their lack of understanding and their lack of caring," Atlas charged.

"They never cared to consider the impact of the policy itself. And the policy itself has been a complete, epic failure, and honestly some people say a crime against humanity. These people should be held accountable," he added.[10]

Just imagine if former president Trump had brought in Dr. Atlas in March of 2020 instead of deferring to Anthony Fauci and others! America might not have been sucked into the futile lockdown madness.

"The Death Rate from Losing Your Democracy"

"As former Soviet citizens can attest, the death rate from COVID is much, much lower than the death rate from losing your democracy." –attorney Michael P. Senger, author of the book *Snake Oil: How Xi Jinping Shut Down the World*[11]

As COVID-19 spread around the world in early 2020, the rallying cry went up for lockdowns. Despite having never been a part of public health strategy before, lockdowns became the go-to response for virtually every government in the world. Videos from China of people allegedly dropping dead in the street from a mysterious virus, followed by clips of Chinese government officials sealing people in their homes—and the subsequent WHO endorsement—were enough to make locking down standard policy in the West. At first the massive lockdowns were sold to Europeans and Americans as a mere "two weeks to flatten the curve," but in reality they went on for months and years and threatened to become permanent.

Meanwhile, numerous studies have shown that lockdowns had little to no impact in stopping the spread of COVID-19—and that the lockdowns themselves have devastating effects of their own.

In 2021 a peer-reviewed study by prominent researchers and Stanford University professors of medicine Eran Bendavid, Christopher Oh, John P. A. Ioannidis, and Jayanta Bhattacharya was published in the *European Journal of Clinical Investigation*. The study found, "There is no evidence that more restrictive nonpharmaceutical interventions ('lockdowns') contributed substantially to bending the curve of new cases in England, France, Germany, Iran, Italy, the Netherlands, Spain, or the United States in early 2020."[13]

"Amazon Made Out Great!"

"Oh, it [COVID-19] was way worse than the flu. It killed tens of thousands of people with overdoses. It cost tens of millions of kids a year of school and left tens of millions of older people isolated and alone. But @amazon made out great!" –Alex Berenson, author of *Pandemia: How Coronavirus Hysteria Took Over Our Government, Rights, and Lives*[12]

And a study in *The Lancet*'s eClinicalMedicine determined that "government actions such as border closures, full lockdowns, and a high rate of COVID-19 testing were not associated with statistically significant reductions in the number of critical cases or overall mortality."[14]

In 2022 a study by two Swedish researchers and professor at Johns Hopkins University concluded that lockdowns had almost no measurable impact on reducing COVID-19 deaths. The paper found "no evidence that lockdowns, school closures, border closures, and limiting gatherings have had a noticeable effect on COVID-19 mortality."[15]

"An analysis of these qualified studies supports the conclusion that lockdowns have had little to no effect on COVID-19 mortality. Lockdown policies are ill-founded and should be rejected as a pandemic policy instrument," explained study coauthor Steve Hanke, a professor of applied economics at Johns Hopkins University.[16]

"Our results are in line with the World Health Organization Writing Group (2006), who state, 'Reports from the 1918 influenza pandemic indicate that social-distancing measures did not stop or appear to dramatically reduce transmission,'" the study reported.

"Overall, we conclude that lockdowns are not an effective way of reducing mortality rates during a pandemic, at least not during the first wave of the COVID-19 pandemic," the researchers wrote in their study titled "A Literature Review and Meta-Analysis of the Effects of Lockdowns on COVID-19 Mortality."[17]

Sweden: Doing Better without Locking Down

"Sweden, which has shunned the strict lockdowns that have choked much of the global economy, emerged from 2020 with a smaller increase in its overall mortality rate than most European countries, an analysis of official data sources showed," Johan Ahlander reported in a 2021 Reuters article titled "Sweden Saw Lower 2020 Death Spike than Much of Europe—Data."

Sweden rejected COVID lockdowns and relied on voluntary measures, keeping restaurants, stores, and schools open, and as a result the nation "spared the economy from much of the hit suffered elsewhere in Europe," according to Reuters.

"Preliminary data from EU statistics agency Eurostat compiled by Reuters showed Sweden had 7.7% more deaths in 2020 than its average for the preceding four years. Countries that opted for several periods of strict lockdowns, such as Spain and Belgium, had so-called excess mortality of 18.1% and 16.2% respectively," Ahlander observed.

"Twenty-one of the 30 countries with available statistics had higher excess mortality than Sweden.... Sweden's excess mortality also came out at the low end of the spectrum in a separate tally of Eurostat and other data released by the UK's Office for National Statistics," Ahlander explained.

Anders Tegnell, Sweden's chief epidemiologist, summed up the results of Sweden's refusal to follow the lockdown herd. "I think people will probably think very carefully about these total shutdowns, how good they really were," Tegnell said.[18]

Overwhelming Evidence

The *European Journal of Clinical Investigation* study concluded that in 75 percent of the comparisons, the lockdown interventions actually increased the spread of the virus. "In summary, we fail to find strong evidence supporting a role for more restrictive NPIs [nonpharmaceutical interventions] in the control of COVID in early 2020. We do not question the role of all public health interventions, or of coordinated communications about the epidemic, but we fail to find an additional benefit of stay-at-home orders and business closures," the Stanford professors who authored the study explained.

"The data cannot fully exclude the possibility of some benefits. However, even if they exist, these benefits may not match the numerous harms of these aggressive measures. More targeted public health interventions that more effectively reduce transmissions may be important for future epidemic control without the harms of highly restrictive measures."[19]

The academic literature has long reported that quarantines and lockdowns were not viable ways to fight viruses.

A key paper refuting lockdowns, "Disease Mitigation Measures in the Control of Pandemic Influenza," published in 2006 in the journal *Biosecurity and Bioterrorism: Biodefense Strategy, Practice, and Science*, slammed any potential societal lockdown–style efforts to contain viruses. Dr. D. A. Henderson, who had led the effort to eradicate smallpox, was a key author of this study, which also included as coauthors infectious disease expert Thomas V. Inglesby, epidemiologist Jennifer B. Nuzzo, and physician Tara O'Toole.

The prescient 2006 paper noted, "There are no historical observations or scientific studies that support the confinement by quarantine of groups of possibly infected people for extended periods in order to slow the spread of influenza.... This mitigation measure should be eliminated from serious consideration."

The study also pointed out:

> Home quarantine also raises ethical questions. Implementation of home quarantine could result in healthy, uninfected people being placed at risk of infection from sick household members.... Travel restrictions, such as closing airports and screening travelers at borders, have historically been ineffective. The World Health Organization Writing Group concluded that "screening and quarantining entering travelers at international borders did not substantially delay virus introduction in past pandemics...and will likely be even less effective in the modern era."...
>
> It is reasonable to assume that the economic costs of shutting down air or train travel would be very high, and the societal costs involved in interrupting all air or train travel would be extreme....

There are many social gatherings that involve close contacts among people, and this prohibition might include church services, athletic events, perhaps all meetings of more than 100 people. It might mean closing theaters, restaurants, malls, large stores, and bars. Implementing such measures would have seriously disruptive consequences....

Schools are often closed for 1–2 weeks early in the development of seasonal community outbreaks of influenza primarily because of high absentee rates, especially in elementary schools, and because of illness among teachers. This would seem reasonable on practical grounds. However, to close schools for longer periods is not only impracticable but carries the possibility of a serious adverse outcome....

Thus, cancelling or postponing large meetings would not be likely to have any significant effect on the development of the epidemic.... The problems in implementing such measures are formidable, and secondary effects of absenteeism and community disruption as well as possible adverse consequences, such as loss of public trust in government and stigmatization of quarantined people and groups, are likely to be considerable.

The study concluded: "Strong political and public health leadership to provide reassurance and to ensure that needed medical care services are provided are critical elements. If either is seen to be less than optimal, a manageable epidemic could move toward catastrophe."[20]

Remember, this paper, which foresaw all of the many woes of mandatory social distancing, lockdowns, and mask mandates, was published in 2006.

Fast-forward to 2020. The COVID lockdowns dragged on for weeks, then months, and then what threatened to be years (with no end in sight), but their full impact could take years to see.

Business Live reported that South African experts called for an end to the lockdown, which they labeled "a humanitarian disaster to dwarf

Covid-19." Mitigation, they said, should "focus on isolating the elderly and allowing children to go back to school, while ensuring the economy restarts so that lives can be saved," the South African analysts explained.

"The lockdown will lead to 29 times more lives lost than the harm it seeks to prevent from Covid-19 in SA [South Africa], according to a conservative estimate contained in a new model developed by local actuaries.

"The model, which will be made public today for debate, was developed by a consortium calling itself Panda (Pandemic ~ Data Analysis), which includes four actuaries, an economist and a doctor, while the work was checked by lawyers and mathematicians."

The South African experts pointed out that "the effects of poverty in terms of death and sickness are well known—so well that they are even modeled by insurance companies when they set their premiums… hunger causes long-term illnesses, retards development and condemns children to lives of misery and dependence."[21]

We're the Guinea Pigs

"In case it's confusing, it is not Sweden that is an 'experiment.' It is the rest of the western world that has abandoned long-established, evidence-based scientific policies & has been experimenting w/catastrophic lockdowns/restrictions at the cost of human lives & mass suffering."
—Kulvinder Kaur, president & cofounder of Concerned Ontario Doctors, lauding Sweden for bucking the lockdown trends of the rest of the world[22]

The South African group deployed a model comparing "years of lives lost" from COVID-19 to "years of lives lost" from the lockdown. Their data revealed that "the impact of the virus on the vast majority of the population, particularly the economically active and schoolchildren, has been massively overstated."

They urged, "We should not incarcerate the masses in their homes, limiting their hard-earned freedoms and decimating the economic system that furnishes their livelihoods. We should be doing everything we possibly can to allow businesses to operate."[23]

A 2020 UK government study estimated the ratio of higher deaths from lockdown impacts versus COVID-19 deaths would be four to one. "Experts from the Department of Health, the Office of National Statistics (ONS), the government's Actuary Department, and the Home

Hospital Déjà Vu

Justin Hart collected reports of overwhelmed hospitals—from the 2018 flu season.

"We had to treat patients in places where we normally wouldn't, like in recovery rooms," states Dr. Bernard Camins, associate professor of infectious diseases at the University of Alabama at Birmingham. "The emergency room was very crowded . . . with sick patients who needed to be admitted.'"

And in California, "several hospitals have set up large 'surge tents' outside their emergency departments to accommodate and treat . . . patients. Even then, the LA Times reported this week, emergency departments had standing-room only, and some patients had to be treated in hallways."

And in news from Fenton, Missouri, "SSM Health St. Clare Hospital has opened its emergency overflow wing, as well as all outpatient centers and surgical holding centers, to make more beds available to patients who need them. Nurses are being 'pulled from all floors to care for them.' . . . 'It's making their pre-existing conditions worse.' . . . 'More and more patients are needing mechanical ventilation due to respiratory failure.'"

In another report, "Dr. Anthony Marinelli says they've seen a major spike in . . . cases. It's so overwhelmed the community hospital that they've gone on bypass at times—that means they tell ambulances to bypass this ER and find another."

Hart commented: "I mean nothing like this has ever happened to our hospitals before?! Except these are all quotes from the 2018 flu season. Healthcare workers are amazing. I know they can do their jobs without the rest of us having to forfeit our lives. No more lockdowns. Get the kids back to school. We got this."[24]

Office forecast the collateral damage from delays to healthcare and the effects of recession arising from the pandemic response," noted Ricardo Bordin at Medium.

The report noted that many Brits were delaying seeking diagnoses and pausing surgeries, and it pointed out that postponing treatment was a "ticking time bomb" that would have unintended consequences.[25]

Investigative journalist Justin Hart of the website Rational Ground summed up numerous studies available in 2021 documenting the negative consequences of COVID lockdowns. Here is the summary in his words:

- 1.4 million additional tuberculosis deaths due to lockdown disruptions
- 500,000 additional deaths related to HIV
- Malaria deaths could double to 770,000 total per year
- 65 percent decrease in all cancer screenings
- Breast cancer screenings dropped 89 percent
- Colorectal screenings dropped 85 percent...
- Increase in cardiac arrests but decrease in EMS calls for them
- 38% decrease in heart disease–related treatments[26]

Unintended Consequences

Chief Swedish epidemiologist Anders Tegnell noted of the lockdowns, "They may have had an effect in the short term, but when you look at it throughout the pandemic, you become more and more doubtful." For his opposition to lockdowns, Tegnell has "received both death threats and flowers as a token of appreciation."[27]

Other data painted the same grim picture of the lockdowns. The UK government's statistical agency reported that in Britain "for every three COVID-19 deaths, lockdowns may have caused another two."

"The national lockdown may have indirectly caused 16,000 excess deaths in two months, according to government analysts," Sky News reported. "The estimates, made by the Office for National Statistics (ONS) and analysts from several government departments, suggest there were 38,500 excess deaths in England connected to COVID-19 between March and 1 May. However, the report concludes 41% of those deaths were the result of missed medical care rather than the virus itself."[28]

"The disruption in healthcare services caused by Covid-19 may have led to an estimated 239,000 maternal and child deaths in South Asia, according to a new UN report," a BBC article stated.[29]

The lockdowns also caused a massive redistribution of wealth to the elite classes, which was too much for the even World Health Organization to let go unnoticed by the end of 2020.

David Nabarro, the World Health Organization's special envoy for COVID-19, called the lockdowns "a terrible, ghastly, global catastrophe" in an interview with the UK magagzine *The Spectator.*

"Look what's happening to poverty levels. It seems that we may well have a doubling of world poverty by next year. We may well have at least a doubling of child malnutrition because children are not getting meals at school and their parents, in poor families, are not able to afford it," Nabarro said.[30]

The lockdowns imposed in the early days of COVID were so devoid of sanity that they seem hard to believe. In April 2020 National Public Radio reported on just how dystopian they were in an article titled "In Spain, Pandemic Restrictions Mean Children Aren't Allowed Outside Their Homes." NPR explained that "millions of children in Spain live in apartments without outdoor space; others live in cramped spaces with large families. All these children haven't been outdoors since mid-March."

"Various regional governments in Spain have introduced local laws that would allow children to go outside—as long as they're accompanied by an adult, wear a face mask (if they're over 3 years old) and leave their homes during permitted times. But these measures must first be approved by the central government in Madrid."[31]

UNICEF (the United Nations International Children's Emergency Fund) warned that lockdowns could kill more children than COVID-19—based on a model predicting "1.2 million child deaths."

As the subhead of the *The Telegraph*'s report on the UN Agency's advice said, "'Indiscriminate Lockdowns' Are an Ineffective Way to Control Covid and Could Contribute to a 45 Per Cent Rise in Child Mortality."[32]

Mask mandates could also pose a health threat to children. A 2020 study published in the journal *Aesthetic Plastic Surgery* found that the mask's "elastics cause constant compression on the skin and, consequently, on the cartilage of the auricle, leading to erythematous and painful lesions of the retroauricular skin when the masks are used for many hours a day. Pre-adolescent children have undeveloped auricular cartilage with less resistance to deformation; prolonged pressure from the elastic loops of the mask at the hollow or, even worse, at the anthelix level can influence the correct growth and angulation of the outer ear."[33]

David Wallace-Wells explained in the *New Yorker* that threat of COVID to kids was minuscule. "Statistically speaking, if a kid who comes down with a coronavirus infection is facing a threat to her life equivalent to the flu—perhaps significantly less—a 90-year-old who does so is treading in the neighborhood of anthrax, the bubonic plague, and certain lighter outbreaks of Ebola," Wallace-Wells wrote in an 2021 article titled "The Kids Are Alright."

"And the risk of children is dramatically smaller still than that CDC baseline; according to one, much-cited paper, the infection fatality rate for those aged 5 to 9 is less than 0.001 percent, about one-tenth the risk of flu for that age group," Wallace-Wells wrote. "It may sound strange, given a year of panic over school closures and reopenings, a year of masking toddlers and closing playgrounds and huddling in pandemic pods, that among children the mortality risk from COVID-19 is actually lower than from the flu."[34]

In contrast to their low risk from COVID-19, kids were at risk from horrible government policies. A 2021 study titled "Impact of the COVID-19 Pandemic on Early Child Cognitive Development" found lockdowns did major damage to children. "We find that children born during the pandemic have significantly reduced verbal, motor, and overall cognitive performance compared to children born pre-pandemic," the study by Sean C. L. Deoni, Jennifer Beauchemin, Alexandra Volpe, Viren D'Sa, and the RESONANCE Consortium found. "Moreover, we find that males and children in lower socio-economic families have been most affected," the authors added.[35]

By February 2022, a full two years into the pandemic, even mainstream news outlets were forced to admit that masks were useless against a respiratory virus.

In an article titled "Mask Mandates Didn't Make Much of a Difference Anyway," Bloomberg opinion columnist Faye Flam wrote that "masks have been the most visible part of America's pandemic response, but one of the least consequential."

"There's no avoiding it: The benefits of universal masking have been difficult to quantify," Flam, who also hosts the podcast *Follow the Science*, wrote. "States with mask mandates haven't fared significantly better than the 35 states that didn't impose them during the omicron wave."[36]

> **"Children to Die Because of What We Did to the Economy"**
> HBO's Bill Maher opposed lockdowns vociferously: "It's almost about what in the long run is going to cause more death. . . . The head of the U.N. said a couple of weeks ago he expects hundreds of thousands of children to die because of what we did to the economy. I know they're not all Americans so they don't count as much to Americans, but I think that matters somewhat."[37]

Let's note once again that it was not COVID-19 that caused this humanitarian disaster; it was the ill-advised lockdowns prescribed to combat the virus and the relentless fear porn peddled by government officials and the media.

As the Colorado Sun reported, "The number of people in Denver who died of cardiac arrests at home in the two weeks following the statewide stay-at-home order was greater than the total number of people who died of COVID-19 in the city during that time."[38]

In the United Kingdom, "The number of deaths due to the disruption of cancer services is likely to outweigh the number of deaths from the coronavirus itself over the next five years," reported *The Times* of London.[39]

Free Funerals

COVID-19 lockdowns kill, but don't worry—the government will pay the funeral expenses.

"I thought this was a myth, but no: the government will pay up to $9,000 for a funeral for someone who dies of #Covid. Which is $9,000 more than it will pay for the funeral of anyone else," former *New York Times* reporter Alex Berenson wrote. "That's not an incentive to report a death as Covid-related AT ALL."[40] The Federal Emergency Management Agency (FEMA) states that in order to get the $9000, applicants need to provide "an official death certificate that attributes the death directly or indirectly to COVID-19 and shows that the death occurred in the United States."[41]

The Atlantic surprised many when it reported on a new study in 2021 revealing that "almost half of those hospitalized with COVID-19 have mild or asymptomatic cases." David Zweig reported that "the study suggests that roughly half of all the hospitalized patients showing up on COVID-data dashboards in 2021 may have been admitted for another reason entirely, or had only a mild presentation of disease."

The title of the article at RealClearPolitics was "Are Pandemic Hospitalization Numbers Misleading Us?" The study was conducted by "researchers from Harvard Medical School, Tufts Medical Center, and the Veterans Affairs Healthcare System."[42]

Suicides and Overdoses

National Public Radio reported the ill effects of lockdowns bluntly. "U.S. Sees Deadly Drug Overdose Spike During Pandemic," read NPR's headline.

"During the pandemic, basically everything is pointed in the wrong direction," said a federal health official quoted by NPR. The official added that the intersection of COVID-19 lockdowns and America's addiction crisis was a nightmare.

As New York substance-abuse counselor Jennifer Austin explained, "The longer people had to isolate it was relapse, relapse, overdose, relapse, overdose." She added, "I've had people who I've never worked with before reach out to me and say, 'Jen, what do I do?'"

The addiction counselor explained, "We tell people not to isolate, that's bad, it's a red flag" for people struggling with substance abuse. But then "the pandemic comes and we're literally told that we're supposed to be isolating, like, stay away from people."[43]

> ### Overdoses "More than Double" Coronavirus Deaths
> "More people died from overdoses than from the coronavirus in San Francisco last year," reported the *New York Times* in April 2021. Deaths from drug overdoses "skyrocketed, claiming 713 lives last year, more than double the 257 people here who died of the virus in 2020."[44]

In Britain, antidepressant consumption raced to record-high levels during the COVID lockdowns. "Calls to mental health helplines and prescriptions for antidepressants have reached an all-time high, while access to potentially life-saving talking therapies has plunged during the coronavirus pandemic," a 2021 investigation by *The Guardian* newspaper discovered. "More than 6 million people in England received antidepressants in the three months [leading up] to September, part of a wider trend and the highest figure on record."

"People are going to their GPs with symptoms of mental illness and being sent away with a bag of medication, having been put on an 18-month waiting list," noted mental health advocate Natasha Devon.

Dr. Esther Cohen-Tovée of the British Psychological Society declared, "I'm shocked and extremely concerned about the massive extent of the reduction in referrals for psychological help during a time of huge anxiety, stress, and distress for the whole population. This is even more concerning when there has been a huge increase in the prescription of antidepressants."[45]

UK Independence Party (UKIP) leader Neil Hamilton summed up the situation. Referring to the record use of antidepressants, Hamilton said, "Locking people in their homes, destroying their livelihoods and preventing them from seeing friends & family will do that."[46]

Flashback to the Holocaust

Researchers whose work was published in the *Journal of Psychiatric Research* in 2021 interviewed 127 Jews who were born before 1945, including nearly one hundred Holocaust survivors, and found that "lockdowns bring back unpleasant memories for Holocaust survivors," according an article on the website Study Finds. "Researchers from Bar-Ilan University say pandemic-related health policy guidelines remind them of conditions that existed during the Holocaust. This includes long periods of isolation and separation from family members."

The article goes on to say, "Rates of loneliness, depression, and suicidal thoughts have increased significantly during the COVID-19 pandemic. According to the CDC, four in 10 U.S. adults reported struggling with mental health and substance abuse issues."[47]

Lefty Celebrities Take Notice

"The next time we have a worldwide pandemic, we have to come up with a better solution than 'everyone becomes Howie Mandel,'" Bill Maher said, referring to a fellow comedian. "[Howie is] the world's most famous germaphobe who was social distancing before it was cool," Maher explained.

"Howie would be the first to tell you he has a disease, OCD, that fucks up your life. He can't touch a doorknob or wear shoes with laces because they might touch the ground. When he excuses himself to go to the bathroom, it's to clean it," Maher said.[48]

"A Completely Neurotic Population"

Americans are "always willing to trade away a little of their freedom in exchange for the feeling, the illusion of security. What we have now is a completely neurotic population obsessed with security and safety and crime and drugs and cleanliness and hygiene and germs," comedian George Carlin said more than two decades before the COVID-19 pandemic, in an HBO stand-up special on February 6, 1999.

"Fear of germs.... What do you think you have an immune system for? It's for killing germs! But it needs practice...it needs germs to practice on. So listen! If you kill all the germs around you, and live a completely sterile life, then when germs do come along, you're not gonna be prepared. And never mind ordinary germs, what are you gonna do when some super virus comes along that turns your vital organs into liquid shit? I'll tell you what you're gonna do . . . you're gonna get sick, you're gonna die, and you're gonna deserve it cause you're f*cking weak and you got a f*cking weak immune system!" Carlin railed.[49]

"We should make it a priority to protect [vulnerable] people. But compulsively washing, being scared of your own hands—that can't become the new normal. In his later years, when he was peeing into jars and wearing Kleenex boxes for shoes, we pitied Howard Hughes because it was pitiful. In the 70s, they made a TV movie with John Travolta about a sick kid called *The Boy in the Plastic Bubble*. And let me tell you—if they start selling these things on Amazon—we're in trouble," Maher added.[50]

"Believe in the Science"

CNN anchor Don Lemon told fellow liberals who were wary of taking off their masks even if fully vaccinated to "believe in the science."

Lemon revealed that his own mother was refusing to spend Mother's Day with him out of fear of COVID-19.

"I'm kind of jealous you've got to spend [Mother's Day] with your mom," Lemon told fellow CNN anchor Chris Cuomo. "Because I would love to spend it with my mom. But my mom won't leave [her home]."

"She is fully vaccinated, Chris," Lemon exclaimed.

"This is real," Lemon stated. "People are having trouble re-emerging into society after COVID-19 lockdowns."[51]

"The past two months have given people the idea that the way to win our million-year war with microbes is to avoid them completely," Maher observed. "And I'm here to tell you—you can't."

Maher posited, "The key to beating covid isn't dining through glass or never going to a concert or a ballgame again, it's your immune system.... You hear people say covid-19 is a new virus so the immune system doesn't know how to handle it. Bullshit, of course, it does, that's why the vast majority of people who've had it either recovered or they didn't even know they had it. What do you think did that? The human immune system."

Maher then argued that "governors should declare keeping our bodies in good health an essential job because that's the only way we're going to win this."[52]

The comedian quipped, "In LA you still can't legally get a haircut, but you can get your dog's hair cut—so he doesn't look stupid in Zoom meetings?"[53]

A "Right against Infection"?

In 2021, Anthony Fauci tried to justify lockdowns by claiming that "even if you are without symptoms, you very well may infect another person.... So in essence, you are encroaching on their individual rights." But attorney Michael Senger was having none of it, calling Fauci's reasoning "a total inversion of the enlightenment: a 'right against infection' that overrides all other rights."[54]

Matt Walsh of The Daily Wire also commented on this type of reasoning. "What you're saying is that nobody has the right to breathe around you. Which is total madness, of course. The kind of statement that should get you locked in an insane asylum. It's the sort of thing that clinical OCD patients would say. Literal insanity."[55]

Exaggerated fears of the virus were documented by *The Atlantic* magazine in "The Liberals Who Can't Quit Lockdown," a May 2021 article by Emma Green. "Liberals who aren't quite ready to let go of pandemic restrictions. For this subset, diligence against COVID-19 remains an expression of political identity—even when that means over-estimating the disease's risks or setting limits far more strict than what public-health guidelines permit."

"Progressive communities have been home to some of the fiercest battles over COVID-19 policies, and some liberal policy makers have left scientific evidence behind," Green explained.[56]

Recommending Summer Vacation Is "Genocide Encouragement"

"After Emily Oster, an economist at Brown University, argued . . . that families should plan to take their kids on trips and see friends and relatives this summer, a reader sent an email to her supervisors at the university suggesting that Oster be promoted to a leadership role in the field of 'genocide encouragement.'" –*The Atlantic*, "The Liberals Who Can't Quit Lockdown"[57]

The *New York Times* profiled people with high anxiety about returning to normal in an article titled "They're Vaccinated and Keeping Their Masks On, Maybe Forever."

As the *Times* reported, "For people like Joe Glickman, a combination of anxiety, murky information about new virus variants and the emergence of an obdurate and sizable faction of vaccine holdouts means mask-free life is on hold—possibly forever."[58]

A Bloomberg News columnist warned of a "permanent pandemic" with "endless cycles of outbreaks and remissions, social restrictions and relaxations, lockdowns and reopenings."

"SARS-CoV-2, protean and elusive as it is, may become our permanent enemy, like the flu but worse. And even if it peters out eventually, our lives and routines will by then have changed irreversibly. Going 'back' won't be an option," Andreas Kluth wrote in a 2021 Bloomberg opinion piece. But don't worry. Kluth claimed that the economy would be damaged less in the coming "endless cycles" of lockdowns "than in the previous one."

"Our Brave New World needn't be dystopian. But it won't look anything like the old world," Kluth reassured his readers in a column titled "We Must Start Planning for a Permanent Pandemic."[59]

Tony Heller of Real Climate Science best summed up the underlying reality: "Viruses kill people. Mass insanity, fear, loathing, paranoia, superstitious ritual and tyranny isn't going to change that."[60]

"We Swam in Raw Sewage"

"Let me tell you a true story about immunization okay? When I was a little boy in New York City in the 1940s, we swam in the Hudson River and it was filled with raw sewage okay? We swam in raw sewage! You know . . . to cool off! And at that time, the big fear was polio; thousands of kids died from polio every year but you know something? In my neighborhood, no one ever got polio! No one! Ever! You know why? Cause we swam in raw sewage! It strengthened our immune systems! The polio never had a prayer; we were tempered in raw shit! So personally, I never take any special precautions against germs. I don't shy away from people that sneeze and cough, I don't wipe off the telephone, I don't cover the toilet seat, and if I drop food on the floor, I pick it up and eat it! Yes, I do. Even if I'm at a sidewalk café! In Calcutta! The poor section!" Carlin joked.

"I got a good strong immune system and it gets a lot of practice. My immune system is equipped with the biological equivalent of fully automatic military assault rifles with night vision and laser scopes."
—comedian George Carlin in a February 6, 1999, HBO stand-up special[61]

In May of 2021, Washington, D.C., decided to reopen, lifting most COVID-19 restrictions. But by that point the idea of leading a "normal" life was alien to many D.C. residents. "This is actually our first time out in about a year and five months of the pandemic. We've been in the house on lockdown," Aarum Hurse told WUSA9. "So it's a little strange to be outside."

D.C. resident Elizabeth Torres noted, "This is the first time I actually have taken my mask off in public, so it's weird. I feel awkward, but I'm trying to tell myself it's okay. Because I'm fully vaccinated."[62]

Alas, D.C. would end up lunging back into more COVID restrictions as it was reported that that the effectiveness of the COVID vaccines would wear off over time.

All of these people were cowering in fear, bowing to a public health bureaucracy that had steered them horribly off course. The evidence shows the opposite of what these social hermits embraced. It was left to comedian Maher to present that evidence to the political left.

"Researchers studied 7,300 COVID cases in China and found just one that was connected to outdoor transmission. Yeah, you've heard people use the phrase 'sunlight is the best disinfectant'? Well, that got to be a metaphor because it was true. The virus doesn't like sun," Maher said.

"Vitamin D is something you get from the sun, not your phone screen. Outdoors, healthy. Unabomber lifestyle, not healthy. Why haven't our top health officials been emphasizing these things? Why haven't they given us any direction on improving our immune systems at a time when we need them the most? Imagine before the virus even existed telling your doctor, 'Hey, doc, I've been locking myself indoors, living in fear, day drinking and eating cheap takeout. Good healthcare plan?" Maher quipped.[64]

Maher's point about the lockdown was vindicated by a study released in 2021. "Researchers Held an Experimental Indoor Concert in Spain with No Social Distancing. No One Contracted Covid," according to the headline of the *Washington Post* report. "In December, [2020] hundreds of people packed into a Barcelona arena to dance and sing along to five hours of live music and D.J. sets, gleefully abandoning social distancing guidelines for the night.

"Researchers found that not one of the concertgoers tested positive for the coronavirus after the event, according to results published Wednesday on the website of the Lancet Infectious Diseases journal," the *Post* reported.[66]

Lockdowns Kill Doctor's Appointments

"Half of Americans say lost insurance and healthcare costs during COVID are keeping them from seeing a doctor," reported the website Study Finds in May 2021. The polling company Tempus surveyed around 1,100 adults between eighteen and seventy and found that "many Americans are still avoiding a trip to the doctor. Aside from the fear of contracting COVID-19, researchers find half the country simply can't afford the visit."

According to Study Finds, "Fifty-nine percent of those surveyed said they experienced adverse health symptoms but did not seek treatment for them. Of this group, 79 percent reported they already suffer from conditions that are considered co-morbid with respect to COVID-19, including obesity, heart conditions, diabetes, cancer, and chronic lung diseases." In addition, "Half of all parents in the survey admit they also missed medical appointments for their children; including routine check-ups and even appointments for ongoing illnesses."[67]

In May of 2021, Alex Berenson presented data showing how "Outside the US and UK, the West had ~NO excess deaths last year in people under 65. And many of those US deaths were lockdown/drug related (as Canada's rise shows)." Berenson pointed out, "We turned the world upside down for a relative handful of people at the end of their lives . . ."[68]

In the United States, deadly health impacts of the lockdowns were flowing out from multiple sources. Drug-overdose fatalities skyrocketed to all-time record levels, according to CDC data.

"New data shows that more Americans died of drug overdoses in the year leading to September 2020 than any 12-month period since the opioid epidemic began," Brian Walsh of Axios reported. "The stubborn increase of such 'deaths of despair' shows that the opioid epidemic still has room to grow and that some of the social distancing steps we took to rein in the pandemic may have brought deadly side effects."

The U.S. saw a 29 percent increase in drug-overdose deaths from 2019 to 2020, according to the CDC. "The biggest spike in deaths occurred in April and May 2020, when shutdowns were strictest," Walsh explained.[69]

Antony Davies and James R. Harrigan of the free-market group Foundation for Economic Education (FEE) commented on the drug-overdose data, "Lawmakers should be keenly aware that every human action has both intended and unintended consequences." As the FEE analysts noted, "Human beings react to every rule, regulation, and order governments impose, and their reactions result in outcomes that can be quite different than the outcomes lawmakers intended. So while there is a place for legislation, that place should be one defined by both great caution and tremendous humility."[70]

Tuberculosis Makes a Comeback

Other diseases were also bolstered by the COVID lockdowns. "'The Biggest Monster' Is Spreading. And It's Not the Coronavirus," read a 2020 headline in the *New York Times*.

"Tuberculosis kills 1.5 million people each year. Lockdowns and supply-chain disruptions threaten progress against the disease as well as H.I.V. and malaria," the paper reported.

"Until this year, TB and its deadly allies, H.I.V. and malaria, were on the run," the *Times* noted. "Yet now, as the coronavirus pandemic spreads around the world, consuming global health resources, these perennially neglected adversaries are making a comeback."

The *Times* article quoted Dr. Pedro L. Alonso, the director of the World Health Organization's global malaria program: "Covid-19 risks [are] derailing all our efforts and taking us back to where we were 20 years ago."[71]

In Australia, where shutdowns seemed to be the most authoritarian in the developed world, the lockdowns led to an "increase in children presenting to hospitals after self-harming." The Australian Broadcasting Corporation reported that "prolonged social isolation and a lack of face-to-face services are being blamed for a concerning increase in the number of young people presenting to emergency departments with self-inflicted injuries."[72]

"US Overdose Deaths Surge to an All-Time High," according to the American Medical Association, which also reported, "The nation's COVID pandemic made the nation's drug overdose epidemic worse.... Every state has reported a spike or increase in overdose deaths or other problems during the COVID pandemic."[73]

Lockdowns lead to economic recessions, which lead to unemployment, and being jobless has a long history of killing people. "A 2011 meta-analysis of international research...found that the risk of death was 63 percent higher during the study periods among those who experienced unemployment than among those who did not," reported the Mises Institute website.[74]

"The Worst Year"

The lockdowns in the United Kingdom were so bad that "Britain's coronavirus-hammered economy...shrank by the most in more than

"A 'Covid Crisis of Stupidity'"

Physicist Denis Rancourt, who studied the impacts of lockdowns and mask mandates, revealed how health bureaucrats used COVID stats to claim lockdown success.

"Public health officials boldly take credit for decreases in transmission, rather than known seasonality. We are in a 'covid crisis of stupidity.' All of science prior to 2020 has been erased," Rancourt said. He offered "a reminder of some prominent causes of death":

- medical practice (third leading cause)
- drug overdoses and suicides
- car crashes
- falling in the home

"Where is the gov to save us from death of all causes?" Rancourt asked.[75]

three centuries in 2020 as a whole, official data showed," Reuters reported. "In 2020, gross domestic product fell by 9.8% from 2019."[76]

Famed scientific pioneer James Lovelock, who had worked in the virus division of the UK National Institute for Medical research, was aghast at Britain's lockdown for COVID-19, which he compared with responses to previous viral outbreaks.

"The flu pandemics were worse in terms of deaths, and no such reaction took place then," Lovelock explained. He pointed out that he could hardly remember the Asian flu, which killed a million people in 1957, or the similarly deadly Hong Kong flu in 1968.

"My impression is that we have overreacted almost everywhere to the [COVID-19] pandemic," he said in June 2021.[77]

Oxford University epidemiologist Dr. Sunetra Gupta railed against imposing "meaningless restrictions on ourselves." Gupta said, "The longer we fail to recognise this, the worse will be the permanent economic damage—the brunt of which, again, will be borne by the disadvantaged and the young."

As Gupta explained, Lockdowns result in "lower childhood vaccination rates, worsening cardiovascular disease outcomes, fewer cancer screenings and deteriorating mental health."[78]

Justin Hart, who publishes at the website Rational Ground, has explained the folly of governments' approach to COVID-19:

> My core #COVID19 mantras:
>
> - lockdowns are bad.
> - masks have little and no effect on case spread.
> - "stopping" cases should NOT be the goal
> - if you are an elected official who think[s] you can STOP the virus you are the problem.[79]

By the end of 2021, nearly two years after COVID lockdowns began, Fauci finally seemed to notice the folly of the policies he and his fellow public health bureaucrats had pushed so hard to implement.

Zero COVID: In Pursuit of a Pipe Dream

Even though lockdowns had a devastating impact on health and no impact on viral spread, some began to call for even longer and more severe lockdowns in pursuit of the impossible goal of "Zero COVID." On January 4, 2021, a feminist activist with the Twitter handle "@zerocovidzoe" demanded:

What we need!
- Long term hard Lockdown STRATEGY (around 24 months)
- Stay at home order by law with a permit system.
- Night Curfew
- Covid eradication plan
- 24 Month Furlough
- All non essentials closed[80]

"When you shut down society, when you shut down the country, there's a lot of deleterious effects that go along with that, that go well beyond the economy, is the availability of people to get things done for their own health. When you shut down the country, you have people who have other diseases who don't have the opportunity to get their HIV test, to get their HIV meds, to get their mammograms, to get the colonoscopies. All the things you do when you shut down," Fauci said. "So I wouldn't just say it's an economic consideration."[81]

Not to be left out, the *New York Times* accelerated the paper's remarkable walk back from the COVID-lockdown narrative with an article by David Leonhardt titled "Do Covid Precautions Work? Yes, but They Haven't Made a Big Difference"—published in March of 2022, two years after the restrictions began.

Leonhardt asked whether "social distancing and masking" had worked and concluded that "the answer is surprisingly unclearM"

As Leonhardt pointed out, "If those restrictions were costless, then their small benefits might still be worth it. But of course they do have costs. Masks hamper people's ability to communicate, verbally and otherwise. Social distancing leads to the isolation and disruption that

No Lockdowns to See Here

You know politicians realize COVID "lockdowns" are unpopular when they start calling them something else. In late 2020, the name "lockdown" was no longer favored by many of the ruling class:

- "Pulling an emergency brake" is how California Gov. Gavin Newsom spun his latest lockdown
- Biden COVID advisor Dr. Celine Gounder talked about a "dimmer switch"
- A two-week "freeze" is what Oregon Governor Kate Brown called her state's lockdown
- "Retightening restrictions" is the euphemism New Jersey Governor Phil Murphy used
- Minnesota issued a COVID "pause to save lives"
- In the United Kingdom they now call lockdowns a "circuit breaker" or "fire break"[82]

have fed so many problems over the past two years—mental health troubles, elevated blood pressure, drug overdoses, violent crime, vehicle crashes and more."

The article in the *Times* ended by noting an "alarming" impact of COVID restrictions: "Learning loss, with the biggest effects on students who are Black, Latino, lower-income, disabled or not fluent in English."[83]

Lockdowns Don't Work—So We Need more Lockdowns

"California has had some of the toughest restrictions in the country to combat the coronavirus, from a complete ban on restaurant dining to travel quarantines and indoor gym closures. It hasn't been enough," reported *POLITICO* in a December 2020 article titled "Locked-Down California Runs Out of Reasons for Surprising Surge."[84]

CHAPTER 6

How "The Science" Was Manipulated to Support Long-Desired Policies

The public health bureaucracy and the "climate community" have become political lobbying organizations, and they are using "The Science" to support their preferred policies—policies that dovetail with the Great Reset and advancing the power of the administrative state.

At this point no researcher looking for government research money would put his name on a study that was against the politically accepted views on COVID lockdowns or mask mandates or climate-crisis claims.

During the COVID-19 panic, public health bureaucrats, politicians, and media figures constantly invoked "The Science" when determining how hard and long to hammer the public with lockdowns and mandates. In reality the Great Reset was underway in 2020, with the promotion of authoritarian COVID-19 "mitigation" measures utilizing decades of corrupted "science."

French president Emmanuel Macron warned that, because of COVID-19, "We must all limit the number of people with whom we're in contact with every single day. Scientists say so."[1]

"Scientists say so." But *which* scientists "say so"? And on what evidence do those scientists base what they say?

In the age of COVID lockdowns and mandates, a pending Green New Deal, and a Great Reset, an insight of renowned economist Thomas Sowell is more valuable than ever: "Experts are often called in, not to provide factual information or dispassionate analysis for the purpose of decision-making by responsible officials, but to give political cover for decisions already made and based on other considerations entirely."[2]

Another name for it—*Science to support the policy.*

As C. S. Lewis warned, "I dread specialists in power because they are specialists speaking outside their special subjects. Let scientists tell us about sciences. But government involves questions about the good for man, and justice, and what things are worth having at what price; and on these a scientific training gives a man's opinion no added value."[3] Lewis was sounding the alarm against the kind of technocracy that we live under thanks to COVID—the control of society by an elite unelected cadre of experts.

"No Longer about Advancing the Truth"

"Since independent thinking is a punishable offense in all government organizations, science is no longer about advancing the truth but about promoting politically preferred ideas," wrote economist Sanjeev Sabhlok.[4]

> **"Science Lost"**
> "There was a clash between two schools of thought, authoritarian public health versus science—and science lost." —renowned Stanford epidemiologist John Ioannidis, expressing his opposition to COVID lockdowns[5]

The entire world of epidemiology and public health was turned on its head as previously rejected remediations for projected future pandemics became part of a "new normal"—allegedly under the guidance of an unquestionable entity known as "The Science." But the pattern had already been set in the climate change debate, which was critical for imposing the Great Reset. "The Science" had already been invoked in the push for "solutions" to the supposed climate crisis by everyone from former vice president Al Gore to teen school-skipper Greta Thunberg, who famously urged the world to "start listening to the science" and "unite behind the science."[6]

Whenever they invoke "The Science," you know something other than science is at play.

"A theory becomes The Science when a mitigation or solution to the theory becomes more important than the theory itself," explained Dr. William M. Briggs, coauthor of *The Price of Panic: How the Tyranny of Experts Turned a Pandemic into a Catastrophe*. "This is, as mentioned, the Cult of Science. Members are easy to spot. Not only do they use phrases like 'We believe in The Science' and 'Denier!'—has there ever been a clearer indication of religious intent than this one word?—but they all evince scientism, the false belief that knowing a ('scientific') fact implies morally what should be done about that fact," Briggs pointed out.

"In plain science theory is made to fit Reality. In The Science this is flipped," he added. "The Science has nothing to do with science and everything to do with solutions and mitigations." Briggs detailed how "how the theory-Reality relationship is reversed" because the "elites benefit from mitigations."

He demonstrated by a thought experiment how "The Science" is not real science. "Say you disbelieve the theory but support the mitigation, and you will be praised. But say you believe all the models of exponential 'cases' and deaths, but you don't think lockdowns and mask mandates should be implemented, and you will be loathed," Briggs wrote.

"Try it with any science that has become The Science. Accept the theory but reject its mitigation. You will very quickly learn The Science has nothing to do with science and everything to do with solutions and mitigations," he added.[7]

Eisenhower Warned Us

We were alerted about being ruled over by scientists and experts. In his 1961 Farewell Address, President Dwight D. Eisenhower bluntly warned of this danger.

Eisenhower explained that "a government contract becomes virtually a substitute for intellectual curiosity" and "the prospect of domination of the nation's scholars by Federal employment, project allocations, and the power of money is ever present and is gravely to be regarded."

According to Eisenhower, "We must also be alert to the equal and opposite danger that public policy could itself become the captive of a scientific-technological elite."[8]

It was in 2020 that Eisenhower's "scientific-technological elite" became a very obvious reality in America. COVID-19 and climate were two sides of the same coin, with coronavirus lockdowns achieving many of the same goals the climate movement has striven for: central planning, loss of individual freedom, economic pain, obedience to authority, and weakened national sovereignty—all happening in a virtual blink of the eye.

Independence, or Slavery?

What would the author of the Declaration of Independence think of America today?

"I prefer dangerous freedom over peaceful slavery." –Thomas Jefferson, letter to James Madison, January 30, 1787[9]

"The natural progress of things is for liberty to yield, and government to gain ground." –Thomas Jefferson, letter to Edward Carrington, May 27, 1788[10]

Epidemiologist Knut Wittkowski also slammed the government-funded "science" used to support COVID lockdowns.

"Shutting down schools, driving the economy against the wall—there was no reason for it," Wittkowski explained in an interview posted on YouTube. YouTube promptly banned Wittkowski for his honesty—a fate, it seems, shared by nearly all lockdown dissenters whose content attracted the attention of the social media censors.

"Governments did not have an open discussion, including economists, biologists and epidemiologists, to hear different voices. In Britain, it was the voice of one person—Neil Ferguson—who has a history of coming up with projections that are a bit odd. The government did not convene a meeting with people who have different ideas, different projections, to discuss his projection," Wittkowski said.

Echoing the point President Eisenhower made in 1961, Wittkowski stated:

> They have the scientists on their side that depend on government funding. One scientist in Germany just got $500 million from the government, because he always says what the government wants to hear.
>
> Scientists are in a very strange situation. They now depend on government funding, which is a trend that has developed over the past 40 years. Before that, when you were a professor at a university, you had your salary and you had your freedom. Now, the university gives you a desk and access to the library. And then you have to ask for government money and write grant applications. If you are known to criticise the government, what does that do to your chance of getting funded? It creates a huge conflict of interest.[11]

Another name for it—Science to support the policy.

Soviet-Style Science

"Communists saw their political beliefs as so all-encompassing that even science was political: if science contradicted the goals of communism, it wasn't science. In today's United States the slow death of liberalism has resulted in the blatant politicisation of science, to the extent that as in Russia, scientists teach things which are obviously untrue because it supports the prevailing ideology. Then there is the media, much of which parrots the party line with almost embarrassing, 'Comrade Stalin has driven pig iron to record production' levels of conformity."—Ed West, deputy editor, UnHerd[12]

Before the CDC's Dr. Anthony Fauci supported "The Science" in favor of lockdowns, he supported "The Science" *against* them. In 2014, Fauci opposed quarantines of health care workers in response to Ebola as "draconian" and warned of "unintended consequences."

Fauci complained about the "unscientific" policies of a number of U.S. governors who had imposed a targeted quarantine on health care workers arriving from Ebola-infected regions. "We have to be careful that there are [not] unintended consequences," Fauci said.

"We need to treat them, returning people with respect," Fauci explained during the outbreak of Ebola in Africa.

"You can monitor them in multiple different ways. You don't have to put them in a confined place," Fauci added.

"Go with the science," he said.

But then the coronavirus came along, and suddenly "The Science" said exactly the opposite.

Journalist Jordan Schachtel summed up Fauci's duplicity on quarantines: "As we've discovered, the 50 year tenured government health bureaucrat wasn't always a fan of quarantines. As recently as 2014, he was emphatically against them. Has 'the science' changed that much in the last 6 years, or is something else afoot?"[13]

Before COVID-19, lockdowns and mask mandates for viruses were not a part of "The Science" of epidemiology. But as we saw in chapter 2, they did show up in the eerily prescient viral-response scenarios in the 2010 Rockefeller Foundation report; the 2018 "Clade X" pandemic event sponsored by the World Economic Forum and the Johns Hopkins Center for Health Security; and Event 201, a joint effort sponsored by the World Economic Forum, the Bill & Melinda Gates Foundation, and the Johns Hopkins Center for Health Security, which portrayed a hypothetical coronavirus pandemic in October 2019—just before COVID-19 began to spread in Wuhan China. The section of the 2010 Rockefeller Foundation report on a future pandemic was titled "Lock Step."[14]

And, remarkably, we did lock down in the pandemic of 2020, the first pandemic to occur after those dry runs—despite, as we have seen,

I AM the Science!

In 2021, Fauci declared that attacks on him are "attacks on science." He claimed, "A lot of what you're seeing as attacks on me, quite frankly, are attacks on science. If you are trying to get at me as a public health official and a scientist, you're really attacking, not only Dr. Anthony Fauci, you're attacking science."[15]

what "The Science" (that is, the accepted public health recommendations up to that point) said. The pandemic of 2020 is unique because the United States did not lock down during previous pandemics.

What Changed?

"We didn't lock down almost the entire country in 1968/69, 1957, or 1949–1952, or even during 1918. But in a terrifying few days in March 2020, it happened to all of us, causing an avalanche of social, cultural, and economic destruction that will ring through the ages," wrote Jeffrey A. Tucker, the editorial director for the American Institute for Economic Research and the author of *Liberty or Lockdown*. "There was nothing normal about it all."[16]

In 1957 the Asian flu pandemic did not prompt lockdowns or mask mandates. "Elvis Was King, Ike Was President, and 116,000 Americans Died in a Pandemic," Tucker explained.

"It's Raining on Prom Night"

"We Didn't Close America in 1957–1958" is the title of an Ed Achorn post about the Asian flu at American Greatness. America dealt with that virus "without doing unacceptably massive damage to our whole society," Achorn summarized. "America in 1957 did not shut down. The National Football League played its games. Elvis Presley kept on wiggling his hips in concerts and TV shows. . . . The economy kept functioning, albeit with a greater number of people than usual calling in sick. . . . The Asian flu arose, quickly spiked, and went away. Unlike the coronavirus, it did not leave behind devastated small businesses, massive unemployment and a shattered economy."[17]

It has been pointed out that the Asian flu was even the theme of a funny song in the 1978 musical *Grease*—"It's Raining on Prom Night":

> I was deprived of a young girl's dream
> By the cruel force of nature from the blue
>
> Instead of a night full of romance supreme
> All I got was a runny nose and Asiatic flu.[18]

"Nothing was shut down. Restaurants, schools, theaters, sporting events, travel—everything continued without interruption," Tucker pointed out. "For staying calm and treating the terrible Asian flu of 1957 as a medical problem to address with medical intelligence, rather than as an excuse to unleash Medieval-style brutality, this first postwar generation deserves our respect and admiration."[19]

According to Tucker, "The mystery of why today vast numbers of governments around the world (but not all) have crushed economies, locked people under house arrest, wrecked business, spread despair, disregarded basic freedoms and rights will require years if not decades to sort out. Is it the news cycle that is creating mass hysteria? Political ambition and arrogance? A decline in philosophical regard for freedom as the best system for dealing with crises?"

As Tucker wrote, "What's remarkable when we look back at this year [1957], nothing was shut down.... Without a 24-hour news cycle with thousands of news agencies and a billion websites hungry for traffic, mostly people paid no attention other than to keep basic hygiene. It was

They Didn't Lock Down Woodstock

"American Life Went on as Normal during the Killer Pandemic of 1969," the headline of a *New York Post* article by Eric Spitznagel pointed out. "H3N2 (or the 'Hong Kong flu,' as it was more popularly known) was an influenza strain that the *New York Times* described as 'one of the worst in the nation's history.'"

"But schools were not shut down nationwide, other than a few dozen because of too many sick teachers. Face masks weren't required or even common. Though Woodstock was not held during the peak months of the H3N2 pandemic (the first wave ended by early March 1969, and it didn't flare up again until November of that year), the festival went ahead when the virus was still active and had no known cure," Spitznagel wrote. "It was like the pandemic hadn't even happened if you look for it in history books."

"I am still shocked at how differently people addressed—or maybe even ignored it—in 1968 compared to 2020," explained Nathaniel Moir, a post-doctoral fellow at Harvard University's Kennedy School of Government.[20]

covered in the press as a medical problem. The notion that there was a political solution never occurred to anyone."[21]

Fauci claimed he was surprised at "how rapidly [COVID-19] just took over the planet." In fact, as author Michael Fumento pointed out, "it appears to spread with the same speed as seasonal flu, which covers the world map annually. And, of course, seasonal flu is also respiratory and has significant mortality."

"The 'Asian flu' of 1957–1958 (H2N2) had a death rate of about 0.67%, well over twice that the CDC estimates for COVID-19. Asian Flu killed an estimated 116,000 Americans and 1.1 million worldwide, according to the CDC. That's 223,000 Americans and 3 million world-wide adjusted to today's population," Fumento noted.

"The 'Hong Kong flu' of 1968–1969 (H3N2) killed an estimated 100,000 Americans and 1 million worldwide, or 165,000 Americans and 2.1 million people worldwide adjusted to today's populations," he added. "Those estimates are not for deaths 'with' the virus or 'suspected' as having been caused by the virus even without a test, as the CDC explicitly allows in its COVID-19 guidelines. They indicate death directly from the flu."

Fumento concluded, "Yet life in those times continued essentially as normal. For neither flu pandemic were there mandatory facemasks in the U.S., no 'social distancing,' no quarantining of the healthy that triggered rises in alcohol and other drug abuse, domestic violence, depression, and suicide, or what Fauci himself described as 'irreparable damage.' They occurred without panic, caused no recessions, much less the possibility of a worldwide depression."[22]

"How Many Lives Were Saved?"

"2020 was the year when I learned that viruses respect directional arrows on supermarket floors." —researcher Tony Heller of Real Climate Science[23]

As Ron Coleman tweeted, "Did they release the official figures yet on how many lives were saved by taping arrows to the floors of supermarket aisles?"[24]

The question looms, how did COVID-19 create a mass panic, starting with "two weeks to flatten the curve" and turning into a massive, unrelenting power grab by all three levels of the U.S. government and countries around the world seemingly acting in unison? Obviously, the Great Reset was in position, with a don't-let-a-crisis-go-to-waste attitude poised to capitalize on COVID-19 fears. Robert F. Kennedy Jr. summed the COVID restrictions as "a coup d'etat against liberal democracy."[25]

How "The Science" Gets Corrupted

But more specifically, how did our most basic human liberties get tossed out seemingly overnight—with government stay-at-home orders, curfews, mask mandates, restrictions on travel, regulations on weddings, funerals, and backyard barbeques, and neighbors encouraged to snitch and be rewarded—all supposedly to fight a virus?

The answer is that the science—"The Science"—has been deeply corrupted. "The fact that the pandemic guidelines of the WHO and nearly every developed nation were simply tossed aside to permit CCP-inspired lockdowns, and the public was neither consulted nor even informed of this decision, suggests to me the corruption of public health runs very deep," attorney and author Michael P. Senger explained.[26]

"Please, Keep to Your Bubbles"

"Stay local. Do not congregate. Don't talk to your neighbors. Please, keep to your bubbles. It comes down again to those very simple principles. We know from overseas cases of the delta variant that it can be spread by people simply walking past one another. So keep those movements outside to the bare minimum. Wear a mask and make sure you keep up that physical distancing." —New Zealand prime minister Jacinda Arder[27]

The *New England Journal of Medicine* put its weight behind lockdowns in an October 2020 editorial. "China, faced with the first outbreak, chose strict quarantine and isolation after an initial delay. These measures were severe but effective," the editors of *NEJM* claimed. The journal even praised New Zealand's "zero COVID" strategy. "New Zealand has used these same measures...to come close to eliminating the disease," the journal claimed.

The *NEJM* did not stop there, but went full political, calling for the ouster of then president Trump because of his administration's unwillingness to support stricter lockdowns.

"This election gives us the power to render judgment," the journal declared. "When it comes to the response to the largest public health crisis of our time, our current political leaders have demonstrated that they are dangerously incompetent. We should not abet them and enable the deaths of thousands more Americans by allowing them to keep their jobs."[28]

"Medical Dictatorship"

In response to *New England Journal of Medicine*'s pro–China–lockdown, political-lobbying editorial, I tweeted a point-by-point rebuttal on October 8, 2020:

NEJM: "China, faced with the first outbreak, chose strict quarantine and isolation after an initial delay. These measures were severe but effective."

Morano Response: Locking people in their homes in dramatic fashion while being filmed for drama is not "effective."

Morano: It is awesome that the U.S. did not have China's "Strict quarantine and isolation." It's amazing you ignore Sweden's rational & scientific approach of avoiding lockdowns!

NEJM: "New Zealand has used these same measures . . . to come close to eliminating the disease."

Response: Trying to zero out cases using fascist govt tactics of quarantining healthy people & isolation & mandatory testing is not something worthy of praise. N. Zealand is wacko.

NEJM: "The U.S. instituted quarantine & isolation measures late & inconsistently, often without any effort to enforce them. . . . "

Response: Yes! That is the beauty of the USA! We don't like locking our people down & using police as viral fascist enforcers of mask mandates & lockdowns.

NEJM: "Our rules on social distancing have in many places been lackadaisical at best . . ."

Response: Great! There should never have been any such "rules" mandated by the govt. End all mandates for lockdowns, social distancing & masks.

NEJM: "Our leaders have stated outright that masks are political tools rather than effective infection control measures."

Response: They are "political tools" & they are NOT "effective" against viruses when the general public wears them. Science says so!

NEJM: "Yet our leaders have largely chosen to ignore and even denigrate experts."

Response: "Experts" like Fauci, Redfield & surgeon gen Adams should be IGNORED & DENIGRATED! They are contradicting themselves & manipulating science to support policies they have already made.

NEJM: "Much of that national expertise resides in government institutions."

Response: No! I have corrected your statement: "Much of the national unelected politicized safety dictators reside in government institutions who no one ever voted for." Unelected public health bureaucrats should not be ruling our lives. Don't blame Americans, they did not vote for Fauci!

NEJM: "U.S. still suffers from disease rates that have prevented many businesses from reopening . . ."

Response: Stop it! The U.S. is "suffering" from a technocracy coup led by the very "experts" you seem to love. The only thing "preventing" businesses from opening is out of control governors, mayors and officials who are acting like dictators.

NEJM: COVID is "the largest public health crisis of our time."

Response: The biggest "crisis" the USA faces is NOT COVID! It is a medical dictatorship of unelected "experts" ruling every aspect of our lives from backyard BBQs to church to restaurants to funerals to weddings, etc. Enough already! We need to STOP public health "experts" & governors who declare a public health "emergency" and then become dictators.[29]

Steve Milloy of Junk Science warned that the government response and suspension of liberty during COVID revealed that "the incompetent, corrupt and politicized public health bureaucracy...want[s] to create a precedent for permanent control of society via 'public health.'"[30]

"As with education, conservatives abandoned public health as a profession decades ago. I don't know any conservatives with expertise in public health. We are now paying the price," Milloy wrote.[31]

"We have ceded the field (of public health) to leftists who have only one tool...government crackdown."[32]

"All public health bureaucrats are Dems and worse sorts of leftists," Milloy wrote.[33] "We can still 'social distance' without devolving into a police state or destroying the economy."[34]

The Surprising Origins of "Social Distancing"

Liberty or Lockdown author Jeffrey Tucker called the origin of the unprecedented COVID lockdowns a "bizarre tale," noting that the first time the phrase "social distancing" had appeared in the *New York Times* was February 12, 2006, during the avian flu scare.[35]

"If the avian flu goes pandemic while Tamiflu and vaccines are still in short supply, experts say, the only protection most Americans will have is 'social distancing,' which is the new politically correct way of saying 'quarantine,'" reported the *Times* in 2006.

"But distancing also encompasses less drastic measures, like wearing face masks, staying out of elevators—and the [elbow] bump. Such stratagems, those experts say, will rewrite the ways we interact, at least during the weeks when the waves of influenza are washing over us."[36]

On April 22, 2020, the *Times* updated its reporting in a revealing exposé on the history of "social distancing":

Fourteen years ago, two federal government doctors, Richard Hatchett and Carter Mecher, met with a colleague at a burger joint in suburban Washington for a final review of a proposal they knew would be treated like a piñata: telling Americans to stay home from work and school the next time the country was hit by a deadly pandemic.

When they presented their plan not long after, it was met with skepticism and a degree of ridicule by senior officials, who like others in the United States had grown accustomed to relying on the pharmaceutical industry, with its ever-growing array of new treatments, to confront evolving health challenges.

"Snap Lockdowns"

"'One Virus Case Puts New Zealand into Nationwide Lockdown'" blared the headline at Bloomberg in 2021. "The snap lockdown will begin at midnight tonight as authorities rush to identify the source of a single infection in largest city Auckland, [New Zealand prime minister Jacinda] Ardern said."[37]

I tweeted: "If you thought lockdowns were bad, get ready for 'snap lockdowns.' They can come at any moment and for any reason. On the whim of a tyrant."[38]

The *New York Times* report, by Eric Lipton and Jennifer Steinhauer, then compared lockdowns to medieval practices.

"Drs. Hatchett and Mecher were proposing instead that Americans in some places might have to turn back to an approach, self-isolation, first widely employed in the Middle Ages. How that idea—born out of a request by President George W. Bush to ensure the nation was better prepared for the next contagious disease outbreak—became the heart of the national playbook for responding to a pandemic is one of the untold stories of the coronavirus crisis."

But the story got more absurd, as the *Times* reported how a high school kid's computer-simulation project became the basis for COVID-19 international policy.

"It required the key proponents—Dr. Mecher, a Department of Veterans Affairs physician, and Dr. Hatchett, an oncologist turned White House adviser—to overcome intense initial opposition. It brought their work together with that of a Defense Department team assigned to a similar task. And it had some unexpected detours, including a deep dive into the history of the 1918 Spanish flu and an important discovery kicked off by a high school research project pursued by the daughter of a scientist at the Sandia National Laboratories.

"The concept of social distancing is now familiar to almost everyone. But as it first made its way through the federal bureaucracy in 2006 and 2007, it was viewed as impractical, unnecessary and politically infeasible."[39]

Let's repeat: Social distancing—the politically correct term for quarantines or lockdowns—was judged "impractical, unnecessary and politically infeasible."

The fourteen-year-old high school student was Laura M. Glass. The *Albuquerque Journal* reported about how her paper would later become law of the land:

> Laura, with some guidance from her dad, devised a computer simulation that showed how people—family members, co-workers, students in schools, people in social situations—interact. What she discovered was that school kids come in contact with about 140 people a day, more than any other group. Based on that finding, her program showed that in a hypothetical town of 10,000 people, 5,000 would be infected during a pandemic if no measures were taken, but only 500 would be infected if the schools were closed.[40]

"Laura's name appears on the foundational paper arguing for lockdowns and forced human separation," Jeffrey Tucker reported. The 2006 paper "set out a model for forced separation and applied it with good results backwards in time to 1957. [The paper's authors] conclude with a chilling call for what amounts to a totalitarian lockdown, all stated very matter-of-factly," Tucker explained.

"In other words, it was a high-school science experiment that eventually became law of the land, and through a circuitous route propelled not by science but politics." Tucker pointed out.[41]

The origin of "The Science" is becoming clearer.

"It Made No Sense"

The plan for this version of lockdowns was viciously criticized in 2006 by Dr. D. A. Henderson, who had led the effort to eradicate smallpox.

Tucker, quoting the *New York Times*, pointed out that "Dr. Henderson was convinced that it made no sense to force schools to close or public gatherings to stop. Teenagers would escape their homes to hang out at the mall. School lunch programs would close, and impoverished children would not have enough to eat. Hospital staffs would have a hard time going to work if their children were at home.... The answer, he insisted, was to tough it out: **Let the pandemic spread, treat people who get sick and work quickly to develop a vaccine to prevent it from coming back**" [emphasis Tucker's].

As Tucker observed in retrospect, "Confronting a manageable epidemic and turning it into a catastrophe: that seems like a good description of everything that has happened in the COVID-19 crisis of 2020."

He added, "Again, the idea was born of a high-school science experiment using agent-based modeling techniques having nothing at all to do with real life, real science, or real medicine."

The April 22, 2020, *New York Times* report explained how, despite the concerns, the Bush Administration approved the lockdown plans.

"The [Bush] administration ultimately sided with the proponents of social distancing and shutdowns—though their victory was little noticed outside of public health circles. Their policy would become the basis for government planning and would be used extensively in simulations used to prepare for pandemics, and in a limited way in 2009 during an outbreak of the influenza called H1N1. Then the coronavirus came, and the plan was put to work across the country for the first time."[42]

Maybe "Science" *Is* a Liberal Conspiracy

A bumper sticker promoted by progressives reads: "Science is not a liberal conspiracy."

"Oh yes it is. Or, yes, it can be, and much of it is. And here is where that bumper sticker is wrong. When the regulatory state—i.e., the Environmental Protection Agency, the United Nations, the U.S. federal government—when they want to regulate, they look for justifications and causes, and that's the natural state of any government. . . . So essentially the regulatory state is using the climate scare now to achieve its ends. . . . The science must support the government policy, and the network of government and academic funding peer-pressure is designed to ensure 'The Science' ends up supporting the politicians' favored policy. Any dissenters have to face intimidation and censorship." —Marc Morano in a 2019 interview[43]

To put politicized science in perspective, we must look at the science before anyone had a political reason to care what the answer was.

The Data on Masks

Just as lockdowns were rejected by health experts before COVID-19, mask mandates on the general public were also viewed as ineffective. Before COVID, masks were determined to be ineffective against infections and viruses in studies going back to the 1970s. But later, when "The Science" needed to be molded to fit the needs of politicians, "The Science" was adjusted through modeling studies and dubious correlations studies to find that mask mandates now miraculously work.

"I'm sure some politicians wish they could take a few things back. Joe Biden might wish he'd never said that thing about the repeal of mask mandates being 'neanderthal thinking,' given that those states have done no worse than any others, but since no reporter has challenged him on it, he's gotten a pass," author Tom Woods commented in 2021.[44]

Some Protests Are More Equal Than Others

Jennifer Nuzzo, a Johns Hopkins epidemiologist, claimed that politically approved gatherings were COVID safe. "In this moment the public health risks of not protesting to demand an end to systemic racism greatly exceed the harms of the virus," Nuzzo tweeted on June 2, 2020, as the George Floyd protests were raging across America.[45]

On April 30, 2020, Michigan governor Gretchen Whitmer declared that no large gatherings would be tolerated: "It is probably not going to be safe to congregate in masses for quite a while and it is heartbreaking.... These big gatherings can't safely happen right now."

But Whitmer changed her tune on June 1, 2020: "The death of George Floyd has once again shown a light on the systematic cycle of injustice in our country. To the overwhelming majority who have taken to the streets and protested peacefully, protesting historic inequities black Michiganders and those across the country are facing, I hear you. I see you. I respect you, and I support your efforts to enact real structural change in America."[46]

More than one thousand "health professionals" signed a public letter supporting the Floyd protests, minimizing the risk of transmitting COVID-19 at such gatherings and declaring that "opposition to racism" was "vital to the public health."[47]

Many studies in the medical literature since the 1970s have revealed that masks, even in medical settings, are not particularly helpful in stopping disease spread and that they serve as contaminated hubs for the spread of bacteria and viruses.

Here is a small sampling of mask studies compiled by Chris Masters in a 2020 article titled "Studies of Surgical Masks Efficacy." In the words of the article:[48]

- Ritter et al., in 1975, found that "the wearing of a surgical face mask had no effect upon the overall operating room environmental contamination."[49]
- Ha'eri and Wiley, in 1980, applied human albumin microspheres to the interior of surgical masks in 20

operations. At the end of teach operation, wound washings were examined under the microscope. "Particle contamination of the wound was demonstrated in all experiments."[50]

- Laslett and Sabin, in 1989, found that caps and masks were not necessary during cardiac catheterization. "No infections were found in any patient, regardless of whether a cap or mask was used," they wrote. Sjøl and Kelbaek came to the same conclusion in 2002....[51]

- A review by Skinner and Sutton in 2001 concluded, "The evidence for discontinuing the use of surgical face masks would appear to be stronger than the evidence available to support their continued use."[52]

- Lahme et al., in 2001, wrote that "surgical face masks worn by patients during regional anaesthesia, did not reduce the concentration of airborne bacteria over the operation field in our study. Thus they are dispensable."...[53]

- Da Zhou et al., reviewing the literature in 2015, concluded that "there is a lack of substantial evidence to support claims that facemasks protect either patient or surgeon from infectious contamination."[54]

And when medical studies turned specifically to mask effectiveness with airborne viruses, the results also showed them to be ineffective. In the words of the Swiss Policy Research group overview of studies:[55]

- A May 2020 meta-study on pandemic influenza published by the US CDC found that face masks had no effect, [either] as personal protective equipment [or] as a source control....[56]

- A Danish randomized controlled trial with 6000 participants, published in the Annals of Internal Medicine in November 2020, found no statistically significant effect of high-quality medical face masks against SARS-CoV-2 infection in a community setting.[57]

- A large randomized controlled trial with close to 8000 participants, published in October 2020 in PLOS One, found that face masks "did not seem to be effective against laboratory-confirmed viral respiratory infections nor against clinical respiratory infection."[58]

- A February 2021 review by the European CDC found no high-quality evidence in favor of face masks and recommended their use only based on the "precautionary principle."[59]

- A July 2020 review by the Oxford Centre for Evidence-Based Medicine found that there is no evidence for the effectiveness of face masks against virus infection or transmission.[60]

- A November 2020 Cochrane review found that face masks did not reduce influenza-like illness (ILI) cases, either in the general population nor in health care workers. . . .[61]

- An April 2020 review by two U.S. professors in respiratory and infectious disease from the University of Illinois concluded that face masks have no effect in everyday life, either as self-protection or to protect third parties (so-called source control). . . .[62]

- A 2015 study in the British Medical Journal BMJ Open found that cloth masks were penetrated by 97% of particles and may increase infection risk by retaining moisture or repeated use.[63]

- An August 2020 review by a German professor in virology, epidemiology, and hygiene found that there is no evidence for the effectiveness of face masks and that the improper daily use of masks by the public may in fact lead to an increase in infections.[64]

As the *Biosecurity and Bioterrorism* study cited in the previous chapter found, "Studies have shown the ordinary surgical mask does little to prevent inhalation of small droplets bearing influenza virus. The pores in the mask become blocked by moisture from breathing, and the air stream simply diverts around the mask."[65]

Former *New York Times* reporter Alex Berenson summed up a 2015 *British Medical Journal* study: "A randomized trial (the gold standard yadda yadda) of 1600 health-care workers showed those wearing masks were 6 times (!) as likely to have flu-like illnesses as those in the control group after 4 weeks."[66]

A May 2020 article in the *New England Journal of Medicine* stated very clearly that masks don't work against viruses. "We know that wearing a mask outside health care facilities offers little, if any, protection from infection," the article said. "The chance of catching Covid-19 from a passing interaction in a public space is therefore minimal. In many cases, the desire for widespread masking is a reflexive reaction to anxiety over the pandemic," the article explained. But the authors of the article essentially recanted these claims in July 2020 as COVID-19 hysteria ramped up and support of mask mandates became—mandatory.[67]

A 2020 CDC report found masks to be ineffective against COVID-19 as well. "A Centers for Disease Control report released in September shows that masks and face coverings are not effective in preventing the spread of COVID-19, even for those people who consistently wear them," reported Jordan Davidson of The Federalist.

"A study conducted in the United States in July found that when they compared 154 'case-patients,' who tested positive for COVID-19, to a control group of 160 participants from health care facilities who were symptomatic but tested negative, over 70 percent of the case-patients were contaminated with the virus and fell ill despite 'always' wearing a mask."[68]

Earlier bouts of mass masking in some parts of the United States during the 1918 Spanish flu outbreak were also deemed "useless." As the *Washington Post* reported in April 2020 (before the great COVID-19 mask flip-flop by public health officials), John M. Barry, author of *The Great Influenza: The Story of the Deadliest Pandemic in History*, had pointed out, "During the influenza pandemic of 1918, officials often advised Americans to wear face masks in public. Doctors believed that masks could help prevent 'spray infections.'" But though millions wore the masks, they "were useless as designed and could not prevent influenza," according to Barry. "Only preventing exposure to the virus could."

Many officials had been eager to enforce mask mandates in 1918. "On Nov. 1, 1918, Eugene C. Caley became the first man in Oakland, Calif., to be arrested for not wearing a mask. He was released on bail, although similar scofflaws in San Francisco had been sentenced to up to 10 days in jail," noted Barry.

"This is only the beginning," said the chief of police, according to the *Oakland Tribune*. "We are going to enforce this mask ordinance if we have to pack the city jail with people. This epidemic is too serious to be taken as a joke, and men arrested…will find that it's no laughing matter when they face the police judges."[69]

"In October 1918, the *San Francisco Chronicle* ran a public service announcement telling readers that 'The man or woman or child who will not wear a mask now is a dangerous slacker'—a reference to the type of World War I 'slacker' who didn't help the war effort. One sign in California threatened, 'Wear a Mask or Go to Jail,'" according to History.com.[70]

Just as in our present era, mask rebellion was prevalent. "I am 75 years old and have been living in this state 67 years," E. Piercy said in police court, according to Los Angeles's *Evening Express*. "I must have my smoke, and I'm not going to give up my tobacco for a cheesecloth muzzle!"[71]

In 1918, a San Francisco health officer shot three people, two of them innocent bystanders, for refusal to comply with the mask mandates, History.com reports.

Also, just as in our present era, hypocrisy abounded. "This was far different from the treatment San Francisco's leaders received when they didn't comply. At a boxing match, a police photographer captured images of several supervisors, a congressman, a justice, a Navy rear-admiral, the city's health officer and even the mayor, all without masks. The health officer paid a $5 fine and the mayor later paid a $50 fine, but unlike other 'mask slackers,' they received no prison time (not to mention no one shot at them)," Becky Little of History.com explained.[72]

Science Rejected Mandatory Masks in 1919

"In 1919, Wilfred Kellogg's study for the California State Board of Health concluded that mask ordinances 'applied forcibly to entire communities' did not decrease cases and deaths, as confirmed by comparisons of cities with widely divergent policies on masking. . . . Kellogg found the evidence persuasive: 'The case against the mask as a measure of compulsory application for the control of epidemics appears to be complete.'

"In a comprehensive study published in 1921, Warren T. Vaughn declared 'the efficacy of face masks is still open to question.' The problem was human behavior: Masks were used until they were filthy, worn in ways that offered little or no protection, and compulsory laws did not overcome the 'failure of cooperation on the part of the public.' Vaughn's sobering conclusion: It is safe to say that the face mask as used was a failure." —E. Thomas Ewing in Health Affairs, May 2021.[73]

"Mask Madness"

Statistician William H. Briggs declared the whole mask phenomenon "Mask Madness." "Having healthy *asymptomatic* people wear masks at what is clearly the end of a *routine* pandemic is asinine," Briggs wrote in 2020.

"We might as well have a tinfoil hat mandate to protect from aliens. It would, at this point, be just as useful," he explained. "This moral panic is like Prohibition. This time not against alcohol, but against breath. Three-quarters of Americans falsely believe death is lurking in people's breath," he added.

"Forcing masks on people in 'passing encounters in public spaces' has no medical justification. None."[74]

The (Political) Science

As coronavirus mask and vaccine mandates started dropping from even blue Democrat states in 2022, the *New York Times* revealed the reason, and that reason had to do with "The Science"—the POLITICAL Science! The *Times* reported that the "easing" of COVID restrictions was in part due to "political focus groups that began in the weeks after the November election."

> ### "Phases of the Moon"
> "I keep seeing people telling journalists that kids can take off masks when case[s]/hospitalizations/deaths fall below some number. That is like tying masking to the phases of the moon. Not a shred of empirical data that shows that masks have benefit above but not below any threshold."
> —Vinay Prasad, associate professor in the Department of Epidemiology and Biostatistics at the University of California San Francisco[75]

New Jersey Democrat governor Phil Murphy was "stunned by the energy of right-wing voters in his blue state" after he nearly lost what was expected to be an easy re-election in 2021, according to the *Times*. "Arranging a series of focus groups across the state to see what they had missed, Mr. Murphy's advisers were struck by the findings: Across the board, voters shared frustrations over public health measures, a sense of pessimism about the future and a deep desire to return to some sense of normalcy," the *Times* reported. "Even Democratic voters, they agreed, were wearying of the toughest restrictions, growing increasingly impatient with mandates and feeling ready to live with the risk that remained."[76]

When You Lose CNN...

"It is so sad but it's true. The CDC has turned into a punch line," said CNN reporter Brian Stelter in 2022. "There's a huge credibility crisis for the CDC," Stelter admitted. "If they hear all these mixed messages and all this confusion, it's all too complicated, they just move on and ignore it."[77]

"Avoid the Showers"

"It's best to avoid the showers if possible, since you can't get masks wet—otherwise they lose their efficacy. If you need to shower at the gym, shower as quickly as possible and only remove your mask when your face and head is [are] going to get wet." –NBC News, "CDC Updates: Wear a Mask while Exercising Indoors at Gyms"[78]

In order to justify the continued mask mandates, the CDC released a study claiming that two masks were more effective than one. Even Anthony Fauci promoted two masks in early 2021. Wearing two masks "just makes common sense that it likely would be more effective," Fauci said.[79]

But the CDC "study" was ridiculed as "nothing more than a handful of experiments on mannequins in a contained environment."

Investigative journalist Jordan Schachtel pointed out, "No human beings were involved in this study. And yes, it was that simple. The CDC sprayed aerosols at mannequins and slapped a science™ label on their experiments."

Schachtel reported, "First and foremost, it is not a completed study at all. These are mere experiments conducted on mannequins, not humans. A proper study on the efficacy of masks needs to be a randomized controlled trial involving human beings in their normal settings—such as the Danish mask study that showed there is no evidence that masks do anything to prevent COVID-19—and not mannequins in a laboratory."[80]

But why stop at double masking? CNBC correspondent Contessa Brewer displayed an onscreen graphic claiming that wearing three masks boosts your viral protection up to 90 percent![81] "A three-layer mask could block up to 90 percent of the particles," Brewer claimed.

NBC News featured guests suggesting wearing four masks.

Dr. Scott Segal, chair of anesthesiology at Wake Forest Baptist Health in Winston-Salem, North Carolina, told NBC News, "If you put three or four masks on, it's going to filter better because it's more layers of cloth."[82]

"Doing Something Virtuous"

"Masks gave meaning to people with meaningless lives. People were led to think they were doing something virtuous by wearing a mask all day. Many don't want the scam to end because it makes people reexamine the sunk costs and entertain the possibility that it was all for nothing."
—investigative journalist Jordan Schachtel[83]

Jeffrey Anderson, former director of the Bureau of Justice Statistics at the U.S. Department of Justice explained why obscuring people's faces should not be dismissed as a minor inconvenience. "Masks hide from view the familiar faces, infectious smiles, and warm glances that bring light and color to everyday life. To dismiss this loss so cavalierly is to devalue human warmth and sociability in a remarkably callous way," Anderson wrote. "In his detailed study of emotions, Charles Darwin observed that human beings' reliance on facial expressions is a key difference between us and animals. He wrote an entire book on the subject, *The Expression of the Emotions in Man and Animals* (1872). Communication, according to Darwin, was 'of paramount importance to the development of man.'"

Anderson also explained how politics corrupted the CDC's science. "Anyone who thinks the CDC is an impartial, politically neutral agency, dedicated solely to the pursuit of scientific truth, should perhaps consider the [2021] e-mail evidence that the teachers union and Joe Biden's White House effectively rewrote sections of the agency's return-to-school guidance."[84]

Masks mandates do work—but not to prevent the spread of the virus. Mask mandates work to embed fear of the virus in the public consciousness, a form of social conditioning. Masks advanced the Great Reset agenda. They were the perfect psyop, instilling fear in the public and confirming the message that the virus was a threat that justified the lockdowns, stay-at-home-orders, and curfews. They were daily and hourly confirmation of the alleged death tolls breathlessly reported through the twenty-four-hour news cycle. Anyone who doubted the viral apocalypse being preached by the cacophony of political leaders, unelected health bureaucrats, the media, and scare family and friends, only had to go to their local Walmart to see the frightening and unprecedented masked faces of the public.

People would inevitably think, *It must be as bad as they (the government-media-corporate complex) are claiming. Look at all these people masked up!* Given the psychological effectiveness of masks—given how they served to grease the COVID-19 panic and the pathway to a Great Reset—there was little incentive for government officials to remove the mandates that everyone wear them.

Anthony Fauci, director of the National Institute of Allergy and Infectious Diseases (NIAID) at the National Institutes of Health (NIH), was against mask mandates before he was for them:

> There's no reason to be walking around with a mask. When you're in the middle of an outbreak, wearing a mask might make people feel a little bit better and it might even block a droplet, but it's not providing the perfect protection that people think that it is. And, often, there are unintended consequences—people keep fiddling with the mask and they keep touching their face.

Fauci said this in a March 8, 2020, interview on *60 Minutes*. He would reverse himself just a few weeks later.[85]

On February 29, 2020, U.S. surgeon general Jerome Adams declared, "Seriously people—STOP BUYING MASKS!" Adams added, "They are NOT effective in preventing general public from catching #Coronavirus." Adams explained, "Folks who don't know how to wear them properly tend to touch their faces a lot and actually can increase the spread of coronavirus." Adams, too, reversed himself on masks a few weeks later, on April 3, 2020.[86]

UK *Daily Mail* columnist Peter Hitchens pointed out that the World Health Organization had caved to politics when it switched its mask recommendations in 2020. "The World Health Organisation (WHO) had reversed its advice on face masks, from 'don't wear them' to 'do wear them.' But the key fact was that it had not done so because of scientific information—the evidence had not backed the wearing of face coverings—but because of political lobbying."

Hitchens quoted BBC medical correspondent Deborah Cohen, who had reported, "We had been told by various sources [that the] WHO committee reviewing the evidence had not backed masks but they recommended them due to political lobbying."

Hitchens called the mask "a badge of subservience and submission" and urged, "Look at the muzzled multitudes, their wide eyes peering out anxiously from above the hideous gag which obscures half their faces and turns them from normal human beings into mouthless, obedient submissives."[87]

Maskless = Mass Murderer

Progressive linguist Noam Chomsky compared anti-maskers to mass shooters. "Chomsky claimed that people who oppose wearing masks are an 'epidemic' in American politics, more concerned about protecting their freedoms than following science," reported The College Fix. "I mean, do you have an individual right to take an assault rifle and go to the supermarket or mall and start shooting randomly?" Chomsky questioned. "That's what it means not to wear a mask. It's a strange kind of individualism."[88]

The COVID Censors

Robert F. Kennedy Jr. pointed out how the government manipulates its citizens to enforce conformity. "If they were told, Here's why you should wear a mask, here's the science that says it will help, here is the science that says it works, that you will stop transmission to other people—everybody would wear [masks] with no problem. But what we know is that we're not being dealt with honestly. We're being told this is 'The Science,' but it's not. It's an appeal to authority," Kennedy said.

"It's science because Tony Fauci and Bill Gates tell us it's science. We want to see the studies. We want to see the studies on hydroxychloroquine.

We want to see the studies on whether the lockdown is killing more people than the coronavirus. We want to see real science and real risk assessments," Kennedy explained.[89]

In a *New York Post* article titled "How Facebook Uses 'Fact-Checking' to Suppress Scientific Truth," former *New York Times* reporter John Tierney detailed how consensus-based "fact checks" suppress science.

"The fact-checkers...ignore the peer-reviewed scientific literature in favor of evidence-free statements from a professional association," Tierney wrote.

A nonprofit group called Science Feedback "has partnered with Facebook in what it calls a 'fight against misinformation.' The group describes itself as 'nonpartisan,' a claim that I would label 'Mostly False' after studying dozens of its fact-checks enforcing progressive orthodoxy on climate change and public health," Tierney explained.

"This is the same tactic used by the tobacco industry last century when epidemiologists observed high rates of lung cancer among people who reported a history of heavy smoking. The industry harped on the limitations of the studies—like their reliance on people's self-reported history of smoking—and insisted that there was no proof that smoking caused cancer because no one had done a sufficiently rigorous controlled study," Tierney pointed out.

"Comical in Its Implausibility"

"Few spectacles are more ridiculous than that of school kids, outside, playing sports, wearing masks. Moreover, the WHO guidance on mask-wearing for children is comical in its implausibility," explained Jeffrey H. Anderson.

The WHO guidance dictates, "Before putting on the mask, children should clean their hands . . . at least 40 seconds if using soap and water. . . . Children should not touch the front of the mask [or] pull it under the chin. . . . After taking off their mask, they should store it in a bag or container and clean their hands."

"Sure. Got that, kids?" Anderson wrote.[90]

"A new breed of censors has been stifling scientific debate about masks on social-media platforms. When Scott Atlas, a member of the Trump White House's coronavirus task force, questioned the efficacy of masks last year, Twitter removed his tweet. When eminent scientists from Stanford and Harvard recently told Florida Gov. Ron DeSantis that children should not be forced to wear masks, YouTube removed their video discussion from its platform," Tierney wrote.

Tierney detailed how the social media "fact-checkers" justified this type of censorship in their "Key Take Away" box claiming, "Masks are safe for children over the age of two years to wear, according to the American Academy of Pediatrics."

Tierney countered: "This pediatric association, known for its advocacy of progressive causes like allowing transgender youths to play in girls' sports, had made that assertion on its Web site along with other questionable statements, like its advice to young athletes to wear a face mask during both training and competition."[91]

Double Trouble?

Los Angeles County banned double features at drive-in movie theatres to keep you SAFE! Watching one film is safe, but two endangers your health! "In accordance with L.A. County guidelines, double features are not permitted," county health-department regulations stated in May 2021."Social Distancing of at least 6' will be enforced. The drive-In will operate at 50% capacity. Customers must leave 9' spacing between vehicles. Customers must remain in their vehicle for the duration of the movie. No sitting outside of the vehicle will be allowed. Each vehicle may only be occupied by members of the same household who have already been in close contact with each other."[92]

One Twitter user commented, "Science my a$$. It is a bunch of lackeys trying to take control of OUR everyday life. Wake up people."[93]

Author Tom Woods commented, "Evidently double features—performed while you're completely isolated in the car—are a driver of infection! I give up trying to figure out how even the most superstitious person can believe this stuff."[94]

Michael Fumento investigated how the media distorted COVID-19's impact on different populations and countries. "Since we're (correctly) under the impression that it's overwhelmingly a disease of the elderly who also have pre-existing conditions, notwithstanding claims that it's 'posing a universal risk,' the MSM sees it as a solemn obligation to find outliers and twist numbers," Fumento wrote.

"It ghoulishly crawls through obits to find someone, *anyone* who doesn't fit that category. And beyond. The *New York Times* wrote of a 27-year-old 'COVID-19 death' on its front page. The guy was murdered. Far from his young age being a red flag, it made it too priceless for fact-checking," Fumento wrote. "We also saw lots of attention given to, as a *Washington Post* headline put it, 'Young and middle-aged people, barely sick with covid-19,...dying of strokes.'

"Turns out it was essentially based on a study comprising five (5) people. A later wider analysis concluded... 'Stroke does not appear to be a major manifestation of Covid-19.'"[95]

Freedom Works

The media also targeted Sweden, the most prominent nation not to impose lockdowns or mask mandates. "It searches abroad for 2nd waves as well, when it's not 'Swede-shaming' for that country not locking down in the first place," Fumento noted, referencing another article he had published under the headline "Media Enraged That More Swedes Aren't Dying."[96]

Journalist Jordan Schachtel made a similar point. "When it comes to the COVID-19 pandemic, more and more evidence is emerging that the laissez-faire approach to the issue—at least on a governmental/'public health' level—was the solution all along. The path chosen by Sweden, Belarus and a select few nations—which put the power in the hands of individuals to make their own health choices, instead of imposing draconian government edicts—appears to have won the day," Schachtel wrote.

"The 'experts' overwhelmingly endorsed these Chinese Communist Party-endorsed 'health' measures, declaring them scientific overnight, despite many of these tools never [having been] utilized in the event of a global pandemic," Schachtel explained.

"If Sweden and Belarus were able to outperform other nations by simply doing nothing, what exactly have all of these 'public health expert' interventions accomplished?"[97]

Death by Ventilator

"WHO cited the guidance by Chinese journal articles, which published papers in January and February claiming that 'Chinese expert consensus' called for 'invasive mechanical ventilation' as the 'first choice' for people with respiratory distress," wrote Attorney Michael P. Senger, author of "China's Global Lockdown Propaganda Campaign."[98]

"Doctors around the world began putting patients on ventilators en masse, killing thousands before a grassroots campaign stopped the practice," Senger added.[99]

Senger also tweeted portions of a *Wall Street Journal* report: "Last spring, doctors put patients on ventilators partly to limit contagion. . . . 'We were intubating sick patients very early. Not for the patients' benefit, but in order to control the epidemic. . . . That felt awful.'"[100]

Dodgy Death Counts and Accusations of "Social Murder"

In an editorial published in the *British Medical Journal* in 2021, Dr. Anne McCloskey explained how the science was altered to create COVID hysteria. "A new directive from the WHO to every doctor changed fundamentally how deaths were attributed. Any death, within 28 days of a positive PCR test (which Kary Mullis, the test's inventor, and Nobel Laureate was clear should not be used as a diagnostic tool) was to be included in the covid fatality total, regardless of the context," McCloskey, a practicing physician who also works with the Ireland-based Freedom Alliance, wrote.

"Where there was no positive test, but clinical symptoms compatible with covid 19 that is fever, shortness of breath, loss of taste and so on, likewise, attribution to the virus on the death certificate was encouraged. Autopsies ceased," McCloskey added.

McCloskey rejected the official COVID-19 death toll in Britain because of this statistical manipulation: "This 100,000 has been played in a loop in every mainstream media outlet for weeks, and it is burned into our psyche," she wrote. The official UK death toll is "a piece of propaganda, an alarmist distortion of the facts. It is not science."[101]

"State of Emergency"

"New York Declares a Health-Care State of Emergency over a Covid Variant That Doesn't Exist in the State," read the 2021 headline at Alex Berenson's Unreported Truths. "Guess what's actually causing the crisis? Hint: it rhymes with 'vaccine schmandate,'" Berenson explained.

"[New York governor Kathy] Hochul says the Xi—I mean Omicron, definitely not Xi!—variant is behind the emergency," quipped Berenson, referring to Chinese president Xi Jinping.[102]

How badly was "The Science" corrupted during the COVID-19 hysteria? A 2021 *British Medical Journal* editorial on COVID suggested "social murder" charges against be brought against anti-lockdown politicians who "wilfully neglect scientific advice...and modelling."

The *BMJ* editorial, by the journal's executive editor, Kamran Abbasi, proposed that "sovereign governments should arguably be held accountable to the international community for their actions and omissions on covid-19."

"The 'social murder' of populations is more than a relic of a bygone age. It is very real today, exposed and magnified by covid-19. It cannot be ignored or spun away. Politicians must be held to account by legal and electoral means, indeed by any national and international constitutional means necessary. State failures that led us to two million deaths are 'actions' and 'inactions' that should shame us all," Abbasi argued.

"When politicians wilfully neglect scientific advice, international and historical experience, and their own alarming statistics and modelling because to act goes against their political strategy or ideology, is that lawful?" the *BMJ* editor asked.[103]

Even the Trump administration allowed the health bureaucracy and their failed COVID doomsday models to dictate the national policy narrative, which paved the way for the lockdowns. Trump economic advisor Larry Kudlow said in April 2020 that it was "up to the health people" when the economy would reopen.

"How much longer? I don't really want to forecast," Kudlow said on Fox News.[104]

Unheeded Warnings

In May of 2020, I lamented to Bloomberg News that the Trump administration had fallen victim to the public health bureaucrats. "[Trump] allowed the greatest economy to essentially be nuked in a matter of weeks because of the Anthony Fauci–CDC scare scenario," he said, pointing out how the Trump administration's allowing politicians to gorge on COVID state-of-emergency powers was the "greatest blunder of his presidency."[105] Looking back, it may have been one of the greatest blunders of any president in the past five decades.

In March 28, 2020, Geoffrey P. Hunt wrote an American Thinker article titled "We've Been Had, and Trump Knows It," explaining how this blunder came about. "Health professionals overwhelmed Trump and his inner circle with doomsday scenarios, bullied by panic-obsessed virologists and epidemiologists—begging for attention and copying the alarmist playbook from the climate/global warming extremists, allied with the MSM Trump-haters."[106]

Columnist Ann Coulter had perhaps the most prescient view of the lockdowns when they first occurred. Coulter wrote a March 25, 2020, column opposing the two weeks to "flatten the curve" on the grounds that it would be very difficult to reopen society. "What mayor, governor or president will be willing to take the blame for causing a coronavirus death?" Coulter asked.

"We need to listen to people other than epidemiologists," Coulter warned. "Playwright Arthur Miller once told a story," Coulter said, "about a geologist who remarked that life was possible even in the vast American desert":

> All you needed was water, he said, and the largest reservoir on the globe was located right under the Rockies.
> But how would he get it?
> Simple—drop a couple of atomic bombs.
> But what about the fallout?
> "Oh," said the geologist, "that's not my field."
> Today, the epidemiologists are prepared to nuke the entire American economy to kill a virus.
> What about the jobs, the suicides, the heart attacks, the lost careers, the destruction of America's wealth?
> *Oh, that's not my field.*[107]

Silly Models

"All models only say what they are told to say, because all models are lists of premises put there by scientists," explained statistician William H. Briggs of scientific models used to predict climate change.

"It's silly because (a) no probability proves a model is true, and (b) model statements get probabilities from the premises scientists choose. They can pick what they like, and make the model's statements appear as sure or as unsure as they like because of these choices," Briggs wrote. "Attribution studies are fundamentally flawed," he added.[108]

Joe Biden said he would listen to the scientists and go along with a second national lockdown to fight COVID. "Asked specifically whether he'd push to shutter economic activity if scientists said it was necessary, Biden replied: 'I would shut it down,'" ABC News reported.[109]

As a Grist subhead on January 29, 2020, said, "'Listen to the Science' Isn't Just a Bumper Sticker Anymore—It's Biden's Official White House

"They're Not People Who Need to Eat"

"Those people at those anti-mask protests—let's not kid ourselves—they're not people who need to eat. They are people who are marching in thinly veiled white-nationalist supremacist, anti-government protests, and they don't deserve that kind of sympathy."
—Naheed Nenshi, mayor of Calgary, Canada[111]

Policy." Associate editor Kate Yoder pointed out that Biden had signed an executive order declaring, "It is, therefore, the policy of my Administration to listen to the science."[110]

The "listen to 'The Science'" narrative has been very effective. It has bullied Republican politicians, conservatives, and many dissenting scientists into silence or submissiveness. You are not going to challenge COVID restrictions if you accept that "The Science" determines whether or not you are a good person, a smart person—or an evil science-denier who deserves to be jailed.

Scientists or Ayatollahs?

"When the coronavirus first arrived in our country last winter, most Americans uncritically accepted what the authorities said about it, they thought they could trust the people in charge. Few imagined that our leaders would leverage a public health emergency for their own political gain. That seemed like the one line that even politicians wouldn't cross. Yet almost immediately, they did cross it.

"Around the country, Democratic governors used quarantine restrictions to reward their allies and punish their opponents. Abortion mills stayed open, but the police kept churches closed. You could buy weed but you couldn't get your knee replaced. Demonstrations against the lockdowns were banned. Riots against Donald Trump were encouraged.... It was partisan politics posing as science, but this was the most amazing part, it was endorsed by actual scientists and that's the part that should worry you.... For those who still believed that American science was on the level, this was a shocking moment. When did the people who are paid to be rational, become corrupt religious zealots? When did their scientists become ayatollahs?" —Tucker Carlson[112]

Dr. Denis Rancourt, a physicist and former professor and environmental-science researcher at the University of Ottawa, ripped the "follow 'The Science'" narrative. "Do not trust science. Practice valid scientific methods. Period. Actual science never asks to be trusted. Science asks you to think independently, and always be willing to re-examine, that's all," Rancourt wrote.[113]

"We're Going to Kill Ourselves because of Stupidity"

Allan Savory trashed consensus science, calling it "stupidity" in the 2020 documentary *Return to Eden*. As Savory, a Zimbabwean ecologist and research biologist, explained, "People talk glibly about science—what is science? People coming out of a university with a master's degree or a Ph.D.; you take them into the field and they literally don't believe anything unless it's a peer-reviewed paper.

"It's the only thing they accept, and you say to them, 'But let's observe. Let's think. Let's discuss.' They don't do it. It's just, 'Is it in a peer-reviewed paper or not?' That's their view of science. I think it's pathetic."

Savory was just getting warmed up: "Gone into universities as bright young people, they come out of them brain dead, not even knowing what science means. They think it means peer-reviewed papers, et cetera. No, that's academia. And if a paper is peer-reviewed it means everybody thought the same therefore they approved it.

"An unintended consequence is that when new knowledge emerges, new scientific insights, they can never ever be peer-reviewed. So we're blocking all new advances in science that are big advances. If you look at the breakthroughs in science, almost always they don't come from the center of that profession—they come from the fringe, people who see it differently. The finest candlemakers in the world couldn't even think of electric lights. They don't come from within, they often come from outside the bricks. We're going to kill ourselves because of stupidity."[114]

Rancourt echoed Savory's sentiments, agreeing that today's academia produces "obedient intellectuals." He explained that professors today are "virtually all service intellectuals. They will not truly critique, in a way that could threaten the power interests that keep them in their jobs. The tenure track is just a process to make docile and obedient intellectuals that will then train other intellectuals."

"You have this army of university scientists and they have to pretend like they are doing important research without ever criticizing the powerful interests in a real way. So what do they look for, they look for elusive sanitized things like acid rain, global warming," Rancourt said.

This system "helps to neutralize any kind of dissent," Rancourt pointed out. "When you do find something bad, you quickly learn and are told you better toe the line on this—your career depends on it."[115]

Renowned Stanford epidemiologist John Ioannidis explained how the powerful, politically determined COVID-19 narrative corrupted science. "The retraction of a highly visible hydroxychloroquine paper from *The Lancet* was a startling example: A lack of sharing and openness allowed a top medical journal to publish an article in which 671 hospitals allegedly contributed data that did not exist, and no one noticed this outright fabrication before publication. *The New England Journal of Medicine*, another top medical journal, managed to publish a similar paper; many scientists continue to heavily cite it long after its retraction," Ioannidis wrote.

Ioannidis, a professor of biomedical science and statistics at Stanford University, explained how his field of specialty became compromised during COVID-19:

The pandemic led seemingly overnight to a scary new form of scientific universalism. Everyone did COVID-19 science or commented on it. By August 2021, 330,000 scientific papers were published on COVID-19, involving roughly a million different authors. An analysis showed that scientists from every single one of the 174 disciplines that comprise what we know as science has published on COVID-19. By the end of

2020, only automobile engineering didn't have scientists publishing on COVID-19. By early 2021, the automobile engineers had their say, too.

At first sight, this was an unprecedented mobilization of interdisciplinary talent. However, most of this work was of low quality, often wrong, and sometimes highly misleading. Many people without subject-matter technical expertise became experts overnight, emphatically saving the world....

Anyone who was not an epidemiologist or health policy specialist could suddenly be cited as an epidemiologist or health policy specialist by reporters who often knew little about those fields but knew immediately which opinions were true. Conversely, some of the best epidemiologists and health policy specialists in America were smeared as clueless and dangerous by people who believed themselves fit to summarily arbitrate differences of scientific opinion without understanding the methodology or data at issue.[116]

When you believe you are saving the world, the only science that matters is "The Science" that supports your preconceived political views.

CHAPTER 7

Censorship and Tech Tyranny

Imposing a Great Reset on the global population requires taking control of all means of communication. The World Economic Forum's Great Reset envisioned by Klaus Schwab requires power over the flow of information.

Let's take a look at how Schwab's vision is playing out in the real world, post–COVID-19. Very well, it turns out. In the years following 2020, we saw major interference in our ability to communicate on a range of topics and a rapid descent toward total control of speech, as cancel culture and suppression of "misinformation" took over social media, government, private business, and the corporate world.

In order to achieve the Great Reset, it is necessary to silence dissent and control information that does not comport with the dear leaders' sweeping vision. The ability to censor and cancel any opposing thought or person or organization at a whim is central to the Great Reset.

German economics professor Antony P. Mueller explained why restrictions on speech are so critical for the advance of tyranny. "Earlier totalitarian regimes needed mass executions and concentration camps to maintain their power. Now, with the help of new technologies, it is believed, dissenters can easily be identified and marginalized. The non-conformists will be silenced by disqualifying divergent opinions as morally despicable."[1]

Event 201

A chilling example of how forward-thinking and prepared the vision-aries of the Great Reset were for the censorship regime that is being imposed now was an exercise that took place in October 2019. As we have seen, a pandemic simulation exercise titled "Event 201" was con-ducted as part of a joint effort sponsored by the World Economic Forum, the Bill & Melinda Gates Foundation, and the Johns Hopkins Center for Health Security in October 2019, just as COVID-19 was beginning to spread in Wuhan.[2]

Event 201 portrayed a hypothetical coronavirus pandemic that would kill sixty-five million people, necessitating a global response coor-dinated between governments, international organizations, and global business concerns. Event 201 hearkened back to the Rockefeller Foundation's 2010 future-scenario event that we discussed in chapter 2. The visions on display at both events were eerily similar.

And when it came to combating the imaginary projected pandemic in Event 201, guess what one of the key takeaways was? A massive, coordinated censorship campaign by governments, Big Tech, and health organizations, all colluding to silence dissenting voices and inconvenient facts—justified by the excuse of "misinformation." In other words, they were planning and practicing the very technique that Twitter, Facebook, and YouTube actually used following COVID's debut in 2020 to keep divergent voices from challenging the ever-changing narrative. What follows are excerpts from the October 2019 "Event 201 Pandemic Exercise: Segment 4, Communications Discussion and Epilogue Video."[3]

A woman playing a newscaster named Chen Huang breathlessly reports, "Alarming news emerging from social media companies today about the CAPS pandemic. Twitter and Facebook are reporting they've identified and deleted a disturbing number of accounts dedicated to spreading this information about the outbreak."

A fictional reporter named Catalina Parks claims, "Countries are reacting in different ways as to how best to manage the overwhelming amounts of dis- and misinformation circulating over the Internet. In some cases, limited Internet shutdowns are being implemented to quell panic."[4]

"Controlling and Reducing Access to Information"

A mock news report and panel discussion about how to stop "misinformation" is presented in the Event 201 video.

"It is clear countries need to make strong efforts to manage both mis- and disinformation.... The task of identifying every bad actor is immense. Experts agree that new disinformation campaigns are being generated every day. This is a huge problem that's going to keep us from ending the pandemic and might even lead to the fall of governments, as we saw in the Arab Spring. If the solution means controlling and reducing access to information, I think it's the right choice," a panelist called Kevin McAleese says in the Event 201 video.

The video of the hypothetical Event 201 pandemic goes on to report, "Some governments have taken control of national access to the Internet. Others are censoring websites and social media content and a small number have shut down internet access completely to prevent the spread of misinformation. Penalties have been put in place for spreading harmful falsehoods, including arrests."

An Event 201 panelist named Matthew Harrington explains: "We're at a moment where the social media platforms have to step forward and recognize their moment to assert that they're a technology platform and not a broadcaster is over. They in fact have to be a participant in broadcasting accurate information and partnering with the scientific and health communities to counterweight, if not flood the zone, of accurate information."[5]

Event 201 makes crystal clear how the architects of the Great Reset were prepared to pounce when COVID-19 appeared on the scene.

And what actually happened in 2020 and 2021, when a real pandemic appeared? Supposed "misinformation" about the coronavirus and the COVID-19 vaccines was censored on social media—and people who spread it were canceled. Twitter, for example, repeatedly warned former *New York Times* reporter Alex Berenson (who had over three hundred thousand followers) against spreading "misinformation" when he posted inconvenient facts about the pandemic. When he persisted in publicizing scientific studies and data about problems with the vaccines, he was permanently suspended.[6]

"A Nation That Is Afraid to Let Its People Judge the Truth"
"We welcome the view of others. We seek a free flow of information across national boundaries and oceans, across iron curtains and stone walls. We are not afraid to entrust the American people with unpleasant facts, foreign ideas, alien philosophies, and competitive values. For a nation that is afraid to let its people judge the truth and falsehood in an open market is a nation that is afraid of its people." —President John F. Kennedy in an address on the 20th Anniversary of the Voice of America on February 26, 1962[7]

"The Rockefeller Foundation, the Bill and Melinda Gates Foundation, and Schwab's World Economic Forum all started planning tabletop pandemic scenarios several years prior to the covid fiasco. Now all of them are involved in the development and implementation of digital vaccine passports, providing the basis for the digital ID and social credit regime that will be at the core of technocratic totalitarianism of the 4th Industrial Revolution, with China leading the way," author Raelle Kaia pointed out in an analysis titled "Why Are They Doing This?"

"We are also increasingly living under a regime of censorship, black-listing, surveillance, and authoritarian measures directed at dissidents and nonconformists," Kaia wrote.

According to Kaia this "fits with the pre-existing aims and activities of these entities, and it also fits with the evidence of a coordinated global media and technocratic covid response, in imitation of China. In addition, this hypothesis helps explain the deeper purpose served by the lockdowns. They provide an excuse for Western democracies to disrupt their societies sufficiently enough to install Chinese-style authoritarian control measures. Social distancing and prohibitions on public gatherings stifle dissent and force much of life into the digital realm. Mask mandates dehumanize the individual and instill fear and disdain for organic human biological processes. This conditions the populace to accept future transhuman biological modifications. Censorship and cancelling regimes encourage silent compliance and obedience to technocratic authority."[8]

"Mass Formation Psychosis"

"How does this happen?" asked virologist Dr. Robert Malone on *The Joe Rogan Experience*. Malone, whose research was instrumental in the invention of the mRNA technology that the Pfizer and Moderna COVID vaccines are based on, was referring to the fact that "a third of the population [is] basically being hypnotized." Malone argued that the public fear of the coronavirus can be explained by looking at Germany in the 1930s. Germany had "a very intelligent, highly educated population, and they went barking mad. And how did that happen? The answer is mass formation psychosis," he explained.

"When you have a society that has become decoupled from each other and has free-floating anxiety—in a sense that things don't make sense, we can't understand it—and then their attention gets focused by a leader or series of events on one small point, just like hypnosis, they literally become hypnotized and can be led anywhere.... The data are

"The Suppression of a People"

"The suppression of a people, of a society, begins—in my mind—with the censorship of the written or spoken word. It was so in Nazi Germany, it is so in many places today where those in power are afraid of the consequences of an informed and educated people. In a mature and incredibly diverse society such as ours, the access to all perspectives of an issue becomes more and more important.... That process cannot and should not be stifled."—songwriter John Denver, testifying about warning labels on music to the U.S. Senate Committee on Commerce, Science and Transportation on September 19, 1985[9] irrelevant. And, furthermore, anybody who questions that narrative is to be immediately attacked; they are the other. This is central to mass-formation psychosis, and this is what has happened."[10]

Biotech entrepreneur Vivek Ramaswamy, author of the book *Woke, Inc.: Inside Corporate America's Social Justice Scam*, warned that the merger of corporate and government power is the greatest threat to freedom. "It is not big government alone," he said, "It is this new hybrid of big government and big business."

"We have spent the last 40 years defending the castle of capitalism from the front door without recognizing that that castle was invaded through the back door from woke activists to the Chinese Communist Party," he explained.[11]

A concept known as "managerialism," which "fuses industry and government" is being implemented, noted Pedro Gonzalez, associate editor at *Chronicles* magazine explained. "Just a handful of billionaires own America's newspapers, for example, while six corporations control virtually all media outlets."[12]

The real-world response to COVID-19 has followed the path laid out in the Event 201 scenarios disturbingly closely. Post-COVID, social media became enforcers for the WHO, the CDC, and other public health bureaucracies to suppress any opinions and even any news not in-line with the approved narrative.

"New Dark Age Cometh"

In the world of the Great Reset, climate change, and COVID-19, no dissent can be allowed. Everyone must support lockdowns, stay-at-home orders, the Green New Deal, UN climate pacts, COVID curfews, mask mandates, church closures, and mandatory vaccines. There must be no questioning the claims about "The Science." If you dare question, you will be promptly silenced, defunded, marginalized, and de-platformed.

Nobel Prize–winning Stanford University chemist Michael Levitt was canceled for his COVID wrongthink.

Professor Levitt, who won the Nobel Prize in Chemistry in 2013, was set to be a keynote speaker at the First International Biodesign Research Conference in December of 2020. But Levitt's invitation was withdrawn after he spoke publicly in opposition to COVID hysteria and lockdown policies.

"My keynote uninvited," Levitt explained. He was told that the "other speakers...all complained about your COVID claims" and were "threatening to quit" unless he was canceled.

"New Dark Age Cometh," Levitt wrote. "I had no intention to talk about COVID19; it is not the theme of the meeting. All my work until 26 Jan. 2020 has been non-COVID computational biology."[13]

Crushing Dissent

"Climate change skeptics have seen this type of crushing of dissent for decades when it comes to 'climate change.' Whether you support COVID lockdowns equates to whether you support the UN Paris Pact or Green New Deal in the climate world. If you oppose mandatory masks, that is like not believing in the alleged '97% consensus' on climate. Can the government 'control' a virus equates to can government 'control' the climate. The COVID/Climate connection runs deep." —Marc Morano, commenting on Stanford University's Michael Levitt's facing cancel culture over COVID-19[14]

Levitt was an early critic of viral panic and lockdowns. "I am a real baby boomer—I was born in 1947, I am almost 73 years old—but I think we've really screwed up.... We've left your generation with a real mess in order to save a relatively small number of very old people," Levitt had said of COVID-19's mass global-lockdown policies.[15]

Dr. Scott Atlas, a member of the Trump White House COVID team, ran afoul of Big Tech censorship as well. Atlas was suspended on Twitter for questioning the effectiveness of masks.

"Atlas, a senior fellow at Stanford's Hoover Institute, not only had his tweets removed, he was banned from tweeting until he deleted the tweets that Twitter for unclear reasons objects to," David Marcus reported at The Federalist.

Atlas explained to Marcus: "In the deleted tweet, I cited the following evidence against general population masks. In Atlas's words:[16]

1. Cases exploded even with mandates: Los Angeles County, Miami-Dade County, Hawaii, Alabama, the Philippines, Japan, the United Kingdom, Spain, France, Israel.
2. Dr. Carl Heneghan, University of Oxford, director of the Centre for Evidence-Based Medicine and editor in chief of *British Medical Journal Evidence-Based Medicine*: "It would appear that despite two decades of pandemic preparedness, there is considerable uncertainty as to the value of wearing masks."[17]
3. The WHO: "The widespread use of masks by healthy people in the community setting is not yet supported by high quality or direct scientific evidence and there are potential benefits and harms to consider."[18]
4. The CDC: "Our systematic review found no significant effect of face masks on transmission of laboratory-confirmed influenza."[19]

Marcus commented, "Notwithstanding this evidence regarding arguably the most important and contentious debate raging in American society—the constant mandate of masks—it appears some 20-something with his pronouns in his Twitter bio just pushed a button and erased scientifically accurate information. For some reason, which hopefully Twitter CEO Jack Dorsey can explain when he is dragged before the Senate, Atlas was silenced by the tech giant."[20]

Former *New York Times* reporter Alex Berenson asked the pertinent question: "Does it seem like the entire elite media speaks with one voice on the [co]ro[navirus]?" And he pointed to the answer: "There's a reason. They've explicitly committed to working together—and with Big Tech, in the 'Trusted News Initiative,' which isn't exactly a secret but isn't exactly well-publicized."[21]

The "Trusted News Initiative" is the Orwellian name for what you might think was a conspiracy theory if the BBC hadn't reported on it.[22]

Government Is "Your Single Source of Truth"

Prime minister of New Zealand Jacinda Ardern's efforts to protect the citizens from COVID-19 "rumors" and misinformation led to her declaring there was only one "single source of truth"—her government! "You can trust us as a source of that information. You can also trust the Director General of Health and the Ministry of Health. For that information, do feel free to visit at any time—to clarify any rumor you may hear—the covid19.govt.nz," Ardern said in 2020. "Otherwise dismiss anything else. We will continue to be your single source of truth."[23]

> ### "Dis Information"
> "Dey won't be giving you dis information, only dat information. Dey know what's best for you! The most dangerous part of this is that it makes news organizations explicit partners with FaceGoogle. Repeat after me: these companies need more independent scrutiny, not less." —Alex Berenson to his hundreds of thousands of followers on Twitter, which eventually banned him for reporting inconvenient facts about COVID-19[24]

The big social media platforms, including YouTube, Facebook, Instagram, and Twitter, implemented COVID-19 "misinformation" policies that became increasingly restrictive as the lockdowns persisted. YouTube, for example, removed any video that violated their policy of medical "misinformation."[25]

That meant any information that was not in-line with the consensus views of the major public health organizations. "YouTube says it doesn't allow content that poses a serious risk of egregious harm, such as videos that contradict the consensus of local and global health authorities regarding the efficacy of masks," according to a report from the Kaiser Family Foundation.

"According to data shared by YouTube in March [2021], the company has removed more than 800,000 videos containing coronavirus misinformation since February of last year. Facebook reported in February that the company and its sister platform, Instagram, had removed more than 1 million pieces of covid misinformation in the last three months of 2020. And last month, Twitter said it had removed more than 8,400 tweets and challenged 11.5 million accounts since the implementation of the covid guidance," Kaiser reported.[26]

Biotech entrepreneur Vivek Ramaswamy detailed the power of Big Tech: "Facebook and Twitter...actually get to determine what ideas we do and don't discuss, and that actually makes them the most powerful companies in the course of history. Not because they're able to make a bunch of profit. I'm okay with that. But because they're able to exercise power over what we can and can't discuss, and to me that was the biggest threat to democracy of all."[27]

Factcheck.org is funded by the Annenberg Foundation, which receives grants from the Bill & Melinda Gates Foundation.[28] The people

---

"Stay Muzzled, Locked Down Forever"

"There is nothing—absolutely nothing—within the Great Barrington Declaration which could possibly breach either Google's or Reddit's terms and conditions and justify closing it down. . . .

"Big Tech has become so shamelessly left-wing that it is now barely capable of embarrassment about its relentless bias. Big Tech supports full lockdowns, enforced mask-wearing, quarantines, curfews and all the other authoritarian baggage because it aligns with its own interests in global rule by a technocratic elite, in ever bigger government, in the globalist new world order promoted by institutions like the World Economic Forum (Davos) and the Chinese-controlled World Health Organisation.

"Increasingly it is flexing its muscles to suppress any dissent." –James Delingpole at Breitbart in an article headlined "Big Tech Wants You to Stay Muzzled, Locked Down Forever"[29]

pushing the Great Reset literally control the fact-checkers who police the public discussion on COVID-19—its origins, treatments, lockdowns, and mask mandates.

In 2021, thousands of Anthony Fauci's emails were released as a result of Freedom of Information Act requests. The emails revealed that, despite past denials, the United States may have funded gain-of-function research for infectious viruses at the Wuhan lab in China and COVID-19 may have been released from the lab—not a bat.

"When Trump began to speak about a possible lab leak in Wuhan last year and calling for an investigation to identify its origin, Fauci roundly dismissed these notions, to the media's delight," wrote William Sullivan in American Thinker in an article titled "The Fall of St. Fauci."

Fauci doubled down, claiming that the evidence "very, very strongly [indicated] this could not have been artificially or deliberately manipulated."[30]

The Wall Came Tumbling Down

The collapse of the zoonotic (animal-to-human) origin theory of COVID-19 in 2021 illustrates just how Big Tech served to block not only the truth but any attempt to ask even basic questions.

Scott McKay described in the *American Spectator* what happened after Fauci's emails caused "the collapse of the narrative on the Wuhan virus lab-leak theory."

"Now that the Narrative Wall has come down in a manner metaphorically quite similar to what happened to the civil infrastructure in Jericho, we can see just how devoid of merit is the American mainstream media," McKay wrote. "For an entire year these people, aided by the totalitarians who run the Big Tech social media sites (and one way to let the market punish those guys is to click here and join us at The Speakeasy), have done everything they could to squelch any notion that COVID-19 is the product of irresponsible, if not downright evil, virology research gone wrong in Wuhan, China."

Before the release of Fauci's emails, "the lab-leak theory was nuttery. It was a conspiracy theory. It was a racist lie" according to our establishment-media overlords, explained McKay.[31]

"Typical of Organized Crime"

Ron Wright, a retired police detective, detailed how the Big Tech acted like "organized crime."

"These people were derided and marginalized for having heretical thoughts. Big Tech aided by deplatforming, silencing, and suppressing these questioning reports of this narrative as conspiracy theories, false, partially false, lacking context, and other trite phrases as not conforming with the Orwellian World of Newspeak," Wright explained at American Thinker.

"What broke the ice was distinguished science reporter Nicholas Wade's, 'Origin of COVID—Following the Clues,' which first was published in the *Bulletin of Atomic Scientists*," Wright wrote. "Wade's article is the metaphorical straw that broke the camel's back. He exposed the lies that were told to the American people by our elected representatives, the administrative deep state, the media, big pharma, and big tech that united together to tell the *big lie* for many self-interested reasons and in many cases were criminal. This behavior is typical of organized crime or a *criminal enterprise* as defined in the federal RICO Act. Organized crime can't exist without corrupt law enforcement," he added.

Since the publication of Wade's investigation, "a tsunami drowned the lies of our media and those who aided and abetted in propagating these lies. No longer can this cabal maintain control of the narrative. Dr. Fauci's almost deity-like shroud was torn asunder," Wright noted.[32]

"This Is Not Fact Checking. This Is Consensus Checking"

PolitiFact explained in 2021 that its "fact-checks" don't actually deal in "facts" but instead in expert "assertions," which may or may not be factual. "When this fact-check [ruling against the lab-leak theory of

COVID-19's origins] was first published in September 2020, Politifact's sources included researchers who asserted the Sars-CoV-2 virus could not have been manipulated. That assertion is now more widely disputed. For that reason, we are removing this fact-check from our database," PolitiFact explained in a May 17, 2021, "Editor's note."

Eric Weinstein, the managing director of Thiel Capital, ripped the flip-flopping "fact-checkers." "Our fact-checkers have one job. Only one reason for being. They are supposed to focus on facts only & check them," Weinstein wrote. "This is not fact-checking Politifact. This is consensus checking. That has nothing to do with facts. You aren't a fact-checker. You opened us all to groupthink."[33]

Did We Say Fact-Check? We Meant to Say Opinion-Check

In 2021, in response to a defamation lawsuit filed by newsman John Stossel, Facebook was forced to reveal in federal court that their fact-checks were in reality opinions. As Facebook admitted in the U.S. District Court for the Northern District of California, "The labels themselves are neither false nor defamatory; to the contrary, they constitute protected opinion."[34]

"I sued them because they defamed me. They, along with one of their 'fact-checkers,' a group called Science Feedback, lied about me and continue to lie about me," Stossel, the founder of Stossel TV, explained. He had been "fact-checked" over a climate change segment he produced. "Now Facebook has responded to my lawsuit in court. Amazingly, their lawyers now claim that Facebook's 'fact-checks' are merely 'opinion' and therefore immune from defamation," Stossel wrote. "I want Facebook to learn that censorship—especially sloppy, malicious censorship, censorship without any meaningful appeal process is NOT the way to go. The world needs more freedom to discuss things, not less."[35]

But perhaps the most jaw-dropping revelation about the "fact-checkers" was a different instance, in which Facebook had cited a scientist linked to the Wuhan lab to debunk the lab-leak theory.

Despite a close relationship with the Wuhan lab, EcoHealth Alliance president Peter Daszak "appeared in multiple media fact-checks and reports over the past year dispelling the notion that the coronavirus accidentally emerged from the lab." "Daszak's organization sent $3.4 million in National Institutes of Health grants to the Wuhan lab between 2014 and 2019," Fox News reported.[36]

Melissa Chen of *The Spectator* raised the obvious question: "Someone at Facebook needs to explain why Peter Daszak, head of EcoHealth & the person with THE MOST glaring conflict of interest, was considered a source for fact-checking content on covid19 origins. It's like asking Ayatollah Khamenei to fact-check content about Iran's nukes."[37]

Don't Listen to *That* Science

"When the media says 'listen to the science,' what they really mean is 'listen to the science that we didn't censor from social media.'" –Dr. Simone Gold, founder of America's Frontline Doctors[38]

Oppose Lockdowns and Mask Mandates? You're Mentally Ill!

According to a study by Dr. Bruce L. Miller published in the *Journal of the American Medical Association* (JAMA) on November 2, 2020, "The US public health response to coronavirus disease 2019 (COVID-19) has been dismal, characterized by antimask behavior, antivaccine beliefs, conspiracy theories about the origins of COVID-19, and vocal support by elected officials for unproven therapies.... The content of false beliefs in dementia with Lewy bodies and frontotemporal dementia differ but may offer insights into the shared neural mechanisms by which humans misperceive information."[39]

Former *New York Times* reporter Alex Berenson commented: "Here's a PHYSICIAN comparing people who disagree with his views on masks or vaccines to patients with Capgras syndrome (a severe psychosis where you believe the people around you are actually imposters)."

Physicist Denis Rancourt also ripped the claim: "This is the most unethical publication I have seen in a scientific journal in my lifetime. Psychosis advanced to 'explain' mask and COVID skeptics! I conclude: Medicine is a sick profession, in need of treatment."[40]

COVID-19 censorship expanded relentlessly. Epidemiologist Knut Wittkowski slammed the coronavirus lockdowns and ripped the "scientific studies" funded to support government policy in 2020. For his honesty, Wittkowski was promptly banned from YouTube, as lockdown dissenters were from all social media platforms.[41]

Big Tech censored the Great Barrington Declaration, a petition calling for an end to government tyranny related to COVID-19, which was signed by more than half a million people including prominent scientists, medical doctors, and public health experts.

The Declaration was authored by three respected public health experts—Harvard professor Martin Kulldorff, Oxford professor Sunetra Gupta, and Stanford professor Dr. Jay Bhattacharya.

"Lockdown is a blunt, indiscriminate policy that forces the poorest and most vulnerable people to bear the brunt of the fight against coronavirus. As an infectious diseases epidemiologist, I believe there has to be a better way," explained Gupta.

"At the heart of our proposal is the recognition that mass lockdowns cause enormous damage. We are already seeing how current lockdown policies are producing devastating effects on short and long-term public health," Gupta added.[42]

The Declaration was censored by Reddit, shadow-banned by Google, and attacked by the mainstream media.[43]

Gupta explained: "When I signed the Great Barrington Declaration on October 4, [2020,] I did so with fellow scientists to express our view that national lockdowns won't cure us of Covid. Clearly, none of us anticipated such a vitriolic response. The abuse that has followed has been nothing short of shameful."

"I was utterly unprepared for the onslaught of insults, personal criticism, intimidation and threats that met our proposal. The level of vitriol and hostility, not just from members of the public online but from journalists and academics, has horrified me," she admitted.

As Gupta pointed out, "Proponents of lockdown policies have seemed intent on shutting down debate rather than promoting reasoned discussion." She added, "This refusal to cherish the value of the scientific method strikes at the heart of everything I, as a scientist, hold dear. To me, the reasoned exchange of ideas is the basis of civilized society."[44]

According to emails that the American Institute for Economic Research obtained in 2021 through the Freedom of Information Act, the two most prominent public health figures in the United States, Dr. Anthony Fauci and Francis Collins (at that time the director of the National Institutes of Health) colluded with the media to help discredit and smear the thousands of signatories to the Great Barrington Declaration.

"In private, the two sainted public-health officials schemed to quash dissenting views from top scientists," the *Wall Street Journal* reported. Dr. Collins wrote to Fauci in an October 8, 2020, email, "This proposal from the three fringe epidemiologists...seems to be getting a lot of attention—and even a co-signature from Nobel Prize winner Mike Levitt at Stanford. There needs to be a quick and devastating published take down of its premises. Is it underway?" Fauci replied that an effort was indeed underway.

"The emails suggest a feedback loop: The media cited Dr. Fauci as an unquestionable authority, and Dr. Fauci got his talking points from the media. Facebook censored mentions of the Great Barrington Declaration. This is how groupthink works," the *Wall Street Journal*'s editorial board concluded.[45]

Stanford University epidemiologist Dr. John Ioannidis ripped the media censorship:

> Big Tech companies, which gained trillions of dollars in cumulative market value from the virtual transformation of human life during lockdown, developed powerful censorship

machineries that skewed the information available to users on their platforms. Consultants who made millions of dollars from corporate and government consultation were given prestigious positions, power, and public praise, while unconflicted scientists who worked pro bono but dared to question dominant narratives were smeared as being conflicted.[46]

"Bullying People into Silence"

"A lot of public figures have been intimidated into not saying what they really think of lockdowns, mandatory masks, continued restrictions because they know of the attacks they'll face if they do. Bullying people into silence/acquiescence/compliance has been a big part of the op."
—UK journalist and broadcaster Neil Clark[47]

Who's Afraid of the Big Bad Wolf?

The censors came for feminist Naomi Wolf, former campaign adviser to Al Gore, in June 2021 when she was banned from Twitter for violating the platform's terms.[48] Wolf, who had almost 150,000 followers, repeatedly spoke out against vaccine passports, lockdowns, and mask mandates. Twitter announced that Wolf's ban was permanent, with no possibility of appeal.[49]

One Twitter user wrote in reaction, "How dare you, Twitter. Naomi Wolf raised damn good questions about the rush to and ramifications of mass vax. This is unAmerican silencing of dissent."[50]

Left-wing journalist Glenn Greenwald called Wolf "a leading soldier" of dissent and explained the forces working behind the scenes to purge voices like hers. "I think a lot of people who constantly disseminate false claims and unhinged and dangerous conspiracy theories—such as MNSBC and CNN hosts—should nonetheless be allowed to remain on Silicon Valley monopolistic social media platforms," Greenwald wrote in response to Wolf's permanent Twitter ban.

"The most passionate, tireless and devoted advocates of online political censorship by the union of state and corporate monopolistic power are found at liberal corporate media outlets. Agitating and cheering for state/corporate censorship is a virtual religious mission there," he concluded.[51]

The silencing of any dissent is doing the bidding of the Great Reset.

> ### "Thinking Is Not Allowed"
> "My post was removed because it made people think: Isn't it odd that the same govt telling us that unpasteurized juice can be harmful to an unborn child is also claiming that an experimental vaccine is safe despite limited data? Thinking is not allowed in a totalitarian state."—Candace Owens on Twitter in 2021[52]

Despite this relentless censorship, COVID dissenters vowed not to be silenced.

"But rest assured. Whatever they throw at us, it won't do anything to sway me—or my colleagues—from the principles that sit behind what we wrote," Gupta wrote.

"I have all but stopped using Twitter, but I am aware that a number of academics have taken to using it to make personal attacks on my character, while my work is dismissed as 'pseudo- science.' Depressingly, our critics have also taken to ridiculing the Great Barrington Declaration as 'fringe' and 'dangerous,'" Gupta explained.

"But 'fringe' is a ridiculous word, implying that only mainstream science matters. If that were the case, science would stagnate. And dismissing us as 'dangerous' is equally unhelpful, not least because it is an inflammatory, emotional term charged with implications of irresponsibility. When it is hurled around by people with influence, it becomes toxic," Gupta added.[53]

Journalist Jordan Schachtel ripped social media giants for their policing policies. "YouTube has an official policy banning people who contradict info from the World Health Organization. For 16 months, YouTube has been deplatforming & censoring people for the act of telling the truth. Tech oligarch suppression has had devastating consequences for the world," Schachtel wrote.[54]

Gupta was surprised at the censorship and smears directed at her. "According to Wikipedia, for instance, the Great Barrington Declaration was funded by a Right-wing think-tank with links to climate-change deniers. It should be obvious to anyone that writing a short proposal and posting it on a website requires no great financing. But let me spell it out, since, apparently, I have to: I did not accept payment to co-author the Great Barrington Declaration," Gupta wrote.

Gupta explained how she was even forbidden to use the name of the Declaration on radio programs because it was purported to be "against the national interest."

"The Great Barrington Declaration represents a heartfelt attempt by a group of academics with decades of experience in this field to limit the harm of lockdown. I cannot conceive how anyone can construe this as 'against the national interest,'" Gupta wrote.[55]

A video published by Grabien Media and featuring Courtney Ann Taylor, a Georgia mother demanding that her local school board drop the mask requirement for schoolchildren, was banned from YouTube in 2021.

Grabien's Tom Elliott reached out to YouTube to ask why the video was deleted.

"The Favored Leftist Narrative"

"Increasingly commentary on coronavirus—as in so many other areas of politics—is being censored by the left-wing media and tech Establishment, not on the basis of whether it's true or untrue, but as to whether or not it accords with the favored leftist narrative," wrote James Delingpole for Breitbart.[56]

David Marcus for The Federalist explained, "Section 230 of the 1996 Communications Decency Act gives Twitter special protection to engage in censorship, but after this week of [COVID-19–related] obviously politically motivated silencing, many in Congress are looking to stripping the company of that protection."

"If [Twitter CEO Jack] Dorsey wants to be a mask busybody while he parties maskless with Beyonce and Jay Z on a yacht, so be it. The mask rules don't apply to him. But the laws of the United States should and must," Marcus added.[57]

"We reviewed your appeal," YouTube responded to Elliot. "We reviewed your content carefully, and have confirmed that it violates our medical misinformation policy. We know this is probably disappointing news, but it's our job to make sure that YouTube is a safe place for all."

Elliot translated YouTube's response thus: "Mothers having opinions about whether their children should be forced into masks 'violates our community guidelines' and our 'medical misinformation policy.'"

"Parents are allowed to express opinions over whether their children should be forced into wearing masks. Parents' perspectives are a valid part of the public debate. This mother does not represent herself as a doctor or medical expert," Elliot wrote. "Incidentally the WHO agrees with this mother that there is currently no scientific basis for compelling all children to wear masks indoors/outdoors as a measure to stop the spread of Covid. So YouTube's 'medical misinformation' claim is entirely false," Elliot added.

"I appealed, noting there's nothing in the WHO guidance this mother is contradicting (supposedly the basis of the video being taken offline). @YouTube has already rejected the appeal. Apparently, the platform must remain 'safe' from concerned mothers," Elliot concluded.[58]

The new media meme seems to be that citizens around the world are either incapable or just plain too unintelligent to evaluate medical information and must be hand-fed oft-repeated government consensus directives hourly. Don't question why you must stay at home or why you are not allowed to go to the park, attend a wedding, host a backyard barbecue, or why you must mask up—you just have to follow orders of the public health experts.

> ### "Please, Everyone, Stop"
>
> "I for one am tired of YouTube or any brick-and-mortar location telling me that my health and safety is their number-one priority. Please, everyone, stop making my health and safety your number-one priority. It generally leads to useless measures that make society weirder and my life less happy, with no discernible health effect.
>
> "How about making not living in a dystopia your number-one priority?"
> —historian and author Tom Woods[59]

Who Are the "Fact-Checkers"?

The media has presented "fact-checkers" as the holy grail of fighting alleged misinformation about COVID, climate change, the Great Reset, and almost any issue.

But who are the fact-checkers and how do they discern their "facts?"

"Fact checkers are just as susceptible to bias and narrative-pushing as any other class of journalist. Despite this, major media organizations treat them as a source of reliably unbiased information—as do social media companies like FaceBook and Twitter, who have granted them the power to flag and remove anything they deem 'misinformation,'" noted Bill D'Agostino of Newsbusters in 2021.[60]

"One of the most common ways in which fact checkers skew their analysis is with selection bias; specifically, they are quick to pounce on any misstep by Republicans, while Democrats are often given a pass," D'Agostino noted. "Two of the biggest names in the fact checking industry—Politifact and Snopes—abuse their role to tilt the scales in Democrats' favor," he added, pointing to a 2021 Media Research Center analysis.[61]

In 2021, the free speech alternative social media platform Parler found itself shut down by tech monopolies.

"Apple banned Parler from the AppStore using a pretext that Parler, which isn't a publisher, didn't stop the spread of dangerous & illegal content," explained Chris Buskirk, the editor and publisher of American Greatness.

"This is a lie. Parler does not permit illegal content. Apple thus relies on 'dangerous' which in their use has no objective meaning," Buskirk wrote. "What they mean is: Parler permits free speech with which they disagree. They also mean that Parler is a competitor that threatens their monopoly which they now use to harm Parler. They also do this as a favor to Democrats who now control all elected branches of government," he added.

"Apple's action against Parler, like Google's, is a pay-off, it's a bribe, or if you like an in-kind contribution to those in control of the state who wish to silence dissent. It is the merger of state power with corporate power against private citizens," he added.

"Devoted to Censorship"

"Facebook has turned its fact-checking in climate and energy over to a partisan group devoted to censorship, not scholarship. They don't fact-check whoppers by the alarmist side, just studies cited by skeptics. . . . Climate Feedback's reasoning is typically superficial and often just plain wrong, and contradicts the data even as compiled by the UN climate change body. . . . It was founded and funded by long-time climate alarmist Eric Michelman for the express purpose of promoting the climate crisis narrative. Indeed, Climate Feedback is tech mogul Michelman's third foray into shutting down a debate that he said, well before he created Climate Feedback, 'is settled.'" —climate statistician Caleb Rossiter, then executive director of the CO_2 Coalition, testifying at a 2020 hearing of the U.S. Senate Committee on Commerce, Science, and Transportation[62]

Both Apple and Google have no problems bowing to countries with poor human rights records. "Apple uses slave labor to make their products. Google worked with the Chinese military to develop technology but refused to work with the US military," Buskirk wrote.[63]

Cancel Culture

Progressive activist Dan Kovalik, the author of the book *Cancel This Book*, lamented the Left's cheering on the censorship and cancel culture we face today. He believes it serves the interest of the powerful against the little guy.

"I'm a longtime peace activist and anti-imperialist," Kovalik explained. Cancel culture "destroys solidarity. The idea that I, as a worker, would unite with the administration to get another worker fired is incredible," he said.

"People seem to think cancelling other people is somehow a form of activism. Real activism and social change have now been eschewed in favour of piling on people to get them fired or de-platformed. That's the problem—you have a movement that cares more about that than about actually winning real gains for working people," Kovalik said.

"Society's cancellers are privileged for the most part. They can sit in their fuzzy slippers in bed and go on their computer and engage in activism by piling on people. It's a very comfortable way to feel good about themselves," he noted.

"It was inevitable that the left's embrace of censorship would come back to bite us.... the Democrats are now taking up the mantle of suppressing speech in the name of social justice. Much of their base supports that. It's happening at the same time as they have abandoned the working class. We are going to see the ability to protest and speak freely start to collapse—and a lot of 'progressives' will be clapping," he added.[64]

As Jeffrey Tucker, the founder and president of the Brownstone Institute, explained, "The purpose of propaganda is not to convince people of lies they do not believe. The purpose is to exhibit the use of power. It's not power merely to say what's true. Power consists of the ability to tell lies that everyone knows are false and still expect compliance."[65]

Anne Applebaum made a similar point in *The Atlantic*: "A decade ago, I wrote a book about the Sovietization of Central Europe in the 1940s, and found that much of the political conformism of the early Communist period was the result not of violence or direct state coercion, but rather of intense peer pressure. Even without a clear risk to their life, people felt obliged—not just for the sake of their career but for their children, their friends, their spouse—to repeat slogans that they didn't believe, or to perform acts of public obeisance to a political party they privately scorned."[66]

Progressive Democrat senator Elizabeth Warren of Massachusetts joined other progressives in admitting that Facebook and other social media outlets are out of control with censorship. "I'm glad that [Trump's] not on Facebook," Warren explained about Trump being banned from the social media giant. "But I don't think that Facebook ought to have this kind of power. We need to break up these giant tech companies, and Facebook is one of them," Warren explained in 2021.

"They are crushing competition," Warren said. "And in cases like Facebook, they're acting like they're bigger than government," she added.

"The New 'Town Square'"—Censored

"The sharing of information with each other as Georgians, as Americans, that is of the highest importance and must be protected," James Taylor, the president of the Heartland Institute, testified to a Georgia House Committee hearing in 2021. According to Taylor, the internet and social media is the new "town square."[67]

"We have the right to free speech not because the government gave it to us in the First Amendment, but because it is an inalienable human right that predates and exists independently of the First Amendment. No government OR private entity can take away that inalienable right. I don't assert that Big Tech is violating the First Amendment, but that it is violating our inalienable right to political free speech in the public discourse," Taylor told me after the hearing.[68]

"They need to be broken up. We need a chance for competition to flourish here, and we need a chance to have some power that balances out what these giants are up to."[69]

"Welcome to Neo-Stalinism"

"Google Promptly Vanishes Greenpeace Co-Founder Dr. Moore from the Enviro Group's History after Then President Trump Tweeted Moore's Skeptical Climate Views," read the headline at Climate Depot on March 16, 2019. "Oh my! Google has removed my photo and name from the 'Founders of @Greenpeace.' It was still there 2 days ago but now I am erased. Tech Tyranny!!" Patrick Moore wrote. Trump had tweeted Moore's statements that "the whole climate crisis is not only Fake News, it's Fake Science." As Moore explained, "I was listed as a founder of Greenpeace on their own websites for 20 years after I left. They only disowned me when I came out in favor of nuclear energy." He also pointed out, Greenpeace "admits they listed me as a founder for 35 years. Then they took me off the list, as if that makes me 'not a founder.' I was also named a founder in countless media reports. Once you are recognized as a founder it cannot be taken away for political purposes." The UK Global Warming Policy Foundation declared "welcome to Neo-Stalinism."[70]

"The Party Is Always Right"

"Every record has been destroyed or falsified, every book rewritten, every picture has been repainted, every statue and street building has been renamed, every date has been altered. And the process is continuing day by day and minute by minute. History has stopped. Nothing exists except an endless present in which the Party is always right." —George Orwell, *Nineteen Eighty-Four*[71]

A Surveillance State

Robert F. Kennedy Jr., the chair of the Children's Health Defense (a nonprofit concerned with the effects of lockdowns, mask mandates, and vaccinations), ran afoul of the censors for his dissident views.

Kennedy warned about how technology was being used for nefarious purposes by governments and international organizations and corporations. "We have 5G, which has created a surveillance state," he explained,[72] noting that phone technology is "not for you and me. It's for Bill Gates, it's for [Mark] Zuckerberg."[73]

"They have biometric facial recognition systems, your GPS, all the satellites that—Bill Gates brags that his satellites will be able to monitor every square inch of the planet twenty-four hours a day," he said.[74] "That's only the beginning. He also will be able to follow you on all of your smart devices, through biometric facial recognition, through your GPS. You think that Alexa is working for you? She isn't working for you. She's working for Bill Gates, spying on you," Kennedy explained.[75]

"They have another innovation, which is digital currency. And once they have digitized our currency and gotten rid of the cash economy, they have absolute control over us because they'll be able to tax every transaction. The banks will be able to cash in on every transfer of wealth, every transaction, no matter how minuscule no matter how small. But also they'll be able to enforce obedience, because if you're disobedient they'll be able to shut down your bank account and starve you, and you'll have no access to cash," Kennedy warned.[76]

For his outspoken criticism of the COVID-19 hysteria and lock-downs, Kennedy faced de-platforming on social media outlets. Instagram banned Robert F. Kennedy Jr. from its platform in 2021 for COVID wrongthink. Kennedy had eight hundred thousand Instagram followers before he was removed.

"We removed this account for repeatedly sharing debunked claims about the coronavirus or vaccines," a spokesperson for Facebook said.[77] Facebook owns Instagram.

The left-wing *Vice* magazine labeled Kennedy "a formerly respected environmentalist who's been best known in recent years for promoting severe vaccine misinformation." The magazine reported indignantly that actor Alec Baldwin had "listened obligingly" during an interview with Kennedy. "Baldwin's Instagram account has 1.8 million followers, and the video, in less than two hours, garnered more than 43,000 views. This is not *precisely* what we need right now," *Vice* fretted.[78]

"Suck the Fun Out of Everything"

Comedian Bill Maher is disgusted with how the those on the Left have become the modern censors. Maher lamented in 2020 that "Democrats are now the party that can't tell the difference between Anthony Weiner and Al Franken," noting how the Left has become more doctrinaire while the Right has become more libertarian.

"Once upon a time the Right were offended by everything. They were the party of speech codes and blacklists and moral panics and demanding some TV show had to go. Well, now that's us. We're the fun-suckers now. We suck the fun out of everything: Halloween, the Oscars, childhood, Twitter, comedy," Maher explained.

"American government works best like a mullet: Republicans do business in the front, Democrats party in the back," he said. "We did fucking in the mud [at Woodstock] and bra-burning and 'turn on and tune in and drop out.' They're the party who won't bake wedding cakes for gay people!" he said. "It's time to switch back because, frankly, you're not good at being us, and being you—sucks."[79]

"The New Puritans"

Anne Applebaum warned in the *The Atlantic* in 2021 that today's Big Tech has evolved into "the New Puritans." She compared today's rigid social media speech codes to the censorship that the elders of the Massachusetts Bay Colony in the 1600s enforced on the fictional character Hester Prynne in Nathaniel Hawthorne's novel *The Scarlet Letter.* "Scarlet letters are a thing of the past. Except, of course, they aren't. Right here in America, right now, it is possible to meet people who have lost everything—jobs, money, friends, colleagues—after violating no laws, and sometimes no workplace rules either. Instead, they have broken (or are accused of having broken) social codes having to do with race, sex, personal behavior, or even acceptable humor, which may not have existed five years ago or maybe five months ago," Applebaum pointed out.[80]

Big Tech Breakup?

A movement is afoot to break up Big Tech's monopoly. "It's indisputable. Big Tech has literally billions of clients and controls a huge chunk of communications in America and around the world. They have either bought up or destroyed competitors," wrote Robert Knight, a former *Los Angeles Times* news editor and a contributor to the *Washington Times*, in an article titled "Breaking Up Big Tech Hard to Do—but It Should Happen."

"Government is far more dangerous since it has a monopoly on force," Knight wrote. "But corporate concentration is dangerous, too. It can become abusive, like Big Tech or Big Media, and more easily be commandeered by malevolent forces than a less centralized marketplace."

"Google, which accounts for more than 90 percent of online searches, has demonetized some conservative news sites and pushed down their articles in their search engine, which could put them out of business," Knight wrote.

"Only information vetted by the World Health Organization, which kowtows to Communist China, gets a pass. Mark Zuckerberg has said so. See the problem here?" he added.[81]

That "problem" is now facing stiff scrutiny.

Republican senator Josh Hawley of Missouri introduced the "Limiting Section 230 Immunity to Good Samaritans Act," which would amend the Communications Act to alter Big Tech's liability exemption. Hawley wrote a book titled *The Tyranny of Big Tech*, which was canceled by his original publisher and found a home at Regnery, the publisher of this book.

"No corporation should be so big and so powerful that it can control the political process, that it can override the will of the voters. And that's exactly what today's mega-corporations who've gotten big and fat with the help of government, what they're trying to do," Hawley said.

Hawley also set his sights on Amazon. "[Amazon] should be broken up," Hawley stated. "No one company should be able to control e-commerce AND privilege its own products on the same platform AND control the cloud."[85]

CHAPTER 8

The New Normal: Immunity Passports and Social-Credit Scores—You Will Exist to Serve the State's Interest

"In order for people to travel in 2021, they may eventually need a COVID vaccine passport," was the breathless opening sentence in a CBS Miami/CNN news article. "Several companies and technology groups have begun developing smartphone apps or systems for individuals to upload details of their COVID-19 tests and vaccinations, creating digital credentials that could be shown in order to enter concert venues, stadiums, movie theaters, offices, or even countries."

Take a guess as to who might be one of the driving forces behind this push for vaccine passports? Yes, you guessed it—the World Economic Forum. "The Common Trust Network, an initiative by Geneva-based nonprofit The Commons Project and the World Economic Forum, has partnered with several airlines including Cathay Pacific, JetBlue, Lufthansa, Swiss Airlines, United Airlines and Virgin Atlantic, as well as hundreds of health systems across the United States and the government of Aruba," CNN reported.[1]

The Rockefeller Foundation is involved as well. The president of The Rockefeller Foundation, Rajiv Shah, is listed as one of The Commons Project General Assembly members.[2] This is the same Rockefeller Foundation that issued the 2010 report *Scenarios for the Future of Technology and International Development*, including the future pandemic scenario entitled "Lock Step."[3]

Assuming their plans come to fruition, if you want to fly again, you will have to comply with the WEF's passport requirements—or you will be grounded.

In the United States, universities led the way in mandating vaccines. "Brown, Notre Dame and Rutgers are among universities warning students and staff they'll need shots in order to return to campus this fall," reported Bloomberg News. "Some sports teams are demanding proof of vaccination or a negative test from fans as arenas reopen. Want to see your favorite band play indoors in California? At bigger venues, the same rules apply. A Houston hospital chain recently ordered its 26,000 employees to get vaccinated."[4]

The European Union set up its immunity passport in Spring 2021, "enabling its population to travel freely once again throughout all 27 member states" using "a Digital COVID Certificate for the nearly 450 million inhabitants of the bloc."

But don't worry, the European Union claims it's not permanent or mandatory. "Officials also stressed that the system is temporary in nature and will be suspended once the World Health Organization declares an end to the emergency," *Fortune* reported. "Importantly, citizens that do not qualify for the certificate still enjoy the right to travel through the EU, but their movement may be subject to limitations such as quarantining upon arrival."[5] So you can move freely if you opt out of the jab, but you are still subject to arbitrary and changing "quarantines."

EU officials were quite proud of their achievement. "Policymakers argued it was no small feat to create a single EU-wide approach due to the extensive coordination required to align IT systems across more than two dozen countries," stated *Fortune* reporter Christiaan Hetzner. "The idea that I can go to Italy, show my mobile phone at a restaurant and a QR reader recognizes my code as proof of vaccination is unique worldwide," Jens Spahn, Germany's health minister, explained.[6]

The World Health Organization (WHO) released a report on its *Digital Documentation of COVID-19 Certificates: Vaccination Status* in 2021. The WHO explained: "A digital vaccination certificate that documents a person's current vaccination status to protect against COVID-19 can...be used for continuity of care or as proof of vaccination for purposes other than health care." The WHO report also revealed that "this work was funded by the Bill and Melinda Gates Foundation, the Government of Estonia, Fondation Botnar, the State of Kuwait, and the Rockefeller Foundation."[7]

You May Be an "Anti-Vaxxer"—Even If You're Vaccinated
Say you have taken all kinds of vaccines—including the COVID vaccines—but you oppose vaccine mandates, or you may not want to get your children an experimental vaccine against a disease that poses virtually no risk to them. You are now officially an "anti-vaxxer." On October 4, 2021, *Merriam-Webster Dictionary* updated the definition of the word "anti-vaxxer" to include anyone opposed to "regulations mandating vaccination" (from the earlier definition, which included opponents of vaccine "laws"). The 2021 "updated entry also adds after the main definition: 'especially: a parent who opposes having his or her child vaccinated.'" According to the Associated Press, this was just "part of the regular updates to the online dictionary."[8]

CNN reported the vaccine passports as good news for Americans. "The CommonPass app...allows users to upload medical data such as a COVID-19 test result or, eventually, a proof of vaccination by a hospital or medical professional, generating a health certificate or pass in the form of a QR code that can be shown to authorities without revealing sensitive information. For travel, the app lists health pass requirements at the points of departure and arrival based on your itinerary."[9]

If you have ever wanted something called a "digital yellow card," you are in luck!

"You can be tested every time you cross a border. You cannot be vaccinated every time you cross a border," Thomas Crampton, chief marketing and communications officer for The Commons Project, explained. So Crampton was pushing the "digital yellow card," to prove your vaccine status.[10]

"If You Are Vaccinated...Here Are the Freedoms That You Have"

"The vaccine is the ticket to pre-pandemic life," Dr. Leana Wen, former Planned Parenthood president turned CNN medical analyst, told then CNN anchor Chris Cuomo in March 2021.

"The window to do that is really narrowing," Wen continued, noting that states are "reopening at 100%. And we have a very narrow window to tie reopening policy to vaccination status."

"Because otherwise, if everything is reopened, then what's the carrot going to be? How are we going to incentivize people to actually get the vaccine? So that's why I think the CDC and the Biden administration need to come out a lot bolder and say, 'If you are vaccinated, you can do all these things. Here are all these freedoms that you have.' Because otherwise, people are going to go out and enjoy these freedoms anyway," Wen said.[11]

Imagine an America where citizens enjoy freedoms even if they disobey the COVID protocols of the WHO and the Biden administration CDC. We can't let that happen!

"Freedom isn't a 'carrot' to force us to do what the government wants," responded Julie Mastrine of the website AllSides. "Wen's thinking is actually an inversion of the ideals that built and sustain this country."[12]

"Inconsistent with the Nuremberg Code"

"Our government is out of control on this and they are lawless. They completely disregard bioethics. They completely disregard the federal common rule. They've broken all the rules that I know, that I've been trained on for years and years and years. These mandates of an experimental vaccine are explicitly illegal. They are explicitly inconsistent with the Nuremberg code. They are explicitly inconsistent with the Belmont Report. They are flat-out illegal and they don't care." —virologist Dr. Robert Malone, whose research was critical in the development of mRNA technology.[13]

"It Feels Vaguely Soviet"

"I'm watching baseball tonight and out of nowhere the announcers start talking about the vaccine, how easy getting it was, how great it is . . . and the stadium signage says 'Take one for the team. Get vaccinated.' . . . Can anyone think of any campaign like this?—not just in the democratic era, but before? It feels vaguely Soviet, sure, but the Soviets didn't have a real private sector or NGOs to play along." —Alex Berenson, former *New York Times* reporter and author of *Pandemia*[14]

The WEF brags to the world that the vaccine passport is its off-spring. "CovidPass is the brainchild of one of the World Economic Forum's Young Global Leaders, Mustapha Mokass," the WEF website announced. (Mokass happens to be a climate change activist and the founder of Climate Finance Advisors. We will discuss the COVID-Climate connection in more detail in chapters 11 and 12.)

The WEF touts the virtues of their vaccine passport:

- A new app acts as a health passport for travellers who are virus-free.
- Using blockchain technology, it provides an encrypted record of test results.
- Its creators say it could allow healthy travellers to avoid quarantine.
- The app could also allow sports and entertainment venues to reopen safely, as well as the global conference and exhibition industry.[15]

But it's not just the WEF and big corporations who want in on this vaccine passport, it's also Big Tech.

"Large tech firms are also getting in on the act. IBM developed its own app, called Digital Health Pass, which allows companies and venues to customize indicators they would require for entry including coronavirus tests, temperature checks, and vaccination records. Credentials corresponding to those indicators are then stored in a mobile wallet," CNN stated.

Of course, there may be a few snags along the way, such as "privacy issues" and "disjointed implementation." But CNN reassures us that we can learn from the previous experience of "contact tracing apps."[16]

Passport Pushback

"Governors and lawmakers in 10 Republican-led states have already banned or limited vaccine passports, including Florida. 'We're not doing any vaccine passports. That's totally unacceptable,' Florida governor Ron DeSantis said [in May 2021] during a press conference on the signing of SB 2006. The bill bans businesses from requiring customers to show proof they have been vaccinated against COVID-19 in order to get service." —Yahoo News[17]

The Great Travel Reset

Michael Svane, the head of the Transport Department of the Confederation of Danish Industry, has embraced the "vaccine passport" as a "way for us to put restrictions behind us and travel by air much more."

As RT reported, "Australia's Qantas Airways earlier announced that proof of Covid-19 vaccination would become mandatory for all international passengers on its flights. Qantas CEO, Alan Joyce, speculated that it's *'going to be a common…in other airlines around the globe.'*"[18]

In the United States, more than thirty Democrat senators and members of Congress implored President Joe Biden to mandate vaccines for all airline passengers. "We ask that you put in place requirements for airline passengers to provide proof of full vaccination against COVID-19 or a negative test to board a domestic flight," the letter read.[19]

For his part, Anthony Fauci, the director of the NIH's National Institute of Allergy and Infectious Diseases and Biden's chief medical officer, was against vaccine mandates before he supported them (just the same as he was on masks).

"You don't want to mandate, and try and force anyone to take a vaccine," Fauci said in August 2020. "We've never done that," Fauci said. He went even further, adding, "It would be unenforceable, and not appropriate."[20]

But in 2021 Fauci had a change of heart about the "unenforceable" and "not appropriate" vaccine mandates. "I would support that if you want to get on a plane and travel with other people that you should be vaccinated," Fauci explained.[22]

> ### "Movement Licenses"
> "They're not 'vaccine passports,' they're movement licenses. It's not a vaccine, it's experimental gene therapy. 'Lockdown' is at best completely pointless universal medical isolation and at worst ubiquitous public incarceration. Call things what they are, not their euphemisms." –Twitter user RoadtoSerfdom in 2021.[21]

Twenty-twenty-one and 2022 saw the push for vaccine passports ramped up steeply, allegedly to combat the delta and omicron variants of COVID-19. "Austria's government announced that police would enforce a lockdown exclusively against unvaccinated citizens. Following days of massive protests, the policy was extended to everyone, with steep

> ### "You Better Get That Vaccine"
> Dr. Leana Wen was frustrated that the Biden administration was so slow to impose an airline vaccine mandate. "I think we really need to make it clear that there are privileges associated with being an American. That if you wish to have these privileges, you need to get vaccinated. Travel, and having the right to travel in our state, it's not a constitutional right as far as I know to board a plane, and so saying that if you want to stay unvaccinated, that's your choice, but if you want to travel, you better go get that vaccine," Wen said.[23]
>
> Fox News host Tucker Carlson ripped Wen for her comments. "So here you have a woman who moved to this country from China sitting authoritatively in a box on CNN, lecturing Americans that their most basic birthright—the right to travel within their own country, the country they were born in—is now, in fact, a privilege that the Democratic Party may decide to grant if you follow its demands," Carlson said.[24]

fines and even prison sentences to be imposed on those who refuse to comply, and a compulsory vaccination requirement tacked on for good measure," reported the website The Gray Zone.

Germany also imposed lockdowns on the unvaccinated, "barring them from almost all public places except for pharmacies and supermarkets," with "Berlin…also weighing a vaccination mandate for all. One German constitutional lawyer has even proposed that refusers of the jab 'be brought before the vaccinator by the police,'" according to The Gray Zone.[25]

Italy and many parts of Europe joined in, allowing only the double-jabbed to fully engage in society and barring unvaccinated Italians from restaurants, theatres, museums, and other public events.[26]

Canadian prime minister Justin Trudeau led a campaign against the unvaccinated. "If you don't want to get vaccinated, that's your choice. But don't think you can get on a plane or a train beside vaccinated people and put them at risk!" Trudeau said.[27]

"F—— Their Freedom"

"When are we going to stop putting up with the idiots in this country and just say it's mandatory to get vaccinated?" Shock jock Howard Stern asked on his SiriusXM program. "F—— them. F—— their freedom. I want my freedom to live," Stern said. "I want to get out of the house. I want to go next door and play chess. I want to go take some pictures. This is bullshit."

"Go f—— yourself," Stern added. "You had the cure and you wouldn't take it."[28]

Mediaite senior columnist John Ziegler commented: "It's truly amazing how many entertainers who made their careers being strongly anti-establishment when they were young have become THE most cowardly/slavish pawns of the state during the pandemic. But it's MORE bizarre how many people STILL think the vaccines stop transmission!"[29]

"Second-Class Citizens"

Attorney Stacey Rudin wrote a devastating analysis of vaccine mandates for the Brownstone Institute titled "First Comply, Then We'll Grant You Some Rights."

"The political establishment intends to make 'the unvaccinated' second-class citizens, to dehumanize them and deny them basic rights many generations have taken for granted. This conditions the population to movement restrictions based on behavior. Compliance gets you rights, like a dog earning treats," Rudin wrote.

"In this system—which is steadily getting underway in country after country—a person who weighs 350 pounds, is completely sedentary and eats a steady stream of Big Macs is considered 'healthy' and accepted in society. The decisive factor is obedience: he dutifully takes all of the 'boosters.' By contrast, a world-class athlete such as Novak Djokovic cannot play tennis at the Australian Open. He is deemed an 'infection risk' because he insists on maintaining his body using eastern-style health practices, the same ones that made him into the greatest tennis player of all time," Rudin continued.

Obesity Passports?

"The Government should not let its drive for health certification stall at Covid-19 passports. If it is serious about saving lives and promoting personal responsibility then it must target the avoidable and identifiable disease of obesity," wrote Tory MP Charles Walker in *The Telegraph*, to illustrate his opposition to vaccine passports. "To understand the dangers of Covid passports, simply imagine an obesity equivalent. Being overweight is a public health epidemic, so why is it that we don't restrict the freedoms and choices of the obese?"[30]

"Australia now has 'quarantine camps.' 'Unvaccinated' Canadians cannot use mass transit. Austrians who refuse the jab cannot leave their homes. *It bears repeating: world governments are holding law-abiding adults in house arrest for refusing to take an injection.* This is not a drill. Combine this real-life dystopia with the twisted 'logic' used to launch the lockdowns, and it is hard to ignore the sinking feeling that lockdown was a preconceived pathway to where we are now: staring down the barrel at permanent, regular, mandatory adult vaccination—your immune system is now a subscription service—and corresponding movement 'passports,'" Rudin concluded.[31]

The Australian prime minister Scott Morrison declared that COVID-mandate protesters were "selfish and self-defeating," adding that protesting "achieves no purpose. It won't end the lockdown sooner." As *The Guardian* reported, "Hundreds of fines have been issued and dozens charged in Sydney after anti-lockdown protesters marched and clashed with police in what one deputy commissioner called 'violent, filthy, risky behaviour.'"[33]

Daniel Andrews, premier of Victoria, Australia, explained how the unvaccinated would be treated. "We're going to move to a situation where, to protect the health system, we are going to lock out people who are not vaccinated and can be. If you're making the choice not to get vaccinated, then you're making the wrong choice.... It's not going to be safe for people who are not vaccinated to be roaming around the place spreading the virus.... But yes, there is going to be a vaccinated economy, and you get to participate in that...if you are vaccinated."[34]

France has seen hundreds of thousands protest vaccine mandates as well, with protesters chanting "Freedom, freedom!" and carrying signs reading "Macron, tyrant," "Big Pharma shackles freedom," and "No to the pass of shame."[36]

"We Will Catch You"

"Teenagers from [a] remote NT [Northern Territory] community [were] arrested after escape from Howard Springs COVID quarantine facility," according to a report by the Australia Broadcasting Company. "At a COVID update press conference, NT Chief Minister Michael Gunner confirmed the teenagers, aged 15, 16 and 17, tested negative for the virus yesterday. He said all three were from the Binjari community near Katherine and had been sent into quarantine as close contacts of positive cases," ABC News reported. "Mr Gunner said the isolation in quarantine was 'pretty hard for some people . . . used to being close to family and community.' He said the escape could mean an extension of the time the teenagers were required to stay in quarantine. 'Absconding from Howard Springs isn't just danger-ous—it is incredibly stupid,' he said. 'Because we will catch you and there will be consequences.'"[37]

In the United States, President Joe Biden tried to push federal vaccine mandates on healthcare workers, federal contractors, and all employees of businesses with more than a hundred workers.[38] But Biden's vaccine mandates took a pummeling in the federal courts as the regulations were suspended, setting up a Supreme Court battle. Across the United States, many hospital workers resigned on account of the mandates, causing some hospitals to "pause baby deliveries after staffers quit over vaccine mandate."[39]

Biden, like Fauci, claimed he was opposed to vaccine mandates before he supported them. "No, I don't think it should be mandatory," Biden asserted in December 2020, adding, "I wouldn't demand it to be mandatory." And Biden press secretary Jen Psaki also asserted that mandating vaccinations is "not the role of the federal government."[40]

But Biden reversed himself in September 2021. "I'm announcing that the Department of Labor is developing an emergency rule to require all employers with 100 or more employees, that together employ over 80 million workers, to ensure their work forces are fully vaccinated or show a negative test at least once a week," Biden said. "I will sign an executive order that will now require all executive branch federal employees to be vaccinated—all. And I've signed another executive order that will require federal contractors to do the same," he added.

Biden also directed ire at the unvaccinated. "Many of us are frustrated with the 80 million people who are still not vaccinated," Biden said. "My message to unvaccinated Americans is this: What more is there to wait for? What more do you need to see? We've made vaccinations free, safe, and convenient.... We've been patient, but our patience is wearing thin."[41]

"The Mother of All Vaccines"

Why is there very little discussion of natural immunity in the vaccine-mandate debate? The inconvenient scientific evidence makes justifying any kind of vaccines problematic.

In 2018 NIH's Dr. Anthony Fauci stated unequivocally to the *New York Times*, "Natural Infection is the mother of all vaccines."[42]

In 2008 *National Geographic* reported on the staying power of natural immunity. "To this day, people who survived the 1918 flu pandemic carry antibodies that can remember and neutralise the murderous strain," Ed Yong explained in an article titled "Flu Survivors Still Immune after 90 Years."[43]

A May 2021 study published by the *The Lancet* found that "SARS-CoV-2 antibody-positivity protects against reinfection for at least seven months with 95% efficacy."[44]

Scapegoating the Unvaccinated

Stanford professor of medicine Jay Bhattacharya criticized the Biden administration's "continued support for vaccine mandates and vaccine segregation. Coercion in support of vaccine uptake is a destructive mistake that—even if it works to increase vax uptake—will cement distrust in public health."

Bhattacharya expressed his displeasure with "the tone of demonization, blaming, and 'othering' of the unvaccinated. Blaming people for getting sick is wrong & bad for public health. It will make many vaccine-hesitant individuals distrust the message & further social division."

"Blaming 'misinformation' for vaccine hesitancy without an acknowledgment that the government & some media have caused great harm to trust in science & the vaccines by their propaganda and silencing of scientific dissidents," Bhattacharya added.

He also noted that coerced vaccination provides "no acknowledgment of the importance of effective immunity possessed by the COVID recovered. This ignorant, anti-science stance destroys confidence in the administration's capacity to effectively convey public health messages."

Bhattacharya was dismayed that the Biden administration offered "no acknowledgment of the catastrophic harms caused by the lockdown-focused policies of the last two years. They were the single most destructive public health policy in living memory. A presidential apology would begin to restore trust in public health."[45]

Naomi Wolf, former advisor to Bill Clinton and Al Gore, was more blunt in her criticism of Biden's vaccine mandates. "It's a coup, it's a bio-fascist coup," declared Wolf. "This is a declaration of war against the American people." Biden was "scapegoating in a way that is right out of Hitler's playbook. And I say this as a granddaughter of survivors of the Holocaust," Wolf said.[46]

The Biden administration was losing even Marxist professors with these mandates. Self-described Marxist Richard Wolff, professor emeritus of economics at the University of Massachusetts at Amherst, ripped vaccine mandates from a "class struggle" perspective. "It's NOT pro- vs anti-vaccine. The issue is class struggle: have employers' dictates/mandates become intolerable for employees? Record job-quitting + strikes + refusals of mask/vaccine mandates say yes," said Professor Wolff, who founded the academic journal *Rethinking Marxism*.[47]

"It is an important opportunity to fight the right and build the left," he wrote.[48] "We're ceding it to the right if we allow the liberals and the others to collapse the people fighting against the mandate," he added. "I am trying to be polite but there's a tragic slippage of these people [supporters of vaccine mandates] into reinforcing the very authoritarian hierarchy that we ought to be critics of," the professor explained.[49]

In an analysis titled "The Medical Objectification of the Human Person," Robert Freudenthal, a psychiatrist in the UK National Health Service, critiqued the underlying philosophy behind COVID-19 mandates. "The pandemic has turbocharged this process of medical objectification," he stated. "The medical system has become the facilitator in converting the complexities of human behavior and range of emotional experience into medicalised data points that can then be fed, as raw material, into the system of surveillance capitalism," Freudenthal wrote.[50]

Opposition to the vaccine mandates was heard from other points along the political spectrum as well. "We underestimate at our peril just how grave an assault on personhood mandatory vaccination represents," argued Brendan O'Neill, chief political writer for Spiked Online.

"We are living through a chilling overhaul of the entire relationship between the state and the individual, with the state empowered to such an extraordinary degree that it can now instruct its citizens on what to inject into their bodies, and the individual so politically emaciated, so denuded of rights, that he no longer even enjoys sovereignty over *himself*, over that tiny part of the world that is his own body and mind. We are witnessing the violent death of European liberalism and the birth pangs of a new and deeply authoritarian era," O'Neill explained.

"Stigmatizing Parts of the Population"

"Historically, both the USA and Germany have engendered negative experiences by stigmatizing parts of the population for their skin color or religion. I call on high-level officials and scientists to stop the inappropriate stigmatization of unvaccinated people, who include our patients, colleagues, and other fellow citizens." —German physician Dr. Günter Kampf in the November 21, 2021, edition of *The Lancet*[51]

O'Neill pointed to the underpinnings of political freedom: "In his *Letter Concerning Toleration* (1689), the great Enlightenment philosopher John Locke sought to 'settle the bounds' between the individual and officialdom. He wrote that even if a man 'neglect the care of his soul' or 'neglect the care of his health,' still the authorities have no right to interfere with him. 'No man can be forced to be...healthful.'"[52]

A Bad Precedent

In the United States the justification for vaccine mandates appears to be on very shaky Constitutional ground. "The United States Supreme Court and its followers have used *Jacobson v. Massachusetts*, a 1905 case in which a man was fined $5 (about $150 today) for refusing a smallpox vaccine, as the precedent justifying all the draconian measures to which Americans have been subject over the past 18 months," explained attorney Michael P. Senger, author of "China's Global Lockdown Propaganda Campaign."

"*Jacobson* has been overruled many times, not least because it was subsequently used to justify eugenics; its resurrection has been compared to 'resurrecting *Dred Scott*, *Plessy v. Ferguson*, or *Korematsu*'—Supreme Court cases referred to as 'anticanon' owing to not only their lack of intellectual rigor but to the unimaginable human tragedies they precipitated," Senger wrote.[53]

"If you like compulsory vaccinations, you'll love child labor and the Espionage Act," Alex Berenson, the author of *Pandemia*, wrote. "*Jacobson*—a 116-year-old ruling about a virus roughly 100 times as deadly as Sars-Cov-2—must be preserved forever and forms the core support for a mandatory vaccination scheme," Berenson noted sarcastically.

"Between *Dred Scott* and the New Deal court, the Supreme Court continuously held that individuals had few if any rights as individuals. The vax decision (*Jacobson*) sits squarely in the middle of a timeline where nine white men in robes loudly scoffed at the idea that there was anything more important than the sheer brute power of business and government. Check out the line-up of horrific cases that surround the alleged 'mandatory vax is permissible' law. Who would want to live in a time and place where this kind of legal thinking held sway?" Berenson wrote. He then summarized the "horrific cases";

- 1883: "Racial discrimination is awesome"—Civil Rights cases (8–1)
- 1895: "Monopolies are awesome"—*U.S. v. E. C. Knight* (8–1)
- 1896: "Separate but equal"—*Plessy v. Ferguson* (7–1)
- 1905: *Jacobson v. Massachusetts* (7–2)
- 1905: "Workers do not have and cannot have any rights vis-à-vis their employer"—*Lochner v. New York* (5–4)
- 1917: "You can go to jail for questioning the government"—*Debs v. U.S.* (9–0)
- 1919: "You can go to jail for speech we don't like"—*Schenck v. U.S.* (9–0)
- 1918: "Child labor is A-OK"—*Hammer v. Dagenhart* (5–4)
- 1923: "Minimum wage laws are illegal"—*Adkins v. Children's Hospital* (5–3)
- 1927: "Your Fallopian tubes belong to us"—*Buck v. Bell* (8–1)[54]

Barcode Tattoos

In December of 2019, *Scientific American* featured an article head-lined "Invisible Ink Could Reveal Whether Kids Have Been Vaccinated. The Technology Embeds Immunization Records into a Child's Skin."[55]

That same month MIT touted the "novel" efforts of Professor Robert Langer and colleagues, funded by Bill Gates, to record and store and the vaccination information of each individual in a marker that would be injected just underneath that person's skin. "Specialized invisible dye, delivered along with a vaccine, could enable 'on-patient' storage of vaccination history," according to the press release.[56]

"Along with the vaccine, a child would be injected with a bit of dye that is invisible to the naked eye but easily seen with a special cell-phone filter, combined with an app that shines near-infrared light onto the skin," Karen Weintraub wrote in the *Scientific American*.[57] "The research was funded by the Bill and Melinda Gates Foundation and the Koch Institute Support (core) Grant from the National Cancer Institute," MIT noted.[58]

Rice University described this Gates-funded vaccine-delivery system as a way to "leave the pattern of tags just under the skin, where they become something like a bar-code tattoo."

A press release from Rice explained how these "bar-code tattoos" came to be. Kevin McHugh, an assistant professor of bioengineering at Rice recounted: "The Bill and Melinda Gates Foundation came to us and said, 'Hey, we have a real problem—knowing who's vaccinated.'... So our idea was to put the record on the person.... This way, later on, people can scan over the area to see what vaccines have been administered and give only the ones still needed."[59]

Pharma Billionaires

"Covid-19 vaccines have created at least nine new billionaires after shares in companies producing the shots soared. Topping the list of new billionaires are Moderna (MRNA) CEO Stéphane Bancel and Ugur Sahin, the CEO of BioNTech (BNTX).... Moderna's share price has gained more than 700% since February 2020, while BioNTech has surged 600%. CanSino Biologics' stock is up about 440% over the same period.... The nine new billionaires are worth a combined $19.3 billion, enough to fully vaccinate some 780 million people in low-income countries, [health] campaigners said. 'These billionaires are the human face of the huge profits many pharmaceutical corporations are making from the monopoly they hold on these vaccines,' Anne Marriott, Oxfam's health-policy manager, said in a statement."—CNN report[60]

A May 2020 "Fact Check" by Reuters verified that this quantum-dot dye technology was funded by the Gates Foundation. Reuters explained that the technology "is similar to a tattoo, which would help provide up-to-date patient vaccine records for professionals in places lacking medical records."[61]

Progressive politicians seemed to love the idea of vaccine barcodes. Former Democrat presidential candidate Andrew Yang suggested in December of 2020 that Americans could have a "barcode" verification system for the COVID-19 vaccine, though at least his idea was to put the codes in people's cell phones, not their bodies. "Is there a way for someone to easily show that they have been vaccinated—like a bar code they can download to their phone?" Yang asked. "There ought to be." Yang claimed that it was "tough to have mass gatherings like concerts or ballgames without either mass adoption of the vaccine or a means of signaling."[62]

Newsweek reported in 2021 that "people in Sweden are increasingly seeking to have microchips inserted into their bodies that contain their COVID-19 vaccination records." In an article titled "People Get Microchips Implanted That Include Vaccine Records amid New COVID

"Stands to Gain Millions"

"No one's laughing at 'The Daily Show' host Trevor Noah's new take on coronavirus vaccine maker Moderna. The late-night comedian appears to be suspicious of Moderna CEO Stephane Bancel. . . . Noah questioned Bancel's intentions as he alleges that the pharma boss may not be the most 'objective source' for pandemic predictions. 'On the one hand, almost all the Omicron cases have been mild so far,' the 37-year-old host began in a clip shared to social media. 'But on the other hand, the guy who stands to gain millions of dollars from new vaccines says we need new vaccines, huh?' As a parody of Bancel, Noah mocked, 'If we don't make a new vaccine, this disease could be with us *Ferrari* . . . I mean "forever." Sorry, I was thinking of something else'—suggesting that the French billionaire businessman might be prioritizing his bank account over epidemiological concerns." —*New York Post*[63]

Restrictions," the magazine reported that "the microchips [are] inserted in their hand, arm or chest. Those individuals then used their smartphone to detect the chip's presence or swiped the portion of their body that contained the chip over door sensors."[64]

Medical Segregation

Feminist Naomi Wolf, CEO of the tech company Daily Cloud and a former political consultant to Vice President Al Gore, testified about the dangers of immunity passports.

"Vaccine passports are not a hypothetical," Naomi Wolf testified to the Michigan legislature in 2021. "Respectfully, they're not a Bigfoot, they're not something in the future. They're not even in development. Vaccine passports are now, they're in use in my home state of New York state. It's called the Excelsior Pass," Wolf explained in her testimony the Michigan House Oversight Committee.

"People cannot go to the Mets game if they don't show their Excelsior Pass by the directive of our governor, Andrew Cuomo, who's been ruling under emergency law month after month after month. So, in New York State I am not free to not be discriminated against already," she added.[65]

"I'm here to share the voices of hundreds of Michiganders who asked me to tell you that they're terrified of this. It transcends party. I'm a lifelong Democrat, and they're all asking you to please stop it from happening preemptively," Wolf concluded.[66]

Wolf has also compared the passports to medical segregation. "So, they're putting an obligation on businesses to police their customers and create a two-tier society exactly like Jim Crow laws," Wolf said. "I don't mean to belittle the horrible history of Jim Crow laws, but it's literally this kind of legislation, some people are better than other people, some people are more equal than others and they get the privilege of removing their masks," she explained.[67]

Wolf said the push for vaccine passports is part of an effort to "recreate a situation that is very familiar to me as a student of history in which it all started with just papers that separated out the population in Germany for instance and then in Central Europe into people who were seen as clean and people who were seen as unclean."[68]

"And that is the start of many, many genocides…and a great deal of very evil times in our—humanity's—history," she added.[69]

Elon Musk on the "Erosion of Freedom"

"You are taking a risk, but people do risky things all the time. . . . I believe we've got to watch out for the erosion of freedom in America." –Elon Musk speaking of the risk taken by the unvaccinated in his *Time* magazine "2021 Person of the Year" interview[70]

The ACLU expressed similar concerns in a May 2020 commentary. "A system of immunity passports in the United States threatens to exacerbate racial disparities and harm the civil liberties of all," the ACLU said.

"We at the ACLU have serious concerns about the adoption of any such proposal, because of its potential to harm public health, incentivize economically-vulnerable people to risk their health by contracting COVID-19, exacerbate racial and economic disparities, and lead to a new health surveillance infrastructure that endangers privacy rights," the ACLU explained.

"An immunity passport system would divide workers into two classes—the immune and the non-immune—and the latter might never be eligible for a given job short of contracting and surviving COVID-19 if an immune worker is available to take the slot," according to the ACLU.[71]

But by September of 2021, the ACLU had changed its tune. On September 7, Joseph Vazquez reported that "ACLU National Legal Director David Cole and ACLU Program on Freedom of Religion and Belief Director Daniel Mach penned an asinine *New York Times* op-ed headlined: 'Want to Enhance Civil Liberties? Embrace Vaccine Mandates.'"[72] The ACLU op-ed explained that "we see no civil liberties problem with requiring Covid-19 vaccines in most circumstances."[73]

Why the change in the ACLU's views on vaccine mandates? "It's worth noting that Soros funded the ACLU with at least $37,359,845 between 2000–2014 alone," Vazquez noted. "Soros's Open Society Foundations has also given $975,000 collectively between the ACLU Foundation and its affiliated organizations in Maryland and Idaho between 2016 and 2019," Vazquez wrote.[74]

Left-wing journalist Glenn Greenwald was agog at the shift in position of the ACLU. Greenwald explained: "The op-ed sounds like it was written by an NSA official justifying the need for mass surveillance (yes, fine, your privacy is important but it is not absolute; your privacy rights are outweighed by public safety; we are spying on you for your own good). And the op-ed appropriately ends with this perfect Orwellian flourish: 'We care deeply about civil liberties and civil rights for all—which is precisely why we support vaccine mandates.'"

Greenwald noted that "in 2008, the ACLU published a comprehensive report on pandemics which had one primary purpose: to denounce as dangerous and unnecessary attempts by the state to mandate, coerce, and control in the name of protecting the public from pandemics."[75]

The Chinafication of the West

Journalist Jordan Schachtel commented that COVID-19 passports and Big Tech surveillance were turning America into a clone of China. "The COVID-19 pandemic began in China, and one of its apparent side effects is that it slowly transforms western governments into China-like surveillance states," Schachtel wrote.[76]

German economics professor Antony P. Mueller echoed those sentiments. "This new world order of digital tyranny comes with a comprehensive social credit system. The People's Republic of China is the pioneer of this method of surveillance and control of individuals, corporations, and sociopolitical entities."[77]

In short, China is demolishing the West from within, and the West is all too willing to commit suicide.

The coronavirus lockdowns herald another step into what is being called "scientism," which is leading us to a technocracy. Technocracy, the public's acquiescence to government by an elite cadre of unelected technical experts who are positioned to call the shots and manage society, is now rapidly becoming a reality in America.

"A One-Party State in America"

"For decades the progressive movement has tried to impose and sought a one-party state in America. Climate activists from Tom Friedman on the pages of the *New York Times* extolled the virtues of China's one-party system. UN climate chiefs talked about a centralized transformation and praised China for getting it right on climate. So what happened was they spent decades trying to scare us about overpopulation, global cooling, the Amazon rainforest [allegedly disappearing], and finally, climate change, and they failed. A virus comes along, and they realized that this cut across ideologies, cut across political affiliation, and they were able to declare an emergency and suspend normal democracy. They were able to achieve, Sebastian, their one-party state with an unelected bureaucracy. . . .

"Fast-forward. The reason Joe Biden can try to impose a vaccine pass-port system in the United States is because of the [COVID-19] emergency declaration where democracy is suspended. We are now in a Chinese-style, one-party state. This is not something that's going to happen in the future, it is being imposed on us now using the COVID-19 emergency declaration. They don't want hearings in Congress, they don't want to vote, they don't want town halls; this is raw authoritarian power that they've sought for decades, and they never thought in their wildest dreams that in a year and a half of COVID they could have this kind of success—but here we are." —Marc Morano, on Newsmax TV with Sebastian Gorka[78]

China's Social-Credit System

"China's social credit system has been compared to Black Mirror, Big Brother and every other dystopian future sci-fi writers can think up. The reality is more complicated—and in some ways, worse," wrote Nicole Kobie for *Wired*.

"China's social credit system expands that idea to all aspects of life, judging citizens' behavior and trustworthiness. Caught jaywalking, don't pay a court bill, play your music too loud on the train—you could lose certain rights, such as booking a flight or train ticket," Kobie described.

"What's troubling is when those private systems link up to the government rankings—which is already happening with some pilots," she added.[79]

As the *Globe and Mail* reported in a 2018 investigation, "First envisioned in the mid-1990s, China's social-credit system would assign a ranking to each of the country's almost 1.4 billion people. Unlike a Western rating based on financial creditworthiness, China's social-credit backers want their system to be all-encompassing, to evaluate not just financial matters but anything that might speak to a person's trustworthiness."[80]

The system is not officially set up yet in China although many pilot programs exist throughout the country in different cities and regions. The pilot systems utilize shopping data to gather information on the habits of citizens to create credit-style scores.

"One city, Rongcheng, gives all residents 1,000 points to start. Authorities make deductions for bad behavior like traffic violations, and add points for good behavior such as donating to charity," Kobie explained. "So far, taking part in both the private and government versions is technically voluntary; in the future, the official social credit system will be mandatory."

Many of these "private systems" link to government rankings, which will allow the two to merge.

"In China, there is no such thing as the rule of law. Regulations that can be largely apolitical on the surface can be political when the Communist Party of China (CCP) decides to use them for political purposes," noted Samantha Hoffman of the Australian Strategic Policy Institute.[81]

The social-credit system will also act as a sort of blacklist—if you owe the government money or you are not in good standing with the government in regard to political issues, you could lose many of your rights.

"China's social credit system is about power and conformity," Republican congressman Mark Green of Tennessee warned. "It's an attempt to shape citizens into the CCP's ideal subject: don't ask questions, disobey or think for yourself." As Green explained, "'Very bad' behavior, such as political dissent, can get someone and their family members blacklisted, making it difficult for them to function in society." The congressman pointed out that "cancel culture in the U.S. might not be as far advanced as China's social credit system, but it has a similar aim—ensuring conformity to one ideology."[82]

The Chinese social-credit system relies on data from every aspect of the lives of the public, and this data is shared with other entities. In China "one infamous example is Sesame Credit linking up with the Baihe dating site, so would be partners can judge each other on their looks as well as their social credit score," noted Kobie.

"A positive rating means discounts and benefits, such as a simplified process with bureaucracies. If you have a low rating, you may have extra paperwork or fees," Kobie explained.[83]

Refuse to wear a mask? Violate lockdown orders? Break the government-imposed curfew? Opt out of a vaccine? Your social-credit score will take a massive hit, and your ability to live as a citizen with full benefits will be restricted.

This social-credit system was visible in real time in California in 2020. Los Angeles Mayor Eric Garcetti issued a plan to shut off utility

---

"List of Dishonest Persons"

"Liu Hu is a journalist in China, writing about censorship and government corruption. Because of his work, Liu has been arrested and fined—and blacklisted. Liu found he was named on a List of Dishonest Persons Subject to Enforcement by the Supreme People's Court as 'not qualified' to buy a plane ticket, and banned from traveling some train lines, buying property, or taking out a loan," reported *Wired* in 2019.

"There was no file, no police warrant, no official advance notification. They just cut me off from the things I was once entitled to," Liu said. "What's really scary is there's nothing you can do about it. You can report to no one. You are stuck in the middle of nowhere."[84]

service to homes in violation of COVID-19 lockdowns on private gatherings. Garcetti authorized "the city-controlled Department of Water and Power (DWP) to shut off utilities to homes and businesses that host unpermitted gatherings in violation of county and city stay-at-home orders." *Reason*'s Christian Britschgi noted that "Los Angeles County's public health order bans family gatherings and parties of any size. The City of Los Angeles' public health order bans gatherings of any size outside of residences, save for several listed exemptions, including protests."[85]

Left Behind in a Volcanic Eruption

To see a glimpse of our possible social-credit–determined future, look no further than the April 2021 volcanic eruption on Saint Vincent in the Caribbean. The volcano La Soufrière erupted and spewed plumes of hot ash into the air, and hot lava flowed, forcing residents to flee their homes and evacuate the island.

"'It's destroying everything in its path,' Erouscilla Joseph, director of the University of the West Indies' Seismic Research Center told the Associated Press. 'Anybody who would have not heeded the evacuation, they need to get out immediately.'"[86]

But only those residents who had already received the COVID-19 vaccine were allowed to exit via the cruise ships standing by to evacuate. *CBS Evening News* with Norah O'Donnell reported it this way: "Nearly twenty thousand people are out of their homes on the Caribbean island of St. Vincent, after the first volcanic eruption there in more than forty years. The volcano sent a thick cloud of smoke twenty thousand feet into the sky, spewing ash for miles. Cruise ships are evacuating people from the island, but only those vaccinated against COVID."[87]

"The Chief Medical Officer will be identifying the persons who are already vaccinated so we can get them on the ship," Prime Minister Ralph Gonsalves explained.[88]

Pennsylvania state representative Andrew Lewis was horrified. "This preferential treatment of populations facing imminent harm and even death—it is absolutely insane. We need to stop this in its tracks and treat all people equally while PROTECTING their medical privacy," Lewis wrote.[89]

But many seemed to be happy with discrimination on the basis of vaccine status. CNN anchor Don Lemon said, "You've got to start telling people, 'If you don't get vaccinated, you can't come into this office or this place of business. If you don't get vaccinated, you can't come to work. If you don't get vaccinated, you can't come into this gym. If you don't get vaccinated, you can't...get onto this airplane.' It, this has nothing to do with freedom. It has nothing to do with liberty. You don't have the freedom and the liberty to put other people in jeopardy," Lemon said.[90]

Democrat New York State assemblyman Patrick Burke proposed a "bill that would allow health insurance companies to deny coverage to those who refuse to get vaccinated against Covid-19." Burke explained, "I'm introducing a bill that allows insurance providers to deny coverage for Covid related treatment to those who refuse to be vaccinated."[91]

Staff writer David Frum of *The Atlantic* suggested hospitals and doctors treat unvaccinated patients last. "Let hospitals quietly triage emergency care to serve the unvaccinated last," Frum tweeted.[92]

Governments around the world seemed eager to punish those who fail to obey their rules. "Pakistan's most populous province, Punjab, has decided to combat residents' COVID-19 vaccination hesitancy by threatening to block cell phone service to anyone who refuses inoculation," CBS News reported in an article titled, "Millions of Pakistanis Threatened with Cell Phone Cut-Off If They Don't Get a COVID Vaccine."[93]

In Nigeria, your ability to enter a bank and conduct financial transactions is at risk. "Edo State Governor Godwin Obaseki gave residents until mid-September to get vaccinated or risk being barred from certain places, including banks, private functions, churches and mosques," according to AfricaNews.com. "We have made adequate arrangements with the security agencies to prevent anyone without a vaccination card from entering these places," Obaseki stated.[94]

In the United States, conservative commentator Candace Owens revealed that a COVID-19 testing lab had denied her service due to opposition to COVID-19 mandates. Aspen Laboratories

> **Freedom**
>
> "Freedom ultimately means the right of other people to do things that you do not approve of."
> —economist Thomas Sowell[95]

cofounder Suzanna Lee wrote to Owens that the testing facility "cannot support anyone who has pro-actively worked to make this pandemic worse by spreading misinformation, politicizing and DISCOURAGING the wearing of masks and actively dissuading people from receiving life-saving vaccinations." Lee's email added, "It would be unfair to them and to the sacrifices we have all made this year to serve you."

"Owens responded that she believes in the 'freedom to choose,' but when health professionals 'begin choosing who is allowed to determine if they have covid—we are no longer in a public health crisis.'"[96]

Entertainer Pat Condell, a self-described "free speech fundamentalist" discussed the new normal of COVID-19 mandates:

> Vaccine passports were the plan from the start. The first step towards a Chinese-style social credit system and digital surveillance of the entire population.
>
> They will keep adding aspects of your life to the app until it knows everything about you and you can't do anything without its permission.
>
> When they get rid of cash and make all financial transactions electronic, the government will decide how and where you can spend your money.
>
> If you drink too much, you're not allowed to buy alcohol today, for your own good. If you're too fat, you can't have that cake. Have an apple instead, for your own good.
>
> If you express opinions that offend the wrong people, you can be prevented from travelling or using the internet, or even buying food, until you change your thinking.

That's how things work in China right now. And it's what they intend to implement here. Vaccine passports are the first step towards total surveillance and control. If we're foolish enough to co-operate, we are signing our culture's death warrant.[97]

Real life validated Condell's warning. The Bank of England urged parliament to weigh in on whether digital currency "should be 'programmable,' ultimately giving the issuer control over how it is spent by the recipient," according to *The Telegraph.*

Tom Mutton, a director at the Bank of England, explained, "There could be some socially beneficial outcomes from that, preventing activity which is seen to be socially harmful in some way. But at the same time it could be a restriction on people's freedoms."

Sir Jon Cunliffe, a deputy governor at the Bank of England, noted, "You could think of giving your children pocket money, but programming the money so that it couldn't be used for sweets. There is a whole range of things that money could do, programmable money, which we cannot do with the current technology."[98]

Meanwhile, Chase Bank canceled the credit cards of former Trump administration national security advisor Lieutenant General Michael Flynn in 2021, citing his "possible reputational risk to our company." As Chase explained to Flynn, "After careful consideration, we decided to close your credit cards on September 18, 2021, because continuing the relationship creates possible reputational risk to our company." Flynn cards were canceled not for COVID-19 related issues, but because he had worked with former president Donald Trump. After an uproar, Chase reversed itself and said it had been a "mistake" to cancel the credit cards.[99]

In 2022, the Biden administration announced support for a U.S. Central Bank Digital Currency.[100]

And Neil Parmenter, the president and CEO of the Canadian Bankers Association, has said "Canada's banks are perfectly situated to help lead the creation of a federated digital ID system between government and the private sector. The World Economic Forum agrees."[101]

The forces pushing the Great Reset see decentralized digital cryptocurrencies like Bitcoin as a threat to the global central banks and their agendas. For the same reasons that corporations and retail chains are much easier to control with woke ideology than small independent businesses, centralized, government-run digital currency is the goal, instead of decentralized cryptocurrencies.

The Canadian truckers' "Freedom Convoy" protest against vaccine mandates and other COVID-19 restrictions provided a preview of the banking aspects of the Great Reset, as Prime Minister Justin Trudeau's administration punished the truckers by freezing their bank accounts and ability to fundraise. "The Canadian government, especially by invoking the Emergencies Act, has ushered in a coming totalitarianism," wrote Annelise Butler of the Center for Technology Policy at The Heritage Foundation. "The act...put into effect to crush the convoy, empowered the Canadian government, according to Business Insider, to 'temporarily override civil rights, restrict travel, forbid public assembly, and force businesses to act without compensation.'"[102]

Donations of $10 million for the trucker's protest to the crowdfunding site GoFundMe were withheld by GoFundMe, acting at the behest of Trudeau's government. An alternative fundraising company, GiveSendGo tried to fill the void and raised millions, but Canadian officials then began to freeze the accounts of anyone who was involved in or donated to the trucker convey. GiveSendGo was forced to refund the donations it received.[103]

For his part, Trudeau revealed he had no self-awareness about the two years of brutal lockdowns he imposed on Canadians. "Individuals are trying to blockade our economy, our democracy, and our fellow citizens' daily lives. It has to stop," Trudeau said of the trucker protest, without a hint of irony.[104]

"Financial deplatforming, or banking censorship, will be a common lever for governments and companies when they decide to silence political opinions," as Butler noted.[105]

Samantha Hoffman, of the Australian Strategic Policy Institute, explained the real motives behind these schemes. "China's social credit system is a state-driven program designed to do one thing, to uphold and expand the Chinese Communist Party's power," Hoffman said.

"In Mao's China, the Mass Line relied on ideological mass mobilization, using Mao Zedong's personal charisma, to force participation," according to Hoffman. "The CCP could no longer, after the Mao era, rely on ideological mobilization as the primary tool for operationalizing social management."

"The west should not copy any aspect of social credit," Hoffman urged. "Often comparisons are drawn between private applications like Uber and its rating system for customers and drivers. While these private company systems are extremely problematic in my view, they are fundamentally different. The People's Republic of China is an authoritarian country, the Chinese Communist Party is responsible for gross human rights violations for decades—just look at the example of Xinjiang now. There is nothing any liberal democratic society should even think about copying in the social credit system."[106]

Naomi Wolf laid out a chilling vision of how close America is to digital tyranny. "It takes half an hour to tweak the back end of a yes-or-no, have-you-been-vaccinated digital product and add Apple Pay or Google Wallet, which is what Microsoft with Oracle and Salesforce have already created. They want to embed—they have embedded the vaccine-status verification digital into Apple Pay and Google Wallet, which means that your income can be switched on or off. Your business can be suspended if you don't comply with whatever the people in power decide."

Wolf presented the reality of the current state of digital surveillance to the legislature: "It takes a half an hour to add AI [artificial intelligence] that reads your social media commentary into this app, so that if you

> **"You Will Never Be Free Again"**
> "Health Passport. Vaccine Certificate. Immunity Card. Society Permit. Freedom Pass. Whatever they call it, if you accept the concept you will never be free again." —Bob Moran, cartoonist for *The Telegraph*[107]

might have said something on social media supportive of conservatives or supportive of liberals, that can dial down or dial up your score on this app in real time. And not only that, within a heartbeat, you can add your credit history, so that your ability to get credit can be suspended or made easier or more difficult digitally so easily, depending on if you've complied with getting vaccinated or not getting vaccinated."

"With a vaccine passport in use—as in my state of New York, as they're rolling out in Southern California, as they're already rolling out in Canada, as the people in Israel are sending us messages saying, save us! Tell the world what's happening to us. We're a two-tier society already—your app can geolocate you," Wolf testified.

Wolf explained that these apps can already track any of their users. "If you gather after this hearing, with your friends in a bar to discuss opposition to the vaccine passport, your app will know who you're meeting with because you'll have to swipe that QR code, which reads who you are, who your friends are."

"I've seen this software. It exists already—maps of your social networks—so that the app will know who you're hanging out with," she added.

"This is not a Chinese Communist–style social-credit system in the future. It's a Chinese Communist–style social-credit system now."[108]

By 2022, even the mainstream media could not miss the strangling of freedom by the COVID-19 restrictions and vaccine mandates. In a moment of clarity, Agence France-Presse (AFP) pointed out, "From a litany of lockdowns to mandatory mask-wearing and Covid passes to access entertainment and sporting venues, the pandemic has led to sweeping restrictions on civil liberties in some of the world's oldest democracies."

As AFP reported, "And from the Netherlands to Austria, Germany, Belgium and France, thousands of people have taken to the streets—sometimes clashing with police—to protest Covid rules and health passes."[109]

> ### "Traitors like You ... Are Going on the No-Fly List"
> Howard University emeritus chemistry professor Josh Halpern smeared me as a "traitor" he hopes is "going on the no fly list." He wrote on Twitter, "Traitors like you and your friends who backed Trump and his goons attacking the Capital [sic] are going on the no fly list anyhow."[110]
> But as I pointed out, "If Bill Gates gets his way 99.99 % of humanity will be on no-fly list since all the commercial airlines will have been bankrupted and out of business."[111]
> As we will see in detail in chapter 12, that's what the climate lobby and the globalists are planning: Closing airports in Britain and essentially making aviation an illegal act.[112]

The proponents of vaccine passports are quick to point out that in many cases it is technically "not the government," but rather private entities mandating them. The problem with this logic is that in requiring the passports the airline industry and other big corporations are doing the governments' bidding—essentially becoming a branch of the federal government. Big Tech and big business are relentlessly collecting all of this data on the basis of immunity status, and those efforts aid the vision of progressive government policies.

Robert F. Kennedy's organization, Children's Health Defense, is wary of the entire COVID-19 vaccination push, which started under President Donald Trump. "News organizations and journalists who raise legitimate concerns about [Operation] Warp Speed will be de-platformed to make way for the 'required' saturation of pro-vaccine messaging across the English-speaking media landscape," noted Whitney Webb in a report on RFK Jr.'s Children's Health Defense News & Views.

"Essentially, the power of the state is being wielded like never before to police online speech and to deplatform news websites to protect the interests of powerful corporations like Pfizer and other scandal-ridden pharmaceutical giants as well as the interests of the U.S. and U.K. national-security states, which themselves are intimately involved in the COVID-19 vaccination endeavor," Webb added.

"Officially a 'public-private partnership,' Operation Warp Speed, which has the goal of vaccinating 300 million Americans by

"Vaccine Refuseniks Could Need Deradicalising like Terrorists"

"Covid: Vaccine Refuseniks Could Need Deradicalising like Terrorists, Expert Says," read a headline at Britain's News Channel. That might be the only way to dissuade some hardcore anti-vaxxers from their beliefs. Professor Stephan Lewandowsky, who holds a chair in cognitive psychology at the University of Bristol, said: "They'll refuse anything—'I'm not going to wear a mask,' 'I'm not going to get vaccinated,' 'I don't think climate change is happening,' 'Covid is a hoax,' and, you know, 'Hillary Clinton is actually a reptilian shapeshifter.'" Lewandowsky argues society must "engage in what is effectively the same as a deradicalisation process for former terrorists, or cult members."[113]

next January, is dominated by the U.S. military and also involves several U.S. intelligence agencies, including the NSA and the Department of Homeland Security (DHS), as well as intelligence-linked tech giants Google, Oracle, and Palantir," Webb explained.[114]

In a speech in Switzerland, Kennedy summed up the global push for these mandates. "When they use the term 'vaccine misinformation,' they are using it as a euphemism for any statement that departs from official government policies and pharmaceutical industry profit taking. It has nothing to do with whether it's true or false; it only has to do with what the political implications are. And who is doing this censorship? It's government officials in league with Bill Gates, with Larry Ellison, with Mark Zuckerberg, with Sergey Brin from Google, and with all of these internet titans," said Kennedy, the author of *The Real Anthony Fauci: Bill Gates, Big Pharma, and the Global War on Democracy and Public Health.*

"They have engineered not only the destruction of our democracy and our civil rights—but they have engineered the biggest shift of wealth in human history: $3.8 trillion from working people to these handfuls of billionaires, many of them from Silicon Valley," he added.[115]

"We Have Lost Our Minds"

Brownstone Institute president Jeffrey Tucker lamented that cosmo-politan cities like New York have been transformed under COVID-19 lockdowns and vaccine passports. "You've got a kind of extreme segregation that's developing there in the city, and it was never voted on by the legislature either.... It was just issued by executive edict from a very unpopular mayor and implemented by public-health officials...who unleashed the cops," noted Tucker, who is the author of the book *Liberty or Lockdown*.

"It's like this machine that's just devouring the city with ever more controls, ever more absurd levels of despotism," he said. "Right now, the crime situation in New York—it is really a very volatile situation. But what are the cops doing? They're going from bars to restaurants and enforcing, with very heavy fines, the vaccine passports."[116]

But former New York City mayor Bill de Blasio was proud of how he used the coercive powers of the government to compel the citizens to comply with the city's vaccine mandates. "We know these mandates work. And we know people respond—look, human beings are pretty predictable. If you say your paycheck depends on it, or your ability to enjoy life and go do the things you want to do, people will make the practical decision overwhelmingly. And they'll go get vaccinated. But we aren't pushing hard enough. We got to go farther," de Blasio said.[117]

These are the kind of government policies and philosophy that enrage Tucker. "We have lost our minds," Tucker explained. "The notion that you would have freedom and normalcy, you know, as the path to greatness seems to not even be part of our public life...anymore.... It feels as if the philosophical foundations of the American republic just kind of got decayed at some point, to the point that they just actually collapsed," Tucker argued. "Somehow this is just lost on people, what's happening in New York. . . .

"We have to really decide as a country and as a society what kind of world we want to live in. And I don't think this is it."[118]

CHAPTER 9

"One of the Greatest Transfers of Wealth in History"

W e're *NOT* "all in this together"!
The earnings of billionaires reached new highs during COVID-19 lockdowns. And the promoters of the Great Reset could not have been happier. Where were the progressives outraged over the COVID-19 lockdowns or expressing any concern about how they were making society less economically equal? The only outrage from the Left was in favor of harder, stricter, more oppressive lockdowns. And advocates of economic "degrowth" and "planned recessions" were buoyed by lockdowns crushing economic growth—despite how they hurt the poor.[1]

"Billionaire wealth reached record high levels amid the COVID-19 pandemic, a report by UBS and PwC found, as a rally in stock prices and gains in technology and healthcare helped the wealth of the world's richest break the $10 trillion mark," Reuters reported.[2]

CNBC business analyst Jim Cramer has said that the lockdowns led to "one of the greatest wealth transfers in history."

As Cramer pointed out, "This is the first recession where big business...is coming through virtually unscathed."[3]

Intended Consequences

In the COVID lockdowns the rich got richer, and the poor got poorer.

Was all of this an unintended consequence of the lockdowns—or a very *intended* consequence?

Regardless of your view on that point, the COVID-19 restrictions served to further advance the Great Reset agenda.

Schwab was very clear that COVID restrictions served his Great Reset. "People assume we are just going back to the good, old world which we had and everything will be normal again in how we are used to normal—in the old fashion. This is, let's say, fiction. It will not happen," Klaus said on July 14, 2020, during a livestream while promoting his book, *COVID-19: The Great Reset.*[4]

Justin Haskins, the director of the Heartland Institute's Stopping Socialism Project warned that the WEF and its allies are using COVID as an excuse to implement "an international, digital currency," Haskins noted. A digital currency will allow "the government to micromanage every aspect of the economy," he said. Haskins, the coauthor of *The Great Reset: Joe Biden and the Rise of Twenty-First Century-Fascism*, also warned the Great Reset is setting up "a China model of capitalism-authoritarianism."[5]

Jay Lehr, writing at CFACT.org, agreed, explaining that the Great Reset's "goal is the complete removal of cash and banks in their previous form and the introduction of digital money from central banks. The end goal says German economist Ernst Wolf is for us all to have a single account through which all transactions are run."[6]

Lockdowns are very effective—but not at stopping viruses. Lockdowns are effective at destroying economies, leveling them down to the ground in order to "Build Back Better," a favorite slogan of the Biden Administration and other politicians. Economist Sanjeev Sabhlok has aptly described what lockdowns really do. "This is like a mass scale bombing of one's own economy," Sabhlok explained.[7]

Economic collapse, runaway inflation, surging unemployment, small businesses decimated, seemingly endless COVID "relief" payments from the federal government to help "solve" a problem the government needlessly created. The more the economy and society are destroyed through strict government lockdowns, the more dependent the citizens are upon government officials to loosen up restrictions and to send stimulus checks. The economic damage from the lockdowns makes people dependent on the very politicians who did this to them and creates more incentives for even bigger government expansion.

Thus the lockdowns have fast-tracked the progressive dream of a government-supplied "universal basic income" for everyone, instead of a job. In 1972 Democrat candidate George McGovern proposed a guaranteed annual income as a presidential candidate. At the time the idea was so out there that even his fellow Democrats like Hubert Humphrey opposed it.

Universal basic income (UBI) advocate Scott Santens describes how the issue played at the May 8, 1972, presidential debate: "On the night of their debate McGovern took the stage against Humphrey with no real understanding of what the net distributive impact of his [federal guaranteed-income proposal] looked like, and so when Humphrey attacked it upon claims it would increase the taxes of middle class families earning $12,000 by $400 ($75,000 by $2,500 in 2019), McGovern couldn't defend it.... When one of the moderators responded in complete surprise, 'But you're asking us to accept a program that you can't tell us how much it's going to cost,' McGovern answered, 'That's exactly right.'"[8]

Fast forward to today. No one seems to care how much anything is going to cost. We have seen broad bipartisan support for massive government "COVID relief" checks to Americans. COVID lockdowns were a gift to the proponents of a universal basic income guaranteed by the government.

Many wondered why governments kept the screws on their populations for years, with lockdowns and other restrictions. Consider this possibility: What if every negative lockdown consequence was actually the desired outcome? Locking down increased the power of the state and gave governors, mayors, and other state and local officials more money from federal bailouts to solve the very problems the government had created in the first place. It was a very attractive move to use a declared "national emergency" to help cover up decades of poor mismanagement of the economy. And the lockdowns were the perfect way to set up the Great Reset.

During the pandemic, states and cities were essentially bribed by the federal government to lock down their local economies. Keeping the declared health emergency was key to ensuring that the federal assistance money spigots kept flowing.[9] It turns out it was not about following the science. It was about following the money.

Los Angeles mayor Eric Garcetti was "ecstatic" when, in March of 2021, his long, brutal lockdown was rewarded with the tidy sum of $1.35 billion in COVID relief from the federal government.[10] In short, the federal bailout of COVID "relief" from the Biden administration was paying for the lockdown that bankrupted the city.

Mayor Eric Garcetti beamed, "Now with this money, we can put that money back into the savings account, we can pay off the credit card, deliver life-saving mental health services, and unarmed response as we reimagine public safety, money to improve our pensions, lower people's healthcare costs, support students with disabilities."[11]

Los Angeles controller Ron Galperin said the huge federal bailout of the city would "transform a very dire financial situation into a much better one, maintain services, build equity and jumpstart the economy."[12]

"Cancel Everything"

Los Angeles mayor Eric Garcetti boldly declared in December 2020, "It's time to cancel everything." He added, "Just be smart and stay apart," and he issued a proclamation to that effect: "All persons living within the City of Los Angeles are hereby ordered to remain in their homes."[13]

Garcetti even banned . . . walking! Okay, only the "unnecessary" kind of walking, The Daily Caller reported. Aside from "limited exceptions," the Los Angeles COVID order prohibited "all travel, including, without limitation, travel on foot, bicycle, scooter, motorcycle, automobile, or public transit."[14]

Amazon was one of the biggest beneficiaries of the lockdowns, doubling its profit to $5.2 billion as stay-at-home orders and curfews created a boom in online shopping.[15]

And in April 2020 Amazon CEO Jeff Bezos suggested that "regular testing on a global scale" was necessary so that "everyone who tests negative could reenter the economy with confidence."[16]

At the time I commented, "Bezos says more testing is necessary before the economy can be reopened. Hmm, might Mr. Bezos have an interest in keeping retail stores closed?"[17]

And Amazon was not alone in profiting during the lockdowns. As *The Guardian* reported, "Tech giants' shares soar as companies benefit from Covid-19 pandemic: Amazon, Apple, Facebook and Google reported positive quarterly results even as overall US economic growth fell by 32.9%."[18]

"Obliterate the Middle Class"

Activist Robert F. Kennedy Jr. was very clear on who benefits from lockdowns and who the victims are. "The pandemic is a crisis of convenience—for the elites who are dictating these policies. It gives them the ability to obliterate the middle class, to destroy the institutions of democracy, to shift all of our wealth, from all of us, to a handful of billionaires to make themselves rich by impoverishing the rest of us," Kennedy declared at an anti-lockdown protest rally in Berlin in 2020.[19]

Amidst the coronavirus lockdowns in October 2020, the Bloomberg Billionaires Index found that "the world's 500 richest people are a combined $813 billion richer now than they were at the beginning of the year."[20]

If lockdowns are imposed for long enough, all that will be left are big corporate businesses. Lockdowns are the greatest and most rapid accelerator of corporate power and the consolidation of our economy in our history. This is all part of the Great Reset. Small businesses are destroyed while billionaires and national corporate-retail chains benefit.

Ironically, this crushing of small businesses, the mom-and-pop operations that drive America, was being pushed and overseen by the very people supposed to be the nemesis of big businesses and the champions of the little guy—progressives and the Democrat Party.

> ### "New York City Is Dead Forever"
>
> In 2020, New York City nightclub owner and former hedge-fund manager James Altucher wrote an epitaph for the Big Apple. New York City is "completely dead," he wrote in an essay for the *New York Post*. "'But NYC always always bounces back.' No. Not this time. 'But NYC is the center of the financial universe. Opportunities will flourish here again.' Not this time," Altucher wrote. "'NYC has experienced worse.' No, it hasn't," he argued.[21]

Why would progressives be copacetic with corporations growing enormously in power? The simple answer that is progressives are no longer opposed to "big business" because they now control the corporate boardrooms with their woke agenda and their green virtue signaling. Why would the Left be opposed to big corporations when those corporations are at the beck and call of the woke left, terrified to offend against any aspect of the progressive agenda—critical race theory, transgenderism, climate change, vaccine passports, lockdowns, and so on.

Biotech entrepreneur Vivek Ramaswamy, author of the book *Woke, Inc.: Inside Corporate America's Social Justice Scam*, explained how financial policy drives the Great Reset. "We're going through this thing that everyone calls The Great Reset, the stakeholder capitalism revolution, where we dissolve the boundaries between government actors and private companies to advance a single progressive globalist agenda," Ramaswamy explained.[22]

And that "progressive globalist agenda" relies on pushing wokeness to achieve its goals. "A bunch of woke millennials get together with a bunch of big banks—together they birth woke capitalism, and then they put Occupy Wall Street up for adoption. And that's really when wokeness met capitalism," Ramaswamy explained.

"It's an arranged marriage, but not of love. It is more like mutual prostitution because each side in this marriage secretly has contempt for the other.... And any marriage in which each side secretly disdains the other isn't going to end well," he added. "This bilateral arranged marriage actually turns into what I call a threesome, which is the Communist Party of China getting in on the act."

Ramaswamy detailed China's role in this arrangement, explaining that China says, "If we can get those companies to criticize the United States in the United States, but stay silent about our actual human rights abuses here in China, we can do the thing that we could have never done with our nuclear arsenal, and that is to undermine the moral standing of the United States on the global stage."[23]

The pro-lockdown forces know it is easier to impose the Great Reset with small businesses destroyed, the middle class decimated, and a dominant and growing corporate culture under the control of progressive activists. While small independent stores could serve as the hotbed of rebellion, it is much easier to get big retail to be compliant to the agenda of academia, Big Tech, and our government overlords. So eliminate the rebels through lockdown policies.

"A Doubling of World Poverty"

By the end of 2020, the evidence of the massive redistribution of wealth to the elite classes was too much to go unnoticed by even the World Health Organization. David Nabarro, the WHO's special envoy for COVID-19, called the lockdowns "a terrible, ghastly global catastrophe" in an interview with *The Spectator*.

"Look what's happening to poverty levels. It seems that we may well have a doubling of world poverty by next year. We may well have at least a doubling of child malnutrition because children are not getting meals at school, and their parents, in poor families, are not able to afford it," Nabarro said.

"We in the World Health Organization do not advocate lockdowns as the primary means of control of this virus," he added. "The only time we believe a lockdown is justified is to buy you time to reorganize, regroup, rebalance your resources, protect your health workers who are exhausted, but by and large, we'd rather not do it."

Nabarro pointed out, "Just look at what's happened to the tourism industry, for example in the Caribbean or in the Pacific, because people aren't taking their holidays. Look what's happened to smallholder farmers all over the world because their markets have got dented."[24]

UNICEF (United Nations International Children's Emergency Fund) warned that lockdowns could kill more than COVID-19. "'Indiscriminate lockdowns' are an ineffective way to control Covid and could contribute to a 45 per cent rise in child mortality," UNICEF explained, according to *The Telegraph*—1.2 million child deaths.[25]

"Covid-19 has reversed years of gains in the war on poverty. Politicians deserve much of the blame," blared *The Economist* in September 2020, adding that the authorities were "failing the poor."

The article stated that the "coronavirus affects everyone, but not equally."

"The rich shrug off the economic shock; the poor cannot. Because of covid-19, the number of extremely poor people (i.e., those making less than $1.90 a day) will rise by 70m–100m this year, the World Bank predicts. Using a broader measure, including those who lack basic shelter or clean water and children who go hungry, the ranks of the poor will swell by 240m–490m this year, says the UN," setting the stage for future years in which "malnutrition will have stunted a tragic number of children's bodies and minds."[26]

Stavroula Pabst and Max Blumenthal, a former writer for *The Nation* and now the editor-in-chief of The Grayzone, detailed the inequity of the lockdowns. "Throughout 2020 in New York City, Black and Latino residents received a whopping 80% of police summonses for supposedly violating social distancing measures, leading civil rights groups including a local chapter of Black Lives Matter to complain that Covid restrictions were being exploited to bring back dreaded 'stop and frisk' policies," they wrote. "For governments across the world, Covid provided an opportunity to pummel their most vulnerable residents, as well as those who dissented from the official order."[27]

In early 2020, the pre–coronavirus-lockdown economy was booming. Black and Hispanic unemployment were at or near record lows.[28] COVID lockdowns changed those facts almost overnight.

As I commented on Twitter on November 6, 2020, Donald Trump "allowed Fauci to set narrative of fear & lockdowns & tanked the economy." I also pointed out that the virus fears stoked by Fauci had justified the mail-in ballots that guaranteed the president's defeat in the 2020 election: "Trump set up his own loss."[29]

Government Shutdowns BAD, COVID Lockdowns GOOD

One of the most telling revelations of the COVID pandemic was how the media and progressives, who freak out when the federal government is shut down for weeks or even days during a budget battle, fully supported the COVID lockdowns that shut down the entire economy and society for months and years. On January 7, 2019, the *New York Times* reported of a government shutdown that at that point had lasted for less than two and a half weeks: "The standoff is beginning to inflict pain on Americans, whose lives are affected, in one way or another, by the federal government" and "delayed mortgage applications, missed paychecks and stymied farmers are among the repercussions of a shutdown with no end in sight."[30]

There seemed to be no similar concern on the part of the media for Americans whose lives were devastated by the seemingly endless COVID lockdowns.

The lockdowns were very good for the wealthy across the globe. "Between April 7 and July 31 this year, billionaires across every industry covered by the study saw their wealth rise by double digits, with billionaires in the technology, healthcare and industrial sectors leading the pack with 36%–44% gains," Reuters reported.[31]

Other studies shed more light on the billionaires' ball. "American billionaires haven't been just immune to the pandemic, they have been thriving in it, drastically increasing their collective wealth," explained Niall McCarthy of Statista.

"An analysis by Chuck Collins at the Institute for Policy Studies found that American billionaires have seen their wealth grow by $1 trillion since March of [2020]—more than 34 percent," Mccarthy reported.

"There were numerous impressive financial gains among notable billionaires on the list with Jeff Bezos growing his fortune by $69.4 billion between March 17 and November 24. The Amazon boss and richest man on the planet is now worth $182.4 billion."

No Equity in the Lockdowns

"Payday, predatory lenders racked up record profits in 2020," said Bloomberg news, of an industry that "often targets Black and Latino communities."

"Charging 589% interest in the Pandemic is a booming business," the news outlet reported. "So good was 2020, in fact, for certain providers of payday and other high-interest loans that they're emerging from the pandemic stronger than perhaps ever before, a development that's encouraging them to aggressively ratchet up lending now as the economy rebounds," Bloomberg noted in May 2021

"Debt collectors had a big year, and so did predatory lenders," Lauren Saunders, associate director at the National Consumer Law Center told Bloomberg.[32]

Interestingly, the COVID lockdowns had a decidedly different impact from past financial downturns.

During "the 2008 financial crisis...it took Forbes' 400 richest people three years to recoup their losses from the Great Recession. The latest findings highlight a wealth gain by a mere 650 individuals that seems obscene at a time when nearly 7 million Americans are at risk of eviction when moratoriums expire at the end of the year," Niall McCarthy explained.[33]

So in 2020, the rich were getting richer during an economic collapse they helped create and support and extend. Nothing like disaster capitalism to bring "equity" to the world.

California governor Gavin Newsom even bragged that his lockdowns were—producing more billionaires!

Newsom rejected criticisms of his California COVID lockdowns harming businesses, citing "all the new billionaires" and bragging that his state's "richest people are doing pretty damn well."[34] Yes, there was never a better time to be a billionaire than during massive government lockdowns.

> ## "Bill Gates Is Not the One in Overalls"
> "Farmers [are being] turned into renters" as Bill Gates becomes the "nation's largest farmland owner" by using "a web of at least 22 limited liability shell companies," reported NBC News in 2021. "Young farmers" are "going up against these billionaire investors. . . . Who can compete with the likes of Bill Gates, right? More and more we are seeing farmers turn into renters," tech reporter April Glaser explained, noting that more farmland could be "gobbled up by an investor class."
>
> "Bill Gates isn't the one in overalls," Glaser pointed out. "He is not the one on the tractor doing the farming. He is the landlord here."[35]

In December 2020 Bill Gates informed the world that COVID lockdowns and mask mandates had to continue "even through early 2022" and warned that the world might never be able to return to "normal." Gates also said that "sadly, that's appropriate" for small businesses like bars and restaurants to be forced to close for yet another "four to six months." Gates warned of the risk of viral "reintroduction" and said we need to keep "big public gatherings" restricted.[36]

The *New York Times* reported in 2022 that remnants of lockdowns continued to decimate the restaurant industry in politically blue areas of the United States. "In the country's most liberal cities, many people are still avoiding restaurants. The number of seated diners last month was at least 40 percent below prepandemic levels in New York, Philadelphia, Minneapolis, San Francisco, Portland, Ore., and Cambridge, Mass., according to OpenTable. By contrast, the number of diners has fully recovered in Las Vegas, Miami, Nashville, Phoenix, Charlotte, N.C., and Austin, Texas, as well as in

Oklahoma, Nebraska and New Hampshire," the *Times* reported on March 3, 2022.[37]

"Good Little Proles"

"Who loves lockdowns? Who makes more money in lockdowns than anyone else? Why, the richest and biggest companies in the world—the tech giants, the mega-retailers, and don't forget Wall Street! Good times. Did you have fun this spring? They did," noted Alex Berenson in October 2020.[38]

"So at what point are the rest of us going to tire of billionaires—whose lives are completely unaffected by lockdowns, school closures, travel restrictions, and all the rest—telling us good little proles that we just have to wait a few more months?" Berenson asked in December 2020.[39]

The lockdowns were quite simply a bonanza for the ruling classes. "Profits on Wall Street reached $27.6 billion in the first six months of the year, an 82% increase over the same period in 2019," is how the media conveyed the revealing report released by New York comptroller Tom DiNapoli's office in 2020.[40] "The profits of the first half of the year are nearly equal to all of 2019's pre-tax earnings of $28.1 billion," Nick Reisman of Spectrum News reported.

However, the rosy picture faded when it came to Main Street. "The report, examining the financial industry's performance in New York, comes as a devastating pandemic has shuttered small businesses, some never to reopen, and created unemployment spikes not seen since the Great Depression," Reisman observed.

Small business owners continued to get hammered by the lockdowns. Even when lockdowns temporarily eased a bit in late spring 2021, as the public health officials attributed the vaccines with reducing the virus, restaurants found it a tough slog to rehire workers due to government policies.

"The food service industry is having a hard time hiring employees, a difficulty owners blame in part on the disincentivizing effects of supercharged federal unemployment benefits, which are paid to individuals on top of their state benefits," reported Just the News.

House Majority Leader Steny Hoyer noted that the "$600 weekly supplemental jobless benefits were 'very, very hard for any employer to replicate.'"

Eric Terry, president of the Virginia Restaurant, Lodging, and Travel Association was more blunt. "I think some people are more comfortable not coming back to the workforce right now and collecting unemployment," Terry said.

> ### "Irreversibly F***ed"
> Podcast host Joe Rogan of *The Joe Rogan Experience* mourned the state of American cities like New York and Los Angeles in 2021. "[Cities] can be irreversibly fucked, like I think some of our cities are right now. I think there's some there's some sections in LA, I don't know how the f**k they're gonna bounce back. You drive down the street and you see everything boarded up. You go, 'How does this come back? How long does it take?'" Rogan vented. "A lot of people are moving out. People are moving out. You get the sense like it's an abandoned ship, like it's a sinking ship."[41]

An Alabama restaurant owner laid out the "new normal" in America. "You've gone on unemployment, and people can sit at home and make the same exact amount sitting on the couch, so it's kind of hard to get people to work," the restaurant owner explained to WVTM 13.[42]

"Workers lost $3.7 trillion in earnings during the pandemic. Women and Gen Z saw the biggest losses," noted Business Insider in 2021, summarizing a report from the International Labour Organization.

Globally, workers lost an estimated $3.7 trillion in earnings during the COVID lockdowns, an 8.3% decline, according to a report from the International Labour Organization. American workers saw the biggest earnings loss, with an "unprecedented" 10.3 percent drop.[43]

Meanwhile, the billionaires kept raking it in. "Billionaires made $3.9 trillion during the pandemic," Business Insider announced, citing an Oxfam report.[44] "The 1,000 richest people on the planet recouped their COVID-19 losses within just nine months, but it could take more than a decade for the world's poorest to recover from the economic impacts of the pandemic," the report explained.[45]

Joel Kotkin, author of the book *The Coming of Neo-Feudalism: A Warning to the Global Middle Class*, detailed how money has been flowing relentlessly to the billionaire class. "Five years ago, around four hundred billionaires owned as much as half of the world's assets. Today, only one hundred billionaires own that share, and Oxfam reduces that number to a mere twenty-six. In avowedly socialist China, the top one percent of the population holds about one-third of the country's wealth, up from 20 percent two decades ago," Kotkin explained in 2022.[46]

No-Fly Zone for Thee, but Not for Me

"Bill Gates just said that . . . we need to continue these lockdowns on bars, restaurants, small businesses. Meanwhile, the billionaire class is reaping all the benefits [of lockdowns]—his pals from Amazon, and Walmart, all other big-box [stores]. But what's interesting is that climate activists are now calling for flying only when it's 'morally justifiable' as the 'new normal' post-pandemic. And Bill Gates is in, sort of in on that. He is saying, well, business travel—he expects 50 percent reduction. So now if you want to fly commercial, if you're not Bill Gates or Leonardo DiCaprio or Al Gore, you need to come up with a 'morally justifiable' reason. This is what the climate activists are doing. So by crushing the airline industry and then by boosting private planes, that's what they're doing—they're living one way for themselves, and they're imposing another set of austerity on the rest of us." —Marc Morano on *Fox and Friends* in January 2021 discussing Bill Gates's $4 billion bid for the world's largest private jet company during global lockdowns[47]

The lockdowns were an important stride for the progressive agenda, and the proponents of the "degrowth" and "planned recessions" movement were pleased. As Axios reported in 2021, "The global economy shrank by an estimated 4.3% in 2020, according to data from the World Bank. That contraction was due both to the direct pain of the pandemic and the effects of social distancing measures, but it also led to a roughly 6% reduction in global carbon dioxide emissions—the biggest annual drop since WWII.... However accidental, 2020 represented perhaps the best example we've ever experienced of degrowthism in action."[48]

My 2021 book, *Green Fraud: Why the Green New Deal is Even Worse Than You Think*, devoted an entire chapter to the movement to impose "planned recessions" and "degrowth" on the economy to save the planet from climate change.[50]

For degrowthers, simply cleaning up the global economy by switching from fossil fuels to zero-carbon sources of energy isn't enough. Economic growth—the goal of essentially every government everywhere—is itself the problem.

> **"Massive Economic Loss"**
> "Turns out staying home is far from safe, not even including the enormous economic cost," wrote Willis Eschenbach, who had predicted "massive economic loss, increased deaths, and young men causing trouble in the streets" in March of 2020.[49]
>
> "Show us a scientific study showing lockdowns saved the health system. They just drove people indoors, and indoor transmission is far higher than outdoor transmission . . . plus the cost in terms of suicides, job loss, mental health, domestic violence, and child abuse was HUGE," Eschenbach tweeted.[51]

The movement now has its own dedicated academic journals, associations, and conferences.

The modern climate change agenda is based on a centrally planned suppression of economic growth. The UN Agenda 21 reads like a rough draft of New York Democratic congresswoman Alexandria Ocasio-Cortez's Green New Deal. Earth Summit chairman Maurice Strong announced at the 1992 UN Summit, "Current lifestyles and consumption patterns of the affluent middle class—involving meat intake, use of fossil fuels, appliances, air-conditioning, and suburban housing—are not sustainable," as Tom DeWeese of the American Policy Center reported.[52]

In order to "save" the Earth, Agenda 21 and the 2015 updated version, Agenda 2030, are very clear that a centrally planned New World Order is necessary. As the UN documents detail, "Effective execution of Agenda 21 will require a profound reorientation of all human society, unlike anything the world has ever experienced. It requires a major shift in the priorities of both governments and individuals, and an unprecedented redeployment of human and financial resources. This shift will demand that a concern for the environmental consequences of every human action be integrated into individual and collective decision-making at every level."[53]

Tom DeWeese explained, "The 350-page, 40-chapter Agenda 21 document was quite detailed and explicit in its purpose and goals." As DeWeese wrote, "From its inception in 1992 at the United Nation's Earth Summit, 50,000 delegates, heads of state, diplomats and non-governmental organizations (NGOs) hailed Agenda 21 as the 'comprehensive blueprint for the reorganization of human society.'"[54]

In 1992, Nancy Pelosi introduced a resolution in Congress to support "a comprehensive national strategy for sustainable development in accordance with the principles of Agenda 21."[55]

And as DeWeese pointed out, "In 1993, President Bill Clinton ordered the establishment of the President's Council for Sustainable Development, with the express purpose of enforcing the Agenda 21 blueprint into nearly every agency of the federal government to assure it became the law of the land."[56]

The powers behind the Great Reset understand how vital the climate change movement and its so-called solutions are to achieving their vision.

And climate activists love lockdowns, as we shall see in detail in chapters 11 and 12.

Meanwhile, many lament that the United States did not lock down sooner and more strictly. "Lockdown delays cost at least 36,000 lives, data show," the *New York Times* reported in 2020, claiming that locking down earlier would have saved lives. "Some 14,000 New Yorkers who died could be alive if New York City was locked down a week earlier than it was, when many parts of California closed up," the *Times* claimed, citing model-based research.[57]

The more their plans failed, the more the planners planned.

CHAPTER 10

Prominent Left-Wing Figures Dissent from the Great Reset

The looming threat of the Great Reset and continuing lockdowns forged unlikely new alliances between people who had seldom if ever been on the same political page. Conservatives and libertarians found themselves aligned with progressives like Naomi Wolf, Robert F. Kennedy Jr., Indian activist Vandana Shiva, and Bill Maher.

As COVID lockdowns helped accelerate the movement toward the Great Reset, the speedy and apparently total abrogation of liberty was too much for many well-known liberals. They objected to how COVID fears were being used to increase censorship and surveillance, and they opposed the inequity of lockdowns.

In an August 2020 speech in Berlin, liberal icon Robert F. Kennedy Jr. spoke out against the COVID-19 fear campaign, the lockdowns, the mask mandates, and the Davos agenda—making explicit comparisons to Nazi tactics.

"The governments love pandemics. They love pandemics for the same reason they love war. Because it gives them the ability to impose controls on the population that the population would otherwise never accept—creating institutions and mechanisms for orchestrating and imposing obedience," Kennedy, who authored the 2021 book *The Real Anthony Fauci: Bill Gates, Big Pharma, and the Global War on*

Democracy and Public Health, told a crowd of thousands protesting the lockdowns.

"Seventy-five years ago, Hermann Göring testified at the Nuremberg Trials. And he was asked, 'How did you make the German people go along with all this?' And he said, 'It's an easy thing. It's not anything to do with Nazism. It has to do with human nature. You can do this in a Nazi regime. You can do it in a Socialist regime. You can do it in a Communist regime. You can do it in a monarchy and a democracy. The only thing the government needs to make people into slaves is fear.'"

Kennedy focused on Dr. Anthony Fauci and Bill Gates during his speech, pointing out that people want "open government" and "leaders who are not going to lie to them" and "make up arbitrary rules and regulations to orchestrate the obedience of the population."

Kennedy said, "It's a mystery to me, that all of these big, important people like Bill Gates and Tony Fauci have been planning and thinking about this pandemic for decades—planning it so that we would all be

All Is Forgiven

Environmental activist Robert F. Kennedy Jr. went from being an advocate of jailing climate skeptics to an anti-lockdown freedom fighter. RFK Jr. told me during an interview in 2014 that he wanted to jail climate skeptics. "I wish there were a law you could punish them under. I don't think there is a law that you can punish those politicians under." At that time Kennedy added, "Do I think the Koch Brothers are treasonous? Yes, I do. . . . Do I think they should be in jail? I think they should be enjoying 'three hots and a cot' at The Hague with all the other war criminals."

But in 2020 I declared RFK Jr. my "new hero."

"RFK JR. SPOT ON about not being obedient to government and against lockdowns!" I wrote. "All is forgiven by me for him wanting to jail climate skeptics after this anti-lockdown speech! Maybe climate skeptics can work with RFK Jr. on opposing climate agenda someday. Climate skeptics have a big tent. We welcomed progressives Michael Moore & Michael Shellenberger, in 2020 and I am ready to welcome RFK Jr. to our issue as well."[1]

safe when the pandemic finally came. And yet, now that it is here, they don't seem to know what they are talking about," Kennedy said.

He urged, "We want health officials who don't have financial entanglements with the pharmaceutical industry—who are working for us and not Big Pharma. We want officials who care about our children's health and not about pharmaceutical profits or government control.

He added, "And the only thing that's between them and our children is this crowd that has come to Berlin.... We are going to demand our democracy back!"[2]

"Philanthro-Imperialism"

Liberal environmental activist Vandana Shiva, executive director of the Navdanya Trust, who has been described as "a physicist, ecofeminist, philosopher," came out strongly against the Great Reset in 2020.

"The Great Reset is about multinational corporate stakeholders at the World Economic Forum controlling as many elements of planetary life as they possibly can. From the digital data humans produce to each morsel of food we eat," explained Shiva, a self-described "food sovereignty advocate."

Shiva accused Bill Gates of "philanthro-imperialism" and said Gates was "emerging as the Columbus of the digital age."[3]

"Why do I call him today's Columbus? Because he is carving out new colonies," she added.

"Bill Gates does both: he takes living resources and our seeds and biodiversity, mines it into data and wants ownership along with his friends. And Mark Zuckerberg mines your data and your behaviors and turns it into the raw material," Shiva explained.

"You have enough data on what happened with Facebook selling data. This is a major threat to democracy," she added.

Shiva is concerned about small farmers in India being displaced and committing suicide at rising rates as their livelihood gives way to big corporations.[4]

"It's beyond Right and Left"

"I am advocating new alliances w/ people we don't agree w/ on lots of issues. It's beyond left & right & all about freedom vs tyranny of permanent lockdowns & rule by a small cadre of elites." –Marc Morano on Twitter in 2021, explaining why old political paradigms don't apply in the Great Reset[5]

Progressive commentator and comedian Jimmy Dore, who was a frequent on-air host for the left-wing show *The Young Turks*, criticized the lockdowns, Anthony Fauci, and Bill Gates during the COVID pandemic.

"Anybody who . . . the news media saw as being against Trump, they embraced. And so they've over-embraced Dr. Fauci, and they'll never give accurate criticisms of him. We do at this show, and other people think we're crazy. Why do you think that? Well, did you watch the segment? *Oh, no. But I just think Fauci's great. Isn't he? Just like Bill Gates. These are all angels sent from heaven to help us*," Dore mockingly explained.[6]

A report titled "The Big Tech Takeover of Agriculture Is Dangerous" at the website Grain explains why activists like Shiva are opposed. "Digital agriculture is building the centralized production systems upstream that will supply Big Tech's evolving operations downstream, which are rapidly displacing the small vendors, hawkers and other local actors who have long served to bring foods from small farmers to consumers. The stage is being set for today's small farmers and vendors to be tomorrow's pieceworkers for Big Tech companies."[7]

Shiva ripped the World Economic Forum's food plans. "WEF is parading fake science," she said, adding, "for Mr. Schwab to promote these technologies [imitation meat] as solutions proves that The Great Reset is about maintaining and empowering a corporate extraction machine and the private ownership of life."

Robert F. Kennedy Jr.'s website, Children's Health Defense, reported that the "WEF has promoted and partnered with an organization called EAT Forum. EAT Forum describes itself as a 'Davos for food' that plans to 'add value to business and industry' and 'set the political agenda.'"

As the report explained, "The organization also assists the United Nations Children's Fund (UNICEF) in the 'creation of new dietary guidelines' and sustainable development initiatives."

Children's Health Defense reported, "EAT network interacts closely with some of the biggest imitation meat companies, including Impossible Foods and other biotech companies, which aim to replace wholesome nutritious foods with genetically modified lab creations.... Impossible Foods was initially co-funded by Google, Jeff Bezos and Bill Gates."

Shiva pointed to a darker purpose behind WEF-sponsored diet plans: "EAT's proposed diet is not about nutrition at all, it's about big business and it's about a corporate takeover of the food system."[8]

Ten Steps to Fascism

We have seen how former Bill Clinton and Al Gore advisor and feminist icon Naomi Wolf spoke out in 2020 as COVID-19 lockdowns persisted past the "fifteen days to flatten the curve."

Wolf said, "If I'd known Biden was open to 'lockdowns'...which is something historically unprecedented...and a terrifying practice, one that won't ever end because elites love it, I would never have voted for him."[9] Wolf authored the 2022 book *The Bodies of Others: The New Authoritarians, COVID-19, and the War Against the Human.*

On her website, Wolf compared the COVID-19 lockdowns to tyranny.

"The 'lockdown'—mislabeled a 'quarantine'—as we are experiencing it now, has actually happened before on this planet: just not in open societies or in the contemporary West. Totalitarian and fascist societies have indeed often used mass restrictions of movement, curfews, and other ways of restricting the free association and free movement of citizens," Wolf wrote.

"But large-scale totalitarian-style restrictions of citizens' movements by the state are new to the postwar democratic West and unheard-of in actual open societies; even past pandemics . . . have not been excuses in such societies to venture into this drastic territory," she pointed out.[10]

Wolf reacted strongly to the United Kingdom's "Tier 3" COVID restrictions, which required, "People must not meet socially indoors or in most outdoor places with anybody they do not live with, or who is not in their support bubble; this includes in any private garden or at most outdoor venues."

"What?? What?? Pure insanity. Madness. You can't sit OUTSIDE with someone you don't LIVE WITH? You can't meet a potential date INDOORS OR OUTDOORS? Or a new friend? You can't meet your grandma OUTDOORS? Am I reading this correctly? England, this is not epidemiology, this is psychological torture on a grand scale," she explained.

"We all need to protect the health of others. But in a free society these measures except for very limited brief and temporary restrictions subject to regular constitutionally legitimate review, are voluntary," Wolf added.[11]

The liberal Wolf blasted both political parties. "The playbook of fascism, I must stress, is nonpartisan, and President Trump did not invent what we are living through now. He merely built upon it. The Ten Steps of Fascism were around long before he was. But turning the Covid-19 pandemic into an opportunity for authoritarianism isn't just an idea, it's happening as I laid out," Wolf explained in 2020.

"During the administration of President Obama, I (and several others) warned that Democrats were taking the authoritarian structures built up by George W. Bush, and adding news levels of oppression on the foundation already laid," she wrote.

"The war on whistleblowers intensified under President Obama's Department of Justice: He subpoenaed reporters such as James Risen. He advanced the prosecution of Chelsea Manning. President Obama went after more people under the Espionage Act than had any previous President, according to the Committee to Protect Journalists. Examples of his push to build up further the structures of fascism he inherited, could go on and on," Wolf explained.

"But since he was a telegenic President with an uplifting rhetorical style, not to mention the otherwise inspiring fact that he was our first

President of color, these abuses of democratic processes went disregarded by the left and by most mainstream media. The problem with Fascistic processes and institutions being built up, though, is that then they are there for the next President, the one you don't like, to use and to abuse. And here we are."

Now, Wolf points out, "We have very little time before we reach a point of no return." She explained in September 2020 that we have reached step ten of the "Ten Steps to Fascism": "Suspend the Rule of Law."[12]

Wolf had originally laid out the "Ten Steps to Fascism" in 2007.[13]

"It Pains Me to Say This"

Susan Collins, liberal Republican senator from Maine, expressed doubts about the Centers for Disease Control. "I used to have the utmost respect for the guidance from the CDC. I always considered the CDC to be the gold standard. I don't anymore," Collins confessed.

According to Dr. Sanjay Gupta of left-leaning CNN, Collins "might be right to question the guidance." Gupta admitted, "It pains me to say this, but I see where she's coming from, Senator Collins, on this."

"In the end, the CDC needs to be just a science-based organization," Gupta asserted. "What does the science say? You don't need to wear a mask outside. It's just one of these things that, again, we've known this for some time."[14]

"In Bed with the Chinese"

We have seen how Glenn Greenwald, an award-winning journalist who worked for Salon and the left-wing UK paper *The Guardian*, took notice of the ACLU's reversal on vaccine mandates. Greenwald seemed to make a significant political shift as the COVID lockdowns accelerated the Great Reset.

When conservative talk show host Glenn Beck interviewed Greenwald in 2021 about the Great Reset, Greenwald compared it to China's social credit system.

"Are you looking into the Great Reset? And if you have... what are your feelings on it?" Beck asked.

"Of course. First of all, that is already being done in China. Right? These kinds of numeric, or quantitative evaluations of various citizens and then determining which rights they do and don't have. It's becoming increasingly digitized so there are no humans making these decisions. It's all done algorithmically."

Greenwald added, "Wall Street and Silicon Valley are in bed with the Chinese, they are tied at the hip."[15]

Greenwald had previously warned about the U.S. government using clandestine surveillance under the guise of counterterrorism. Greenwald earned wide recognition for his reporting on whistleblower Edward Snowden, a former contractor for the U.S. National Security Agency.[16]

In 2020, Greenwald faced censorship head-on from his own media outlet, The Intercept, which he had cofounded in 2013. "The same trends of repression, censorship and ideological homogeneity plaguing the national press generally have engulfed the media outlet I co-founded, culminating in censorship of my own articles," Greenwald wrote in his October 29, 2020, resignation letter.[17]

Greenwald's concern focuses on the expansion of authoritarianism in the United States. "Go back to the debate right after the 9/11 attack when all of these radical proposals were introduced to increase power in the hands of the government like the PATRIOT Act, and the argument at the time was don't worry, these are temporary measures, they are only going to be in place for as long as is necessary to get this crisis, this emergency, under control," he explained.

"20 years later, the PATRIOT Act is very much in place. Every four years it's renewed without any opposition, its uses and application have wildly expanded beyond its original intention, it's almost never used for terrorism, it's used for all varieties of other means for the government to spy on its citizenry," Greenwald added.

"When you start building these bureaucratic apparatuses that vest power in the hands of the state to control the lives of citizens in the name of some temporary crisis, it never is temporary, it never goes away, there's never a political motive to dismantle it," he offered. "These powers once vested are going to be very difficult to pry out of the hands of government."[18]

"This Has Gotta Stop"

Musician Van Morrison, known for such hit singles as "Brown Eyed Girl," released three songs to protest the COVID-19 lockdowns: "No More Lockdown," "Born to Be Free," and "As I Walked Out."

"No More Lockdown" included these lyrics:

> No more taking of our freedom
> And our God-given rights
> Pretending it's for our safety
> When it's really to enslave.[19]

Morrison also collaborated with Eric Clapton on a fourth song against lockdowns called "Stand and Deliver."[20] In August, Clapton, known for songs such as "I Shot the Sheriff," released another anti-lockdown song: "This Has Gotta Stop."[21] In May 2021 he had said, "I've been a rebel all my life, against tyranny and arrogant authority, which is what we have now."[22]

"The Nazis Didn't Just Show Up One Day"

Commentator Dave Rubin, former host of the progressive show *The Young Turks* railed against the lockdowns. Rubin said he had been "a lifelong Democrat" but finally voted for the GOP in 2020.

"I have been a lifelong Democrat. I have voted for Obama twice, I voted for Gore, I voted for John Kerry, this is the first time I ever voted for a Republican president," the host of *The Dave Rubin Show* explained in October of 2020.[23]

Rubin did not hold back his disdain for the COVID lockdowns. "I don't think it's hyperbolic at this point to say there was virtually no science behind any of this—that the lockdowns did absolutely nothing. I mean, we know that. We absolutely know that the lockdowns did nothing. They have inflicted a psychological condition on people to now make us afraid of each other, to make us turn on each other," Rubin said in 2021.

"The irony is these are the people who call all of us Nazis. But the Nazis didn't just show up one day.... It is a process of othering people, saying the worst things about people. And now it's not just that our political views are odious and should be silenced and kicked off Big Tech and everything else. It's that we are literally killing people by not wearing masks," Rubin explained.[24]

Elon Musk Takes the Red Pill

Tesla founder Elon Musk, a climate change activist who endorsed Hillary Clinton for president in 2016 and Andrew Yang for the Democratic presidential nomination in 2020,[25] turned politics on its head in 2020.

"Give people their freedom back!" Musk demanded in spring of 2020, when the coronavirus lockdowns were in full swing.

"FREE AMERICA NOW," he declared in all caps on Twitter.

On the COVID lockdowns, Musk held nothing back. "The extension of shelter-in-place—or as I would call it, forcibly imprisoning people in their homes, against all constitutional right, and in my opinion infringing on people's freedoms in ways that are horrible and wrong, and not why people came to America or pulled this country—what the fuck?" Musk asked.[26]

Musk attacked virus-modeler professor Neil Ferguson over his "absurd fake science."[27] He also ripped CNN. "What I find most surprising is that CNN still exists," Musk wrote.[28] "Take the red pill," he urged, calling the lockdowns "fascist."

"This is not freedom—give people back their goddamn freedom!" he demanded.

Musk fully supported the protests in Canada against vaccine requirements and COVID lockdowns. "Canadian truckers rule," Musk tweeted. "If you scare people enough, they will demand removal of freedom. This is the path to tyranny," Musk wrote later the same day.[29]

"Take the red pill" was Musk going full *Matrix*. The 1999 film depicts the character Neo, played by Keanu Reeves, taking a red pill that opens his eyes to the reality that the world he lives in is a fake creation.

Musk even defiantly took on Alameda County, California, officials and announced he was going to defy the lockdowns and open up his production line. "Tesla is restarting production today against Alameda County rules. I will be on the line with everyone else. If anyone is arrested, I ask that it only be me," Musk wrote. Alameda County relented and re-opened.[30]

Stand-up comic, mixed martial arts commentator, and popular podcast host Joe Rogan ran afoul of social media censors and rose to even greater prominence by featuring guests challenging the COVID narrative.

Rogan has held politically left views for years. "I am not right-wing at all," Rogan declared.[31] "I think I'll probably vote for Bernie . . . He's been insanely consistent his entire life," Rogan announced in early 2020.[32]

But like many other figures on the Left, Rogan expressed shock about the digital-ID agenda of the Great Reset. "This is going to introduce the social credit score system," Rogan said in a 2021 episode of *The Joe Rogan Experience*, his podcast on Spotify. "That's a bizarre thing to do, to openly do. Why do you think they openly discuss it that way? . . . Because the Great Reset has always been this gigantic conspiracy theory among the online folks, 'Like this is all part of the Great Reset.' Well, when he [Klaus Schwab] wrote a fucking book called *The Great Reset*, you're like, 'Hey man, shouldn't you be hiding this?'"[33]

Comedian Jimmy Dore also spoke out publicly about the Great Reset. Dore expressed concern over digital vaccine passports and showed clips of the World Economic Forum's Klaus Schwab bragging about how he has trained young leaders like Canadian prime minister Justin Trudeau. "So now you know . . . the rest of the story. . . . Justin Trudeau has been groomed. . . . Everything will be on your digital ID, and you see . . . they want to do that so now they can control you. . . . As soon as you start to go against the establishment, they can use that because now they've got you, and they can shut you down," Dore said on his program, *The Jimmy Dore Show*.

"Why do you think that it doesn't matter if you vote Democrat or Republican or for Justin Trudeau? Because they all serve the same corporatist neoliberal agenda that serves Wall Street, the military-industrial complex, Big Pharma, fossil fuel companies. That's who runs our country. We're not a democracy," Dore explained.[34] "The quicker people realize that, that both parties are not on their side—they only serve the oligarchy; we are in fact in an oligarchy...."[35]

Civil liberties activist Jenin Younes joined the chorus of figures on the political left speaking out against the COVID mandates. Younes has described herself as "formerly left-leaning, now politically homeless."[36]

"How do people not see the dangers of 'show me your papers' regimes? We're just implementing a system where petty bureaucrats have total control over our freedom of movement?" Younes, an attorney with the D.C.–based New Civil Liberties Alliance, wrote.[37] "Yesterday someone I went to college with wrote and told me how sad it was to see I've joined the alt right. If opposing government tyranny and public health coercion that has no basis in logic, science, or ethics makes me alt right, then call me Marjorie Taylor Greene," she quipped.[38]

English actor and comedian Russell Brand has gotten attention attacking COVID mandates and exposing the Great Reset. Brand has a long history as a left-wing activist; in 2013 he declared, "I'm a bit of a tree-hugging, Hindu-tattooed, veggie meditator"[39] and said he supported "a socialist egalitarian system based on the massive redistribution of wealth, [with] heavy taxation of corporations."[40]

In 2022, Brand called out the World Economic Forum's Great Reset as having an "evil malicious agenda" and trying "to implement a set of policies that will lead to centralized power that facilitates an ongoing march towards dystopia." Brand mocked the annual Davos meetings. "If you want to improve the state of the world, don't invite the people that are most responsible for ruining the fucking thing in the first place. These are the people that are causing the bloody problem," he said.[41] "We've talked about how both Democrats and Republicans have increased surveillance and government emergency powers—all over the world this has taken place.... Maybe it's time to forget the right wing and the left wing and to focus on the bird in the middle, and hopefully that bird can fly us to something approaching freedom because you know what I want most of all is that you stay free," Brand suggested.[42]

The WEF wants to implement "a dumb idiom like 'You will own nothing and you will be happy.' No I won't. I'm going to keep holding of my stuff," Brand said. "They will exploit that opportunity to own more and more things till eventually you're left with nothing, creating a more and more unequal society with a tiny, tiny elite, where everybody else is just out in some barren wasteland owning nothing, having no resources, and forced to just be pitted against one another like it's a bloody hunger games or something in order to survive for an oligarchy of the increasingly powerful," he explained.[43]

Former Democrat congresswoman Cynthia McKinney and 2008 presidential nominee for the Green Party—the first African American woman to hold a U.S. congressional seat from Georgia—also spoke out vociferously against the Great Reset. "WEF Puppets and Core Members are kooks with power," McKinney tweeted.[44]

"Imagine you have an idea to make everyone a serf; it means you must bankrupt the middle class—take their land, their property; shutter their small and medium-sized businesses; bankrupt them. Lockdowns: the perfect solution for your idea to come true," McKinney wrote.[45]

In another tweet, she revealed her weekend movie choice. "Weekend Watching: Aldous Huxley's 'Brave New World' Ready for the Great Reset??" she asked.[46]

"'Leftugees' Flee Blue States"

"Democrats have implemented the harshest, most authoritarian restrictions on freedom of movement, freedom to participate in society, freedom to have an education, freedom to run a business, and more. People are moving to Republican-run states to be allowed to eat in restaurants, run their businesses, and educate their children in classrooms." –talk show host Kim Iversen of *The Hill*, in a YouTube clip subtitled "'Leftugees' Fly Blue States amid HORRIBLE Dem Policies, DIRE Need for Self-Reflection"[47]

264 THE GREAT RESET

Journalist Max Blumenthal, editor in chief of The Grayzone and former writer for *The Nation* and Media Matters for America, came out against the Great Reset and called out "the Lockdown Left" for supporting endless COVID mandates.[48]

Blumenthal summed up the WEF's vision this way during an interview on *The Jimmy Dore Show*: "You will own nothing and be happy. You'll just be stuck at home in your rented house getting, like, some crumbs off the Davos table.... You'll go crazy and fantasize about suicide and fall into addiction and miss your routine medical appointments, and you won't be able to organize any social movement because your protests are forbidden under lockdown."[49] Blumenthal and Stavroula Pabst wrote a lengthy article titled "Flattening the Curve or Flattening the Global Poor? How Covid Lockdowns Obliterate Human Rights and Crush the Most Vulnerable" for The Grayzone.[50]

"[BlackRock CEO] Larry Fink was advising the Trump administration on its COVID response, and BlackRock has experienced like a wet dream, where all these small businesses close, commercial real estate in 2020 collapsed, and they snap up at bargain-basement rate commercial real estate. They buy homes from people who've been...forced into foreclosure. I mean this has been the greatest time for BlackRock," Blumenthal said.

"Bill Gates's business empire is ten, twenty times bigger than the Koch brothers' and the lockdowns were a boon for him. Bill Gates's dream is to end in-person education because then everyone will be forced onto Microsoft technology, stuck at home," he added.

Blumenthal criticized many of his colleagues on the political left for being "Klaus Schwab's useful idiots. They're Bill Gates's useful idiots. They're Big Pharma's useful idiots, and they've never been forced to examine the logical contradictions of their own arguments," he said. "What is the agenda here? COVID's not going away, so everyone has to be locked down at home forever and given some UBI [universal basic income]? Is that the agenda?" he asked.

The Left "is not concerned with the construction of a biomedical security state where a healthy population has been defined as a public-health risk because they have not obeyed state mandates to take a Big Pharma product that does not prevent viral transmission," Blumenthal lamented.[51]

Joe Rogan to Bill Gates: "You Look like Shit"

In 2022, talk show host Joe Rogan called out Bill Gates for pushing fake meat and not presenting the look of a man concerned about public health. "You look like shit. If you're eating those plant-based burgers, or whatever you're doing, you're obese. A guy like that telling people about—he's got these breasts and this gut, and I'm like, this is crazy, you're one of the richest guys on earth. You have access to the best nutrients, the best amazing trainer, you could be in phenomenal shape, and you're giving out public health advice and you're sick," Rogan said of Gates. "Your health is piss poor. I'm not a doctor, but when you've got man boobs and a gut and you're walking around with these toothpick arms. I'm like, hey buddy, you're not healthy."[52]

"Whiter than Usual"

"Your dinners in Midtown and your shows at Webster Hall are going to be whiter than usual this fall, thanks to a new policy by New York City Mayor Bill De Blasio, which will disproportionately lock Hispanics and blacks out of indoor venues," Timothy P. Carney of the *Washington Examiner* pointed out in a 2021 article titled "Disparate Impact: Bill de Blasio's Vaccine Passport Rule Is Racist according to the Left's Definition."[53]

Black Lives Matter even targeted Mayor de Blasio's mandate. "Seventy-two percent of black people in this city from ages 18 to 44 are unvaccinated. So what is going to stop the Gestapo, I mean the NYPD, from rounding up black people, from snatching them off the train, off the bus?" said Chivona Newsome, a cofounder of BLM NYC, following a protest at a New York City restaurant.[54]

Even many in the left-wing media began speaking out about the racial inequity of lockdown restrictions and enforcement. "People in non-white communities will be more familiar with this feeling of being over-policed, but for many in the suburbs, the experience of being policed and fined without discretion was novel and unwelcome. It made them aware—some for the first time—of their civil liberties," wrote Brigid Delaney, a columnist for *The Guardian*.[55]

Hugh de Kretser, the executive director of the Human Rights Law Centre in Australia noted, "Before this pandemic, for many people living safe, comfortable lives, rights violations were things that happened to other people in other places. The pandemic changed that. People who never had to worry much about police were suddenly being stopped and fined for driving to an exercise location. A pregnant woman was arrested and handcuffed in front of her family over a Facebook post. Many people have had a taste of the kind of policing that Aboriginal people and migrants have been experiencing for decades," de Kretser said.[56]

Mixed Reactions

Some progressives had mixed feelings about the Great Reset. Liberal activist Naomi Klein, the chair of the media, culture, and feminist studies at Rutgers University and the author of *On Fire: The (Burning) Case for a Green New Deal* and *This Changes Everything: Capitalism vs. the Climate*, shrugged off concerns over the Great Reset.

"A viral conspiracy theory blends together legitimate critiques with truly dangerous anti-vaccination fantasies and outright coronavirus denialism," Klein wrote in December 2020 for The Intercept.

"I've been doing my best to ignore it for months, even when various Reset 'researchers' have insisted that all of this is an example of the shock doctrine, a term I coined a decade and a half ago to describe the many ways that elites try to harness deep disasters to push through policies that further enrich the already wealthy and restrict democratic liberties," Klein wrote.

"Search for the term 'global reset' and you will be bombarded with breathless 'exposés' of a secret globalist cabal, headed by Schwab and Bill Gates, that is using the state of shock created by the coronavirus (which is probably itself a 'hoax') to turn the world into a high-tech dictatorship that will take away your freedom forever."

Klein argued that both the Right and the Left are obsessing over the Great Reset, but in different ways.

If the Great Reset fears emanate from "the far right," it is portrayed as a "green/socialist/Venezuela/Soros/forced vaccine dictatorship," Klein wrote.

"If the exposé hails from the far left," it is seen as "a Big Pharma/GMO/biometric implants/5G/robot dog/forced vaccine dictatorship," she continued.

"Less a conspiracy theory than a conspiracy smoothie, the Great Reset has managed to mash up every freakout happening on the internet—left and right, true-ish, and off-the-wall—into one inchoate meta-scream about the unbearable nature of pandemic life under voracious capitalism," she explained.

But Klein does have some concerns about what she labeled the "reset conspiracy smoothie."

"What Schwab and the WEF are doing with the Great Reset is both more subtle and more insidious. Schwab is, of course, absolutely right when he says that the pandemic has revealed many deadly structural failures of capitalism as usual, as does the accelerating climate crisis and the hoovering of the planet's wealth up toward the Davos class, even in the midst of a global pandemic. But like the WEF's earlier big themes, the Great Reset is not a serious effort to actually solve the crises it describes," Klein wrote.

"On the contrary, it is an attempt to create a plausible impression that the huge winners in this system are on the verge of voluntarily setting greed aside to get serious about solving the raging crises that are radically destabilizing our world."[57]

The Anti-Defamation League fretted that concern about the Great Reset could undermine "faith in democratic institutions by casting its leaders as part of a globalist plot and can even lead to further threats of violence against government officials," a 2020 ADL commentary stated.

"As is so often the case with conspiracy theories, one can find anti-semitic sentiments in the Great Reset, with some believers going so far as to accuse Jews of orchestrating the plot or invoking George Soros and the Rothschild family," the ADL warned.[58]

The BBC labeled the Great Reset a "conspiracy theory" and explained why it is coalescing the political left and right. "The nebulous-ness of this conspiracy theory means it has found followers among anti-vaccine activists, anti-lockdown campaigners, new-age healers, and those on the far right and far left," the BBC Reality Check reported. "Experts say similar ideas about the emergence of a totalitarian world government have been circulating since the 1960s under the umbrella term New World Order, which itself borrows ideas from conspiracy theories of the 18th Century," according to the BBC.

"The term 'Great Reset' has received more than eight million interac-tions on Facebook and been shared almost two million times on Twitter since the initiative was launched," the BBC explained, noting that push-back from both the Left and Right had forced the World Economic Forum to admit the "messaging around the Great Reset didn't quite go to plan."[59]

The WEF issued a statement explaining: "Conspiracy theories replace reason with fantasy. They are a noisy but peripheral part of the public sphere.... We encourage rationally grounded, fact-based debate."[60]

In 2021 the WEF released a video responding to the global outcry over its plans. "It's not surprising that people who've been disenfran-chised by a broken system and pushed even further by the pandemic, will suspect global leaders of conspiracy, but the world's not that simple," the WEF video explained. The video went on to mock the idea that the Great Reset is "masking some nefarious plans for world domination" but acknowledged that the Great Reset "slogan hasn't gone down well."[61]

"Believing Such a Bunch of Crap"

After liberal icon Bill Maher left the COVID-lockdown fear nar-rative in 2021,[62] he slapped down mainstream media for COVID disinformation, asking, "If the right-wing media bubble has to own things like climate change denial, shouldn't liberal media have to answer for, 'How did your audience wind up believing such a bunch of crap about COVID?'"

"Liberals often mock the Republican misinformation bubble," the comedian pointed out. "But what about liberals, you know, the high-information, by-the-science people?"

As Maher explained, "If you lie to people—even for a very good cause—you lose their trust."

He raged, "[Democrats] also have a greatly exaggerated view of the danger of COVID to, and the mortality rate among, children, all of which explains why today the states with the highest share of schools that are still closed are all blue states."

Maher even praised GOP governors in Texas and Florida and ripped New York governor Andrew Cuomo.

Maher called Republican Florida governor Ron DeSantis "a voracious consumer of the scientific literature, and maybe that's why he protected his most vulnerable population, the elderly, way better than did the governor of New York."

Maher was infuriated when the mainstream media was using photos of packed Florida beaches to attack those not submitting to lockdowns. "The media won't stop putting pictures of the beach on stories about COVID even though it's looking increasingly like the beach is the best place to avoid it. Sunlight is the best disinfectant, and vitamin D is the key to a robust immune system. Texas lifted its COVID restrictions recently and their infection rates went down in part because of people getting outside to let the sun and wind do their thing. But to many liberals, 'That can't be right, because Texas and beach-loving Florida have Republican governors.' But life is complicated!" Maher said.[63]

"Panic Porn"

Maher ripped what he called "nonstop gloom and doom" from the media and government officials. "At some point, the daily drumbeat of depression and terror veers into panic porn," Maher said. "Enough with the 'life will never be the same' headlines."[64]

Maher nailed the public health bureaucracies' practice of playing politics to manipulate the public. "Over the past year the pandemic has prompted the medical establishment, the media, and the government to take a scared straight approach to getting the public to comply with their recommendations," he explained.

"When all of our sources for medical information have an agenda to spin us, yeah, you wind up with a badly misinformed population including on the Left," Maher said.[65]

Maher urged millennials to reject fear and lockdowns and instead lead the United States back to a "life not dominated by fear."

"This is your time," he said. "Just storm the beaches. And the malls. Go buy pants. Live your pre-corona life because you are the least likely to die from it."

He admitted, "Safety is a virtue. But if it was the only one, nothing would ever get done."[66]

Maher expressed serious doubts about Fauci. "I think Dr. Fauci is honorable, smart, and sincere. But I also thought that about Robert Muller, and I worry liberals are once again falling into the same trap of lionizing someone just because they're the anti-Trump," Maher said.[67]

Maher was incensed at how misinformed his fellow liberals were when it came to COVID. "In a recent Gallup survey, Democrats did much worse than Republicans in getting the right answer to the fundamental question: What are the chances that someone who gets COVID will need to be hospitalized? The answer is between 1 and 5 percent. Forty-one percent of Democrats thought it was over 50 percent; another 28 percent put the chances at 20 to 49 [percent]," Maher explained. "Those are just facts. I know it's irresponsible of me to say them. Look, here's what I'm saying: I don't want politics mixed in with my medical decisions."[68]

In 2022 Maher became increasingly agitated at the Left he once felt comfortable being a part of. "Let's get this straight: It is not me who's changed. It's the Left—who is now made up of a small contingent who have gone mental and a large contingent who refused to call them out for it. But I will," Maher said. "Democrats have become a parody of themselves just making rules to make rules because it makes you feel like you're a better person.... Democrats have to stop thinking that what the voters dream about is to be hassled."[69]

Maher dismissed lockdowns as an effective strategy to battle viruses and suggested a focus on reducing obesity, a huge risk factor of COVID-19.

"Instead we were told to lock down. Unfortunately, the killer was already in the house, and her name is Little Debbie," Maher quipped.[70]

CHAPTER 11

The COVID-Climate–Reset Connection

n 2010 MIT climate scientist Dr. Richard S. Lindzen summed up the climate debate perfectly. "For a lot of people, including the bureaucracy in government and the environmental movement, the issue is power," Lindzen, a climate skeptic, explained.

"It's hard to imagine a better leverage point than carbon dioxide to assume control over a society.... It's essential to the production of energy, it's essential to breathing.... If you demonize it and gain control over it, you, so-to-speak, control everything. That's attractive to people," Lindzen said.[1]

"If you ever wanted a leverage point to control everything from exhalation to driving, this would be a dream. So it has a kind of fundamental attractiveness to bureaucratic mentality," he added.[2]

"It's hard to imagine a better leverage point than carbon dioxide to assume control over a society."

They "imagined" something better. A virus turned out to be an even "better leverage point than carbon dioxide."

After decades of trying to scare the public on climate change to help empower the administrative state, COVID-19 came along and, seemingly overnight, stole the thunder from the climate change activists without an effort. The year 2020 saw a drastic shift away from the climate momentum that the Green New Deal was riding when COVID-19 showed up on the global scene. Suddenly the public was genuinely scared about—not a long-hyped climate "emergency"—but a viral pandemic. Most of the world, including the United States, went into max-fear and lockdown mode in March 2020, and climate activists watched helplessly as their issue was supplanted by COVID.

"The Powers They Were Unable to Achieve with Climate Fears Fell into Their Hands"

The climate change activists have watched the governments around the world and their responses to the COVID-19 pandemic with awe. Global warming campaigners have been taking notes as the virus-induced societal shutdowns have enacted much of the climate activists' long-sought-after agenda. The austere lockdowns and economic collapse inspired climate activists.

As Peter Barry Chowka observed at the American Thinker, "Overnight, our society is doing what radical leftist Rep. Alexandria Ocasio Cortez (D-NY) and her fellow Green New Deal fanatics have demanded: An almost total end to air travel; personal automobile travel down to a trickle; promises of free health care for all quickly becoming the new status quo; and the ability of people to sit at home without working and receive a paycheck from the government. The Democrats want that to continue indefinitely."[3]

In 2021 Joel Kotkin reported at UnHerd on the "woke oligarchs" who hoped to get more control over society by means of the climate agenda. "Eric Heymann, a senior executive at Deutsche Bank, suggests that to reach the climate goals of Davos, corporations will have to embrace 'a certain degree of eco-dictatorship.' After all, it would be difficult to get elected officials to approve limits on such mundane popular pleasures as affordable air travel, cars, freeways and suburbs with single-family houses, unless they were imposed by judicial or executive fiat."[4] But the powers they were unable to achieve with climate fears fell into their hands in the pandemic panic.

How the Green Great Reset Aids China

The 2021 G7 Summit's plan "to 'counter China' involves forcing themselves and their partners to adopt unreliable energy and let China completely off the hook," noted journalist Jordan Schachtel. "One leader after another pledged $100 billion a year to force developing countries to remain impoverished and rely on unreliable 'clean energy' to solve the 'climate crisis,' which they declared the greatest issue of our time. Of course, their solutions all involved increasing the power of the state over its citizens and embracing creepy one-world U.N. affiliated organizations."[5]

IS THE CORONAVIRUS LOCKDOWN **THE FUTURE** ENVIRONMENTALISTS WANT?

COVID lockdowns have great appeal to the climate change activists. *Courtesy of Christina Norman, the Committee for a Constructive Tomorrow (CFACT)*

World Economic Forum founder and chairman Klaus Schwab seized on the opportunity that the COVID lockdowns brought to advance government powers. "The changes we have already seen in response to COVID-19 prove that a reset of our economic and social foundations is possible," Schwab said in June 2020. "In short, we need a 'Great Reset' of capitalism," he declared.

"One silver lining of the pandemic is that it has shown how quickly we can make radical changes to our lifestyles. Almost instantly, the crisis forced businesses and individuals to abandon practices long claimed to be essential, from frequent air travel to working in an office.... A Great Reset agenda would ensure that investments advance shared goals, such as equality and sustainability," Schwab claimed.[6]

Thomas Schomerus, professor of public law at Leuphana University in Germany, was optimistic about the opportunities COVID-19 and

> **"Climate Change Is the Greatest Health Challenge"**
> "Climate change is the greatest health challenge of the 21st century, and threatens all aspects of the society in which we live."
> —2018 WHO report for the UN climate summit in Poland titled *Health and Climate Change*[7]

climate change gave governments. "Both the corona crisis and the climate crisis require freedom-limiting measures. The earlier and more vigorously these are defined and implemented, the sooner the success that is vital for survival can be expected. In this respect, corona and climate protection measures do not differ in principle, but only on the time axis," Schomerus wrote.[8]

No matter how much the climate activists tried to scare the public, they were never able to accomplish their goal. Polling from Pew, Gallup, and Harris have all shown that the public was just never that concerned or afraid or willing to sacrifice in order to fight global warming. But then the upstart COVID-19 came on the scene, and just about every utopian wish list of the administrative state of the climate activists became a reality overnight.

At first when the COVID lockdowns happened, the climate activists were palpably jealous. They were beside themselves, asking, How is this happening? But then everyone from Greta Thunberg to John Kerry noted the similarities between climate and COVID-19, regrouped, and started taking notes. As the world endured an unprecedented lockdown for a virus, they began demanding that we do the same for climate change.

Climate activists even proposed the idea of adding "climate change" to death certificates as a cause of death to mimic the daily death tolls of COVID-19. The final step is a merging of COVID and climate, with climate alarmism being subservient to viral fears.

The Chinese-inspired lockdowns were music to the ears of the proponents of the Great Reset, including WEF founder Klaus Schwab.

In *COVID-19: The Great Reset*, the 2020 book he coauthored with Thierry Malleret, Schwab literally stated that climate activists might want to "take advantage" of COVID to achieve their agenda, "not letting the crisis go to waste." According to Schwab, "Some leaders and decision-makers who were already at the forefront of the fight against climate change may want to take advantage of the shock inflicted by the pandemic to implement long-lasting and wider environmental changes. They will, in effect, make 'good use' of the pandemic by not letting the crisis go to waste."

No Deal For Nature campaigner Paul Cudenec wrote at the website Winter Oak, "When any tyrant declares the right to rule over a population without taking their views into account, they like to justify their dictatorship with the claim that they are morally entitled to do so because they are 'enlightened.'"

"The same is true of the Covid-fuelled tyranny of Schwab's great reset, which the book categorises as 'enlightened leadership,' Cudenec said of Schwab's book *COVID-19: The Great Reset.*[9]

And Schwab and Malleret weren't the only ones. Others saw this same chance to make "good use" of the COVID-19 lockdowns.

At the G7 Speakers' Meeting in 2020, Sir Lindsay Hoyle, the Speaker of the House of Commons, declared his amazement at how "compliant" the public had been in accepting COVID lockdowns. "No-one could ever imagine that we would be wearing masks so readily and that we would all be so compliant," he said. "People were prepared to accept limitations on personal choice and lifestyle—for the good of their own family and friends."

Hoyle suggested that that same compliance might also work on the climate issue. "If one lesson from the pandemic is that taking serious action in a timely manner is key—then shouldn't this also be true in terms of climate change?" Hoyle asked. "Surely, it is in our hands to rescue it, if we have got the will to do it?"[10]

The "will to do it" means the public—so "compliant" in accepting the COVID lockdowns—should be ready for climate lockdowns. The fact is that a "compliant" public and ambitious politicians and bureaucrats are a grave threat to liberty. The coronavirus lockdowns are being hailed by climate activists across the spectrum as the model for climate lockdowns and the path to the Great Reset.

Former vice president Al Gore is also fully committed to the Great Reset: "I think this is a time for a 'Great Reset,'" Gore said. "We've got to fix a lot of these problems that have been allowed to fester for way too long." Gore added, "So this is a time for a Reset to fix a bunch of challenges, first among them the climate crisis."[11]

> ### "Why We Might Be Eating Insects Soon"
> The World Economic Forum has touted eating bugs to save the planet. In a 2018 article titled "Good Grub: Why We Might Be Eating Insects Soon," World Economic Forum senior writer Sean Fleming explained, "The global market for edible insects could grow to $1.18 billion by 2023. That's almost triple its current level." According to Fleming, "Per kilo of live weight, bugs emit less harmful gas than more mainstream farm animals. A cow, for example, produces 2.8 kg of greenhouse gas per kilo of live body weight. Insects, on the other hand, produce just 2 grams," WEF claimed.[12]

"The Parallels Are Screaming at Us"

"This pandemic has provided an opportunity for a Reset. This is our chance to accelerate our pre-pandemic efforts to re-imagine economic systems that actually address global challenges like extreme poverty, inequality, and climate change," noted Canadian prime minister Justin Trudeau, speaking to a UN conference in September 2020.[13]

Former secretary of state John Kerry noted that "the parallels are screaming at us, both positive and negative."[14] According to Kerry, "You could just as easily replace the words *climate change* with *COVID-19*; it is truly the tale of two pandemics deferred, denied, and distorted, one with catastrophic consequences, the other with even greater risk if we don't reverse course."[15]

Kerry was correct: the discussion about COVID has aped the climate debate in many key ways.

"Both the climate and COVID movements share these features—hypocrisy and hysteria, models and money, fear and false prophets, and inevitability. This is also how dictatorships begin," noted Brian C. Joondeph in American Thinker.

"One can see numerous parallels between COVID and climate policy. Both create fear, to a frenzy level, of the world ending, massive death and destruction, all due to a warming planet or an aggressive flu virus. If we don't wear a mask, we are murderers and should be imprisoned. If we don't believe in man-made global warming, we should also be locked away in jail," Joondeph wrote.

COVID-19 was the basis for "six months of lockdowns, mandates, and restrictions previously unfathomable in a free society.... Question the dogma of either the virus or climate movement and prepare to have your life, if not disrupted, then ruined. There is only one politically correct viewpoint on both issues," Joondeph explained.

Scientifically, COVID-19 and climate share other similarities. "Both global warming and the Wuhan flu rely on models. Many climate models predicted rising sea levels and flooded cities, along with catastrophic storms, none of which has materialized. Virus models predicted 2.2 million U.S. deaths, only to be scaled down as reality was nowhere close to the predictions. Both relied on flawed models and failed to adjust their prognostications accordingly," he added.

"Climate and COVID share the commonality of government control. From electric car and fuel efficiency mandates to the entire economy busting Green New Deal, the 'benevolent' government seeks to control all aspects of our lives," Joondeph concluded.[16]

Tony Heller, who runs the Real Climate Science website, summed up the twin threats of COVID lockdowns and climate "solutions." As Heller wrote, "We have arrived at the end game. Totalitarianism and economic depression. And a compliant public which has begged for it to happen."[17] Heller pointed out, "The COVID-19 response was the implementation of the Green New Deal."[18]

As astrophysicist and philosopher Martín López Corredoira noted, "Neither Greenpeace, nor Greta Thunberg, nor any other individual or collective organization have [sic] achieved so much in favor of the health of the planet in such a short time."

"It is certainly not very good for the economy in general, but it is fantastic for the environment," Corredoira opined.[19]

In May 2020 Washington State governor Jay Inslee said the following about his plan to rebuild the state's economy with a "green initiative": "We should not be intimidated when people say, 'Oh you can't use this COVID crisis to peddle a solution to climate change.' No, we have to recognize the necessity of this moment." Inslee added, "These are two things we have to deal with, and we can deal with both, because they're so similar."[20]

New York Times "climate desk" reporter John Schwartz drew parallels between COVID and climate. "Social Distancing? You Might Be Fighting Climate Change, Too," blared the headline. The article cited Kimberly Nicholas, a researcher at the Lund University Center for Sustainability Studies in Sweden, who asserted, "Any time you can avoid getting on a plane, getting in a car or eating animal products, that's a substantial climate savings."[21]

Climate activist Mark Hertsgaard and Kyle Pope, the editor in chief of the *Columbia Journalism Review*, also drew comparisons. "The similarities between the causes of and solutions to the coronavirus and the climate crisis are nothing short of eerie," they wrote. "As awful as the coronavirus is, it is something of a test run for the challenges of a climate crisis that continues to accelerate."[22]

Gore explained, "The scientists have warned us about the coronavirus, and they've warned us about the climate crisis; and we've seen the dangers of waiting too late to heed the warnings of the doctors and scientists on this virus.... Fossil fuels are a pre-existing condition for COVID-19."[23]

Environmental journalist Emily Atkin was more blunt. "I'm sorry," she said, "but if you still refuse to see parallels between climate change and coronavirus then honestly you're just stupid." As she explained, "Both are global crises which threaten millions of lives with clear science on how to solve them which governments have been too slow to act on; the same people who promote climate denial are refusing to accept the science of coronavirus, too." Atkins claimed, "Coronavirus makes climate change worse, and vice versa.... We can't

> **"A Nightmare Mix"**
>
> "Lockdown feels like the new Climate Change. A nightmare mix of bogus science, woke political posturing and economic lunacy,"
> —UK filmmaker Martin Durkin in June 2020[24]

do our research on climate because of it, we've had to cancel the UN climate summit for international negotiations."[25]

The "Ecological Benefits" of the COVID Lockdowns

The COVID lockdowns and mandates were a gift to climate activists. The climate movement may now be poised to plan and dictate a new "Earth-friendly" world in the aftermath of the heavy-handed government response to the coronavirus. The climate activists quickly began to strategize about how to use the coronavirus pandemic as a model for the climate scare—as a dry run for what they hope to achieve.

> **"It Is Unthinkable to 'Go Back to Normal'"**
>
> "Pollution, climate change, and the destruction of our remaining natural zones has brought the world to a breaking point. For these reasons, along with increasing social inequalities, we believe it is unthinkable to 'go back to normal.' The radical transformation we need—at all levels—demands boldness and courage. It will not happen without a massive and determined commitment. We must act now." —letter signed by Hollywood celebrities, including Robert De Niro, Madonna, Cate Blanchett, Barbra Streisand, Jane Fonda, Juliette Binoche, Ralph Fiennes, Eva Green, Adam Driver, Penélope Cruz, Willem Defoe, and Joaquin Phoenix[26]

Progressive environmentalists lauded the lockdowns as having "ecological benefits" but lamented that they were not in control of the shutdown. Jason Hickel, a lecturer in economic anthropology at Goldsmiths University and member of the advisory board of the Green New Deal for Europe, explained his thoughts on COVID and climate in April 2020. "When you do scale down energy use and industrial production, then it does have these ecological benefits. But the crucial thing to observe here is that this is happening in an unplanned, chaotic way that's hurting peoples' lives. We would never advocate for such a thing in climate policy. What we need is a planned approach to reducing unnecessary industrial activity that has no connection to human welfare…and that also disproportionately benefits already wealthy people as opposed to ordinary people."

In other words, while Dr. Hickel likes the "ecological benefits" of the COVID-19 lockdowns, he wants future lockdowns to be more "planned"—so that he and his academic colleagues can be in charge, crafting their vision of a utopian world by "reducing unnecessary industrial activity." The climate campaigners envision a post-COVID world defined by fear of "climate change," and they are seeking to remake societies from their university offices instead of letting free people and free economies thrive.[27]

> ### "This Is the Moment They've Been Waiting For"
> "If you thought the nightmare was going to end once the coronavirus scare passed, think again: it's only just beginning. The greens and the globalists aren't about to let a crisis go to waste. This is the moment they have been waiting for. And don't expect much resistance from politicians—even ones wearing the 'Conservative' label, like Boris Johnson. They're part of the problem." –James Delingpole in May 2020.[28]

The warmists' repeated calls for "global government" have been inserted into the COVID shutdown debate.[29]

Former UK prime minister Gordon Brown exhorted world leaders to create "a temporary form of global government" to take on the coronavirus. "This is not something that can be dealt with in one country," Brown argued. "There has to be a coordinated global response."[30]

The goals of the climate activists have been advanced by the total shutdown of society. Climate activists know that if the U.S. government and other Western nations can shut down all aspects of society to deal with a virus, they can do the same for climate change.

Climate activists must have been pleased to see a conservative Republican president—Donald Trump—at least temporarily support a near-complete shutdown of the economic engine of the United States for public safety purposes. The climate campaigners know that a precedent has been set, and they will exploit future presidents and Congresses more agreeable to their climate agenda to impose similar restrictions for our "safety" in the supposed climate crisis.

As we discussed in chapter 6, the Trump administration allowed speculative catastrophic COVID-death models to drive the implementation of a national lockdown. Trump economic advisor Larry Kudlow even admitted he did not know when the economy would not reopen because that decision was "up to the health people."[32]

> **"A More Feminine Way"**
> At the 2021 G7 Summit, UK prime minister Boris Johnson told the world: "We're building back better together, and building back greener, and building back fairer, and building back more equal, and . . . in a more gender-neutral—and, perhaps, in a more feminine way."[31]

> **Print Your Own "Meat"**
> "Machines can currently print up to 6kg of meat an hour," claimed an video included in a World Economic Forum article by senior writer Sean Fleming. "A start-up firm in Israel, Redefine Meat, is using industrial-scale 3D-printing to produce a plant-based 'alt-steak' that it says has a structure and texture similar to that of the real thing," and "the use of 3D-printing technology . . . creates layers of interwoven fibres that more closely mimic the real thing."[33]

Never-Ending Crisis

Climate activists are now increasingly linking viruses to "climate change" and thus make fighting climate change a part of fighting deadly viruses.

Former secretary of state and presidential candidate John Kerry, for example, has argued, "Climate change is a threat multiplier for pandemic diseases, and zoonotic diseases—70 percent of all human infections—are impacted by climate change and its effect on animal migration and habitats."[34]

And a science reporter at the *Washington Post* claimed, "Climate change affects everything—even the coronavirus.... No aspect of life on this planet has been untouched by climate change—viruses included."[35]

"To Permanently Change the Way We Live"

Before compelling evidence came out that COVID had originated in a Chinese lab—and that he was aware of that probability—Dr. Anthony Fauci sought to claim that the virus was due to "extreme backlashes from nature" and that "creative harmony with nature" would be necessary to prevent future outbreaks.

Fauci claimed, "Living in greater harmony with nature will require changes in human behavior as well as other radical changes that may take decades to achieve: rebuilding the infrastructures of human existence."

"Dr. Anthony Fauci, the 36 year head of the National Institute of Allergy and Infectious Diseases (NIAID), appears to have embraced something resembling an enviro de-growth movement, arguing in a new 'scientific' paper that we need to go back to living in 'creative harmony with nature' in order to avoid future health issues such as pandemics, which have existed since the beginning of the human species," wrote journalist Jordan Schachtel. He described Fauci as going "full pseudoscience."

Schachtel explained, "Fauci and crew seem to believe that we are living in a permanent pandemic era, which is the fault of human progress, and one that requires immense, but untold, regressive action to combat. Simply put, they are now blatantly attempting to leverage the pandemic to permanently change the way we live."[36]

Actress Jane Fonda waded into the COVID-climate debate. "Climate change guarantees that COVID-19 will not be the last pandemic we will see," she warned. "The melting of the Arctic ice sheet is releasing untold pathogens to which humans are not immune. Climate change guarantees that COVID-19 will not be the last pandemic we will see."[37]

The activists are now sure to attempt to piggyback their efforts like the Green New Deal onto future virus-fighting strategies. In fact, climate activist Laurie Macfarlane of Open Democracy has already urged that the COVID response needs to be "a Global Green New Deal" to "decarbonise the global economy as fast as is feasibly possible."[38]

Science Isn't on Their Side

"In reality, if a modestly warming Earth has any impact on viruses and pandemics, it is to make them less likely and less severe. . . . Historically, we know that the Black Plague arose and ran rampant in Europe and elsewhere during the Little Ice Age," wrote H. Sterling Burnett in an article on ClimateRealism.com in 2020.

"Transmissible diseases like the flu and the coronavirus are far more prevalent and deadly during the late-fall, winter, and early spring, when the weather is cold and damp, rather than in the summer months when it is warm and dry. That is the primary reason that flu season runs from fall through early spring, and then peters out. Similarly, colds are called colds because they are less common in the summer, as well," Burnett pointed out.[39]

"Shut Down the Whole Global Economy"

A 2013 comment from a former high-level UN climate official sheds light on why climate activists are so enthusiastic about the worldwide COVID-19–inspired lockdowns of the economy.

"There is nothing that can be agreed in 2015 that would be consistent with the 2 degrees," said Yvo de Boer, who was UNFCCC (United Nations Framework Convention on Climate Change) executive secretary in 2009, when attempts to reach a deal at a summit in Copenhagen crumbled, with a rift between industrialized and developing nations. "The only way that a 2015 agreement can achieve a 2-degree goal is to shut down the whole global economy."[40]

Today, now that we have experienced the COVID lockdowns grinding the world economy to a halt, de Boer's words sound prophetic.

On April 22, 2020, climate activist Eric Holthaus made this observation about the effect of the COVID lockdowns on global CO_2 emissions: "This is roughly the same pace that the IPCC says we need to sustain every year until 2030 to be on pace to limit global warming to 1.5C and hit the Paris climate goals. This is what 'rapid, far-reaching and unprecedented changes in all aspects of society' looks like."[41] So cheer up, this is good news, right? Just ten more years of full lockdowns, and we can meet our UN Paris climate goals! Hurray!

"Medieval Lords"

"Even as they push austerity on the masses, they live like medieval lords, indulging in lavish weddings and building estates reminiscent of the Habsburgs'. Jeff Bezos just spent $100 million (£80 million) on a Hawaiian retreat. Bill Gates's daughter just enjoyed a $2 million (£1.5 million) wedding. John Kerry, president Biden's chief climate scold and beneficiary of an heiress's fortune, travels on a private jet that use[s] thirty times the energy of the average American vehicle." –Joe Kotkin in the United Kingdom's *The Spectator*[42]

But the reality is that even with lockdowns and shutdowns of most aspects of society, global CO_2 emissions still didn't seem to notice. Climatologist Roy Spencer explained why: "It would be difficult to see a downturn in the anthropogenic source of CO_2 unless it was very large (say, over 50%) and prolonged (say over a year or longer)."[43]

In fact, human activity is responsible for only a small proportion of the CO_2 in our atmosphere. But that didn't deter the climate alarmists.

"The coronavirus pandemic makes what we've already known clear: we need a Green New Deal to stop climate change, provide desperately needed jobs, and halt future mass pandemics," claimed the Democratic Socialists of America in March 2020.[44]

Holthaus welcomed COVID-19 restrictions and hoped they would continue beyond the pandemic: "This is a really heartening trend. All around the world, cities are closing key roads to cars, to make more space for pedestrians and bikes. After the pandemic, this needs to become permanent."[45]

Nations Mull a Radical "Pandemic Treaty"

Permanent is exactly what the public health bureaucrats and the Davos crowd are seeking. The World Health Organization agreed to negotiate a "pandemic treaty" complete with a "legally binding" agreement to deal with future viruses, reported the *Washington Post* in 2021.[46]

WHO director general Tedros Adhanom Ghebreyesus was all in, noting that a "global accord" would help streamline "pandemic prevention, preparedness and response" and "help to keep future generations safer from the impacts of pandemics."[47]

At Climate Depot, I explained why a "pandemic treaty" is a very bad idea:

> This will be a virus version of the UN IPCC and Paris climate style pacts. The pandemic "crisis" will become permanent just like the "climate crisis." Attempts to impose lockdowns for future COVID variants or new viruses may be internationally imposed instead of national, state, or local. If you don't like your governor, mayor, or school board, you can vote them out, but if a "radical" WHO "pandemic treaty" that is "legally binding" becomes reality, global mandates may be coming your way and local elections will cease to matter as unelected bureaucrats will be yielding the real power over your life, liberty, and pursuit of happiness....
>
> Once a "pandemic treaty" is set in place, COVID mandates will become permanent as elite officials fly around the world to discuss how to further crush freedom to wage war on viruses. Just like the UN Intergovernmental Panel on Climate Change, the architects of a "pandemic treaty" will seek more and more power and control and become a self-interested lobbying organization all while doing squat to prevent or mitigate future viruses. A "radical" WHO "pandemic treaty" may be just the ticket for the administrative

state to reign in rogue anti-lockdown governors like [Florida's] Ron DeSantis.[48]

Cause of Death: Climate Change

Say what you will about climate activists, they are a quick study. Seeing the scary and emotional daily COVID-19 death counts on television and all the media attention that the virus received inspired climate activists to play copycats in order to draw attention back to their pet climate cause.

In 2021 a doctor from British Columbia clinically diagnosed a patient as suffering from "climate change." "For the first time in his 10 years as a physician, the ER doctor picked up his patient's chart and penned in the words 'climate change,'" reported the *Times Colonist* of Canada. "If we're not looking at the underlying cause, and we're just treating the symptoms, we're just gonna keep falling further and further behind," explained Dr. Kyle Merritt, the head of the Kootenay Lake Hospital's emergency department.

Merritt's colleagues, including forty doctors and nurses, later formed a group that is calling on governments to declare an "ecological emergency" to battle climate change.[49]

Meteorologist Anthony Watts penned a direct response to Doctor Merritt's "climate change" diagnosis in an article titled "REBUTTAL to Doctor Merritt: 'Climate Change' Does Not Affect Human Health, Weather Does." Watts explained that **"this is an absurd claim**, because the doctor is simply making the mistake of conflating short-term weather events with long-term climate change."[50]

The bending of medical standards did not end with doctors diagnosing patients with "climate change."

Perhaps the wackiest climate story to come out of the climate campaigners' COVID envy was about the call, in a study published in May 2020 in *Lancet Planetary Health*, to put "climate change" on death certificates as a cause of death. Academics in Australia were demanding that "climate change" be added to death certificates as a "pre-existing condition."

Arnagretta Hunter of the Australian National University (ANU) Medical School, a coauthor of the study, said, "Climate change is a killer, but we don't acknowledge it on death certificates.... Climate change is the single greatest health threat that we face globally even after we recover from coronavirus."[51]

"Far, far more people have died from climate change than are dying from COVID-19—far more," noted Mary Robinson, former president of Ireland. "We have to get out of COVID in a way that helps us get out of climate—meaning, go green," Robinson added.[52]

Bill Gates echoed those sentiments in August 2020, noting, "The actual economic and death toll from climate change will be much, much, much greater than what we have with this pandemic."[53]

But climate skeptics were having none of it. Ron Clutz of Science Matters ridiculed the *Lancet Planetary Health* study. "No doubt they noticed how powerful were the Covid19 death statistics in getting the public to comply with lockdown regulations. Their logic is clear: When people die with multiple diseases, pick the one that's politically useful. ('Never let a crisis go to waste.')"[54] Statistician William M. Briggs also poked fun at the study. "They discovered a way to boost fear and keep control!" he said "Daily body counts blasted from the evil media, 'Over 100 people died from climate change today, raising questions about... blah...'"[55]

The possibilities are endless. Federal research has posited a link between "climate change" and "fatal [car] crashes." A 2016 U.S. Department of Transportation study asked, "How might climate change increase the risk of fatal crashes in a community?"[56] Is it possible that anyone dying in a car crash could be listed as a "climate change" death?

And will cancer deaths also be listed on death certificates as "climate change" deaths? A 2020 study in an *American Cancer Society* journal claimed that "climate change is already increasing cancer risk."[57]

Organ failure at the time of death could also prompt a climate change death certificate listing. In 2017, Al Gore warned that "every organ system can be affected by climate change."[58]

If someone dies from a car crash, cancer, or organ failure, "climate change" could be listed as a cause of death on a death certificate. Expect daily "climate change" death tolls to someday soon be hyped by the media.

"Just wait for the headlines about 'Millions killed by climate change.' And 'Climate change death toll mounts.' If it bleeds, it leads. Politicized science is now a fact of life in the Western world, undermining the very foundations of the technological and material progress that liberated the mass of humanity from permanent poverty, the normal state of affairs until the scientific and industrial revolutions changed the state of civilization," Thomas Lifson said at the American Thinker.

"Stalin was the pioneer in bending science in service of a political agenda, and under him, Trofim Lysenko led the charge to corrupt science,

"Cold Is a Bigger Killer Than Warmth"

"Your notion of a 'climate crisis' . . . though fashionable among the classe politique, is misplaced," wrote Christopher Monckton, former advisor to Margaret Thatcher, in a 2020 letter to the medical journal *The Lancet*.

"Your suggestion that warmer worldwide weather has caused net loss of life, particularly among the world's fast-declining population of poor people, is fashionable but misplaced. Cold is a bigger killer than warmth. Research conducted three years ago for the European Commission found that, for this reason, even if there were 5.4 C° global warming from 2020–2080, there would be 100,000 more Europeans than with no warming at all," Monckton wrote.

"With respect, *The Lancet* should study more science and economics, however unfashionable, and peddle less totalitarian politics, however fashionable and profitable—and deadly," he concluded. —Christopher Monckton's response to a *Lancet* editorial titled "Climate and COVID-19: Converging Crises"[59] which ended disastrously when agriculture was forced to accept practices based on phony science. Lysenkoism is the name given to the practice of bending science to politics," he wrote.[60]

The real science of climate-related deaths does not appear to matter to climate activists. "New data shows the global climate-related death risk has dropped by over 99% since 1920. Despite the near constant caterwauling from climate activists that we are in a 'climate emergency,' real-world data, released at the end of 2020 shows that climate related deaths are now approaching zero," reported meteorologist Anthony Watts.[61]

Just imagine MSNBC and CNN daily tallies of the climate change "death toll" and calls for "climate action" to stop the deaths. The climate death tolls and doctor diagnoses have arrived just in time.

CNN technical director Charlie Chester was caught on undercover cameras by Project Veritas revealing the media's next focus after COVID fades. Because of "COVID fatigue," CNN is "going to start focusing mainly on climate," Chester said in 2021. "It [COVID] will taper off to a point that it's not a problem anymore. Climate change can take years, so [CNN will] probably be able to milk that quite a bit.... Climate change is going to be the next COVID thing for CNN," he explained, adding, "Fear sells."[62]

Global Warming Made the Public "Docile"?

A 1941 theory linking warmer temperatures to the rise of Hitler and Mussolini could explain the modern-day public's obedience to COVID lockdowns. "Increasingly warmer temperatures throughout the world may produce a trend toward dictatorial governments, in the opinion of Dr. Clarence A. Mills, professor of experimental medicine at the University of Cincinnati," explained a United Press report in the Iowa newspaper the *Mason City Globe-Gazette* on March 27, 1941. "In fact, Dr. Mills believes that the rise to power of Adolf Hitler in Germany and Benito Mussolini in Italy may be due in part to the gradually warming temperature of the world. People are more docile and easily led in warm weather than in cold, Dr. Mills insists."[63]

Many in the climate-action community would like the public to become conditioned to living under some sort of perpetual lockdown. They want these governmental lockdown powers to remain and be used for climate change after worry over COVID-19 fades. Activists want the public to get used to the travel restrictions, to get used to the quarantines, to get used to the limits in their personal freedom—all of which will come in handy as lower emissions are mandated to "solve" the "climate emergency."

Former Obama administration U.S. Treasury official Mark Mazur said the quiet part out loud in 2022 in the lead-up to the Russian invasion of Ukraine. "We don't want lower prices for fossil-fuel buyers, we prefer higher prices" to achieve "climate change goals," Mazur explained.[64]

High energy prices are *not* the unintended consequences of Great Reset and Green New Deal-style policies; they are the *intended* consequences.

"For some, the lockdowns served as a 'test run' for necessary measures to realize their preferred climate-change policies. In the new schema, the real class enemy is not the excesses of the ultra-rich, or even wasteful spending by government: it's the consumption patterns of the masses," explained Joel Kotkin of Chapman University, author of the book *The Coming of Neo-Feudalism: A Warning to the Global Middle Class*.

"The early-twentieth-century Italian sociologist Robert Michels noted that complex issues—climate, for instance—reinforce what he called the 'iron law of oligarchy': the more dependent on expertise a society becomes, the greater the need for elite-driven solutions that bypass popular input—and the greater the force the elite will apply to attain its goals," Kotkin wrote.

"The conscious policy of degrowth as a means of forcibly reducing greenhouse gas emissions will require getting most people out of their cars, and forcing them to travel far less and to live in tiny apartments. Enforcement will be necessarily intrusive as well," Kotkin explained, adding that "your right to free movement is subject to government approval."[65]

The United States and the world have taken a great leap toward the Great Reset, and the COVID-Climate–Reset connection has deepened as politicians and the unelected public health bureaucracy have resisted relinquishing many of the COVID-19 restrictions. The next chapter will reveal how they plan to keep the COVID lockdowns going in a new form...climate lockdowns.

CHAPTER 12

COVID Lockdowns Morph to Climate Lockdowns

The next crisis is already waiting for us around the corner, and it is the climate crisis.
—Klaus Schwab on July 14, 2020, during the World Economic Forum
livestream on "COVID-19: The Great Reset"

The COVID lockdowns greatly accelerated the Great Reset, giving a major boost to the program of the progressive left and the climate activists, who want you to get used to living a restricted life where your everyday actions have to be approved by the government or okayed by a bureaucratic official. Our current virus-inspired government lockdown is the perfect template for the future the climate campaigners envision, with all of us living under a coercive government that takes the "climate emergency" seriously.

A "BBC Reality Check" claimed that the Great Reset has been "hijacked by conspiracy theories," in part by "online activists who deny the existence of climate change."

The BBC quoted Melanie Smith, an analyst who researches "disinformation," explaining that climate skeptics focus on the Great Reset theory to "dismiss sustainability and renewable energy initiatives as an elite agenda for control."[1]

Why would anyone believe that the climate agenda is about an "elite agenda for control"?

Stay tuned for the answer.

In 2021 *The Guardian* blared this headline: "Global Lockdown Every Two Years Needed to Meet Paris CO_2 Goals—Study." The article, by Fiona Harvey, reported, "Carbon dioxide emissions must fall by the equivalent of a global lockdown roughly every two years for the next decade for the world to keep within safe limits of global heating, research has shown."[2]

A prescient government-funded report by five universities in the United Kingdom (Cambridge, Imperial College, Oxford, Bath, Nottingham, and Strathclyde) titled *Absolute Zero*, released in November 2019, envisions what a society locked down for the sake of the climate would look like. "Stop doing anything that causes emissions regardless of its energy source.... Stop eating beef and lamb.... Either use 60% fewer cars or they will be 60% the size," urged the report, funded by the United Kingdom's Engineering and Physical Sciences Research Council. By 2050, "All remaining airports close.... All shipping declines to zero."

According to the report's executive summary, there is no choice but to follow this draconian path because it is "the law."

"We have to cut our greenhouse gas emissions to zero by 2050: that's what climate scientists tell us, it's what social protesters are asking for and it's now the law in the UK. But we aren't on track."

Absolute Zero continues, "The big actions are: travel less distance, travel by train or in small (or full) electric cars and stop flying; use the heating less and electrify the boiler when next upgrading; lobby for construction with half the material for twice as long.... Each action we take to reduce emissions, at home or at work, creates a positive ripple effect....

"In addition to reducing our energy demand, delivering zero-emissions with today's technologies requires the phasing out of flying, shipping, lamb and beef, blast-furnace steel and cement."

Page 39 of the report bluntly states, "Ensuring carbon is at zero is a regulation issue, with prohibitions on the use of carbon similar to prohibitions on the use of asbestos."[3] Just to be clear, humans inhale oxygen and exhale carbon dioxide.

"Let's Not Let This Crisis Go to Waste"

The Ecologist magazine's Gareth Dale summed up *Absolute Zero*: The "report recommends a radical transformation to the way we live. All shipping must be phased out by 2050, and likewise all use of cement-based mortar or concrete. In Britain, all airports except Heathrow and Glasgow will have to close by 2029, and those two by 2049. Aviation must become illegal by then."[4]

"Dismantle Capitalism"

"The world's top scientists just gave rigorous backing to systematically dismantle capitalism as a key requirement to maintaining civilization and a habitable planet." –climate activist Eric Holthaus welcoming the UN IPCC's 2018 climate report[5]

But despite the radical nature of the report, the House of Lords debated *Absolute Zero* in February 2020, and many members gave the report glowing reviews.

Lord Browne of Ladyton was enthusiastic: "Apart from the fact that *Absolute Zero* is the most accessible reading on this subject that I have come across, this report is important in three respects. First, net zero is a misleading concept. The true target is absolute or real zero. There are no significant technologies to create negative emissions.... We are beyond the 11th hour on this issue and academics are screaming for the Government to show more leadership in this regard."

As was Baroness Walmsley: "The Climate Change Act commits us only to 'net zero' within the UK territory. That will not do. We need absolute zero and we must count all the emissions for which we are responsible."

Lord Lipsey had misgivings: "I am not a denier at all; I strongly believe in dealing with climate change. But if we were to put this report before the British people, it would be received in much same way as was the Labour manifesto: 'Oh, you cannot be serious.'"[6]

But they were serious. Very serious.

"No One Wants to Become Climate Roadkill"

Canadian banker Mark Carney, a climate advisor to both UK prime minister Boris Johnson and Canadian prime minister Justin Trudeau, has a plan to financially lockdown businesses that don't adhere to the dictates of the climate agenda. "Carney's Brave New World will be one of severely constrained choice, less flying, less meat, more inconvenience and more poverty: 'Assets will be stranded, used gasoline powered cars will be unsaleable, inefficient properties will be unrentable,' he promises," wrote Peter Foster, columnist for the *National Post* and the author of *Why We Bite the Invisible Hand: The Psychology of Anti-Capitalism.*

"The agenda's objectives are in fact already being enforced, not primarily by legislation but by the application of non-governmental—that is, non-democratic—pressure on the corporate sector via the ever-expanding dictates of ESG (environmental, social and corporate governance) and by 'sustainable finance,' which is designed to starve non-compliant companies of funds, thus rendering them, as Carney puts it, 'climate roadkill.' What ESG actually represents is corporate ideological compulsion. It is a key instrument of 'stakeholder capitalism.'

"Carney's Agenda is promoted by the United Nations and other international bureaucracies and a vast and ever-growing array of non-governmental organizations and fora, especially the World Economic Forum (WEF), where Carney is a trustee. Also, perhaps most surprisingly, by its corporate victims. No one wants to become climate roadkill," Foster wrote.[7]

In September 2020 the forces behind the Great Reset raised the threat of a literal "climate lockdown." Mariana Mazzucato, a WHO and UN advisor and Professor in the Economics of Innovation and Public Value at University College London, wrote a paper titled "Avoiding a Climate Lockdown."[8]

"As COVID-19 spread earlier this year, governments introduced lockdowns in order to prevent a public-health emergency from spinning out of control. In the near future, the world may need to resort to lockdowns again—this time to tackle a climate emergency," Mazzucato wrote.[9]

"Under a 'climate lockdown,' governments would limit private-vehicle use, ban consumption of red meat, and impose extreme energy-saving measures, while fossil-fuel companies would have to stop drilling," Mazzucato explained. "To avoid such a scenario, we must overhaul our economic structures and do capitalism differently."[10]

"Let's not let this crisis go to waste," Mazzucato pleaded.[11]

Mazzucato is not just any university professor. She serves on the United Nations Committee for Development Policy and was an advisor to the Scottish and Italian governments and the European Commissioner for Research, Science and Innovation. She heads the Council on the Economics of Health for All, a division of the World Health Organization.[12]

Mazzucato's website reveals that her research has been funded by the Ford Foundation, the Rockefeller Foundation, the Institute for New Economic Thinking, and George Soros's Open Society Foundations.[13]

Mazzucato's article "Avoiding a Climate Lockdown" "was first published in October 2020 by Project Syndicate, a non-profit media organization that is (predictably) funded through grants from the Open society Foundation[s], the Bill & Melinda Gates Foundation, and many, many others," noted Kit Knightly of the OffGuardian news outlet.

"After that, [Mazzucato's climate-lockdown article] was picked up and republished by the World Business Council for Sustainable Development (WBCSD), which describes itself as '*a global, CEO-led organization of over 200 leading businesses working together to accelerate the transition to a sustainable world.*' The WBCSD's membership is essentially every major company in the world, including Chevron, BP, Bayer, Walmart, Google and Microsoft. Over 200 members totaling well over 8 TRILLION dollars in annual revenue," Knightly wrote.

"In short: an economist who works for the WHO has written a report concerning 'climate lockdowns,' which has been published by both a Gates+Soros backed NGO AND a group representing almost every bank, oil company and tech giant on the planet. Whatever it says, it clearly has the approval of the people who run the world," Knightly explained.

"The whole article is not an argument, so much as an ultimatum. A gun held to the public's collective head. *'Obviously we don't want to lock you up inside your homes, force you to eat processed soy cubes and take away your cars,'* they're telling us, *'but we might have to, if you don't take our advice,'*" Knightly concluded.[14]

"Death by 1,000 Climate Faucis"

Kevin Hassett, the former chairman of the president's Council of Economic Advisers, warned that "the government's pandemic power grab should make us more skeptical of climate policy."

In an article titled "Death by 1,000 Climate Faucis," Hassett explained that "the section of our ruling class" that is seeking "to take away our freedoms and control our lives found, in Tony Fauci, the perfect device for mass oppression."

Hassett noted "the similarities between the apocalyptic rhetoric about COVID and that about climate change, often spouted by the same people." He concluded that "the oppressive behavior of emboldened leftists . . . would unleash a thousand climate Faucis on us if they could."[15]

In May 2021 an International Energy Agency *Net Zero* report urged "behavioural changes" to fight climate change. The IEA report called for "a shift away from private car use," a reduction in "upper speed limits," government-mandated thermostat "controls," and limits on "hot water," among many other restrictions.

The IEA report, titled *Net Zero by 2050: A Roadmap for the Global Energy Sector*, explained how COVID lockdowns had inspired recommendations for climate-based restrictions. "The Covid-19 pandemic has increased general awareness of the potential effectiveness of behavioral changes, such as mask-wearing, and working and schooling at home. The crisis demonstrated that people can make behavioral changes at significant speed and scale if they understand the changes to be justified, and that it is necessary for governments to explain convincingly and to provide clear guidance about what changes are needed and why they are needed," the report stated.

"Regulations and mandates could enable roughly 70% of the emissions saved by behavioral changes in the NZE [net zero emissions]." These are the key points, in the words of the IEA report:

- Keeping air travel for business purposes at 2019 levels. Although business trips fell to almost zero in 2020, they accounted for just over one-quarter of air travel before the pandemic....
- Keeping long-haul flights (more than six hours) for leisure purposes at 2019 levels. Emissions from an average long-haul flight are 35 times greater than from a regional flight (less than one hour)....
- Upper-speed limits, which are reduced over time in the NZE from their current levels to 100 km/h, cutting emissions from road vehicles by 3% in 2050.
- Appliance standards, which maximize energy efficiency in the buildings sector.
- Regulations covering heating temperatures in offices and default cooling temperatures for air conditioning units.[16]

In 2022, the International Energy Agency followed up on their *10-Point Plan to Cut Oil Use* report in response to the Russian invasion of Ukraine and the skyrocketing energy prices.

My headline at Climate Depot summed up the 2022 report: "Intl Energy Agency Urges ENERGY LOCKDOWNS: 'Banning Use of Private Cars on Sundays…Reducing Highway Speed Limits…More Working from Home…Cutting Business Air Travel' & SUV 'Tax.'" I commented:

COVID 2.0 has arrived?! The 2022 International Energy Agency's (IEA) report sounds an awful lot like an energy version of COVID lockdowns. Instead of opening America back up for domestic energy production, we are told to suffer and do with less and are prescribed the same failed lockdown-style policies we endured for COVID. It is odd how COVID "solutions" also allegedly helped the climate and now the same solutions are being touted to deal with Russia's invasion of Ukraine. As a bonus, IEA tells us these measures will also help "achieve vital climate goals." Let's simplify this: The proposed "solutions" to climate change, COVID, and now the Russian war are all exactly the same—hammer the poor and middle class with more restrictions on travel, less freedom, and even more surrendering of power to unelected government regulators.[17]

Time magazine's April 2021 issue was devoted to celebrating the COVID lockdowns and urging climate lockdowns on that model. "The Pandemic Remade Every Corner of Society. Now It's the Climate's Turn," blared the headline. The phrase "Climate is Everything" appeared at the top of the magazine's the cover.

Time claimed that COVID "can lead us to a better, greener world." According to the article, which read like a press release from the World Economic Forum, "the COVID-19 pandemic has given the E.U. the perfect opportunity to accelerate the remaking of its economic agenda with climate at its core." The magazine quoted Rachel Kyte, dean of the Fletcher School at Tufts University, saying, "We are at the point where climate change means systems change—and almost every system will change."[18]

Climate activists have welcomed the economic slowdown. After all, climate campaigners have long wanted "planned recessions." Warmist professor Alice Bows-Larkin, for example, has said, "Economic growth needs to be exchanged" for "planned austerity" and "whole system change."[19]

Brian Walsh reported in 2021 at Axios that the "degrowth" movement and advocates of "shrinking the economy" were buoyed to see COVID lockdowns crush the old normal. "Some environmentalists and economists are pushing for 'degrowth'—stabilizing or even shrinking the economy—to avert environmental catastrophe," Walsh explained.

"We Must Embrace...Ecological Leninism"

In 2020 Lund University professor Andreas Malm urged, "We must find a way of turning the environmental crisis into a crisis for fossil capital itself." Malm pointed to Lenin as the model. "The whole strategic direction of Lenin after 1914 was to turn World War I into a fatal blow against capitalism. This is precisely the same strategic orientation we must embrace today—and this is what I mean by ecological Leninism."

"State power should definitely be used to prevent luxury emissions perpetrated by the rich—private jets should be banned outright, as should SUVs and other vehicles that consume completely indefensible amounts of fuel. This is low-hanging fruit for the climate justice movement, as these sources of emissions are among the least socially necessary," Malm continued.

"Some forms of consumption will indeed have to be limited or abolished outright—this cannot be done through markets or appeals to ethical consumption, but only through state regulation," Malm added.[20]

"For degrowthers, simply cleaning up the global economy by switching from fossil fuels to zero-carbon sources of energy isn't enough. Economic growth—the goal of essentially every government everywhere—is itself the problem," Walsh reported.

Walsh noted that environmental activist Greta Thunberg berated delegates at a UN climate summit in 2019, saying, "We are in the beginning of a mass extinction, and all you can talk about is money and fairy tales of eternal economic growth. How dare you!"

"The [degrowth] movement now has its own dedicated academic journals, associations and conferences," Walsh wrote. "The global economy shrank by an estimated 4.3% in 2020, according to data from the World Bank,"

"The Absolute Power to Suspend Society"

"The green blob and its 'High Level Climate Action Champions' have wet dreams about Lockdown. They have long sought the absolute power to suspend society: to hold people in their places, and to only permit what is convenient to the blob." –UK climate skeptic Ben Pile in July 2020[21]

Walsh reported. "That contraction was due both to the direct pain of the pandemic and the effects of social distancing measures, but it also led to a roughly 6% reduction in global carbon dioxide emissions—the biggest annual drop since WWII."

"However accidental, 2020 represented perhaps the best example we've ever experienced of degrowthism in action," Walsh wrote.[22]

And massive recessions, collapsing economies, and the resulting social unrest are just the ticket for the Great Reset and the progressive agenda. The more the pain and the more the nasty consequences of the lockdowns, the more government solutions will be required.

"To Overhaul American Capitalism"

The *New York Times* let slip the truth about the Biden administration's new "infrastructure" bill in 2021, calling it "the first step in a two-part agenda to overhaul American capitalism, fight climate change."[23]

Emergency Powers

"Progressive environmentalists" urged then president-elect Joe Biden to "go beyond naming a climate czar and declare an environmental national emergency," reported Bloomberg News in December 2020.

"Invoking a climate emergency could give Biden the authority to circumvent Congress and fund clean energy projects, shut down crude oil exports, suspend offshore drilling and curtail the movement of fossil fuels on pipelines, trains, and ships, according to a research note by consulting firm ClearView Energy Partners. 'The president's powers to address climate change through an emergency are very, very large,' said Kassie Siegel, an attorney with the environmental group Center for Biological Diversity, which is lobbying Biden's team to act. 'This is No. 1 on the list of things the Biden administration should do.'"[24]

Democratic senator Jeff Merkley of Oregon also urged Biden "to declare a national climate emergency" and use "every tool available to him."

"We cannot wait. We need bold executive action that treats this crisis—quite literally—as the emergency it is," Merkley said.[25]

Shortly after Joe Biden was inaugurated as president, Democrat senate majority leader Chuck Schumer beseeched Biden "to call a climate emergency."

"I think it might be a good idea for President Biden to call a climate emergency," Schumer said. "Then he can do many, many things under the emergency powers...that he could do without legislation." Schumer said an emergency declaration would give Biden "more flexibility."[26]

In 2022 House Democrats urged President Biden to transition from the COVID emergency to a "climate emergency." The Congressional Progressive Caucus demanded Biden declare a "climate emergency" using the executive powers of the presidency.[27]

Jean Su and Maya Golden-Krasner of the Center for Biological Diversity explained "the case for declaring a national climate emergency" in *The Nation* and claimed "there is no greater emergency" facing the world today, urging that Biden could use his presidential power under the Defense Production Act (DPA). "The Defense Production Act, or DPA, is a wartime statute that permits a president to marshal domestic industries to manufacture critical materials needed for the national defense," Su and Golden-Krasner wrote. "The confluence of the climate emergency and Russia's war in Ukraine make this moment an ideal opportunity for Biden to declare a national climate emergency."

The environmentalists even claimed Biden could help solve racism with these "climate emergency" powers. "The DPA also permits the president to allocate these technologies domestically where they're needed most: in partnership with environmental justice communities that have borne the brunt of climate harms and a racist energy system, helping actualize the president's environmental justice priorities," they explained.[28]

Steve Milloy of Junk Science warned of one crucial way that climate lockdowns would be even worse than COVID lockdowns: "The #coronavirus police state is only temporary (I hope!). The climate police state would be permanent."[29]

A Cure Worse Than the Disease?

The BBC featured an analysis examining "when governments abuse emergency powers" in April 2021. "There is emerging evidence that emergency powers are usually used to benefit governments rather than save lives. One study of natural disasters and the use of constitutional emergency provisions found that the more powers given to the executive, the higher the body count (controlling for disaster severity and size)," wrote Luke Kemp, a research associate at the Centre for the Study of Existential Risk at the University of Cambridge[30]

You're Going Nowhere Fast

Climate activists are eyeing "climate emergency" limits on travel modeled after the COVID travel restrictions. They don't want to let you fly unless you have a "morally justifiable" reason.

COVID Lockdown: "People wishing to travel must first make a declaration as to why they need to travel." In January 2021, Reuters reported that "Britain announced new measures to reduce travel on Wednesday with a requirement that people wishing to leave the country must fill in a form to explain why they are travelling, as well as introducing new hotel quarantine stays for some arrivals."

"It is clear that there are still too many people coming in and out of our country each day," Home Secretary Priti Patel said. "We will introduce a new requirement so that people wishing to travel must first make a declaration as to why they need to travel."[31]

Proposed Climate Lockdown: "We can't continue to treat cheap air travel as something compatible with a habitable planet." According to meteorologist and climate activist Eric Holthaus, "seeing loved ones is pretty much the only morally justifiable use for luxury aviation emissions in a climate emergency." Holthaus sets the rules: "It turns out, nearly all of those business trips weren't necessary," he wrote in 2020.[32]

Under these proposed climate lockdowns, you will presumably need to get a government official's approval to fly. You may be allowed to see your family or attend a wedding or funeral, but your travel plans may be rejected if you are merely seeking to go on a vacation or attend a business meeting.

Pierre L. Gosselin of the No Tricks Zone commented that the "USA [is] morphing into communist East Germany! Back then citizens [were] required to apply for an 'Ausreisegenehmigung' (permission to travel abroad) if they wanted to travel out of country. Now it's to be taken a step further by new Marxists: Even domestic travel has to be permitted!"[33]

And the climate campaigners are targeting U.S. air travelers for having the biggest carbon footprint in the world. "If you want to resolve climate change and we need to redesign [aviation], then we should start at the top, where a few 'super emitters' contribute massively to global warming," said Stefan Gössling of Linnaeus University in Sweden. "We should see the [COVID-19] crisis as an opportunity to slim the air transport system," Gössling added.[34]

"The coronavirus may finally cause us to see air travel for what it is, a fuse burning in the climate bomb," wrote a hopeful Christopher Ketcham for the *Los Angeles Times*. "As it happens, a lot less flying is required if we are to stabilize a non-nightmarish planetary climate for our children, our grandchildren and their children.... We must embrace a world that the coronavirus, perversely, is laying out for us. It is a world of less travel, less consumption," Ketcham wrote.[35]

These climate lockdowns are not theoretical. In April 2021 France announced that the nation was going to ban domestic flights where trains are available in a move to battle "climate change." As CNN reported, "France is set

Bill Gates, Climate Hypocrite

Bill Gates "was listed in 2019 as the number one carbon footprint of all the celebrities.... He spoke to the World Economic Forum about we have to change every aspect of our lives to fight global warming, but Bill Gates himself is not willing to do it. The last estimate, by the way, in 2010, was he paid $30,000 a month in his electricity bill at his home then. And since he has now recently bought a $43 million oceanfront property, [he is] not very worried about sea-level rise apparently." —Marc Morano on *Fox and Friends* on January 10, 2021[36] to ban short domestic flights in favor of train services, after lawmakers approved a plan that will see several air routes discontinued to reduce emissions. MPs voted late on Saturday to suspend some flights by domestic airlines that can be made by train in less than two-and-a-half hours, as part of a wider climate bill." CNN noted that France "will join a number of European countries seeking to move away from short flights."[37]

And forget driving to the destination you're banned from flying to. Eliminating private car ownership is a top priority of the climate activists. Democrat presidential candidate Andrew Yang suggested in 2019 that because of climate change "we might not own our own cars." Yang explained, "Our current car ownership and usage model is really inefficient and bad for the environment." The solution? A "constant roving fleet of electric cars that you would just order up, then you could diminish the impact of ground transportation on our environment very, very quickly."[38]

"They're Going after Freedom of Movement"

"In the UK they've proposed CO_2 ration cards that the government or employers would monitor your CO_2 levels . . . your energy use. . . . A CO_2 budget for every man, woman, and child on the planet has been proposed by a German climate advisor. This is what we're looking at," I explained.

"We have a major UK report coming out, we have an International Energy Agency report that came out, calling for essentially the same type of lockdowns—everything from restrictions on your thermostat to restrictions of moving. You can only fly in a climate emergency when it's 'morally justifiable.' . . .

"They're going after freedom of movement; they're going after private car ownership; they're going after everything it means to be a free person and turning it over to the administrative state." –Marc Morano on *Tucker Carlson Tonight*, June 22, 2021[39]

Automobiles are in the crosshairs of the climate agenda. "Social planners, ecologists look to exploit coronavirus as golden opportunity to permanently remove cars from the road—hope 'to save city dwellers...

from the auto-centric culture' and 'remake cities,'" tweeted CFACT author Craig Rucker, referencing a *Wired* magazine article in April 2020.[40]

No More Beer Runs

Flashback to 1975: future Obama science czar John Holdren warned that the United States was "threatened" by "the hazards of too much energy" and chastised Americans for driving cars to the store for a six-pack of beer. "The U.S. is threatened far more by the hazards of too much energy, too soon, than by the hazards of too little energy, too late," Holdren wrote in 1975. Holdren lamented that American society "uses its 5,000 pound automobiles for half-mile round trips to the market to fetch a six-pack of beer, consumes the beer in buildings that are overcooled in summer and overheated in winter, and then throws the aluminum cans away at an energy loss equivalent to a third of a gallon of gasoline per six-pack."[41]

Environmentalists, leftists, and authoritarians in general have long been horrified to see people enjoying the normal pleasures of life. But the COVID lockdowns gave them new opportunities to thwart those pleasures. In New South Wales, Australia, government officials prevented citizens from leaving their homes to shop—and then rationed the amount of beer and wine they could have delivered.[42]

"If We Can Shut Down the World"

Climate campaigners were very excited that the COVID lockdowns spread globally and set up this Reset of society.

"The brakes placed on economic activities of many kinds, worldwide, have led to carbon emission cuts that would previously have been unthinkable.... What was once impossible (socialist, reckless) now turns out not to be, at all," gushed the editors of *The Guardian* about the lockdowns.[43]

Prominent climate activists have made it clear that they expect the COVID lockdowns to usher in a new era of lockdown-type regulations in the name of climate change.

In a TikTok video, youth activist Jamie Margolin asserted, "If we can shut the world down to stop a virus, that means that it's also possible to do the same for climate change! Treat ALL emergencies like emergencies!"[44] In a *Teen Vogue* article titled "Coronavirus Response Should Be a Model for How We Address Climate Change," Margolin asked, "What would it look like when the world actually decides to take on the climate crisis? It would look like what we're seeing right now.... Everyone stopping everything and putting the world on pause to deal with the immediate crisis at hand."[45]

Bill McKibben, founder of the climate group 350.org, sounded downright envious of the global response to COVID. "Who, now that we've seen how fast good governments can move, wouldn't want to use this moment to help avert the even more dangerous crises that global warming is sending our way?"[46]

"This Is the End of Capitalism"

The climate activists are pushing hard to implement ESG or Environmental, Social, & Governance responsibility into our financial systems—a "climate credit score" for businesses. The American Enterprise Institute's Ben Zycher testified to Congress that this is nothing short of "a blatant effort to use private-sector resources for ideological purposes."[47]

Talk show host Glenn Beck was even more blunt, declaring, "This is the end of capitalism." As Beck explained, "It is basically at the barrel of a gun. The government and the big businesses have decided who's going to get the money."[48]

Alex Epstein of the Center for Industrial Progress called ESG a "financially ruinous, and deeply immoral movement that perpetuates poverty . . . and threatens the security of the free world." Epstein argued that "ESG was a movement cooked up at the UN" to coerce investors to "divest from fossil fuels in every way possible, and associate . . . with 'renewable' solar and wind in every way possible."[49]

The climate activist community had been lobbying for decades for this kind of coercive government intervention in the economy and society. The activists have long sought the opportunity to impose their worldview, implement central planning with a comprehensive administrative state, ban anything and everything in our lives that they deem insufficiently friendly to the climate, and remake society in their image.

Climate activists are eager to extend emergency declarations to climate change—and were also eager to use the Russian invasion of Ukraine and skyrocketing energy prices to further their agenda and condition the public to accept constant crises and deprivation.

Coronavirus "revealed what governments are capable of doing," declared Michael Marmot, the chair of the World Health Organization's Commission on Social Determinants of Health. "With Covid-19, everything [on austerity] went out of the window. It turns out austerity was a choice," stated Marmot. "The government can spend anything [in the context of the coronavirus crisis], and they have socialised the economy."[50]

Ed Conway, the economics editor of Sky News and a columnist for *The Times* of London could not contain his excitement about the world shutdown. "Don't take this the wrong way but if you were a young, hardline environmentalist looking for the ultimate weapon against climate change, you could hardly design anything better than coronavirus," Conway wrote. "Unlike most other such diseases, it kills mostly the old who, let's face it, are more likely to be climate skeptics. It spares the young. Most of all, it stymies the forces that have been generating greenhouse gases for decades."[51]

Your financial institution and your own money will also be devoted to fighting "climate change" under the United States' embrace of the financial New World Order.

"Large U.S. banks would have to integrate climate financial risk assessments into every aspect of their work under sweeping new draft supervisory guidance proposed by a top U.S. banking regulator," according to *U.S. News & World Report.* "The principles touch on everything from how climate change affects boardroom governance, liquidity, credit, and operational risk, to the way banks project hypothetical future losses on their books and their ability to service poorer communities."[52]

In 2022, President Biden issued an "Executive Order on Ensuring Responsible Development of Digital Assets" that cited "climate" six times and called for the study and eventual creation of a U.S. "central bank digital currency." In public remarks at the time of the order, Biden stressed that "digital assets" have profound implications for "financial inclusion and equity; and climate change and pollution."[53]

The Biden administration was working with environmental groups, industry, and labor unions to develop a new climate-friendly and equity-based "central bank digital currency."

"Why would you be working with all of these people...on a new currency? The only reason you would be working with them on that is because the currency is going to be programmable. It's going to be programmable, controllable, trackable, traceable, and you'll be able to manage it, set restrictions for it—anytime you want," warned Justin Haskins, the director of the Heartland Institute's Stopping Socialism Project.[54]

Climate change concerns are also being used to manipulate the financial system in other ways. Biotech entrepreneur Vivek Ramaswamy, the author of the book *Woke, Inc.: Inside Corporate America's Social Justice Scam*, explained how BlackRock founder and CEO Larry Fink is the "King of the Woke Industrial Complex" and acts as "the puppet master behind the scenes of Corporate America."

"He is CEO of the world's largest asset manager and what they do is they cause companies to bend the knee to woke orthodoxy because BlackRock says that we won't invest in your company, unless you abide by these progressive standards, or we will dock the pay of a CEO or fire a CEO who refuses to bend the knee," Ramaswamy explained.[55]

Fink has publicly admitted that he believes coercion is necessary to achieve his agenda. "Behaviors are going to have to change, and this is one thing we are asking companies. You have to force behaviors, and at BlackRock we are forcing behaviors," Fink explained in 2017 at a *New York Times* forum. "You have to force behaviors, and if you don't force behaviors, whether it's gender or race or just any way you want to say the composition of your team, you're gonna be impacted," Fink said. He added, "We're gonna have to force change."[56]

BlackRock uses other people's money to force this ideology on companies, according to Ramaswamy. "It is not their money. That $10 trillion doesn't belong to BlackRock. Say what you will about George Soros, at least it's his money. In this case, it is money that belongs to you, to everyday Americans in this country whose blood would boil if they actually knew the way their own money was being used to force a progressive social orthodoxy back onto them."[57]

"Master Level Ponzi Scheme"

"You're watching a master level ponzi scheme. 2020 crash gets laundered through covid bailouts. Covid bailouts laundered through inflation. Inflation laundered through war in ukraine. The war and its effects on the globe will be laundered through climate change. The perps walk." —Class Redux Killa (@BLCKD_COM_PlLLD) on Twitter[58]

"The three largest asset managers in this country, State Street, Vanguard, and the king of them all, BlackRock...together manage today over $20 trillion. That's more than the GDP of the United States," he said. They "are aggregating the money of everyday pensioners and retirees, et cetera," Ramaswamy detailed. "They are using the private sector to effectuate a left-wing social agenda that they could not directly effectuate through Congress."

"ESG [environment, social, and governance], DEI (diversity, equity, inclusion), CSR (corporate social responsibility); there are three-letter acronyms—word salads—that are designed to hide the essence of what is going on," he said.

"That is not the free market in action. It's even worse than a monopoly or an ideological cartel. They're working hand in glove with the party in power to be able to do their bidding through the private sector," Ramaswamy explained.

"If you couldn't get the Green New Deal through Congress, guess what John Kerry is doing. He's getting every major banking CEO to sign the so-called climate pledge," he added, calling it a "form of crony capitalism."

"And here's the kicker...they apply that to the U.S. companies, but they don't apply it to the Chinese companies. So in the United States, they preach ESG. In China, they supplicate to the CCP," he said.[59]

"It is the defining scam of our time," he concluded.[60]

Tesla CEO Elon Musk agreed. Musk, who drew considerable scrutiny from the establishment after his bid to purchase Twitter in 2022 and turn it into a free speech outlet, called ESG "an outrageous scam" after his electric car company was demoted on the S&P Global index that tracks ESG standards.

"Exxon is rated top ten best in world for environment, social & governance (ESG) by S&P 500, while Tesla didn't make the list! ESG is a scam. It has been weaponized by phony social justice warriors," Musk tweeted.[61]

Fall of the Dollar?

"One of the pillars of the dollar's status is the use of the dollar in the international oil market. The 'petrodollar,' though, may soon be replaced. Saudi Arabia is considering selling some oil for Chinese yuan instead of US dollars. India is considering using Russian rubles and Indian Rupees instead of US dollars in trade with Russia, including for the purchase of Russian oil. This will help get around US sanctions." —former Texas GOP congressman Ron Paul in 2022[62]

Credit Card Tracks "Carbon Footprint on Every Purchase"

Get ready for a China-style social-credit system when it comes to your personal spending habits and how they impact "climate change." A new credit card called Doconomy is "working in tight collaboration with Mastercard" and in alliance with the UN Framework Convention on Climate Change (UNFCCC). The credit card was released in 2021 so you can monitor the effect of every purchase you make on your personal CO_2 budget.

The Doconomy credit card enables "all users to track, measure and understand their impact by presenting their carbon footprint on every purchase."

The World Economic Forum praised the CO_2 monitoring card. "While many of us are aware that we need to reduce our carbon footprint, advice on doing so can seem nebulous, and keeping a tab is difficult. DO monitors and cuts off spending, when we hit our carbon max," the WEF statement on the Doconomy website reads.[63]

Other credit card companies are getting into the climate conduct monitoring business as well. "FIGHT CLIMATE CHANGE WITH EVERY SWIPE," declares one new climate change debit card called the Aspiration Impact Measurement (AIM). "Our AIM feature shows you your own personal sustainability score based on your purchases—and the Planet and People scores of the places you're shopping so that you can decide where to spend your money," AIM's website explains.[64]

Currently these new CO_2-monitoring cards are all "voluntary." The question is how long until they are mandated by big corporations in collusion with governments? Will this kind of credit card become mandatory under a declared "climate emergency"?

Meanwhile, prestigious scientific journals have published studies on using climate change as a vehicle in service of more centralization of power, along the lines of the curtailment of rights in the COVID lockdowns. A 2021 paper in the online journal Nature Sustainability argued that COVID lockdowns were the key to beginning "personal carbon allowances" in order to place "restrictions on individuals…that were unthinkable only one year before."

The paper, with four academic coauthors, argued that the COVID lockdowns had conditioned the public to be "more prepared to accept tracking and limitations" in order to "achieve a safer climate." The paper was titled, "Personal Carbon Allowances Revisited."

"In particular, during the COVID-19 pandemic, restrictions on individuals for the sake of public health, and forms of individual accountability and responsibility that were unthinkable only one year before, have been adopted by millions of people. People may be more prepared to accept the tracking and limitations related to PCAs (Personal Carbon Allowances) to achieve a safer climate," the authors explained.[65]

The Independent promoted the idea of "personal carbon quotas" as "demonstrably do-able" and suggested that "every person in the UK be given a monthly carbon budget to balance between heating, travel, energy and food."[66]

Climate skeptic Ron Clutz of Science Matters rejected these calls for government monitoring of your carbon emissions. "Enamoured by lockdown, the puritans wish for a perma-pandemic in which no-one, nowhere, will be happy," Clutz explained. "This all sounds like **one's entire life would be recorded and regulated and monitored and meddled with** by politicians who'll punish or praise, all in pursuit of a vague utopia," Clutz wrote. "**What happens when we reach Net Zero and the weather doesn't change?** I can only guess... 'That wasn't real Net-Zero. Real Net-Zero has never been tried [emphasis in the original].'"[67]

Another respected journal, the *American Political Science Review*, published a paper in 2021 lamenting "democracy" and calling for "authoritarian environmentalism" modeled after COVID lockdowns to fight a climate "emergency." The paper, titled "Political Legitimacy, Authoritarianism, and Climate Change," was written by Ross Mittiga, a politics professor at the Catholic University of Chile. Mittiga argued that during the COVID-19 "severe limitations on free movement and association have become legitimate techniques of government. Climate change poses an even graver threat to public safety. Consequently, I argue, legitimacy may require a similarly authoritarian approach."[68]

Another 2021 study, authored by a team of European researchers and published in the journal *Global Environmental Change*, also argued for a version of climate lockdowns. *Reason* author Ronald Bailey summarized the authors claims: "Americans must cut energy use by 90 percent, live in 640 square feet, and fly once every three years."[69] The authors advocated for limiting "new clothing," eating a "plant-based diet," and using "'collective transport." They also promoted economic "degrowth" and a universal basic income. The study was titled "Socio-Economic Conditions for Satisfying Human Needs at Low Energy Use."[70]

One of New Zealand's top COVID public health officials praised the government's COVID lockdowns and urged the same solution for climate change. "We can do this for the other diseases that we have here in New Zealand. We can do this for climate change," microbiologist Dr. Siouxsie Wiles said on New Zealand television in 2021. "Why wouldn't we do this for other things?" she asked.[71]

This COVID-climate connection all started back in 2020, not long after "two weeks to flatten the curve." The climate activists even co-opted that phrase. In May 2020, the *Washington Post* featured the headline: "We're Flattening the Coronavirus Curve. We Can Flatten the Climate Curve, Too."[72]

Here is a small sampling, from Climate Depot reports, of even more calls to morph COVID and climate and impose similar restrictions on human freedom:

- "Climate is 'greatest threat' to global public health, say 230 medical journals: declare COVID-19 'response' be 'template' for climate response'"[73]
- "Climate lockdown: 'It's time to ban the sale of pickup trucks'—'shift away from relying on private vehicles entirely'"[74]
- "British Medical Journal study calls for meat & dairy price hikes to fight 'climate change'—meat consumption in N. America must fall 79%—'substantially fewer journeys by car'"[75]
- "Foreign Policy mag: 'What if democracy & climate mitigation are incompatible?—democracy 'is not necessarily the path to a solution. It might, instead, be part of the problem'"[76]
- "Business Insider mag: 'Electric vehicles won't save us—we need to get rid of cars completely'"[77]

- "Owning a car is outdated '20th-century thinking' & we must move to 'shared mobility' to cut carbon emissions, UK transport minister says"[78]
- "First, they came for energy, then your SUV—& now: 'Houses pose more danger to climate than vehicles'"[79]
- "Vogue article asks, 'Is having a baby in 2021 pure environmental vandalism?'"[80]

In short, if you like living under the COVID lockdowns, then you'll love living under government mandates to "solve" the "climate emergency." The seeds of climate lockdowns were planted before COVID-19.

"We Can Actually Take Military Measures"

In 2020 Democratic presidential primary candidate and mega–climate funder Tom Steyer laid out his plan for a climate police state. "I will declare...a state of emergency on climate on the first day of my presidency. I will use the executive emergency powers of the presidency

Big Tech Treats Climate Skeptics like Russia

In 2022, in response to the Russian invasion of Ukraine, *Newsweek* reported that "Google, which owns YouTube, has now suspended monetization on videos for all users in Russia."[81]

As I commented at the time, "Big Tech does not differentiate between Russia & climate skeptics.... Google [had previously] demonetized skeptical meteorologist Dr. Roy Spencer's website for allegedly 'unreliable & harmful' climate information.... To all of you cheering on Big Tech and corporations banning and de-platforming anything 'Russian' right now, you may want to think again. If you ever find yourself on the wrong end of the official state narrative on climate, war, or COVID policies, this could be your free speech and your personal bank cards being banned. The coordination and speed of the censorship cancel culture are frightening and will be used against anyone including private citizens who dare dissent."[82]

to tell companies how they can generate electricity, what kind of cars they can build on what schedule, what kind of buildings we're gonna have, how we are going to use our public lands," Steyer declared. "We need to rebuild this country in a climate-smart way.... We don't have a choice on this."[83]

There have been calls for military enforcement of climate regulations. In 2019, University of Copenhagen international relations professor Ole Wæver explained, "If there was something that was decided internationally by some more centralized procedure and every country was told 'this is your emission target, it's not negotiable, we can actually take military measures if you don't fulfil it,' then you would basically have to get that down the throat of your population, whether they like it or not."[84]

Making Us Dependent on China

"The net effect of a Green New Deal distills to replacing domestic energy production (and exports) of hydrocarbons with an unprecedented level of energy mineral imports.... China, for example, supplies about 90% of rare-earths for the world. On the cobalt front, China has also quietly gained control over more than 90% of the battery industry's cobalt refining, without which the raw ore is useless." —energy analyst Mark P. Mills, senior fellow at the Manhattan Institute[85]

Other climate activists have demanded a World War II–style climate mobilization that would convert "a large portion of U.S. military into a kind of climate mobilization force."

In 2016 Stan Cox, the author of the book *Any Way You Slice It: The Past, Present, and Future of Rationing*, urged widescale rationing to ward off the climate threat. "Necessary steps will include phasing out fossil-fuel use within a decade," Cox claimed, and "deeply cutting meat and dairy consumption; and converting a large portion of the U.S. military into a kind of climate mobilization force." The climate "Victory Plan," according to Cox, "calls for a declaration of a 'national climate and sustainability emergency.'"[86]

"For the Rich"

"If their crusade succeeds, cars, meat, and seaside holidays will be for the rich, just as they were a hundred years ago." –Czech publisher and political analyst Alexander Tomský[87]

Christopher Bedford of The Federalist summed up the COVID-climate connection perfectly. "Wouldn't it be grand, our technocrats think, if they could turn the COVID-19 emergency into a permanent emergency over climate? The possibilities are limitless," Bedford explained, adding that "the leadership class has realized there's a lot of value to keeping society permanently in crisis."[88]

CHAPTER 13

The Great Reject—Mass Defiance Can Defeat the Great Reset

This Great Reset is designed to fail because those who planned it do not understand that there are still people ready to take to the streets to defend their rights, to protect their loved ones, to give a future to their children and their grandchildren.

—Carlo Maria Viganò, *former apostolic nuncio representing the Vatican in the United States*

F ormer Czech president Václav Klaus, who lived under communism most of his life, compared the dystopian locked-down world of the past few years to the old Soviet system and offered advice on how to fight to regain freedom. "The communist system really wanted to separate us. It was not called socially distancing, but practically it was the same idea and the same logic. Not to let us go together and to talk to and potentially to prepare a revolution to destroy communism," Klaus explained in the *Planet Lockdown* documentary. "People should oppose all kinds of government restrictions. This is the only—the only lesson which we have learned from the history and especially which we have learned from our communist era."[1]

But if we don't resist it, the Great Reset could soon be unstoppable: limited holidays; restricted weddings; reduced family celebrations; regulated live music; restrictions on live sports, nights out, cinema, and theatre; no bustling bars; and no buzzing restaurants. The COVID lockdowns were just a practice run. This time, the elites' tyranny over every aspect of our lives—and our enslavement to them—will be permanent.

In the post-COVID world, the agenda of the Great Reset is advancing unfettered in the halls of governments around the globe. The greatest challenge in battling the Great Reset is that much of the sinister agenda is hidden from public view, coursing through the veins of obscure policy mandates and arcane banking and financial regulations, hiding in plain sight from a clueless public—who may not realize until it's too late that their liberties are being chipped away by an administrative state that has mastered deception and lack of accountability.

As energy prices and shortages increase and blackouts become routine, how many people will identify the root cause—the preplanned

---

"Homeownership Should Be Seriously Questioned...If We Want to Keep Cities Safe in the Face of Climate Change"

The climate activists endorsing the Green New Deals don't want us to own our own homes. They're calling for ending construction of new houses unless they meet green mandates. During the 2020 presidential primary campaign, Democrat senator Elizabeth Warren said she wanted to ban the construction of new homes in America unless they were built with "zero carbon footprint." As she explained, "By 2028, no new buildings, no new houses, without a zero carbon footprint."[2]

"UCLA urban planning professor Kian Goh also pushed the green assault on home ownership. 'We need to seriously question the ideal of private homeownership,' she wrote for *The Nation* in 2019. 'Cheap energy is untenable in the face of a climate emergency. And individual homeownership should be seriously questioned. . . . If we want to keep cities safe in the face of climate change, we need to seriously question the ideal of private homeownership.' Goh lamented how the 'idealization of individual homeownership has created the scorching landscapes we face today.'" –Marc Morano, *Green Fraud: Why the Green New Deal Is Even Worse Than You Think*[3] curtailment of their lives to force them to behave as they "should," that is, according to the Great Reset's preplanned vision?

As politicians and unelected public health officials warn of new virus variants, necessitating prolonged emergency declarations and more restrictions on freedom of movement and association and speech, how many of the general public will call BULLSHIT?

As Bill Gates and BlackRock buy up farmland and single-family homes, driving up food prices and turning more and more citizens into renters, who will realize the root causes of the higher cost of living? Will the public just accept the goal of the Great Reset: "You will own nothing and you will be happy"?

As vaccine passports and Chinese Communist Party–style social-credit systems are put in place, and surveillance of our lives continues to expand, who will realize this was all set up by the forces of the Great Reset?

How many people in once-free nations will recognize that their rights—not just to free speech but to independent thoughts—are being stripped away at a rapid pace?

It's Not Inevitable

Remember when "Defund the Police" seemed to have unstoppable momentum? And yet less than two years after George Floyd's death and the rioting in major cities that led seemingly every Democratic politician to pledge to defund and hamstring urban police departments, the movement is now almost moribund.

On the floor of the United States Congress for his 2022 State of the Union address, President Biden declared, "The answer is not to defund the police. It's to fund the police." This line was met with a standing ovation from his fellow Democrats, including House Speaker Nancy Pelosi and Vice President Kamala Harris. "Fund them. Fund them. Fund them with resources and training. Resources and training they need to protect their communities," Biden emphasized, plunging a dagger into the heart of what was once the progressives' top-tier political issue.[4] It was easy to be for defunding the police until we saw the consequences in every major city: massive crime spikes and chaos.

The virtue signaling about defunding the police had consequences; it ran into reality in a span of less than two years. The narrative changed when the public realized the real-world consequences of the rhetoric. In the same way, we can hope that as the Great Reset is implemented, the consequences will be so palpable and unpleasant that the public will not tolerate these incursions on our freedom. Much like defunding the police, the Great Reset agenda to take away human dignity and freedom can face a serious reckoning. If the Great Reset can awaken the sleeping bear of the great middle in America, the apparently irresistible force of central planning will have met with an immovable object.

We must expose how wannabe authoritarians have infiltrated every level of our government, from the school board to the executive branch and are working furiously below the radar to expand their iron grip on all levels of government—and the whole of society.

In his opinion in *County of Butler v. Wolf*, a September 14, 2020, case on the legality of COVID-19 lockdowns, U.S. federal district judge William S. Stickman IV summed up the battle we face for our liberties:

> Even in an emergency, the authority of government is not unfettered. The liberties protected by the Constitution are not fair-weather freedoms—in place when times are good but able to be cast aside in times of trouble. There is no question that this Country has faced, and will face, emergencies of every sort. But the solution to a national crisis can never be permitted to supersede the commitment to individual liberty that stands as the foundation of the American experiment. The Constitution cannot accept the concept of a "new normal" where the basic liberties of the people can be subordinated to open-ended emergency mitigation measures. Rather, the Constitution sets certain lines that may not be

crossed, even in an emergency. Actions taken by Defendants crossed those lines.

"It is the duty of the Court to declare those actions unconstitutional," he concluded.[5]

"Superstition and Darkness"

"I have a foreboding of an America in my children's or my grandchildren's time—when the United States is a service and information economy; when nearly all the key manufacturing industries have slipped away to other countries; when awesome technological powers are in the hands of a very few, and no one representing the public interest can even grasp the issues; when the people have lost the ability to set their own agendas or knowledgeably question those in authority; when, clutching our crystals and nervously consulting our horoscopes, our critical faculties in decline, unable to distinguish between what feels good and what's true, we slide, almost without noticing, back into superstition and darkness." —Carl Sagan, in his prescient 1995 book, *The Demon-Haunted World: Science as a Candle in the Dark*[6]

The whole point—and benefit to would-be dictators—of emergency declarations is to bypass constitutional government, to punish and control anyone who defies their plans. Canadian prime minister Justin Trudeau smeared those who chose not to get the COVID vaccines. "There are also people who are fiercely against vaccination," Trudeau said. "They are extremists who don't believe in science, they're often misogynists, also often racists. It's a small group that muscles in, and we have to make a choice in terms of leaders, in terms of the country. Do we tolerate these people?"[7]

HBO's Bill Maher responded to Trudeau, "Tolerate these people? Now you do sound like Hitler."[8]

Trudeau made the logic-torturing claim that vaccine mandates were "the way to avoid further restrictions."[9] How about instead we recognize that freedom is the way to avoid endless tyranny? And Trudeau knows tyranny.

French president Emmanuel Macron declared that those who declined the COVID vaccines were not worthy of being called citizens of his nation. "Someone irresponsible is not a citizen," Macron said of the unvaccinated. "As for the non-vaccinated, I really want to piss them off. And we will continue to do this, to the end. This is the strategy," Macron explained.[10]

Ottawa police chief Steve Bell proclaimed that Canadian law enforcement would crack down on the truckers' "Freedom Convoy" protesting COVID mandates with "financial sanctions and criminal charges."[11]

As a result of the measures the Canadian government took to crush the truckers' protest, "some family members of convoy folks have had difficulty banking because a family member has been involved in the protest," according to CTV National News.[12]

Entrepreneur Balaji Srinivasan, former chief technology officer of the cryptocurrency exchange platform Coinbase, noted that "the concept of punishing an entire family for the acts of one person has certainly existed in other civilizations before. But none of them would be considered democratic." Srinivasan pointed to a 2008 study on Joseph Stalin's "Practices of Collective Punishment," published by Cambridge University Press.[13] The study documented how "the Soviet security police or OGPU-NKVD issued detailed instructions regarding the punishment that should be assigned to the spouses, children, siblings, parents, and even ex-wives of state enemies."[14]

Things that appear to happen overnight—lockdowns, new curricula, spikes in gas prices, supply chain issues, skyrocketing inflation, restrictions on speech, and limits on movement—are in reality decades in the making. When you peek behind the curtain, you find a well-organized network of nonprofits, nongovernment organizations, and community agitators who have been busy at work behind the scenes planning to overthrow the founding principles of freedom and democracy. We must expose, fight, and stop the insidious organizations and leaders who are conspiring to impose a permanent one-party state and thwart the will of the people to empower and enrich themselves.

When an outsider and a rebel like Donald Trump became president and tried to curtail portions of the administrative state, the resistance he faced was massive. And when Joe Biden came into office, the Great Reset was ramped up to high speed, with every cabinet department becoming a climate agency and the banking system being utilized to coerce compliance. The expansion of government power may become so entrenched that a future president bent on dismantling it will face an impenetrable wall of bureaucracy.

The Biden administration, which has been under intense pressure to declare a national "climate emergency," has learned from the COVID lockdowns and has begun implementing the Green New Deal without a vote of Congress. No hearings, no town halls, no calls to legislators—instead, the administration is just imposing the plan on the United States.[15]

We are fast approaching a time when elections *won't* have consequences. In other words, you won't be able to effect change by voting for mayor, city council, governor, or president because the real power will be in the one-party state—the unelected bureaucracy empowered by endless emergency declarations.

Case in point, former New York Democrat governor Andrew Cuomo declared gun violence in his state to be a "public health crisis." Cuomo bragged that the emergency declaration was "just like we did with COVID" as he touted his "first-in-the-nation disaster emergency on gun violence."[16]

The Biden administration declared "misinformation" a crisis and worked with Big Tech to cancel specific individuals from social media.[17]

Statistician William M. Briggs, coauthor of the book *The Price of Panic: How the Tyranny of Experts Turned a Pandemic into a Catastrophe*, believes, "There will be no voting away of the Expertocracy. The Expert ruling class will allow voting only over limited choices, and if the vote is 'wrong,' it will be openly changed or fortified. The idea of voting might remain, but it will be used, like journalism, only to manipulate." Briggs wrote, "The road to this takeover is not straight, or even well demarcated. Power in the Expertocracy is diffuse, not concentrated in any one man, or woman, or even in any one small group. This is why replacing one senator with another, or one president with another, of the country or an institution, does so little. The Expertocracy is Hydra without a central head."[18]

Declaring an emergency and then imposing your preferred "solutions" without a vote on those "solutions" is a dream for politicians who want to bypass the gridlock of democracy. They want a permanent one-party rule.

How do we fight this plan to control, plan, and mastermind every aspect of our lives—from our home thermostat; to our home appliances; to attempts to eliminate private car and homeownership; to targeting the suburbs, freedom of association, freedom of travel, and physical autonomy; to the general crushing of economic liberty?

The answer is the Great Reject.

Feminist Naomi Wolf urged the following on Twitter (before she was permanently banned): "'The Great Reject': everyone needs to engage in civil disobedience All. Day. Long. History shows that only that and criminal charges can stop what's coming next."[19]

Wolf is correct.

Defy the Reset, defy the lockdowns, resist the new normal. The police can't arrest everyone. The Berlin Wall did not come down because the East German government passed a law that said, "Let's remove the wall." It came down because the people no longer consented to live under tyranny. When the people no longer give their consent to live under the Great Reset, energy poverty, censorship, limits on travel, coerced medical procedures, and lockdowns, they will defy the restrictions on their freedom with mass civil disobedience—mass ignoring of whatever edict our betters in government impose on us. That will be the beginning of how we fight and defeat the Great Reset.

A heroic example of the Great Reject is San Diego mom Britt Mayer, who has been a bane to the existence of her local board of supervisors by fighting their COVID mandates. "This is a constitutional republic.... San Diego is not a hospital floor that we collectively have checked into that subjects all patients to equitably prescribed medical care with no due process," Mayer told her elected officials. "We remove consent from treating us like we are patients in a hospital ward. We are done! The consent of the governed is removed. We will not comply. We do not consent.... You are on notice: we will constitutionally remove all petty tyrants beginning now!"[20]

"We Can Grab Our Freedom Back"

"We are the people, we are the 99%, and together we can grab back our freedom from the deadly jaws of the fascist machine!" –Paul Cudenec at the website Winter Oak[21]

But defiance is not enough.

The Great Resist: the way forward is to live your life by exercising your ability to drive a private vehicle, eat meat, live where you wish, own things, be free, and be happy.

We need to develop a series of reforms—checks and balances—for the county, state, and federal health authorities. We need a complete overhaul of the time limits and justifications for executive emergency powers. We need state legislatures to severely limit governors' abilities to operate under emergency declarations. We need a way to ensure they can never do this to us again.

We need a game plan to fight the technocratic state. Talk show host Glenn Beck offered a sample letter to Congress for concerned Americans to send to their representatives spelling out exactly what is needed from our elected leaders in order to thwart the encroaching tyranny. The June 8, 2021, letter to Congress read:

> The foundation of the American way of life is freedom from tyranny, which can only exist in a nation that defends the rights, powers, and property of individuals and families. Over the past two centuries, the greatest threats to liberty have come from governments, both foreign and domestic. And from the beaches of Normandy to the civil rights movement of the 1960s, Americans have repeatedly conquered the

challenges placed before them by those seeking to extinguish or limit individual rights.

However, over the past few years, a new, potentially catastrophic danger has emerged, but not primarily from the halls of Congress or state capitols. This threat to freedom has largely emanated from the boardrooms of the world's wealthiest, most powerful corporations, large financial institutions, central banks, and international organizations like the United Nations and World Economic Forum....

Our free society and the American way of life will not survive this "great reset" unless policymakers put rules into place that ensure banks and corporations, which benefit immensely from special legal and tax advantages, cannot unjustly discriminate against nonviolent individuals and legal businesses. If powerful financial institutions, international organizations, corporations, and governments are allowed to work together to control society to their benefit, then our "rights" will become nothing more than meaningless scribbles on old, fading pieces of parchment.

As a member of Congress, you are duty-bound to defend the rights of all Americans against such attacks on freedom. Failing to do so would be an egregious violation of the oath you swore upon entering Congress. I write this letter to you today to ask that you work as quickly as possible to stop this "great reset" of the United States—before it's too late to reverse course.[22]

We must demand that allegedly "conservative" or "libertarian" or Republican politicians are on the side of freedom: we need to insist that the side that purports to stand for limited government begins to openly challenge the premise of a COVID "emergency" power or the authorization of a "climate emergency." We must reclaim the liberties that inspired previous generations to fight for the demise of the Soviet Union, Nazi Germany, and fascist Italy.

We cannot allow politicians on the "smaller government" label to pander to COVID alarm, climate fears, and other alleged "crises." We cannot allow so-called "conservative" politicians to allow vaccine passports or lockdowns to ever happen again. We must demand that politicians who should be on "our side" stand up and reject the totalitarian premises of "Zero COVID" and "Net Zero CO_2." We cannot allow the alleged "friends" of limited government to just argue around the margins of the big questions surrounding the Great Reset.

"Strident Jackasses"

"Historians of the future will have a hard time figuring out how so many organized groups of strident jackasses succeeded in leading us around by the nose and morally intimidating the majority into silence."—economist Thomas Sowell[23]

Author Joel Kotkin offered a way to battle the Great Reset in his essay "Welcome to the End of Democracy":

> H. G. Wells dreamed of a "new republic" run by a virtuous few. Our digital elites are anointing themselves, and being anointed by their fellow elites in business and media. . . . We have already seen pushback from the right and left in both Europe and America. Many people do not want to accept a life of subsidized dependency, made bearable by the digital equivalent of Rome's bread and circuses. . . . If we as citizens, whatever our political orientation, are not vigilant, our democracy will become an increasingly hollow vessel.[24]

Is there a silent majority that will awaken and fight back against climate and the Great Reset? Are there elected officials in either party ready to lead? We must fight Big Tech and media censorship. We must join other platforms where information can flow freely, and we must not accept the Great Reset in any of its forms.

Daily Mail columnist Peter Hitchens laid bare what is at stake in standing up to resist. "If you have at any time wondered if you would have conformed or rebelled against the consensus, at *any* of the great turning points of the last century and a bit, I think you now know," Hitchens wrote in 2020.[25]

A defiant Robert F. Kennedy Jr., one of my new political heroes, vowed not to relent to the Great Reset. "We are not going to let you take our democracy away. We are not going to let you take our health away. We are not going to let you take our freedoms away," Kennedy said in Berlin in 2020.[26]

Reject the Reset

"The time has come for Canadians to reject the immoral and illegitimate use of government power; to reject the quasi-science of politicized health mandates; to reject opaque policy formulation and decision-making practices; to reject the double-standards and two-faced rhetoric of public servants; to reject politicians who value their careers over their constituency; to reject the wasteful and ineffective spending of taxpayer money; to reject the fear and insecurity of cancel culture; to reject the deployment of police as a tool for intimidation rather than to protect the peace; to reject the prioritization of an indiscernible 'common good' over the rights of all individuals; to reject unwarranted invasions into peoples' private affairs and associations; to reject censorship and conformity over freedom of expression and open debate; and to reject those responsible for undermining our national heritage and sovereignty."–financial expert and author Jesse Berger[27]

If left unfettered, the World Health Organization, which is a Bill Gates tool and a vehicle for Chinese propaganda, will never let go of its power and influence. As we have seen, the WHO is seeking to grab permanent pandemic powers modeled after the UN climate process.

If the "experts," the bureaucrats, and the global elites have their way, the crises will never end. And neither will their "emergency" powers.

"The pandemic is a long way far from over," the WHO declared. "It will not be over anywhere until it's over everywhere."[28]

A never-ending "pandemic" ensures the Great Reset continues unabated.

Statistician William M. Briggs believes that the people can defeat the "managed one-world Expertocracy," and he urges that "the only possible hope of blunting the force of the Great Reset in the regions where it will come is to replace *their* Experts with *our* Experts. Not just in government by (good grief) 'elections,' but everywhere."[29]

"Leaders Who Dared to Defy the So-Called Scientific Consensus"

Investigative journalist Jordan Schachtel issued a special report on The Dossier on the importance of confronting the "pseudoscientific insanity" that was presented as the "consensus" by our political, scientific, and medical establishment.

Schachtel credited "a small group of leaders who dared to defy the so-called scientific consensus on lockdowns," including governors Kristi Noem of South Dakota and Brian Kemp of Georgia.

But "no American politician has been as relentless as [Florida's] Gov. [Ron] DeSantis when it came to making the case against the draconian madness that is lockdowns, school closures, mask mandates, vaccine movement passes, and a number of other disastrous COVID-related restrictions," Schachtel wrote in the 2021 report titled "How Ron DeSantis Saved America from COVID tyranny."

For a model of how to fight the Great Reset, one needs to look no further than the actions of Governor DeSantis. "DeSantis made it a point to showcase that his policy decisions instinctively leaned on liberty in addition to being evidence-based. He elevated the voices of some of the preeminent experts in the field to make the case that these restrictions were not just fundamentally anti-American, but they were also based on fraudulent science," Schachtel explained. "He made the case for freedom, backed by science."

The importance of DeSantis's actions cannot be underestimated. Any plan for resisting the looming tyrannical technocracy would be incomplete without an understanding of what the Florida governor's actions meant at a key time.

Schachtel explained:

> What separates Gov. DeSantis from his gubernatorial colleagues across America is that he was willing to fight both battles and engage both the moral and scientific arguments against lockdowns at the same time. In doing so, DeSantis became the de facto leader of the resistance against COVID tyranny in America, defying corrupt, hyper-politicized U.S. Government Health institutions like the CDC and the NIH, the Biden Administration, the "expertise" of career bureaucrats like Anthony Fauci and the recently "retired" Deborah Birx, and power drunk lockdown governors like Andrew Cuomo (D-NY) and Gavin Newsom (D-CA)....
>
> Moreover, Florida's anti-lockdown success was critical to the policies of fence-sitting governors like Doug Ducey in Arizona and Greg Abbott in Texas, who finally, after months of catering to the supposed science behind restrictions, came around to embrace Florida's roadmap to reopening....
>
> Gov. DeSantis may not have been the first man through the door on opposing lockdowns, but he made the case for freedom against COVID tyranny louder, more succinctly, and with more passion and persistence than any of his counterpart political allies across the nation.

Schacthel explained the effects of DeSantis's stand: "The Florida success caused the Biden Administration and pro-lockdown governors to scramble for answers. After months of having claimed the moral high ground, they were put on defense. It became more and more difficult for these authoritarian forces to continue to justify their power grabs."[30]

The right actions and words by the right leader at the right time can have reverberations far beyond their immediate context. Many countries have had it with forces of the Great Reset.

Brazil has stood up strongly to the global media, academia, and the political establishment. Ernesto Araújo, formerly Brazil's minister of foreign affairs, rejected the World Economic Forum's Great Reset, telling a UN special session in 2020 that "totalitarian social control is not the remedy for any crisis."

A Necessary Reckoning

"A reckoning on the catastrophe of lockdowns is especially important. A narrow group of powerful scientists must never again be permitted to panic the population into lockdown. Checks and balances need to [be] instituted." —Stanford professor of medicine Dr. Jay Bhattacharya[31]

"Those who dislike freedom always try to benefit from moments of crisis to preach the curtailing of freedom. Let's not fall for that trap," Araújo said.

"Brazil is a founding member of the UN, and hence, is committed to its basic principles: peace and security, cooperation among nations, respect for human rights, and fundamental freedoms," Araújo said in his speech to the UN. "COVID-19 must not be taken as a pretext to advance agendas that extrapolate from the constitutional structure of the UN system," he argued.

The Brazilian minister added: "Fundamental freedoms are not an ideology. Human dignity requires freedom as much as it requires health and economic opportunities."[32]

Author and satirist C. J. Hopkins noted that the forces behind the Great Reset "underestimated the potential resistance to the Great Reset, and the time it would take to crush that resistance." Hopkins, who authored the 2020 book *The War on Populism*, observed, "As Klaus Schwab said: 'the pandemic represent[ed] a rare but narrow window of opportunity to reflect, reimagine, and reset our world.'" But, Hopkins pointed out, "it isn't over, but that window is closing, and our world has not been 'reimagined' and 'reset,' not irrevocably, not just yet." He then asserted, "And now the clock is running down, and the resistance isn't crushed...on the contrary, it is growing."[33]

"We Do Not Consent"

Dr. Anne McCloskey, a practicing physician who also works with the Ireland-based Freedom Alliance, explained how to battle the Great Reset. "We do not consent," McCloskey said in a video.

"Across the world, there are millions of people who are awakening to the understanding that this current health crisis, this so-called pandemic, is a Trojan Horse which has been used to introduce a new era for humanity—the Great Reset, the Fourth Industrial Revolution, Building Back Better—whatever catchy, chirpy name the bankers and billionaires are calling it, it's not good for you and me, for the ordinary people," McCloskey said.

"This was not about health; it never was about health. It's smoke and mirrors," a passionate McCloskey declared. "It's over. The lie has been exposed. We must stand together. We do not consent."

McCloskey helped coordinate a worldwide rally for freedom against lockdowns. Given "the removal of our most basic inalienable rights," she urged, we must "stand together to say enough is enough. We do not consent."[34]

McCloskey also wrote a powerful letter to the editor that was published by *British Medical Journal* in 2021.[35]

On the website Winter Oak, Paul Cudenec wrote a profile of the WEF's founder Klaus Schwab that is also an action plan for defeating the Great Reset.

"The majority of the world's population have already been excluded from decision-making processes by the lack of democracy which Schwab wants to accentuate through his stakeholderist corporate domination, his 'agile governance,' his totalitarian 'system management of human existence,'" wrote Cudenec, a No Deal For Nature campaigner who opposes the World Economic Forum's agenda to financialize nature.

"What degree of 'force' and 'coercive measures' would he be prepared to accept in order to ensure the dawning of his technocratic new age? The question is a chilling one, but we should also bear in mind the historical example of the 20th century regime into which Schwab was born. Hitler's new Nazi normal was meant to last for a thousand years, but came crashing down 988 years ahead of target. Just because Hitler said, with all the confidence of power, that his Reich would last for a millennium, this didn't mean that it was so," Cudenec stated.

"Just because Klaus Schwab and Thierry Malleret and their friends say that we are now entering the Fourth Industrial Revolution and our world will be changed forever, this doesn't mean that it is so. We don't have to accept their New Normal. We don't have to go along with their fearmongering. We don't have to take their vaccines. We don't have to let them implant us with smartphones or edit our DNA. We don't have to walk, muzzled and submissive, straight into their transhumanist hell," Cudenec said.

"Klaus Schwab is not a god, but a human being. Just one elderly man. And those he works with, the global capitalist elite, are few in number. Their aims are not the aims of the vast majority of humankind. Their transhumanist vision is repulsive to nearly everyone outside of their little circle and they do not have consent for the technocratic dictatorship they are trying to impose on us. That, after all, is why they have had to go to such lengths to force it upon us under the false flag of fighting a virus. They understood that without the 'emergency' justification, we were never going to go along with their warped scheme," Cudenec pointed out.[36]

Cudenec was making the essential point. We the people have the power, if we are willing to use it.

"They are scared of our potential power because they know that if we stand up, we will defeat them. We can bring their project crashing down before it has even properly started," Cudenec urged.

"We can denounce their lies! Expose their agenda! Refuse their narrative! Reject their toxic ideology! Resist their fascism!"[37]

ACKNOWLEDGMENTS

This book was greatly aided by the tireless efforts of a band of tireless activists, researchers, journalists, and academics who supplied oftentimes minute-by-minute and hour-by-hour updates of all COVID-lockdown insanity and subsequent efforts to promote aspects of the Great Reset. Here is a partial honor roll of those whose work was invaluable in writing this book:

Jordan Schachtel
Michael P. Senger
Naomi Wolf
Robert F. Kennedy Jr.
Kim Iversen
Glenn Beck
Justin Haskins
Jimmy Dore
Russell Brand
Alex Berenson
Tom Elliot
Anthony Watts
Jenin Younes
Glenn Greenwald
Patrick Wood
Derek Hunter
Max Blumenthal
William M. Briggs
Keean Bexte
Alex Newman
Denis Rancourt
James Delingpole

Steve Milloy
Joel Kotkin
Paul Cudenec
Ezra Levant
Michael Fumento
Justin Hart
Thomas Woods
Liz Wheeler
Tony Heller
Peter Hitchens
James Corbett
Jeffrey A. Tucker
Sanjeev Sabhlok

NOTES

Epigraph

"The Obsolete Man," Twilight Zone Wiki, https://twilightzone.fandom.com/wiki/The _Obsolete_Man; MellowTorch, "Rod Serling Was Prophetic with This Warning," YouTube, June 22, 2017, originally broadcast June 2, 1961, https://www.youtube.com /watch?v=FMLWXsV0E-M

Chapter 1: The Great Reset

1. Klaus Schwab, "Now Is the Time for a Great Reset," World Economic Forum, June 3, 2020, https://www.weforum.org/agenda/2020/06/now-is-the-time-for-a-great-reset.

2. Maurice Newman, "Dangerous Elites Planning 'the Great Reset,'" *The Spectator*, October 10, 2020, https://www.spectator.com.au/2020/10/dangerous-elites-planning -the-great-reset/.

3. "'You'll Own Nothing, and You'll Be Happy': World Economic Forum Propaganda Video Gets Deleted—but We've Got a Copy," Rebel News, November 10, 2020, https:// www.rebelnews.com/ezra_levant_show_november_10_2020; Marc Morano, "Watch 2016 Video: World Economic Forum's Utopian Great Reset Vision of 2030—'You'll Own Nothing, and You'll Be Happy'—'Whatever You Want You'll Rent & It'll Be Delivered by Drone'—Meat Will Be 'an Occasional Treat,'" Climate Depot, November 3, 2020, https://www.climatedepot.com/2020/11/03/watch-2016-video-world-econo mic-forums-utopian-great-reset-vision-of-2030-youll-own-nothing-and-youll-be-hap py-whatever-you-want-youll-rent-itll-be-delivered-by-drone-meat/.

4. "'You'll Own Nothing.'"

5. This post has since been deleted. World Economic Forum (@wef), "Welcome to 2030. I own nothing …," Twitter, November 10, 2017, 10:48 a.m., https://twitter.com/wef /status/929012781550112768.

6. Peter Barry Chowka, "Will the Covid-19 PsyOp Succeed?," American Thinker, April 19, 2020, https://www.americanthinker.com/blog/2020/04/will_the_covid19_psyop _succeed.html.

7. Jokebidenisapos,"I'm Selfish?," America's Best Pics and Videos, May 18, 2020, https:// americasbestpics.com/picture/i-m-selfish-you-force-others-to-inject-themselves-with -GnieQuPc8.

8. Tom Tap, "Los Angeles Coronavirus Update: Mayor Eric Garcetti Says DWP Will Shut Off Water and Power at Homes That Throw Large Parties," Deadline, August 5, 2020, https://deadline.com/2020/08/los-angeles-coronavirus-garcetti-shut-off-water-large -parties-1203005621/.

9. OldenWeddellSeal, "The Year is 2043 Covid Variant Phi Beta Epsilon Is Ravaging 0.0026% of the Population," Reddit, August 2021, https://www.reddit.com/r/copypa sta/comments/otxui4/the_year_is_2043_covid_variant_phi_beta_epsilon/.

10. Marc Morano, "NBC News Urges Wearing 4 Masks! CNBC Goes for 3 Masks—But Wash Post & CNN Only Go for Wearing 2 Masks ," Climate Depot, January 28, 2021, https://www.climatedepot.com/2021/01/28/nbc-news-cites-doctor-urging-wearing -4-masks-cnbc-goe-for-3-masks-but-wash-post-cnn-only-go-for-wearing-2-masks/; Lucía Benavides, "In Spain, Pandemic Restrictions Mean Children Aren't Allowed Outside Their Homes," NPR, April 17, 2020, https://www.npr.org/sections/coronavi rus-live-updates/2020/04/17/837248837/in-spain-pandemic-restrictions-mean-childr en-arent-allowed-outside-their-homes; Catie Perry, "New Jersey Gym Owner Takes Coronavirus Shutdown Revolt National with Business Directory," Fox Business, December 9, 2020, https://www.foxbusiness.com/money/new-jersey-gym-coronavir us-shutdowns-national-coalition.

11. *Climate Hustle* 2, produced and directed by Christopher Rogers, written by Marc Morano, featuring Kevin Sorbo, Marc Morano, and Brian Sussman (CFACT Presents, 2020).

12. Brett Samuels and Rebecca Klar, "Trump: We Can't Let the Cure Be Worse Than the Problem Itself," *The Hill*, March 23, 2020, https://thehill.com/homenews/administra tion/488965-trump-hints-at-changes-to-restrictions-we-cant-let-the-cure-be-worse.

13. Vinay Prasad, "What's the Evidence Guiding CDC's Latest Mask Policy?," Medpage Today, July 29, 2021, https://www.medpagetoday.com/opinion/vinay-prasad/93803.

14. C. S. Lewis, *God in the Dock: Essays on Theology and Ethics*, ed. Walter Hooper (Grand Rapids: Eerdmans, 1970), 292.

15. Tim Hinchliffe, "Brazil Says 'No' to Great Reset: 'Totalitarian Social Control Is Not the Remedy for Any Crisis," The Sociable, December 8, 2020, https://sociable.co/governme nt-and-policy/brazil-says-no-great-reset-totalitarian-social-control-not-remedy-crisis/, quoting Mariana Mazzucato, "It's 2023. Here's How We Fixed the Global Economy," *Time*, October 21, 2020, https://time.com/5900739/fix-economy-by-2023/.

16. Ida Auken, "Welcome to 2030: I Own Nothing, Have No Privacy and Life Has Never Been Better," *Forbes,* November 10, 2016, https://www.forbes.com/sites/worldecono micforum/2016/11/10/shopping-i-cant-really-remember-what-that-is-or-how-differen tly-well-live-in-2030/?sh=59105bc41735 (originally at https://www.weforum.org/age nda/2016/11/how-life-could-change-2030/, which is now a broken link); Tim Hinchliffe, "A Skeptical Look at the 'Great Reset': A Technocratic Agenda That Waited Years for a Global Crisis to Exploit," The Sociable, November 2, 2020, https://sociable.co/tech nology/skeptical-great-reset-technocratic-agenda-waited-years-crisis-exploit/; Tim Hinchliffe, "Your Digital Identity Can Be Used against You in the Event of a Great Reset," The Sociable, November 23, 2020, https://sociable.co/technology/your-digital -identity-used-against-you-great-reset/.

17. Hinchliffe, "Brazil Says 'No' to Great Reset."

18. Robert F. Kennedy Jr., "People in Authority Lie," Children's Health Defense, August 28, 2020, https://childrenshealthdefense.org/wp-content/uploads/08-31-20-RFK-Jr.-P ress-Conference-Transcript.pdf; OneSilentJoy, "Robert F Kennedy Jr in Berlin 28 Aug 2020," YouTube, August 28, 2020, https://www.youtube.com/watch?v=wM7NLlW ZD5I&t=4s.

19. Anthony Mueller, "From Lockdowns to 'The Great Reset,'" Mises Institute, August 1, 2020, https://mises.org/wire/lockdowns-great-reset.

20. Joel Kotkin, "How the Democrats Fell for Mussolini," UnHerd, July 5, 2021, https:// unherd.com/2021/07/how-the-democrats-fell-for-mussolini/.

21. Joel Kotkin, "Welcome to the End of Democracy," *The Spectator*, January 8, 2022, https://www.spectator.co.uk/article/welcome-to-the-end-of-democracy.

22. "Aldous Huxley and *Brave New World*: The Dark Side of Pleasure," Academy of Ideas, June 21, 2018, https://academyofideas.com/2018/06/aldous-huxley-brave-new-world -dark-side-of-pleasure/.

23. Kotkin, "Welcome to the End."

24. Kotkin, "How the Democrats."

25. Jon Hersey, "Statist Responses to Covid-19: An Interview with Michael Fumento," *Objective Standard*, April 3, 2020, https://theobjectivestandard.com/2020/04/statist -responses-to-covid-19-an-interview-with-michael-fumento/.

26. Luke Kemp, "The 'Stomp Reflex': When Governments Abuse Emergency Power," BBC News, April 28, 2021, https://www.bbc.com/future/article/20210427-the-stomp-refl ex-when-governments-abuse-emergency-powers.

27. Ibid.

28. "National Terrorism Advisory System Bulletin," Homeland Security, February 7, 2022, https://www.dhs.gov/ntas/advisory/national-terrorism-advisory-system-bulletin-febru ary-07-2022; Alex Berenson, "Extremely Urgent: The Biden Administration Says I'm a Terrorist Threat," Unreported Truths (Substack), February 9, 2022, https://alexbere nson.substack.com/p/extremely-urgent-the-biden-administration/comments.

29. Michael P Senger (@MichaelPSenger), "As a rule of thumb…," Twitter, February 8, 2022, 7:58 a.m., https://twitter.com/MichaelPSenger/status/1491078998507417601 (Twitter has deleted Senger's account, but this tweet is available at the Internet Archive's Wayback Machine: https://web.archive.org/web/20220208160011/https://twitter.com /MichaelPSenger/status/1491078998507417601).

30. Justin Haskins, "How the European Union Could Soon Force America into the 'Great Reset' Trap," *Townhall*, June 21, 2021, https://townhall.com/columnists/justinhaski ns/2021/06/21/how-the-european-union-could-soon-force-america-into-the-great-re set-trap-n2591253.

31. Anne McCloskey, "Rapid Response: Re: Covid-19: Social Murder, They Wrote— Elected, Unaccountable, and Unrepentant," *British Medical Journal*, March 24, 2021, https://www.bmj.com/content/372/bmj.n314/rr-33.

32. Peter Hitchens, "Face Masks Turn Us into Voiceless Submissives—and It's Not Science Forcing Us to Wear Them—It's Politics," *Daily Mail*, July 19, 2020, https://hitchensb log.mailonsunday.co.uk/2020/07/peter-hitchens-face-masks-turn-us-into-voiceless-su bmissives-and-its-not-science-forcing-us-to-wear-.html.

33. Anna (@AnnaGraceWood), "In less than 12 months…," Twitter, January 11, 2021, 2:52 p.m., https://twitter.com/AnnaGraceWood/status/1348719557305917450.

34. Carlo Maria Viganò, "Open Letter to President Donald Trump," *Catholic Family News*, October 30, 2020, https://catholicfamilynews.com/blog/2020/10/30/open-lett er-to-president-donald-trump/.

35. John Smith, "Dr Anne McCloskey," YouTube, March 16, 2021, http-s://www.youtu be.com/watch?v=CG-jmnz6MK4 (This video was removed when YouTube terminated the account, but the video is available here: Trenutnoueu, "Dr. Anne McCloskey— World Wide Rally for Freedom 20th March 2021," BrandNewTube, March 16, 2021, https://www.brandnewtube.com/watch/dr-anne-mccloskey-world-wide-rally-for-free dom-20th-march-2021_HibpQJzUxykZ3ED.html?lang=spanish).

36. Klaus Schwab and Thierry Malleret, *COVID-19: The Great Reset* (Geneva, Switzerland: World Economic Forum, 2020), quoted in "Covid-19—The Great Reset,"

The Real Truth Network, August 22, 2020, https://therealtruthnetworkcom.wordpre ss.com/2020/08/22/the-great-reset/; Louie, "The Only Solution to the Great Reset," AKA Catholic, April 12, 2021, https://akacatholic.com/great-reset/.

37. RISE OR DIE (@altern8ending), "Netherlands Dutch Politician Thierry Baudet drops some massive COVID truth bombs…," Twitter, June 5, 2021, 12:16 a.m., https://twi tter.com/altern8ending/status/1401075443600527360 (Twitter has deleted the account, but this tweet is available at the Internet Archive's Wayback Machine: https://web.arc hive.org/web/20210605071859/https://twitter.com/altern8ending/status/1401075443 60052736; and a transcript of part of the speech is available at Andy Pickett, "Memorandum: Public Comment Submitted for June 8, 2021 Butte County Board of Supervisors Meeting Item 5.02A—COVID-19 Update by the Public Health Director," June 10, 2021, https://buttecounty.granicus.com/MetaViewer.php?view_id=2&clip_id =982&meta_id=151631).

38. "Alex Berenson (@AlexBerenson), "On Memorial Day, we recall our war dead…," Twitter, May 22, 2020, 6:00 p.m., https://mobile.twitter.com/AlexBerenson/status/12 63953008691421188 (Twitter has deleted Berenson's account, but the text of this tweet is available here on Reddit: u/AmigoDeIan, "On Memorial Day, we recall our war dead….," Reddit, May 26, 2020, https://www.reddit.com/r/AntiHateAlliance/comm ents/gqtx9e/on_memorial_day_we_recall_our_war_dead_a_good/).

39. Marc Morano, "Canadian PM Trudeau Confirms Great Reset: 'This Pandemic Has Provided an Opportunity for a Reset'—We Need 'To Re-Imagine Economic Systems' by 'Building Back Better,'" Climate Depot, November 16, 2020, https://www.climate depot.com/2020/11/16/canadian-pm-trudeau-confirms-covids-great-reset-this-pande mic-has-provided-an-opportunity-for-a-reset-we-need-to-re-imagine-economic-syste ms-by-building-back-better/.

40. James Delingpole, "Only Donald Trump Can Save Us from the Great Reset," Breitbart, November 1, 2020, https://www.breitbart.com/politics/2020/11/01/delingpole-only -donald-trump-can-save-us-from-the-great-reset/.

41. James Melville (@JamesMelville), "'So we penetrate the cabinets'…," Twitter, February 1, 2022, 6:21 a.m., https://twitter.com/jamesmelville/status/1488472558425063430 ?lang=en.

42. James Delingpole, "The Great Reset Is Trending. Here's Why…," November 18, 2020, https://www.breitbart.com/europe/2020/11/18/the-great-reset-is-trending-heres-why/.

43. "Trudeau under Fire for Expressing Admiration for China's 'Basic Dictatorship,'" CTV News, November 8, 2013, https://www.ctvnews.ca/politics/trudeau-under-fire-for-ex pressing-admiration-for-china-s-basic-dictatorship-1.1535116; John Talks, "Justin Trudeau Actually Said This…," YouTube, February 16, 2022, https://m.youtube.com /watch?v=lnitEXJ0bwo.

44. Delingpole, "Only Donald Trump Can Save Us."

45. Tim Haines, "President Biden: There's Going to Be a New World Order, It Hasn't Happened in a While and America Has to Lead It," RealClearPolitics, March 21, 2022, https://www.realclearpolitics.com/video/2022/03/21/president_biden_theres_going _to_be_a_new_world_order_and_america_has_to_lead_it.html.

46. Justin Haskins, "John Kerry: 'Great Reset' Will Happen," RedState, November 30, 2020, https://redstate.com/heartlandinstitute/2020/11/30/john-kerry-great-reset-will -happen-n286949.

47. Phillip Inman, "Pandemic Is Chance to Reset Global Economy, Says Prince Charles," *The Guardian*, June 3, 2020, https://www.theguardian.com/uk-news/2020/jun/03/pandemic-is-chance-to-reset-global-economy-says-prince-charles.

48. Jonathan Sumption, "Tyranny of the Covid Experts: Finger-Wagging SAGE Scientist Jeremy Farrar Penned a Book about How HE'S the Only Person Boris Johnson Should Ever Have Listened to, Writes ex–Supreme Court Judge Jonathan Sumption," *Daily Mail*, August 1, 2021, https://www.dailymail.co.uk/debate/article-9847775/Tyranny-Covid-experts-JONATHAN-SUMPTION.html.

49. Paul Cudenec,"Klaus Schwab and His Great Reset," WinterOak, October 5, 2020, https://winteroak.org.uk/2020/10/05/klaus-schwab-and-his-great-fascist-reset/; Cory Morningstar and Paul Cudenec, "Klaus Schwab and His Great Fascist Reset–An Overview," Wrong Kind of Green, October 14, 2020, https://www.wrongkindofgreen.org/2020/10/14/klaus-schwab-and-his-great-fascist-reset-an-overview/.

50. Glenn Beck, "Letter to Congress: How You Can Fight Back against the Great Reset," Glenn, June 8, 2021, https://www.glennbeck.com/glenn-beck/how-you-can-fight-back-against-the-great-reset.

51. Justin Haskins, "How the European Union Could Soon Force America into the 'Great Reset' Trap," *Townhall*, June 21, 2021, https://townhall.com/columnists/justinhaskins/2021/06/21/how-the-european-union-could-soon-force-america-into-the-great-reset-trap-n2591253.

52. Alexandros Marinos (@alexandrosM), "So what are Central Bank…," Twitter, March 15, 2022, 9:20 a.m., https://twitter.com/alexandrosM/status/1503722793086554118.

53. Alexandros Marinos (@alexandrosM), "How far are we from a world…," Twitter, March 15, 2022, 9:37 a.m., "https://twitter.com/alexandrosM/status/1503727165103255552.

54. Forever Inspired, "Edward Snowden 2021 Will It Be Mandatory? It Is Happening Now!!," YouTube, March 3, 2021, https://youtu.be/BWBUVUqSKHk (The video has been removed but can be seen here: Motivation TV, "It Is Happening Now!! I Edward Snowden 2021 Will It Be Mandatory?," March 10, 2021, https://www.youtube.com/watch?v=c7Ib3pkWeGI).

55. "Klaus Schwab Releases 'The Great Narrative' as Sequel to 'The Great Reset,'" World Economic Forum, January 7, 2022, https://www.weforum.org/press/2022/01/klaus-schwab-releases-the-great-narrative-as-sequel-to-the-great-reset/.

56. "Belarus President Unwilling to Accept Additional Terms to Get Foreign Loans," BELTA, June 19, 2020, https://eng.belta.by/president/view/belarus-president-unwilling-to-accept-additional-terms-to-get-foreign-loans-131164-2020/ (This link no longer works, but the quotation can be found here: "World Bank/IMF Exposed COVID Aid Conditional on Imposing Extreme Lockdowns, Curfews," Europe Reloaded, July 28, 2020, https://www.europereloaded.com/world-bank-imf-exposed-covid-aid-conditional-on-imposing-extreme-lockdowns-curfews/).

57. Klaus Schwab, "Now Is the Time for a 'Great Reset,'" World Economic Forum, June 3, 2020, https://www.weforum.org/agenda/2020/06/now-is-the-time-for-a-great-reset/.

58. Delingpole, "Only Donald Trump Can Save Us"; Kyta (@kyta), "It's not a conspiracy when they tell you what they are doing," (comment on "The Great Reset") The Daily Sceptic, October 31, 2020, https://dailysceptic.org/forums/general-discussion/the-great-reset/paged/14/.

59. Michael P Senger (@MichaelPSenger), "Lockdowns, mandates, curfews, closures, states of emergency...," Twitter, December 20, 2021, 12:13 p.m., https://twitter.com/Mich aelPSenger/status/1472978432996765698 (Twitter has deleted Senger's account, but this tweet is available at the Internet Archive's Wayback Machine: https://web.archive .org/web/20211220171437/https://twitter.com/MichaelPSenger/status/14729784329 96765698.)

60. Klaus Schwab and Nicholas Davis, *Shaping the Future of the Fourth Industrial Revolution* (New York: Currency, 2018), 233.

61. "The Global Risks Report 2019," World Economic Forum, http://www3.weforum.org /docs/WEF_Global_Risks_Report_2019.pdf, 70.

62. Kit Knightly, "Climate is the New Covid," OffGuardian, April 23, 2021, https://off-gu ardian.org/2021/04/23/climate-is-the-new-covid/.

63. Tony Heller (@Tony_Heller), "A few rich billionaires bought academia....," Twitter, December 25, 2020, 12:12 p.m., https://twitter.com/Tony__Heller/status/134251860 6257479680 (Twitter has deleted Heller's account, but this tweet is available at the Internet Archive's Wayback Machine: https://web.archive.org/web/20201225171250 /https://twitter.com/Tony__Heller/status/1342518606257479680).

64. William Jasper, "The Great Reset," *New American* 36, no. 17, September 7, 2020, https://thenewamerican.com/magazine/tna3617/page/66758/.

65. Ivan Wecke, "Conspiracy Theories Aside, There Is Something Fishy about the Great Reset," openDemocracy, August 16, 2021, https://www.opendemocracy.net/en/ourec onomy/conspiracy-theories-aside-there-something-fishy-about-great-reset/.

66. Bill Sardi, "Who Runs the World? BlackRock and Vanguard," LewRockwell.com, April 21, 2021, https://www.lewrockwell.com/2021/04/bill-sardi/who-runs-the-wor ld-blackrock-and-vanguard/.

67. Ryan Dezember, "If You Sell a House These Days, the Buyer Might Be a Pension Fund," *Wall Street Journal*, April 4, 2020, https://www.wsj.com/articles/if-you-sell-a-house-th ese-days-the-buyer-might-be-a-pension-fund-11617544801.

68. Mike Danes, "The Great Reset: BlackRock Is Fueling A $120 Trillion Transformation On Wall St.," OilPrice, December 28, 2020, https://oilprice.com/Energy/Energy-Gen eral/The-Great-Reset-BlackRock-Is-Fueling-A-120-Trillion-Transformation-On-Wall -St.html.

69. CulturalHusbandry (@APhilosophae), "Thread. Blackrock is buying every single family house...," (thread) Twitter, June 8, 2021, 9:15 p.m., https://twitter.com/APhilosophae /status/1402434266970140676.

70. Josh Wingrove, "Biden Says to Expect 'Real' Food Shortages due to Ukraine War," Bloomberg, March 24, 2022, https://www.bloomberg.com/news/articles/2022-03-24 /biden-says-to-expect-real-food-shortages-due-to-ukraine-war.

71. Ryan McCrimmon, "China Is Buying Up American Farms. Washington Wants to Crack Down," *POLITICO*, July 19, 2021, https://www.politico.com/news/2021/07 /19/china-buying-us-farms-foreign-purchase-499893.

72. April Glaser, "McDonald's French Fries, Carrots, Onions: All of the Foods That Come from Bill Gates Farmland," NBC News, June 8, 2021, https://www.nbcnews.com/te ch/tech-news/mcdonald-s-french-fries-carrots-onions-all-foods-come-bill-n1270033.

73. James Temple, "Bill Gates: Rich Nations Should Shift Entirely to Synthetic Beef," *MIT Technology Review*, February 14, 1012, https://www.technologyreview.com/2021/02 /14/1018296/bill-gates-climate-change-beef-trees-microsoft/.

74. Sean Fleming, "This 3D-Printed Steak Could Help Us Reduce Meat Consumption," World Economic Forum, July 8, 2020, https://www.weforum.org/agenda/2020/07/3d -printed-steak-cut-meat-consumption; Marc Morano, "The Great Diet Reset: World Economic Forum Promotes Fake Meat from a Printer in Video—'Machines Can Currently Print up to 6kg of Meat an Hour,'" Climate Depot, December 31, 2020, https://www.climatedepot.com/2020/12/31/the-great-diet-reset-world-economic-for um-.promotes-fake-meat-from-a-printer-in-video-machines-can-currently-print-up-to -6kg-of-meat-an-hour/.

75. Sean Fleming, "Good Grub: Why We Might Be Eating Insects Soon," World Economic Forum, July 16, 2018, https://www.weforum.org/agenda/2018/07/good-grub-why-we -might-be-eating-insects-soon/; Marc Morano, "Reset Your Diet! World Economic Forum Touts Eating Bugs to Save the Planet! 'Good Grub: Why We Might Be Eating Insects Soon,'" Climate Depot, December 31, 2020, https://www.climatedepot.com /2020/12/31/reset-your-diet-world-economic-forum-touts-eating-bugs-to-save-the-pl anet-good-grub-why-we-might-be-eating-insects-soon/.

76. Robert Freudenthal, "The Medical Objectification of the Human Person," Brownstone Institute, December 3, 2021, https://brownstone.org/articles/the-medical-objectificati on-of-the-human-person/.

77. Delingpole, "Only Donald Trump Can Save Us."

78. Jeremy Loffredo, "'Dr. Fauci, Mr. Hyde': RFK, Jr. Shares Details about New Book on 'The Corbett Report,'" The Defender, November 24, 2021, https://childrenshealthdef ense.org/defender/james-corbett-robert-f-kennedy-jr-the-real-anthony-fauci/; The Corbett Report Official LBRY Channel, "The REAL Anthony Fauci with Robert F. Kennedy, Jr.," odysee, November 19, 2021, https://odysee.com/@corbettreport:0/rfk jr-fauci720p:e.

79. Tucker Carlson, "The Elites Want COVID-19 Lockdowns to Usher in a 'Great Reset' and That Should Terrify You," Fox News, November 16, 2020, https://www.foxnews .com/opinion/tucker-carlson-coronavirus-pandemic-lockdowns-great-reset.

80. NO Suger Added, "Robert F Kennedy Jr. Speaks to Switzerland—Press Conference— 12th Nov 2021," BitChute, November 14, 2021, https://www.bitchute.com/video/5c gQUzOLPW4D/.

81. "Dan Hannan Asks—'Are We in Danger of Permanently Tilting the Bounds So That We Have Preemptive State at Home Orders or Other Restrictions on the Off Chance?," Britannia News, December 16, 2021, https://web.archive.org/web/20211216145014 /https://britannianews.co.uk/2021/12/16/dan-hannan-asks-are-we-in-danger-of-perm anently-tilting-the-bounds-so-that-we-have-preemptive-stay-at-home-orders-or-other -restrictions-on-the-off-chance/; Daniel Hannan, "Health Protection (Coronavirus, Restrictions) (Self-Isolation) (England) (Amendment) (No. 6) Regulations 2021— *Motion to Approve*—in the House of Lords at 11:45 am on 15th December 2021," TheyWorkforYou, December 15, 2021, https://www.theyworkforyou.com/lords/?id= 2021-12-15a.255.2&s=speaker%3A25975#g264.0.

82. Jan Jekielek, "Jeffery Tucker: How the Working Class Was Betrayed by Lockdowns, Vaccine Mandates," *Epoch Times*, November 18, 2021, https://www.theepochtimes .com/jeffrey-tucker-how-the-working-class-was-betrayed-by-lockdowns-vaccine-man dates_4109859.html.

83. Jeffrey Tucker, "A President Betrayed by Bureaucrats: Scott Atlas's Masterpiece on the Covid Disaster," Brownstone Institute, November 27, 2021, https://brownstone.org/ar

ticles/a-president-betrayed-by-bureaucrats-scott-atlass-masterpiece-on-the-covid-disa
ster/.

84. "Scottish Government Seeks to Make Emergency Covid Powers Permanent," *The National*, August 17, 2021, https://www.thenational.scot/news/19518599.scottish-go vernment-seeks-make-emergency-covid-powers-permanent/.

85. London Real, "You Are the Nazi—Jordan Peterson on Lessons We Learned from WW2 | London Real," YouTube, September 14, 2018, https://www.youtube.com/watch?v= eP_wE0fdlGE.

86. Harry Kretchmer, "Resetting Education: Lessons from Sesame Street on Helping a Generation at Risk. This Week's Great Reset Podcast," World Economic Forum, October 2, 2020, https://www.weforum.org/agenda/2020/10/sesame-and-the-muppe ts-the-great-reset-podcast/.

87. Armchair Quarterback, "Subversive Sesame Street 'Great Reset' Propaganda," YouTube, October 16, 2020, https://www.youtube.com/watch?v=QBLUxXJNQUw.

88. Kotkin, "Welcome to the End."

Chapter 2: The Origins of the Great Reset

1. BasicEconomics, "Milton Friedman vs Bill Clinton (1999) Debunking Climate Policy, The FDA & More!," YouTube, May 28, 2012, https://youtu.be/UlNxIc9gUMc.

2. "Administrative State," Ballotpedia, https://ballotpedia.org/Administrative_state.

3. William Alan Hodson and John M. Carfora, "Stuart Chase," *Harvard Magazine*, September–October 2004, https://www.harvardmagazine.com/2004/09/stuart-chase -html.

4. Stuart Chase, *When the War Ends: The Road We Are Traveling 1914–1942* (New York: The Twentieth Century Fund, 1942), https://ia802600.us.archive.org/29/items /TheRoadWeAreTraveling/TheRoadWeAreTraveling_text.pdf, 95–96.

5. Noah Rothman, "The Greenest Generation," *Commentary*, January 2, 2019, https:// www.commentary.org/noah-rothman/green-new-deal-envy/.

6. William M. Briggs, "Capitalism Is Dead: Long Live the Expertocracy. Burnham's *The Managerial Revolution* at 80," William M. Briggs: Statistician to the Stars!, September 9, 2021, https://wmbriggs.com/post/37075/.

7. Neil Clark, "Twenty Years on from 9/11, the 'War on Terror' Has Morphed into a 'War' against the West's Own Populations," RT, September 14, 2021, https://www.rt .com/op-ed/534789-911-tragedy-war-terror/.

8. Maurice Newman, "Dangerous Elites Planning 'the Great Reset,'" *Spectator Australia*, October 10, 2021, https://spectator.com.au/2020/10/dangerous-elites-planning-the-gr eat-reset/.

9. Tim Hinchliffe, "A Timeline of the Great Reset Agenda: From Foundation to Event 201 and the Pandemic of 2020," The Sociable, November 17, 2020, https://sociable.co /government-and-policy/timeline-great-reset-agenda-event-201-pandemic-2020/.

10. Klaus Schwab and Hein Kroos, *Moderne Unternehmensführung im Maschinenbau* (Franfurt: Verein Deutscher Maschinenbau-Anstalten e.V., 1971); Klaus Schwab and Hein Kroos, *Modern Company Management in Mechanical Engineering* (Franfurt: Verein Deutscher Maschinenbau-Anstalten e.V., 1971).

11. Paul Cudenec, "Klaus Schwab and His Great Fascist Reset," Winter Oak, October 5, 2020, https://winteroak.org.uk/2020/10/05/klaus-schwab-and-his-great-fascist-reset/.

12. Eben Shapiro, "'It's the Right Thing to Do': Walmart CEO Doug McMillon Says It's Time to Reinvent Capitalism Post-Coronavirus," *Time*, October 21, 2020, https://time .com/collection/great-reset/5900765/walmart-ceo-reinventing-capitalism/.

13. Associated Press, "Klaus Schwab on the World Stage," *Hindustan Times*, January 28, 2006, https://www.hindustantimes.com/india/klaus-schwab-on-the-world-stage/sto ry-cBf09I8Wo3QUfBzV6iwxDP.html.

14. Peter S. Goodman, "'He Has an Incredible Knack to Smell the Next Fad': How Klaus Schwab Built a Billionaire Circus at Davos," *Vanity Fair*, January 18, 2022, https:// www.vanityfair.com/news/2022/01/how-klaus-schwab-built-a-billionaire-circus-at -davos.

15. Cory Morningstar and Paul Cudenec, "Klaus Schwab and His Great Fascist Reset: An Overview," Wrong Kind of Green, October 14, 2020, https://www.wrongkindofgreen .org/2020/10/14/klaus-schwab-and-his-great-fascist-reset-an-overview/.

16. "2030Vision," World Economic Forum, https://www.weforum.org/projects/frontier -2030.

17. Raelle Kaia, "Why Are They Doing This?," Medium, March 25, 2021, https://raellek aia.medium.com/why-are-they-doing-this-73963183a502 (Medium has deleted Kaia's account, but this article is available at Open Heart, Open Mind (Substack): https:// raellekaia.substack.com/p/why-are-they-doing-this-73963183a502).

18. IWantTheTruth.ca, "Klaus Is Saying He Has Indoctrinated Leaders and Placed Them in Positions," BitChute, January 26, 2022, https://www.bitchute.com/video/Ikvdeu71 zyNl/.

19. Klaus Schwab and Nicholas Davis, *Shaping the Fourth Industrial Revolution* (New York: Currency, 2018), 42.

20. Klaus Schwab, "The Fourth Industrial Revolution," World Economic Forum, https:// www.weforum.org/about/the-fourth-industrial-revolution-by-klaus-schwab; World Economic Forum, "Davos 2017—An Insight, an Idea with Sergey Brin," YouTube, January 19, 2017, https://www.youtube.com/watch?v=ffvu6Mr1SVc; "Flashback: Klaus Schwab Imagines 'Ten Years in Future' We'll All Have Brain Implants," Miami Standard, April 27, 2022, https://miamistandard.news/2022/04/27/flashback-klaus-sc hwab-imagines-10-years-in-future-well-all-have-brain-implants/.

21. Morningstar and Cudenec, "Klaus Schwab and His Great Fascist Reset."

22. James Corbett, "Episode 403—Meet the World Economic Forum," *The Corbett Report*, June 12, 2021, https://www.corbettreport.com/wef/.

23. Sanjeev Sabhlok (@sabhlok), "Australia's bureaucracy has performed.... ," Twitter, July 27, 2020, 11:52 p.m., https://twitter.com/sabhlok/status/1288004318499491840 (Twitter has deleted Sabhlok's account, but this tweet is available at the Internet Archive's Wayback Machine: https://web.archive.org/web/20200728065253/https:// twitter.com/sabhlok/status/1288004318499491840); Marc Morano, "The 'Great Reset': Rule by Unelected 'Experts'—COVID-Climate Technocracy Has Arrived— 'The Danger of Letting Lab Coats Run the World'—Special Report," Climate Depot, October 13, 2020, https://www.climatedepot.com/2020/10/13/the-great-reset-rule-by -unelected-experts-covid-climate-technocracy-has-arrived-the-danger-of-letting-lab -coats-run-the-world-special-report/.

24. World Economic Forum, *Annual Report 2018–2019* (Geneva, Switzterland: World Economic Forum,September 10, 2019), https://www3.weforum.org/docs/WEF_Ann ual_Report_18-19.pdf, 25.

25. Sanjeev Sabhlok, "Xi Jinping's Use of Hysteria as Warfare Part 3," *Times of India*, January 6, 2021, https://timesofindia.indiatimes.com/blogs/seeing-the-invisible/xi-jin pings-use-of-hysteria-as-warfare-part-3/.

26. Sanjeev Sabhlok, "Xi Jinping's Use of Hysteria as Warfare Part 1," *Times of India*, January 6, 2021, https://timesofindia.indiatimes.com/blogs/seeing-the-invisible/xi-jin pings-use-of-hysteria-as-warfare-part-1/.

27. Patrick Wood, "Chinese Technocratic Authoritarianism Rising, Western Democracy Eroding," Technocracy News, May 21, 2021, https://www.technocracy.news/chinese -technocratic-authoritarianism-rising-western-democracy-eroding/.

28. Mark Moore, "Fauci Defends China, Claims It's 'Far Out' COVID Was Created in a Lab," *New York Post*, June 3, 2021, https://nypost.com/2021/06/03/fauci-defends-ch ina-claims-its-far-out-covid-was-created-in-a-lab/.

29. Ilya Somin, "Remembering the Biggest Mass Murder in the History of the World," *Washington Post*, August 3, 2016, https://www.washingtonpost.com/news/volokh-co nspiracy/wp/2016/08/03/giving-historys-greatest-mass-murderer-his-due/.

30. Derek Hunter (@derekahunter), "Yes a communist regime currently committing genocide…," Twitter, June 3, 2021, 9:53 a.m., https://twitter.com/derekahunter/status /1400450532599209987?s=20&t=vvFiaF10G_wK79afe1TpCg.

31. J. Brooks Spector, "The Rise of Chinese Technocratic Authoritarianism and the Erosion of Western Democracy," Daily Maverick, April 14, 2021, https://www.dailymaverick .co.za/article/2021-04-14-the-rise-of-chinese-technocratic-authoritarianism-and-the -erosion-of-western-democracy/.

32. Stacy Rudin, "What's Behind the WHO"s Lockdown Mixed-Messages," American Institute for Economic Research, October 14, 2020, https://www.aier.org/article/wha ts-behind-the-whos-lockdown-mixed-messaging/.

33. Abhijit Iyer-Mitra, "WHO and China Covered Tedros' Past—but What Is Worrying Is How India Fell for It," The Print, April 13, 2020, https://theprint.in/opinion/who -and-china-tedros-past-worrying-how-india-fell-for-it/400945/.

34. James Corbett, "Who is Bill Gates?" *The Corbett Report*, January 5, 2020, https:// www.corbettreport.com/gates/; Donald McNeil Jr., "Candidate to Lead the W.H.O. Accused of Covering Up Epidemics," *New York Times*, May 13, 2017, https://archive .is/vgOWw.

35. "WHO Director-General's Statement on IHR Emergency Committee on Novel Coronavirus (2019-nCoV)," World Health Organization, January 30, 2020, https:// www.who.int/director-general/speeches/detail/who-director-general-s-statement-on -ihr-emergency-committee-on-novel-coronavirus-(2019-ncov); see also Andrew Joseph and Megan Thielking, "WHO Praises China's Response to Coronavirus, Will Reconvene Expert Committee to Assess Global Threat," Stat News, January 29, 2020, https://www.statnews.com/2020/01/29/who-reconvene-expert-committee-coronavi rus/.

36. Michael P Senger (@MichaelPSenger), "By corrupting global institutions…," Twitter, January 10, 2021, 12:44 p.m., https://twitter.com/MichaelPSenger/status/134832483 8167908352 (Twitter has deleted Senger's account, but this tweet is available at the Internet Archive's WayBack Machine: https://web.archive.org/web/20220221125914 /https://twitter.com/MichaelPSenger/status/1348324838167908352).

37. Senger updated his profile, and Twitter subsequently deleted his account, but a screenshot is available at https://pbs.twimg.com/media/EraNbeGXAAMp-rI?format =jpg&name=large.

38.   Michael P Senger (@MichaelPSenger), "Snake oil: How Xi Jiping shut down the world…," (thread) Twitter, October 31, 2021, https://twitter.com/MichaelPSenger/st atus/1454831901173186561 (Twitter has deleted Senger's account, but this tweet is available at the Internet Archive's WayBack Machine: https://web.archive.org/web/20 211102132049/https://twitter.com/MichaelPSenger/status/1454831901173186561).

39.   Robert F. Kennedy Jr., "People in Authority Lie," Children's Health Defense, August 28, 2020, https://childrenshealthdefense.org/wp-content/uploads/08-31-20-RFK-Jr.-P ress-Conference-Transcript.pdf; OneSilentJoy, "Robert F Kennedy Jr in Berlin 28 Aug 2020," YouTube, August 28, 2020, https://www.youtube.com/watch?v=wM7NLlW ZD5I&t=4s.

40.   Freddie Sayers, "Neil Ferguson Interview: China Changed What Was Possible," UnHerd, December 26, 2020, https://unherd.com/thepost/neil-ferguson-interview-ch ina-changed-what-was-possible/.

41.   Michael P. Senger, "The Masked Ball of Cowardice," Tablet, August 29, 2021, https:// www.tabletmag.com/sections/news/articles/masked-ball-cowardice.

42.   Jon Hersey, "Statist Responses to COVID-19: An Interview with Michael Fumento," Objective Standard, April 3, 2020, https://theobjectivestandard.com/2020/04/statist -responses-to-covid-19-an-interview-with-michael-fumento/.

43.   Bill Bostock, "How 'Professor Lockdown' Helped Save Tens of Thousands of Lives Worldwide—and Carried COVID-19 into Downing Street," Business Insider, April 25, 2020, https://www.businessinsider.com/neil-ferguson-transformed-uk-covid-resp onse-oxford-challenge-imperial-model-2020-4.

44.   Bostock, "How 'Professor Lockdown' Helped."

45.   Edward Peter Stringham, "Was Lockdown Architect and Theoretical Physicist Neil Ferguson Morally Right to Defy the Lockdown?," American Institute for Economic Research, May 18, 2020, https://www.aier.org/article/was-lockdown-architect-and-theo retical-physicist-neil-ferguson-morally-right-to-defy-the-lockdown/; Will Feuer and Noah Higgins-Dunn, "Cuomo Orders Most New Yorkers to Stay Inside—'We're All under Quarantine Now,'" CNBC, March 20, 2020, https://www.cnbc.com/2020/03/20/new -york-gov-cuomo-orders-100percent-of-non-essential-businesses-to-work-from-home .html; Zac Anderson, "Delayed Lockdown Decision Could Haunt Gov. DeSantis," Tallahassee Democrat, April 3, 2020, https://www.tallahassee.com/story/news/2020/04 /03/delayed-lockdown-decision-could-haunt-gov-desantis/2938720001/.

46.   Howard Bauchner, "Interview with Anthony S. Fauci, MD, author of Coronavirus Infections—More than Just the Common Cold," Conversations with Dr Bauchner, January 23, 2020, https://edhub.ama-assn.org/jn-learning/audio-player/18197306; Gregg Re, "Coronavirus Timeline Shows Politicians,' Media's Changing Rhetoric on Risk of Pandemic," Fox News, April 20, 2020, https://www.foxnews.com/politics/fr om-new-york-to-canada-to-the-white-house-initial-coronavirus-responses-havent-ag ed-well.

47.   Hersey, "Statist Responses to COVID-19."

48.   Bostock, "How 'Professor Lockdown' Helped."

49.   Hersey, "Statist Responses to COVID-19."

50.   "Gates Foundation Awards $14.5 Million for Global Healthcare Access," Philanthropy News Digest, December 13, 2018, https://philanthropynewsdigest.org/news/gates-fou ndation-awards-14.5-million-for-global-healthcare-access.

51.   "Imperial College London," Gates Foundation, July 2020, https://www.gatesfoundat ion.org/about/committed-grants/2020/07/inv016635.

52. Kennedy, "People in Authority Lie"; OneSilentJoy, "Robert F Kennedy Jr in Berlin."
53. Bostock, "How 'Professor Lockdown' Helped."
54. Michael P Senger (@MichaelPSenger), "The purpose of lockdowns prior to vaccination…," Twitter, May 2, 2021, 11:31 a.m., https://twitter.com/MichaelPSeng er/status/1388878836956241924 (Twitter has deleted Senger's account, but this tweet is available at the Internet Archive's WayBack Machine: https://web.archive.org/web /20210502153150/https://twitter.com/MichaelPSenger/status/138887883695624 1924.)
55. Michael Fumento, *The Myth of Heterosexual AIDS* (New York: Basic Books, 1990).
56. Adam Andrzejewski, "Dr. Anthony Fauci: The Highest Paid Employee in the Entire U.S. Government," *Forbes*, January 25, 2021, https://www.forbes.com/sites/adaman drzejewski/2021/01/25/dr-anthony-fauci-the-highest-paid-employee-in-the-entire-us -federal-government/?sh=60fff6af386f; Gina Kolato, "Fauci Wants to Make Vaccines for the Next Pandemic before It Hits," *New York Times*, July 25, 2021, https://www .nytimes.com/2021/07/25/health/fauci-prototype-vaccines.html.
57. Michael Fumento, "The Two Horsemen of the Apocalypse: Fauci and Redfield," Issues & Insights, August 4, 2020, https://issuesinsights.com/2020/08/04/the-two-horsemen -of-the-apocalypse-fauci-and-redfield/?fbclid=IwAR3jaqG5NzOSkx7Ddoci96MBQ SiqDB_c7hMIskgUc6ooUepp3VL30E3PIdA.
58. Isaac Schorr, "Video Resurfaces of Fauci Warning 'Household Contact' with AIDS Patients Could Put Kids at Risk," Yahoo!Life, November 9, 2021, https://www.yahoo .com/lifestyle/video-resurfaces-fauci-warning-household-180945365.html.
59. Justin Hart (@justin_hart), "This is Fauci talking about AIDS…," Twitter, November 9, 2021, 11:43 a.m., https://twitter.com/justin_hart/status/1458113043968102401.
60. Fumento, "The Two Horsemen of the Apocalypse."
61. Naomi Wolf, "COVID-19 Policies Are a War on Humanity," Wolf: Author and Journalist, January 4, 2021, https://web.archive.org/web/20210711162351/https://dr naomiwolf.com/covid-war-on-humanity/.
62. Michael Fumento, "Fauci Finally, Falsely, Invokes the 'Spanish Flu,'" *American Spectator*, July 21, 2021, https://spectator.org/fauci-new-york-did-it-correctly-covid-19 -spanish-flu/.
63. Fumento, "The Two Horsemen of the Apocalypse."
64. Robert F. Kennedy Jr., "Dear CHD Friend…," Children's Health Defense, https://chi ldrenshealthdefense.salsalabs.org/therealanthonyfauci-rfk?.
65. "Global Health Leaders Launch Decade of Vaccines Collaboration," World Health Organization, https://www.who.int/immunization/newsroom/press/news_release_de cade_vaccines/en/ (This article is no longer at the World Health organization link, but it is available at the Internet Archive's Wayback Machine: https://web.archive.org/web /20210308031649/https://www.who.int/immunization/newsroom/press/news_relea se_decade_vaccines/en/); "Bill and Melinda Gates Pledge $10 Billion in Call for Decade of Vaccines," Gates Foundation, https://www.gatesfoundation.org/Media-Center/Pre ss-Releases/2010/01/Bill-and-Melinda-Gates-Pledge-$10-Billion-in-Call-for-Decade -of-Vaccines.
66. Kelly Davio, "NIH, Bill and Melinda Gates Foundation Collaborate to Develop Gene-Based HIV Treatment," *American Journal of Managed Care*, October 28, 2019, https:// www.ajmc.com/newsroom/nih-bill-and-melinda-gates-foundation-collaborate-to-de velop-genebased-hiv-treatment.

67. World Economic Forum, "Davos Annual Meeting 2008—Bill Gates," YouTube, January 25, 2008, https://www.youtube.com/watch?v=Ql-Mtlx31e8.

68. Corbett, "Who is Bill Gates?"

69. Michael Fumento, "Why the WHO Faked a Pandemic," *Forbes*, https://www.forbes .com/2010/02/05/world-health-organization-swine-flu-pandemic-opinions-contribut ors-michael-fumento.html (This article is no longer at the *Forbes* link, but it is available at the Internet Archive's Wayback Machine: https://web.archive.org/web/201002081 82828/https://www.forbes.com/2010/02/05/world-health-organization-swine-flu-pa ndemic-opinions-contributors-michael-fumento.html); Margaret Chan, "Address to the Regional Committee for Europe (59th Session)," World Health Organization, September 15, 2009 (This article is available at the Internet Archive's Wayback Machine: https://web.archive.org/web/20100208182828/http://www.who.int/dg/speeches/2009 /euro_regional_committee_20090815/en/index.html).

70. "Voluntary Contributions by Fund and by Contributor," World Health Organization, May 9, 2019, https://www.who.int/about/finances-accountability/reports/A72_INF5 -en.pdf (This article is no longer at the WHO link, but it is available at the Internet Archive's Wayback Machine: https://web.archive.org/web/20211215043326/https:// www.who.int/about/finances-accountability/reports/A72_INF5-en.pdf); "Voluntary Contributions by Fund and by Contributor, 2017," World Health Organization, April 19, 2018.

71. TED, "Innovating to Zero! | Bill Gates," YouTube, February 20, 2010, https://www.yo utube.com/watch?v=JaF-fq2Zn7I.

72. Bill Gates, "Does Saving More Lives Lead to Overpopulation?" YouTube, February 13, 2018, https://www.youtube.com/watch?v=obRG-2jurz0.

73. Ryan Saavedra, "Bill Gates, Worth Nearly $120 Billion, Advocates for Keeping Some Businesses Closed during the Pandemic," The Daily Wire, December 14, 2020, https:// www.dailywire.com/news/bill-gates-worth-nearly-120-billion-advocates-for-keeping -some-businesses-closed-during-pandemic.

74. Yoni Heisler, "Bill Gates Says the Coronavirus Could Kill Millions of People Who Aren't Even Infected," BGR, August 22, 2020, https://bgr.com/science/bill-gates-coro navirus-deaths-china-masks/; The Economist, "Covid-19: Zanny Minton Beddoes Interviews Bill Gates," YouTube, August 19, 2020, https://www.youtube.com/watch ?v=m7StkvQ7kos.

75. Corbett, "Who Is Bill Gates?"

76. Raelle Kaia, "Why Are They Doing This?" Medium, March 25, 2021, https://raellek aia.medium.com/why-are-they-doing-this-73963183a502 (Medium has deleted Kaia's account, but this article is available at Open Heart, Open Mind (Substack): https:// raellekaia.substack.com/p/why-are-they-doing-this-73963183a502).

77. "Where Our Money Comes From," BBC Media Action, https://www.bbc.co.uk/med iaaction/about/funding.

78. "About This Site," *The Guardian*, October 25, 2011, https://www.theguardian.com /global-development/2010/sep/14/about-this-site.

79. "Committed Grants," Gates Foundation, https://www.gatesfoundation.org/How-We -Work/Quick-Links/Grants-Database/Grants/2018/10/OPP1180191.

80. "How We're Funded," Our World in Data, https://ourworldindata.org/supporters.

81. Bill Carter, "Gates Foundation Backs ABC News Project," *New York Times*, October 6, 2010, https://mediadecoder.blogs.nytimes.com/2010/10/06/gates-foundation-backs -abc-news-project/.

82. "Gates Foundations Awards $3.5 Million to PBS's 'NewsHour' to Expand Global Health Coverage," Philanthropy News Digest, December 7, 2008, https://philanthrop ynewsdigest.org/news/gates-foundation-awards-3.5-million-to-pbs-s-newshour-to-ex pand-global-health-coverage.

83. "Bill Gates on Where the COVID-19 Pandemic Will Hurt the Most," *PBS NewsHour*, April 7, 2020, https://www.pbs.org/video/bill-gates-1586294450/.

84. Jeremy Lofredo and Michele Greenstein, "Why the Bill Gates Global Health Empire Promises More Empire and Less Health," Grain, July 18, 2020, https://grain.org/en/ar ticle/6511-why-the-bill-gates-global-health-empire-promises-more-empire-and-less-pu blic-health.

85. The Late Show with Stephen Colbert, "Bill Gates: Global Innovation Is the Key to Achieving a Return to Normal," YouTube, April 24, 2020, https://www.youtube.com /watch?v=dNiuaKKEPu8.

86. Corbett, "Who Is Bill Gates?"; "Bill and Melinda Gates Foundation Expands Commitment to Global COVID-19 Response, Calls for International Collaboration to Protect People Everywhere from the Virus," Gates Foundation, April 15, 2020, https://www.gatesfoundation.org/Media-Center/Press-Releases/2020/04/Gates-Foun dation-Expands-Commitment-to-COVID-19-Response-Calls-for-International-Coll aboration.

87. "What Has the Gates Foundation Done for Global Health?" *The Lancet* 373, no. 9675 (May 2009): https://doi.org/10.1016/S0140-6736(09)60885-0.

88. The Rockefeller Foundation and Global Business Network, *Scenarios for the Future of Technology and International Development* (New York: The Rockefeller Foundation, May 2010), http://www.nommeraadio.ee/meedia/pdf/RRS/Rockefeller Foundation.pdf.

89. Jason Puckett, David Tregde, and Terry Spry Jr., "VERIFY: 'Rockefeller Document,' Doesn't Prove Theory Coronavirus Pandemic Was Planned in 2010," WUSA9, July 15, 2020, https://www.wusa9.com/article/news/health/coronavirus/rockefeller-document -pandemic-scenario-2010/507-00197d1f-4f92-40ee-a0c7-2f5fe9d3b3cb.

90. *Scenarios for the Future of Technology and International Development.*

91. Chelsey Cox, "Fact Check: 'Rockefeller Playbook' and 'Operation Lockstep' Are Hoaxes," *USA Today*, January 14, 2021, https://www.usatoday.com/story/news/fact check/2021/01/14/fact-check-operation-lockstep-covid-19-conspiracy-theory/656723 1002/.

92. Puckett, Tregde, and Spry Jr., "Verify: 'Rockefeller Document.'"

93. Tim Hinchcliffe, "A Timeline of the Great Reset Agenda: From Foundation to Event 201 and the Pandemic of 2020," The Sociable, November 17, 2020, https://sociable.co /government-and-policy/timeline-great-reset-agenda-event-201-pandemic-2020/. Hinchcliffe cites World Economic Forum, *World Economic Forum Annual Meeting 2014* (Geneva, Switzerland: World Economic Forum, 2014), http://www3.weforum .org/docs/AM14/WEF_AM14_Public_Report.pdf; "We Need to Press Restart on the Global Economy," World Economic Forum, November 10, 2015, https://www.wefor um.org/agenda/2015/11/we-need-to-press-restart-on-the-global-economy/; "How to Reboot the Global Economy?" World Economic Forum, 2016, https://www.weforum .org/open-forum/event_sessions/how-to-reboot-the-global-economy; Homi Kharas and John W. McArthur, "We Need to Reset the Global Operating System to Achieve the SDGs. Here's How," World Economic Forum, January 13, 2017, https://www.we

forum.org/agenda/2017/01/we-need-to-upgrade-the-sustainable-development-goals
-here-s-how/.

94. Center for Health Security, "Clade X Pandemic Exercise: Segment 4," YouTube, May
18, 2018, https://youtu.be/tqa7NHq73xM.

95. Tom Inglesby, "6 Ways Countries Can Prepare for the Next Infectious Disease
Pandemic," World Economic Forum, July 18, 2018, https://www.weforum.org/agen
da/2018/07/infectious-disease-pandemic-clade-x-johns-hopkins/.

96. "Event 201," Center for Health Security, https://www.centerforhealthsecurity.org/eve
nt201/.

Chapter 3: How the COVID-19 Response Accelerated the Great Reset

1. Klaus Schwab and Thierry Malleret, *COVID-19: The Great Reset* (New York:
Currency, 2020), 89.

2. Adam Wagner (@AdamWagner1), "I am not one for melodramatic comparisons...,"
Twitter, September 30, 2020, 4:51 a.m., https://twitter.com/AdamWagner1/status/131
1277952777293825.

3. Marc Morano (@ClimateDepot), "Mayor from East Germany?...," Twitter, April 8,
2020, 11:54 a.m., https://twitter.com/ClimateDepot/status/1247915651487973378.

4. Ron Gant, "Rahm Emanuel 'Never Let a Good Crisis to Waste,'" YouTube,
October 30, 2012, https://www.youtube.com/watch?v=Pb-YuhFWCr4.

5. Robert F. Kennedy Jr., "People in Authority Lie," Children's Health Defense, August
28, 2020, https://childrenshealthdefense.org/wp-content/uploads/08-31-20-RFK-Jr.-P
ress-Conference-Transcript.pdf; OneSilentJoy, "Robert F Kennedy Jr in Berlin 28 Aug
2020," YouTube, August 28, 2020, https://www.youtube.com/watch?v=wM7NLlW
ZD5I&t=4s.

6. Bill Dunne, "The Danger of Letting Lab Coats Run the World," American Thinker,
May 14, 2020, https://www.americanthinker.com/articles/2020/05/the_danger_of_le
tting_lab_coats_run_the_world.html.

7. Rebecca Klar, "France's Macron Calls for All Citizens to Remain Confined in Homes:
'We're at War,'" *The Hill*, March 16, 2020, https://thehill.com/policy/international/48
7870-frances-macron-calls-for-all-citizens-to-remain-confined-in-homes-were.

8. C. S. Lewis, *God in the Dock* (Grand Rapids: Eerdmans, 1970), 315. This passage is
available at archive.org: https://archive.org/details/godindockessayso0000lewi/page
/314/mode/2up.

9. Jeffrey A. Tucker, "What Were Lockdowners Thinking? A Review of Jeremy Farrar,"
Brownstone Institute, August 1, 2021, https://brownstone.org/articles/what-were-loc
kdowners-thinking-a-review-of-jeremy-farrar/.

10. "Dr. Donald A Henderson," Pan American Health Organization, https://www.paho
.org/en/public-health-heroes/dr-donald-henderson.

11. Thomas V. Inglesby et al., "Disease Mitigation Measures in the Control of Pandemic
Influenza," *Biosecurity and Bioterrorism: Biodefense Strategy, Practice, and Science*
4, no. 4 (2006), https://s3.documentcloud.org/documents/6841076/2006-11-Disease
-Mitigation-Measures-in-the.pdf.

12. Mary Harrington, "The American Right's Civil War," UnHerd, November 6, 2021,
https://unherd.com/2021/11/the-american-rights-civil-war/.

13. Michael P Senger (@MichaelPSenger), "By corrupting global institutions...," Twitter,
January 10, 2021, 12:44 p.m., https://twitter.com/MichaelPSenger/status/134832483

8167908352 (Twitter has deleted Senger's account, but this tweet is available at the Internet Archive's WayBack Machine: https://web.archive.org/web/20220104234631 /https://twitter.com/MichaelPSenger/status/1348324838167908352).

14. Ibid.

15. Michael P Senger, (@MichaelPSenger), "In February 2020, a team from Imperial College London…," Twitter, January 10, 2021, 1:19 p.m., https://twitter.com/michae lpsenger/status/1348333750342488064 (Twitter has deleted Senger's account, but this tweet is available at the Internet Archive's WayBack Machine: https://web.ar chive.org/web/20210110182546/https://twitter.com/michaelpsenger/status/13483337 50342488064).

16. "Tucker Carlson Guest Tells Fox Viewers That Covid Vaccines Are 'Declining in Effectiveness Very Quickly,'" Media Matters for America, July 16, 2021, https://www .mediamatters.org/tucker-carlson/tucker-carlson-guest-tells-fox-viewers-covid-vaccin es-are-declining-effectiveness.

17. Michael P Senger (@MichaelPSenger), "By corrupting global institutions, promoting hysterical data…," (thread) Twitter, January 10, 2021, 12:44 p.m., https://twitter.com /MichaelPSenger/status/1348324838167908352 (Twitter has deleted Senger's account, but this tweet is available at the Internet Archive's Wayback Machine: https://web.arc hive.org/web/20220104234631/https://twitter.com/MichaelPSenger/status/1348324 838167908352).

18. Anne McCloskey, "Rapid Respose Re: COVID-19: Social Murder, They Wrote– Elected, Unaccountable, and Unrepentent," British Medical Journal, March 4, 2021, https://www.bmj.com/content/372/bmj.n314/rr-33.

19. Ibid.

20. County of Butler v. Wolf, 486 F. Supp. 3d 883, 926 (W.D. Pa. 2020) https://casetext .com/case/cnty-of-butler-v-wolf-1.

21. Greg Ip, "New Thinking on COVID Lockdowns: They're Overly Blunt and Costly," Wall Street Journal, August 24, 2020, https://www.wsj.com/articles/covid-lockdowns -economy-pandemic-recession-business-shutdown-sweden-coronavirus-11598281419.

22. "Wuhan Lockdown 'Unprecedented,' Shows Commitment to Contain Virus: WHO Representative in China," Reuters, January 23, 2020, https://www.reuters.com/artic le/us-china-health-who/wuhan-lockdown-unprecedented-shows-commitment-to-con tain-virus-who-representative-in-china-idUSKBN1ZM1G9.

23. "Statement on the Second of the International Health Regulations (2005) Emergency Committee Regarding the Outbreak of Novel Coronavirus (2019-nCoV)," World Health Organization, January 30, 2020, https://www.who.int/news/item/30-01-2020 -statement-on-the-second-meeting-of-the-international-health-regulations-(2005)-em ergency-committee-regarding-the-outbreak-of-novel-coronavirus-(2019-ncov).

24. Jeffrey H. Anderson, "The Masking of America," Claremont Review of Books, Summer 2021, https://claremontreviewofbooks.com/the-masking-of-america/.

25. "WHO Director-General's Statement on IHR Emergency Committee on Novel Coronavirus (2019-nCoV)," World Health Organization, January 30, 2020, https:// www.who.int/director-general/speeches/detail/who-director-general-s-statement-on -ihr-emergency-committee-on-novel-coronavirus-(2019-ncov).

26. Andrew Joseph and Megan Thielking, "WHO Praises China's Response to Coronavirus, Will Reconvene Expert Committee to Assess Global Threat," Stat News, January 29, 2020, https://www.statnews.com/2020/01/29/who-reconvene-expert-co mmittee-coronavirus/.

27. "WHO Director-General's Statement."

28. Stacey Rudin, "What's Behind the WHO's Lockdown Mixed-Messaging," American Institute for Economic Research, October 14, 2020, https://www.aier.org/article/wha ts-behind-the-whos-lockdown-mixed-messaging/.

29. "Statement on the Second of the International Health Regulations (2005)."

30. Michael P. Senger, "The Masked Ball of Cowardice," Tablet, August 29, 2021, https:// www.tabletmag.com/sections/news/articles/masked-ball-cowardice.

31. Jeffery A. Tucker, "Why Masks? Control, Power, and Revenue," Brownstone Institute, October 5, 2021, https://brownstone.org/articles/why-masks-control-power-and-reve nue/.

32. Frances Eve, "China's Reaction to the Coronavirus Outbreak Violates Human Rights," *The Guardian*, February 2, 2020, https://www.theguardian.com/world/2020/feb/02/ chinas-reaction-to-the-coronavirus-outbreak-violates-human-rights.

33. WHO-China Joint Mission, *Report of the WHO-China Joint Mission on Coronavirus Disease 2019 (COVID-19)*, February 16–24, 2020, https://who.int/docs/default-sour ce/coronaviruse/who-china-joint-mission-on-covid-19-final-report.pdf.

34. Tom Grundy, "Video: Top WHO Doctor Bruce Aylward Ends Video Call after Journalist Asks about Taiwan's Status," Hong Kong Free Press, March 29, 2020, https:// hongkongfp.com/2020/03/29/video-top-doctor-bruce-aylward-pretends-not-hear-jou rnalists-taiwan-questions-ends-video-call/.

35. "Subject: Press Conference of WHO-China Joint Mission on COVID-19," World Health Organization, February 24, 2020, https://www.who.int/docs/default-source/co ronaviruse/transcripts/joint-mission-press-conference-script-english-final.pdf?sfvrsn= 51c90b9e_2.

36. Daniel Harries, "'Copy China's Response to COVID-19,' WHO Expert Urges Rest of the World," China Global Television Network (CGTN), February 26, 2020, https://ne wseu.cgtn.com/news/2020-02-26/-Copy-China-s-response-to-COVID-19-WHO-ex pert-urges—OnNfwORI3u/index.html.

37. Senger, "By corrupting global institutions."

38. Christopher Bedford, "How COVID Lockdowns Handed Global Warming Extremists the Tools to Crush Freedom," The Federalist, November 15, 2021, https://thefederali st.com/2021/11/15/how-covid-lockdowns-handed-global-warming-extremists-the-to ols-to-crush-freedom/.

39. Washington Free Beacon, "Biden Surrogate Jane Fonda Calls Covid 'God's Gift to the Left,'" YouTube, October 7, 2020, https://www.youtube.com/watch?v=BSFx7PxfVLI.

40. Oliver Smith (@ollysmithtravel), "No holidays, no weddings, no family celebrations…," Twitter, October 8, 2020, 2:50 a.m., https://twitter.com/ollysmithtravel/status/13140 95805888958466.

Chapter 4: Following "The Science"—or the Chinese?

1. Anthony P. Mueller, "From Lockdowns to 'the Great Reset,'" Mises Institute, August 1, 2020, https://mises.org/wire/lockdowns-great-reset.

2. Thomas T. Siler Jr., "Let's Demand a Recount…of COVID Deaths," American Thinker, May 12, 2021, https://www.americanthinker.com/articles/2021/05/lets_de mand_a_recountof_covid_deaths.html.

3. Ibid.

4. "Robert F. Kennedy, Jr. Speaks at Berlin Rally for Freedom and Peace," Children's Health Defense, August 29, 2020, https://childrenshealthdefense.org/news/robert-f-k

ennedy-jr-speaks-at-berlin-rally-for-freedom-and-peace/; Natural Health Media Project, "Bobby Kennedy to Berlin Freedom Rally: Ich Bin Ein Berliner!...," Facebook, August 29, 2020, 6:57 p.m., https://www.facebook.com/NaturalHealthMediaProject /photos/a.751078158385449/1587913198035270/?type=3.

5. Danielle Chavira, "Grand County Coroner Raises Concern on Deaths among COVID Cases," CBS4, December 15, 2020, https://denver.cbslocal.com/2020/12/15/grand-co unty-covid-deaths/.

6. Siler Jr., "Let's Demand a Recount."

7. Michael P. Senger, "The Masked Ball of Cowardice," Tablet, August 29, 2021, https:// www.tabletmag.com/sections/news/articles/masked-ball-cowardice.

8. Henry Ealy et al., "COVID-19 Data Collection, Comorbidity, & Federal Law: A Historical Retrospective," *Science, Public Health Policy, and the Law* 2, no. 4–22 (October 2020): 1, https://www.ratical.org/PandemicParallaxView/C19dataCollecti on-C+FL-HistPerspec.pdf.

9. Siler Jr., "Let's Demand a Recount."

10. Matt Vespa, "Sorry, Fauci, Johns Hopkins Doctor Declares We're Close to COVID Herd Immunity," *Townhall*, March 29, 2021, https://townhall.com/tipsheet/mattves pa/2021/03/29/wsj-oped-herd-immunity-is-hereeven-if-fauci-doesnt-want-to-admit-it -n2587026.

11. Siler Jr., "Let's Demand a Recount."

12. Cheryl K. Chumley, "Anthony Fauci Plummets in Polls," *Washington Times*, May 21, 2021, https://www.washingtontimes.com/news/2021/may/21/anthony-fauci-plumme ts-polls/.

13. Washington Examiner (@dcexaminer), ".@Jim_Jordan: "You don't think Americans' liberties...," Twitter, April 15, 2021, 1:48 p.m., https://twitter.com/dcexaminer/status /1382752798069112833.

14. David Catron, "A Mitigation Disaster," *American Spectator*, April 6, 2020, https://sp ectator.org/a-mitigation-disaster/.

15. Lord Sumption, "Locking Up the Elderly until Coronavirus Is Defeated Is a Cruel Mockery of Basic Human Values: Former Supreme Court Judge Lord Sumption Gives a Withering Critique of the Government's Lockdown," *Daily Mail*, May 3, 2020, https://www.dailymail.co.uk/debate/article-8281007/amp/Former-Supreme-Court-ju dge-LORD-SUMPTION-gives-withering-critique-Governments-lockdown.html?__t witter_impression=true.

16. Luboš Motl, "Physicist: 'Lockdown Madness Is a Triumph of the Precautionary Principle,'" Climate Depot, May 11, 2020, https://www.climatedepot.com/2020/05 /11/physicist-lockdown-madness-is-a-triumph-of-the-precautionary-principle-denoun ces-the-flat-curve-society/.

17. Marc Morano (@ClimateDepot), "Indian economist Sanjeev Sabhlok...," Twitter, May 5, 2020, 7:51 p.m., https://twitter.com/ClimateDepot/status/1257820119511810048.

18. Sky News Australia, "Australians Made 'Prisoners in a So-Called Democracy': Alan Jones," YouTube, October 7, 2020, https://www.youtube.com/watch?v=QdF2d-cucjI.

19. Conor Friedersdorf, "Australia Traded Away Too Much Liberty: How Long Can a Democracy Maintain Emergency Restrictions and Still Call Itself a Free Country?," *The Atlantic*, September 2, 2021, https://www.theatlantic.com/ideas/archive/2021/09 /pandemic-australia-still-liberal-democracy/619940/.

20. Megan Sauer, "Bill Gates: 'If Every Country Does What Australia Did,' the World Could Prevent the Next Pandemic," CNBC, February 24, 2022, https://www.cnbc

.com/2022/02/24/bill-gates-australia-covid-blueprint-could-help-prevent-next-pande
mic.html.

21. Victor Davis Hanson, "The Gathering Storm in the West," American Greatness,
February 20, 2022, https://amgreatness.com/2022/02/20/the-gathering-storm-in-the
-west/.

22. Julie Kelly, "One Year Later, Vindication for Lockdown Skeptics," American Greatness,
March 11, 2020, https://amgreatness.com/2021/03/11/one-year-later-vindication-for
-lockdown-skeptics/.

23. Andrew Napolitano, "Napolitano: The Government's Emergency Powers Myth,"
Standard-Examiner, May 21, 2021, https://www.standard.net/opinion/national-com
mentary/2021/may/21/napolitano-the-governments-emergency-powers-myth/.

24. Naomi Wolf, "Fascism's Step Ten: 'Lockdown' Is Not a 'Quarantine,'" Wolf: Author
and Journalist, October 3, 2020, https://web.archive.org/web/20210506060133/http
s://drnaomiwolf.com/lockdown-is-not-a-quarantine/.

25. Peter Hitchens, "Face Masks Turn Us into Voiceless Submissives—and It's Not Science
Forcing Us to Wear Them, It's Politics," *Daily Mail*, July 19, 2020, https://hitchensbl
og.mailonsunday.co.uk/2020/07/peter-hitchens-face-masks-turn-us-into-voiceless-su
bmissives-and-its-not-science-forcing-us-to-wear-.html.

26. Peter Hitchens, "Is Shutting Down Britain—with Unprecedented Curbs on Ancient
Liberties—REALLY the Best Answer?," *Daily Mail*, March 21, 2020, https://www.da
ilymail.co.uk/debate/article-8138675/PETER-HITCHENS-shutting-Britain-REALLY
-right-answer.html.

27. Albert Biderman, "Communist Attempts to Elicit False Confessions from Air Force
Prisoners of War," *Bulletin of the New York Academy of Medicine* 33, no. 9 (September
1957): 616–25, https://www.ncbi.nlm.nih.gov/pmc/articles/PMC1806204/?page=1;
Marc Morano, "COVID Lockdowns Compared to Coercion and Torture Methods to
Break the Will of Prisoners of War," Climate Depot, December 7, 2020, https://www
.climatedepot.com/2020/12/07/covid-lockdowns-compared-to-bidermans-chart-of-co
ercion-on-torture-methods-to-break-the-will-of-prisoners-of-war/.

28. Denis Rancourt (@denisrancourt), "COVID = Large-scale application of the Biderman
chart of coercion…," Twitter, December 4, 2020, 6:15 p.m., https://twitter.com/denis
rancourt/status/1334999923612405760.

29. Sanjeev Sabhlok (@sabhlok), "Someone's shared this.…," Twitter, November 18, 2020,
https://twitter.com/sabhlok/status/1328890135392387073?ref_src=twsrc%5Etfw
(Twitter has deleted Sabhlok's account, but this tweet is available at Morano, "COVID
Lockdowns Compared to Coercion & Torture Methods").

30. "No Selves to Defend: Curriculum for Marissa Alexander Teach-In," NIA Dispatches,
September 26, 2013, https://niastories.wordpress.com/2013/09/26/no-selves-to-defend
-curriculum-for-marissa-alexander-teach-in/, including the link to "Biderman's Chart
of Coercion," https://niastories.files.wordpress.com/2013/09/bidermans_chart_of_co
ercion.pdf.

31. Larry Siems, "Document a Day: Old Torture Made New," ACLU, June 14, 2010,
https://www.aclu.org/blog/national-security/torture/document-day-old-torture-made
-new.

32. Freddie Sayers, "Inside Australia's Covid Internment Camp," UnHerd, December 2,
2021, https://unherd.com/thepost/inside-australias-covid-internment-camp/.

33. NYC Angry Mom (@angrybklynmom), "But lockdowns were something completely
out of our control…," (thread) Twitter, May 19, 2021, 5:00 a.m., https://twitter.com

/angrybklynmom/status/1394941127262883840; Monica Humphries, "NYC Parents Unleash Fury after News that Schools Will Close as Restaurants, Gyms Remain Open," *Business Insider*, November 19, 2020, https://www.businessinsider.nl/nyc-parents-un leash-fury-after-news-that-schools-will-close-as-restaurants-gyms-remain-open/.

34. Devin Balkind, "New Yorkers Must Break Free from Our Stockholm Syndrome," *Gotham Gazette*, June 16, 2020, https://www.gothamgazette.com/opinion/9496-new -yorkers-must-break-free-stockholm-syndrome-cuomo-de-blasio-coronavirus.

35. Sam Dorman, "Anthony Fauci Praises New York's Coronavirus Response: 'They Did It Correctly,'" Fox News, July 18, 2020, https://www.foxnews.com/politics/anthony -fauci-praises-new-york-coronavirus-response.

36. Simon Kelner, "I'm Loath to Admit It, but Part of Me Is Frightened of Leaving Lockdown," *i*, February 24, 2021, https://inews.co.uk/opinion/lockdown-leaving-frig htened-covid-roadmap-885567.

37. Rhys Blakely and Kat Lay, "NHS Will Be Plagued by Covid 'for at Least Five Years," *The Times*, December 3, 2021, https://www.thetimes.co.uk/article/nhs-will-be-plagu ed-by-covid-for-at-least-five-years-7v90l05l6.

38. The Fly in the Ointment, "'Lockdown Stockholm Syndrome' Sets in as Restrictions Ease," *Northwich Guardian*, April 16, 2021, https://www.northwichguardian.co.uk /news/19237367.big-test-country/.

39. Robby Soave, "Many Epidemiologists Want Social Distancing and Masks Forever," *Reason*, December 4, 2020, https://reason.com/2020/12/04/epidemiologists-masks-so cial-distancing-vaccine-forever-new-york-times/.

40. William M. Briggs, "Coronavirus Update—Calm Yourselves," William M. Briggs: Statistician to the Stars!, March 24, 2020, https://www.climatedepot.com/2020/03/28 /statistician-dr-matt-briggs-coronavirus-update-calm-yourselves-raise-your-hand-if-yo ure-tired-of-hearing-from-experts/.

41. William M. Briggs, "Stay Inside Or Die," William M. Briggs: Statistician to the Stars!, March 30, 2020, https://www.wmbriggs.com/post/30006/.

42. Will Feuer, "New Jersey Gym Owners Arrested after Defying Coronavirus Order: 'We Will Not Be Backing Down,'" CNBC, July 27, 2020, https://www.cnbc.com/2020/07 /27/new-jersey-gym-owners-arrested-after-defying-coronavirus-order-we-will-not-be -backing-down.html.

43. Lee Brown, "NJ Gym Famed for Defying COVID-19 Lockdown Orders Fined More than $1.2 Million," *New York Post*, December 14, 2020, https://nypost.com/2020/12 /14/nj-gym-that-defied-covid-19-lockdown-fined-more-than-1-2m/.

44. Nikolas Lanum, "Virginia Restaurant Owner Who Defied COVID Orders Labeled 'Imminent Threat' to the Community," Fox Business, March 26, 2021, https://www .foxbusiness.com/small-business/virginia-restaurant-owner-covid-orders-coronavirus -threat; "Virginia Restaurant Owner Sued for Defying Coronavirus Restrictions," Fox Business, March 26, 2021, https://video.foxbusiness.com/v/6244515169001#sp=show -clips.

45. Roger Koops, "The Covid Cult's Attack on Science and Society," Brownstone Institute, August 30, 2021, https://brownstone.org/articles/the-covid-cults-attack-on-science-and -society/.

46. Robert F. Kennedy Jr., "People in Authority Lie," Children's Health Defense, August 28, 2020, https://childrenshealthdefense.org/wp-content/uploads/08-31-20-RFK-Jr.-P ress-Conference-Transcript.pdf; OneSilentJoy, "Robert F Kennedy Jr in Berlin 28 Aug

2020," YouTube, August 28, 2020, https://www.youtube.com/watch?v=wM7NLlW ZD5I&t=4s.

47. Twitter has deleted Wolf's account, but see Marc Morano, "Feminist Icon Naomi Wolf: 'If I'd Known Biden Was Open to "Lockdowns"…Which Is Something Historically Unprecedented…& a Terrifying Practice, One That Won't Ever End Because Elites Love It, I Would Never Have Voted for Him,'" Climate Depot, November 14, 2020, https://www.climatedepot.com/2020/11/14/progressive-feminist-icon-naomi-wolf-if -id-known-biden-was-open-to-lockdowns-which-is-something-historically-unprecede nted-a-terrifying-practice-one-that-won/.

48. Michael P. Senger (@MichaelPSenger), "Greater Sydney, Australia, extends lockdown…," Twitter, August 22, 2021, 1:44 p.m., https://twitter.com/MichaelPSen ger/status/1429499725384884224 (Twitter has deleted Senger's account, but this tweet is available at the Internet Archive's Wayback Machine: https://web.archive.org/web /20220105203700/https://twitter.com/MichaelPSenger/status/142949972538488 4224).

49. Peter Imanuelsen (@PeterSweden7), "Australia. Army deployed to enforce lockdown…," Twitter, August 21, 2021, 1:45 p.m. https://twitter.com/PeterSweden7/status/1429137 600217030657.

50. Kennedy, "People in Authority Lie"; OneSilentJoy, "Robert F Kennedy Jr in Berlin."

51. Michael Haskoor, "Bill Maher Calls COVID-19 Lockdowns 'Reckless Experiment' That Accelerated George Floyd Protests on 'Real Time,'" Decider, June 6, 2020, https:// decider.com/2020/06/06/bill-maher-says-covid-19-lockdowns-accelerated-george-flo yd-protests/.

52. "Bill Maher's Audience Cheers as He Trashes Young People with Far-Left Views: 'Your Ideas Are Stupid,'" The Daily Wire, April 24, 2021, https://www.dailywire.com/news /bill-mahers-audience-cheers-as-he-trashes-young-people-with-far-left-views-your-ide as-are-stupid.

Chapter 5: A Solution Worse than the Disease: Lockdowns Kill

1. Victor Morton, "George Soros Sees 'Revolutionary Moment' in Coronavirus Pandemic," *Washington Times*, August 12, 2020, https://www.washingtontimes.com /news/2020/aug/12/george-soros-sees-revolutionary-moment-coronavirus/.

2. Joseph Vazquez, "George Soros in *NY Times*: I'm Trying to Bend 'Arc of History' in Right Direction," mrcNewsBusters, October 28, 2019, https://www.newsbusters.org /blogs/business/joseph-vazquez/2019/10/28/george-soros-ny-times-im-trying-bend-arc -history-right.

3. "Dr. Atlas: Prolonged Coronavirus Lockdowns a 'Complete Disaster,'" Fox News, October 14, 2020, https://video.foxnews.com/v/6200409821001#sp=show-clips.

4. Sanjeev Sabhlok, "Who Am I?" Sanjeev Sabhlok's Blog, https://www.sabhlokcity.com /who-am-i/.

5. Sanjeev Sabhlok, (@sabhlok), "Australia's bureaucracy has performed as badly…," Twitter, July 27, 2020, 11:52 p.m., https://twitter.com/sabhlok/status/128800431849 9491840 (Twitter has deleted Sablok's account, but the tweet is available at the Internet Archive's Wayback Machine: https://web.archive.org/web/20200728065253/https:// twitter.com/sabhlok/status/1288004318499491840).

6. Sanjeev Sabhlok, "Xi Jinping's Use of Hysteria as Warfare—Part 1," *Times of India*, January 6, 2021, https://timesofindia.indiatimes.com/blogs/seeing-the-invisible/xi-jin pings-use-of-hysteria-as-warfare-part-1/.

7. William M. Briggs, "Paper Says Social Distancing Doesn't Work; Lockdowns Don't Work; Deaths at Yearly Low; More—Coronavirus Update LXIII," William M. Briggs: Statistician to the Stars!, April 27, 2021, https://wmbriggs.com/post/35380/.

8. Sanjeev Sabhlok, "Xi Jinping's Use of Hysteria as Warfare—Part 2," *Times of India*, January 6, 2021, https://timesofindia.indiatimes.com/blogs/seeing-the-invisible/xi-jin pings-use-of-hysteria-as-warfare-part-2/.

9. Colin's Tweet's (@GovPolicyDoubt), "Covid is a true killer….," Twitter, January 18, 2021, 9:07 am., https://twitter.com/GovPolicyDoubt/status/1351169468941139970.

10. Marc Morano, "White House Advisor Dr. Scott Atlas: 'Lockdowns Are a Complete Disaster'—'Off the Rails'—Ridicules 'Public Health Experts'—'They Have Killed People'—Public Health Experts Presided over a 'Gross Failure'—Policies 'Complete Epic Failure,'" Climate Depot, October 14, 2020, https://www.climatedepot.com/20 20/10/14/white-house-advisor-dr-scott-atlas-lockdowns-are-a-complete-disaster-off -the-rails-ridicules-public-health-experts-they-have-killed-people-public-health-exper ts-presided-over/; "Dr. Atlas: Prolonged Coronavirus Lockdowns."

11. Michael P Senger (@MichaelPSenger), "As former Soviet citizens can attest…," Twitter, October 21, 2021, 11:24 a.m., https://twitter.com/MichaelPSenger/status/145120781 1182907393 (Twitter has deleted Senger's account, but this tweet is available at the Internet Archive's WayBack Machine: https://web.archive.org/web/20211021152720 /https://twitter.com/MichaelPSenger/status/1451207811182907393).

12. Alex Berenson (@AlexBerenson), "Oh, it was way worse than the flu….," Twitter, March 3, 2021, 12:13 p.m., https://twitter.com/AlexBerenson/status/1367161167911 792647 (Twitter has deleted Berenson's account, but this tweet is available at the Internet Archive's Wayback Machine: https://web.archive.org/web/20210425221708 /https://twitter.com/AlexBerenson/status/1367161167911792647).

13. Eran Bendavid et al., "Assessing Mandatory Stay-at-Home and Business Closure Effects on the Spread of COVID-19," *European Journal of Clinical Investigation* 51, no. 4 (January 2021), https://doi.org/10.1111/eci.13484.

14. Rabail Chaudhry et al., "A Country Level Analysis Measuring the Impact of Government Actions, Country Preparedness and Socioeconomic Factors on COVID-19 Mortality and Related Health Outcomes," eClinicalMedicine 25, no. 100464 (August 2020), https://doi.org/10.1016/j.eclinm.2020.100464.

15. Jonas Herby, Lars Jonung, and Steve H. Hanke, "A Literature Review and Meta-Analysis of the Effects of Lockdowns on COVID-19 Mortality," *Studies in Applied Economics*, January 2022, https://sites.krieger.jhu.edu/iae/files/2022/01/A-Literature -Review-and-Meta-Analysis-of-the-Effects-of-Lockdowns-on-COVID-19-Mortality .pdf.

16. Emel Akan, "Do Lockdowns Reduce Covid-19 Mortality," *Epoch Times*, February 2, 2022, https://www.theepochtimes.com/do-lockdowns-reduce-covid-19-mortality_42 32386.html.

17. Herby et al., "A Literature Review."

18. Johan Ahlander, "Sweden Saw Lower 2020 Death Spike Than Much of Europe— Data," Reuters, March 24, 2021, https://www.reuters.com/article/us-health-coronavi rus-europe-mortality-idUSKBN2BG1R9.

19. Bendavid et al., "Assessing Mandatory Stay-at-Home and Business Closure Effects."

20. Thomas V. Inglesby et al., "Disease Mitigation Measures in the Control of Pandemic Influenza," *Biosecurity and Bioterrorism: Biodefense Strategy, Practice, and Science*

4, no. 4 (2006): 366–75, http://citeseerx.ist.psu.edu/viewdoc/download?doi=10.1.1.552 .1109&rep=rep1&type=pdf.

21. Katharine Child, "Exclusive: Lockdown Disaster Dwarfs Covid-19, Say SA Actuaries: Model Shows 10% of South Africans Will Become Poorer and Lose a Few Months of Their Lives," Business Live, May 5, 2020, https://www.businesslive.co.za/fm/features /2020-05-05-lockdown-disaster-dwarfs-covid-19-say-sa-actuaries/.

22. Kulvinder Kaur MD (@dockaurG), "In case it's confusing, it is not Sweden….," Twitter, September 26, 2020, 10:19 a.m., https://twitter.com/dockaurG/status/130986022802 0736008.

23. Child, "Exclusive: Lockdown Disaster."

24. Justin Hart, "Thread: I Need to Rethink Things…," Threadreader, August 2, 2021, https://threadreaderapp.com/thread/1422243808536715265/.

25. Ricardo Bordin, "Lockdown May Cost 200,000 Lives, Government Report Shows," Medium, July 20, 2020, https://medium.com/@rickbordan/lockdown-may-cost-200 -000-lives-government-report-shows-dcb68604f66d.

26. Justin Hart, "The List: Lockdown Impact," Rational Ground (Substack), October 17, 2021, https://covidreason.substack.com/p/the-list-lockdown-impact?s=r.

27. Ahlander, "Sweden Saw Lower 2020 Death Spike."

28. Tom Rayner, "Coronavirus: For Every Three COVID-19 Deaths, Lockdown May Have Caused Another Two," Sky News, August 8, 2020, https://news.sky.com/story/coron avirus-lockdown-may-have-indirectly-caused-16-000-excess-deaths-study-12044923.

29. "COVID-19 Disruptions Killed 228,000 in South Asia, Says UN Report," BBC News, March 17, 2021, https://www.bbc.com/news/world-asia-56425115.

30. The Spectator (@spectator), "Watch: Dr David Nabarro, the WHO's Special Envoy on Covid-19…," Twitter, October 9, 2020, 8:27 a.m., https://twitter.com/spectator/stat us/1314573157827858434?s=.

31. Lucía Benvides, "In Spain, Pandemic Restrictions Mean Children Aren't Allowed Outside Their Homes," NPR, April 17, 2020, https://www.npr.org/sections/coronavi rus-live-updates/2020/04/17/837248837/in-spain-pandemic-restrictions-mean-childr en-arent-allowed-outside-their-homes.

32. Sarah Newey, "Unicef Warns Lockdown Could Kill More Than COVID-19 as Model Predicts 1.2 Million Child Deaths," The Telegraph, May 13, 2020, https://www.teleg raph.co.uk/global-health/science-and-disease/unicef-warns-lockdown-could-kill-cov id-19-model-predicts-12/.

33. Bruno Zanotti et al., "Can the Elastic of Surgical Face Masks Stimulate Ear Protrusion in Children?" Aesthetic Plastic Surgery 44, no. 5 (2020): 1947–50, https://doi.org/10 .1007/s00266-020-01833-9.

34. David Wallace-Wells, "The Kids Are Alright: Why Now Is the Time to Rethink COVID Safety Protocols for Children—and Everyone Else," Intelligencer, July 12, 2021, https:// nymag.com/intelligencer/2021/07/the-kids-were-safe-from-covid-the-whole-time.html.

35. Sean C. L. Deoni et al., "Impact of the COVID-19 Pandemic on Early Child Cognitive Development: Initial Findings in a Longitudinal Observational Study of Child Health," MedRxiv, (August 11, 2021), https://www.medrxiv.org/content/10.1101/2021.08.10 .21261846v1.

36. Faye Flam, "Masks Mandates Didn't Make Much of a Difference Anyway," Bloomberg, February 11, 2022, https://www.bloomberg.com/opinion/articles/2022-02-11/did-ma sk-mandates-work-the-data-is-in-and-the-answer-is-no.

37. Joe Concha, "Bill Maher: 'Reckless Experiment' of Coronavirus Shutdowns May Have Fueled Floyd Protests," *The Hill*, June 6, 2020, https://thehill.com/homenews/media/501460-bill-maher-reckless-experiment-of-coronavirus-shutdowns-may-have-fueled-floyd.

38. John Ingold, "Denver Doctors May Have Found the Answer to a Pandemic Mystery: What Happened to All the Heart Attacks?" Colorado Sun, August 17, 2020, https://coloradosun.com/2020/08/17/denver-coronavirus-deaths-heart-attack/.

39. Alice Thomson, "Cancer Treatment Will Be the Next NHS Crisis," *The Times*, April 14, 2020, https://www.thetimes.co.uk/edition/comment/forgotten-illnesses-will-be-the-nhss-next-crisis-lxtqggt8l.

40. Alex Berenson (@AlexBerenson), "I thought this was a myth, but no: the government will pay up to $9,000 for a funeral....," Twitter, April 26, 2021, https://twitter.com/alexberenson/status/1386766224353370115?lang=en (Twitter has deleted Berenson's account, but this tweet is available at the Internet Archive's WayBack Machine: https://web.archive.org/web/20210426193700/https://twitter.com/AlexBerenson/status/1386766224353370115).

41. "FEMA to Help Pay Funeral Costs for COVID-19-Related Deaths in Virginia," Virginia Department of Emergency Management, April 6, 2021, https://www.vaemergency.gov/fema-to-help-pay-funeral-costs-for-covid-19-related-deaths-in-virginia/.

42. David Zweig, "Our Most Reliable Pandemic Number Is Losing Meaning," *The Atlantic*, September 13, 2021, https://www.theatlantic.com/health/archive/2021/09/covid-hospitalization-numbers-can-be-misleading/620062/ (aggregated by RealClearPolitics at this link: https://www.realclearpolitics.com/2021/09/13/are_pandemic_hospitalization_numbers_misleading_us_551642.html).

43. Brian Mann, "U.S. Sees Deadly Drug Overdose Spike during Pandemic," NPR, August 13, 2020, https://www.npr.org/sections/coronavirus-live-updates/2020/08/13/901627189/u-s-sees-deadly-drug-overdose-spike-during-pandemic.

44. Thomas Fuller, "San Francisco Contends with a Different Sort of Epidemic: Drug Deaths," *New York Times*, April 23, 2021, https://www.nytimes.com/2021/04/23/us/fentanyl-overdoses-san-francisco.html.

45. Pamela Duncan and Sarah Marsh, "Antidepressant Use in England Soars as Pandemic Cuts Counselling Access," *The Guardian*, January 1, 2021, https://www.theguardian.com/society/2021/jan/01/covid-antidepressant-use-at-all-time-high-as-access-to-counselling-in-england-plunges.

46. Neil Hamilton (@NeilUKIP), "Locking people in their homes...," Twitter, January 3, 2021, 7:31 a.m., https://twitter.com/NeilUKIP/status/1345709297951506433?ref_sr.

47. Embriette Hyde, "Researchers Discover COVID-19, Lockdowns Bring Back Unpleasant Memories for Holocaust Survivors," Study Finds, April 7, 2021, https://www.studyfinds.org/covid-19-holocaust-survivors/; Amit Shrira, Ruth Maytles, and Maya Frenkel-Yosef, "Suffering from Infectious Diseases during the Holocaust Relates to Amplified Psychological Reactions during the COVID-19 Pandemic," *Journal of Psychiatric Research* 130 (2020): 421–23, https://doi.org/10.1016/j.jpsychires.2020.08.024.

48. Bill Maher, "Immunity Booster," Facebook, May 1, 2020, https://www.facebook.com/watch/?v=2645287895711290; see also Tommy Christopher, "Bill Maher Bravely Tells America Not to Be Afraid of Germs—While Quarantined in His Backyard," Mediaite, May 2, 2020, https://www.mediaite.com/tv/bill-maher-bravely-tells-america-not-to-be-afraid-of-germs-while-quarantined-in-his-back-yard/.

49. First ellipsis added, other ellipses in the original. "George Carlin: You Are All Diseased—Transcript (1999)," Scraps from the Loft, April 6, 2018, https://scrapsfrom theloft.com/2017/04/06/george-carlin-you-are-all-diseased-transcript/.
50. Maher, "Immunity Booster."
51. Ben Johnson, "Don Lemon Tells Liberals: 'Believe in the Science,' Take Off Your Mask," The Daily Wire, May 12, 2021, https://www.dailywire.com/news/don-lemon -tells-liberals-believe-in-the-science-take-off-your-mask.
52. Christopher, "Bill Maher Bravely Tells America Not to Be Afraid."
53. Real Time with Bill Maher, "New Rule: America Out of Order | Real Time with Bill Maher (HBO)," YouTube, June 9, 2020, https://www.youtube.com/watch?v=DqSAR DDdlsw.
54. Michael P Senger (@MichaelPSenger), "Fauci: 'Even if you are without symptoms…,'" Twitter, August 2, 2021, 12:52 p.m., https://twitter.com/MichaelPSenger/status/1422 238955483779078 (Twitter has deleted Senger's account, but this tweet is available at the Internet Archive's Wayback Machine: https://web.archive.org/web/20210802165 321/https://twitter.com/MichaelPSenger/status/1422238955483779078).
55. Matt Walsh (@MattWalshBlog), "What you're saying is that nobody has the right to breathe around you….," Twitter, August 2, 2021, 6:40 a.m. (This tweet was deleted by the author, but it is available at the Internet Archive's Wayback Machine: https:// web.archive.org/web/20210802134030/https://twitter.com/MattWalshBlog/status/14 22190507732635648).
56. Emma Green, "The Liberals Who Can't Quit Lockdown," The Atlantic, May 4, 2021, https://www.theatlantic.com/politics/archive/2021/05/liberals-covid-19-science-deni al-lockdown/618780/.
57. Ibid.
58. Sarah Maslin Nir, "They're Vaccinated and Keeping Their Masks On, Maybe Forever," New York Times, May 17, 2021, https://www.nytimes.com/2021/05/17/nyregion/vac cinated-masks-cdc.html?smid=tw-nytmetro&smtyp=cur.
59. Andreas Kluth, "We Must Start Planning for a Permanent Pandemic," Bloomberg, March 24, 2021, https://www.bloomberg.com/opinion/articles/2021-03-24/when-wi ll-covid-end-we-must-start-planning-for-a-permanent-pandemic.
60. Tony Heller (@Tony_Heller), "Viruses kill people….," Twitter, January 3, 2021, 9:06 p.m. (Twitter has deleted Heller's account, but this tweet is available at the Internet Archive's Wayback Machine: https://web.archive.org/web/20210104020654/https:// twitter.com/Tony__Heller/status/1345914469612834822).
61. "George Carlin: You Are All Diseased."
62. Jess Arnold, "DC Businesses and Neighbors Cautiously Embrace Full Reopening," WUSA9, May 22, 2021, http://www.wusa9.com/article/money/business/small-busine ss/dc-businesses-neighbors-reopening-covid-restrictions-rollback/65-0409e8ae-e648 -4326-8d2c-3d8c5e272750.
63. Jan Hennop, "Covid, Cocaine Take Europe to 'Breaking Point': Europol," Barron's, April 12, 2021, https://www.barrons.com/news/covid-cocaine-take-europe-to-breaki ng-point-europol-01618218305.
64. Real Time with Bill Maher, "New Rule: America Out of Order."
65. Tom Elliott, "Fauci in 2019: Best Way to Avoid Infectious Disease Is to Eat Healthy, Exercise, Get Good Sleep," GrabienNews, September 13, 2021, https://news.grabien .com/story-fauci-2019-best-way-avoid-infectious-disease-eat-healthy-exe.

66. Antonia Noori Farzan, "Researchers Held an Experimental Indoor Concert in Spain with No Social Distancing. No One Contracted Covid," *Washington Post*, May 28, 2021, https://www.washingtonpost.com/world/2021/05/28/spain-coronavirus-conce rt-experiment/.

67. Chris Melore, "Half of Americans Say Lost Insurance and Healthcare Costs During COVID are Keeping Them from Seeing a Doctor," Study Finds, May 11, 2021, https://www.studyfinds.org/insurance-healthcare-costs-covid/.

68. Alex Berenson (@AlexBerenson), "1/ Stunning chart. Outside the US and UK …," Twitter, May 1, 2021, 2:33 p.m., https://twitter.com/AlexBerenson/status/138856233 5170768896 (Twitter has deleted Berenson's account, but this tweet is available at the Internet Archive's Wayback Machine: https://web.archive.org/web/20210513043715 /https://twitter.com/AlexBerenson/status/1388562335170768896).

69. Bryan Walsh, "Drug Overdose Deaths Surged during Coronavirus Pandemic," Axios, April 14, 2021, https://www.axios.com/drug-overdose-record-coronavirus-pandemic -opioids-8657bd57-ab9a-4c1b-9666-76ed7254df55.html.

70. Antony Davies and James R. Harrigan, "The Cobra Effect: Lessons in Unintended Circumstances," The Foundation for Economic Education, September 6, 2019, https:// fee.org/articles/the-cobra-effect-lessons-in-unintended-consequences/.

71. Apoorva Mandavilli, "'The Biggest Monster' Is Spreading. And It's Not the Coronavirus," *New York Times*, August 3, 2020, https://www.nytimes.com/2020/08 /03/health/coronavirus-tuberculosis-aids-malaria.html.

72. Rachel Clayton, "Statistics Show Increase in Children Presenting to Hospitals after Self-Harming," ABC News (Australia), August 8, 2020, https://www.abc.net.au/news /2020-08-08/young-people-self-harming-end-up-in-hospital-emergency-rooms/1253 2040; https://search-beta.abc.net.au/index.html?siteTitle=news#/?configure%5BgetR ankingInfo%5D=true&configure%5BclickAnalytics%5D=true&configure%5Buser Token%5D=anonymous-3edb43ec-8b8e-46ed-8796-2ca173bcc727&configure%5B hitsPerPage%5D=10&query=prolonged%20isolation%20and%20a%20lack%20of %20face&page=; https://www.abc.net.au/news/2020-08-08/young-people-self-harm ing-end-up-in-hospital-emergency-rooms/12532040..

73. "Issue Brief: Drug Overdose Epidemic Worsened During COVID Pandemic," American Medical Association, November 12, 2021, https://www.ama-assn.org/system/files/20 20-12/issue-brief-increases-in-opioid-related-overdose.pdf; Jake Zuckerman, New Data: Fatal Overdoses Leapt 22% in Ohio Last Year," Ohio Capital Journal, July 15, 2021, https://ohiocapitaljournal.com/2021/07/15/new-data-fatal-overdoses-leapt-22 -in-ohio-last-year/.

74. Ryan McMaken, "Unemployment Kills: The Longer Lockdowns Last, the Worse It Will Get," Mises Institute, April 30, 2020, https://mises.org/wire/unemployment-kills -longer-lockdowns-last-worse-it-will-get.

75. Denis Rancourt (@denisrancourt), "Public health officials boldly take credit for decreases in transmission…," Twitter, June 3, 2021, 9:18 a.m., https://twitter.com/de nisrancourt/status/1400441727039807492; Denis Rancourt (@denisrancourt), "A reminder of some prominent causes of death…," Twitter, June 3, 2021, 8:53 a.m., https://twitter.com/denisrancourt/status/1400435596980543492.

76. William Schomberg and Andy Bruce, "UK Economy Grew More than Thought at End of Miserable 2020," Reuters, March 31, 2021, https://www.reuters.com/article/uk-he alth-coronavirus-britain-economy-idUSKBN2BN0L8.

77. Marlowe Hood, "A World Redrawn: Worry about Climate Not COVID, Says James 'Gaia' Lovelock," Phys.org, June 16, 2020, https://phys.org/news/2020-06-world-red rawn-climate-covid-james.html.

78. Sunetra Gupta, "A Contagion of Hatred and Hysteria: Oxford Epidemiologist Professor Sunetra Gupta Tells How She Has Been Intimidated and Shamed for Backing Shielding Instead of Lockdown," *Daily Mail,* October 30, 2020, https://www.dailymail.co.uk /debate/article-8899277/Professor-Sunetra-Gupta-reveals-crisis-ruthlessly-weaponis ed.html.

79. Justin Hart (@justin_hart), "My core #COVID19 mantras…," Twitter, November 12, 2020, 5:51 p.m., https://twitter.com/justin_hart/status/1327021332790267904.

80. Zoe #ZeroCovid (@zerocovidzoe), "What we need…," Twitter, January 4, 2021, 3:24 p.m., https://twitter.com/zerocovidzoe/status/1346190828423798793.

81. Mr Producer Media, "Fauci Now Realizes Shutting Down Economy Makes Things Worse," Rumble, December 29, 2021,https://rumble.com/vrmk8k-fauci-now-realizes -shutting-down-economy-makes-things-worse.html.

82. Marc Morano, "COVID Lockdowns No Longer Called 'Lockdowns': 'Dimmer Switch,' 'Emergency Brake,' 'Freeze,' 'Retightening,' 'Disruptions' & 'Pause' Make Debut as Politicians Avoid Word 'Lockdown,'" Climate Depot, November 16, 2020, https://www.climatedepot.com/2020/11/16/covid-lockdowns-no-longer-called-lockd owns-dimmer-switch-freeze-emergency-brake-make-debut-as-politicians-avoid-word -lockdown/.

83. David Leonhardt, "Do Covid Precautions Work? Yes, but They Haven't Made a Big Difference," *New York Times,* March 9, 2022, https://www.nytimes.com/2022/03/09 /briefing/covid-precautions-red-blue-states.html (The article is also available at https:// milled.com/nytimes/the-morning-do-covid-precautions-work-Gh4T0il0_AUg1W_g).

84. Victoria Colliver, "Locked-Down California Runs Out of Reasons for Surprising Surge," *POLITICO,* December 23, 2020, https://www.politico.com/news/2020/12 /23/california-covid-surge-450315; POLITICO (@politico), "California has had some of the toughest restrictions in the country…," Twitter, December 23, 2020, 11:00 p.m., https://twitter.com/politico/status/1341956884488744960.

Chapter 6: How "The Science" Was Manipulated to Support Long-Desired Policies

1. Rebecca Klar, "France's Macron Calls for All Citizens to Remain Confined in Homes: 'We're at War,'" *The Hill,* March 16, 2020, https://thehill.com/policy/international/48 7870-frances-macron-calls-for-all-citizens-to-remain-confined-in-homes-were.

2. Thomas Sowell, *Intellectuals and Society* (New York: Basic Books, 2009), 24.

3. C. S. Lewis, *God in the Dock* (Grand Rapids: William B. Eerdmans Publishing Company, 1970), 315.

4. Sanjeev Sabhlok (@sabhlok), "The Problem with Science Today Is That It Is Effectively Just Another Branch of Government," Twitter, July 16, 2020, 6:03 a.m., https://twitt er.com/sabhlok/ status/1283703789111795714 Twitter has deleted Sabhlok's account, but a quotation from it is preserved in Marc Morano, *Green Fraud: Why the Green New Deal Is Even Worse Than You Think* (Washington, D.C.: Regnery, 2021), 265).

5. John P. A. Ioannidis, "How the Pandemic Is Changing the Norms of Science," Tablet, September 8, 2021, https://www.tabletmag.com/sections/science/articles/pandemic-sc ience.

6.   E. J. Ward, "Donald Trump, 73, Takes Swipe at Greta Thunberg, 17, during Davos Speech," LBC, January 21, 2020, https://amp.lbc.co.uk/world-news/greta-thunberg -donald-trump-climate-davos/; Penny Starr, "Watch Live: Climate Kid Greta Thunberg Testifies in Congress," Breitbart, September 18, 2019, https://www.breitbart.com/pol itics/2019/09/18/watch-live-climate-kid-greta-thunberg-testifies-in-congress/.

7.   William M. Briggs, "How a Science Becomes The Science," William M. Briggs: Statistician to the Stars!, April 5, 2021, https://www.wmbriggs.com/post/35136/.

8.   Dwight D. Eisenhower, "President Dwight D. Eisenhower's Farewell Address (1961)," National Archives, https://www.ourdocuments.gov/doc.php?flash=false&doc=90&p age=transcript.

9.   Translated from the original Latin quotation. Thomas Jefferson to James Madison, January 30, 1787, Library of Congress, https://www.loc.gov/resource/mtj1.006_1110 _1119/; Marc Morano (@ClimateDepot), "I prefer dangerous freedom...," (thread) Twitter, April 21, 2020, 12:03 p.m., https://twitter.com/ClimateDepot/status/1252629 158670237699.

10. Thomas Jefferson to Edward Carrington, May 27, 1788, National Archives: Founders Online, https://founders.archives.gov/documents/Jefferson/01-13-02-0120.

11. "'We Could Open Up Again and Forget the Whole Thing,'" Spiked, May 15, 2020, https://www.spiked-online.com/2020/05/15/we-could-open-up-again-and-forget-the -whole-thing/.

12. Ed West, "America Has Become Its Own Worst Enemy," UnHerd, August 3, 2021, https://unherd.com/2021/08/america-is-turning-into-the-soviet-union/.

13. Jordan Schachtel, "Flashback: Fauci Describes Ebola Quarantines as 'Draconian,' Warns of 'Unintended Consequences,'" The Dossier (Substack), February 19, 2021, https://dossier.substack.com/p/flashback-fauci-describes-ebola-quarantines?s=r.

14. The Rockefeller Foundation and Global Business Network, *Scenarios for the Future of Technology and International Development* (New York: The Rockefeller Foundation, May 2010), http://www.nommeraadio.ee/meedia/pdf/RRS/Rockefeller Foundation.pdf; Center for Health Security, "Clade X Pandemic Exercise: Segment 4," YouTube, May 18, 2018, https://youtu.be/tqa7NHq73xM.

15. Marc Morano (@ClimateDepot), "Fauci says attacks on him are 'attacks on science...,'" (thread) Twitter, June 9, 2021, 9:32 p.m., https://twitter.com/ClimateDepot/status/14 02800828226879491.

16. Jeffrey A. Tucker, "The 2006 Origins of the Lockdown Idea," American Institute for Economic Research, May 15, 2020, https://www.aier.org/article/the-2006-origins-of -the-lockdown-idea/.

17. Ed Achorn, "We Didn't Close America in 1957–1958," American Greatness, May 25, 2020, https://amgreatness.com/2020/05/25/we-didnt-close-america-in-1957-1958/.

18. Jim Jacobs and Warren Casey, "It's Raining on Prom Night," performed by Cindy Bullen, *Grease* (Los Angeles: Paramount Pictures, 1978).

19. Jeffrey A. Tucker, "Elvis Was King, Ike Was President, and 116,000 Americans Died in a Pandemic," American Institute for Economic Research, May 4, 2020, https://www .aier.org/article/the-2006-origins-of-the-lockdown-idea/.

20. Eric Spitznagel, "Why American Life Went On as Normal during the Killer Pandemic of 1969," *New York Post,* May 16, 2020, https://nypost.com/2020/05/16/why-life-we nt-on-as-normal-during-the-killer-pandemic-of-1969/.

21. Tucker, "Elvis Was King, Ike Was President."

22. Michael Fumento, "The Two Horsemen of the Apocalypse: Fauci and Redfield," Issues & Insights, August 4, 2020, https://issuesinsights.com/2020/08/04/the-two-horsemen -of-the-apocalypse-fauci-and-redfield/.

23. Tony Heller (@Tony_Heller), "2020 was the year when I learned that viruses respect directional arrows on supermarket floors…," Twitter, June 10, 2021, 6:00 p.m., https:// twitter.com/Tony__Heller/status/1403155039665852417 (Twitter has deleted Heller's account, but this tweet is available at the Internet Archive's Wayback Machine: https:// web.archive.org/web/20210611011824/https://twitter.com/Tony__Heller/status/1403 155039665852417).

24. Ron Coleman (@RonColeman), "Did they release the official figures yet…," Twitter, September 5, 2021, 12:39 p.m., https://twitter.com/RonColeman/status/1434556900 327280655.

25. Jeremy Loffredo, "'Dr. Fauci, Mr. Hyde': RFK, Jr. Shares Details about New Book on 'The Corbett Report,'" The Defender, November 24, 2021, https://childrenshealthdef ense.org/defender/james-corbett-robert-f-kennedy-jr-the-real-anthony-fauci/.

26. Michael P Senger (@MichaelPSenger), "The fact that the pandemic guidelines of the WHO…," Twitter, June 12, 2021, 9:53 a.m., https://twitter.com/MichaelPSenger/sta tus/1403711946466107393 (Twitter has deleted Senger's account, but this tweet is available at the Internet Archive's WayBack Machine: https://web.archive.org/web/20 210612140245/https://twitter.com/MichaelPSenger/status/1403711946466107393).

27. Michael P Senger (@MichaelPSenger), "New Xiland goes back into lockdown…," Twitter, August 17, 2021, 12:15 p.m., https://twitter.com/MichaelPSenger/status/142 7665297431928834 (Twitter has deleted Senger's account, but this tweet is available at the Internet Archive's WayBack Machine: https://web.archive.org/web/202108171 63149/https://twitter.com/MichaelPSenger/status/1427665297431928834).

28. "Dying in a Leadership Vacuum," (editorial), *New England Journal of Medicine* 383, no. 15 (October 8, 2020): 1479–80, https://www.nejm.org/doi/full/10.1056/NEJMe2 029812.

29. Marc Morano (@ClimateDepot), "NEJM: 'Our rules on social distancing have in many places been lackadaisical at best…," (thread) Twitter, October 8, 2020, 9:42 a.m., https://twitter.com/ClimateDepot/status/1314199586546868230.

30. Steve Milloy (@JunkScience), "We need herd immunity and for the virus to burn itself out….," Twitter, August 2, 2020, 11:51 a.m., https://twitter.com/JunkScience/status /1289952045122727936.

31. Steve Milloy (@JunkScience), "Conservative politicians are now at the mercy of the leftist-run public health bureaucracy….," Twitter, March 22, 2020, 10:51 a.m., https:// twitter.com/JunkScience/status/1241739320546988034.

32. Steve Milloy (@JunkScience), "We are all paying a very steep price…," Twitter, April 12, 2020, 6:27 p.m., https://twitter.com/JunkScience/status/1249464090063507456.

33. Steve Milloy (@Junk Science), "This is what's coming…," Twitter, March 18, 2020, 10:27 a.m., https://twitter.com/JunkScience/status/1240283663029415937.

34. Steve Milloy (@JunkScience), "We can still 'social distance' without devolving…," Twitter, April 12, 2020, 5:58 p.m., https://twitter.com/JunkScience/status/124945683 2046936067.

35. Tucker, "The 2006 Origins of the Lockdown Idea."

36. Donald G. McNeil Jr., "Greetings Kill: Primer for a Pandemicic," *New York Times*, February 12, 2006, https://www.nytimes.com/2006/02/12/weekinreview/greetings-ki ll-primer-for-a-pandemic.html.

37. Tracy Withers, "One Virus Case Puts New Zealand into Nationwide Lockdown," Bloomberg, August 17, 2021, https://www.bloomberg.com/news/articles/2021-08-17 /new-zealand-puts-nation-into-lockdown-on-single-covid-case.

38. Marc Morano (@Climate Depot), "If you thought lockdowns were bad…," Twitter, August 17, 2021, 2:36 p.m., https://twitter.com/ClimateDepot/status/142770097728 1474566.

39. Eric Lipton and Jennifer Steinhauer, "The Untold Story of the Birth of Social Distancing," *New York Times,* April 22, 2020, https://www.nytimes.com/2020/04/22 /us/politics/social-distancing-coronavirus.html.

40. Ollie Reed Jr., "Social Distancing Born in ABQ Teen's Science Project," *Albuquerque Journal,* May 2, 2020, https://www.abqjournal.com/1450579/social-distancing-born -in-abq-teens-science-project.html.

41. Tucker, "The 2006 Origins of the Lockdown Idea."

42. Ibid.; Lipton and Steinhauer, "The Untold Story."

43. Marc Morano, "Viral Video: Watch Morano's 1-Hour Interview Debunking 'Global Warming' & Explaining How the Climate Scare Became a Tool for the Regulatory State," Climate Depot, August 27, 2019, https://www.climatedepot.com/2019/08/27 /watch-morano-in-1-hour-interview-debunks-global-warming-explains-how-the-clim ate-scare-became-a-tool-for-the-regulatory-state/.

44. Tom Woods, "Now That Our Overlords Have Graciously Allowed Us to Discuss the Possibility That the Virus Originated in a Lab, They've Had to Cover Their Tracks a Bit," Mailchimp, https://mailchi.mp/tomwoods/wapoheadline?e=5c84172ffc.

45. Dan Diamond, "Suddenly, Public Health Officials Say Social Justice Matters More Than Social Distance," *POLITICO,* June 4, 2020, https://www.politico.com/news /magazine/2020/06/04/public-health-protests-301534; Jennifer Nuzzo, DrPH (@JenniferNuzzo), "We should always evaluate the risks and benefits…," Twitter, June 2, 2020, 2:25 p.m., https://twitter.com/JenniferNuzzo/status/12678850766978 12993.

46. Tucker Carlson, "Scientists Who No Longer Believe in Science Is a Real Problem for Civilization," Fox News, May 28, 2021, https://www.foxnews.com/opinion/tucker-ca rlson-scientists-who-no-longer-believe-in-science-is-a-real-problem-for-civilization.

47. Mallory Simon, "Over 1,000 Health Professionals Sign a Letter Saying, Don't Shut Down Protests Using Coronavirus Concerns as an Excuse," CNN, June 5, 2020, https:// www.cnn.com/2020/06/05/health/health-care-open-letter-protests-coronavirus-trnd /index.html.

48. Chris Masters, "Studies of Surgical Masks Efficiency," August 12, 2020, http://12160 .info/m/blogpost?id=2649739:BlogPost:2035264; Marc Morano, "Shock Research Shows Masks Ineffective During Surgeries," Climate Depot, August 13, 2020, https:// www.climatedepot.com/2020/08/13/shock-research-shows-masks-ineffective-during -surgeries-a-lack-of-substantial-evidence-to-support-claims-that-facemasks-protect-ei ther-patient-or-surgeon-from-infectious-contamination/.

49. M. A. Ritter et al., "The Operating Room Environment as Affected by People and the Surgical Face Mask," *Clinical Orthopaedics and Related Research* 111 (September 1975): 147–50, https://journals.lww.com/clinorthop/Citation/1975/09000/The_Oper ating_Room_Environment_as_Affected_by.20.aspx.

50. G. B. Ha'eri and A. M. Wiley, "The Efficacy of Standard Surgical Face Masks: An Investigation Using 'Tracer Particles,'" *Clinical Orthopaedics and Related Research* 148 (May 1980): 160–62, https://pubmed.ncbi.nlm.nih.gov/7379387/.

51.   Lawrence J. Laslett and Alisa Sabin, "Wearing of Caps and Masks Not Necessary during Cardiac Catheterization," *Catheterization and Cardiovascular Diagnosis* 17, no. 3 (July 1989): 158–60, https://pubmed.ncbi.nlm.nih.gov/2766345/; Anette Sjøl and Henning Kelbaek, "[Is use of surgical caps and masks obsolete during purcutaneous heart catheterization?]," *Ugeskrift for Laeger* 164, no. 12 (March 18, 2002): 1673–75, https://pubmed.ncbi.nlm.nih.gov/11924291/.

52.   M. W. Skinner and B. A. Sutton, "Do Anaesthetists Need to Wear Surgical Masks in the Operating Theatre? A Literature Review with Evidence-Based Recommendations," *Anaesthesia and Intensive Care* 29, no. 4 (August 2001): 331–38, https://journals.sag epub.com/doi/10.1177/0310057X0102900402.

53.   T. Lahme et al., "[Patient surgical masks during regional anesthesia. Hygenic necessity or dispensable ritual?]," *Der Anaesthesist* 50, no. 11 (November 2001): 846–51, https:// pubmed.ncbi.nlm.nih.gov/11760479/.

54.   Charlie Da Zhou, Pamela Sivathondan, and Ashok Handa, "Unmasking the Surgeons: The Evidence Base behind the Use of Facemasks in Surgery," *Journal of the Royal Society of Medicine* 108, no. 6 (June 2015): 223–28, https://journals.sagepub.com/doi /10.1177/0141076815583167.

55.   "Are Face Masks Effective? The Evidence," Swiss Policy Research, July 2020, https:// swprs.org/face-masks-evidence/. (The bullet point that begins, "An April 2020 review by two U.S. professors . . ." has been removed from the page, but this bullet point is available at the Internet Archive's Wayback Machine: https://web.archive.org/web/20 210901062031/https://swprs.org/face-masks-evidence/.)

56.   Jingyi Xiao et al., "Nonpharmaceutical Measures for Pandemic Influenza in Nonhealthcare Settings—Personal Protective and Environmental Measures," *Emerging Infectious Diseases* 26, no. 5 (May 2020): 967–75, https://wwwnc.cdc.gov/eid/article /26/5/19-0994_article.

57.   Henning Bundgaard et al., "Effectiveness of Adding a Mask Recommendation to Other Public Health Measures to Prevent SARS-CoV-2 Infection in Danish Mask Wearers," *Annals of Internal Medicine* (March 2021), https://www.acpjournals.org/doi/10.7326 /M20-6817.

58.   Mohammad Alfelali et al., "Facemask against Viral Respiratory Infections among Hajj Pilgrims: A Challenging Cluster-Randomized Trial," *Public Library of Science One* 15, no. 10 (October 13, 2020), https://journals.plos.org/plosone/article?id=10.1371/journ al.pone.0240287.

59.   Agoritsa Baka et al., *Using Face Masks in the Community: First Update* (Stockholm: European Centre for Disease Control and Prevention, February 15, 2021), https://www .ecdc.europa.eu/sites/default/files/documents/covid-19-face-masks-community-first-up date.pdf.

60.   Tom Jefferson and Carl Heneghan, "Masking Lack of Evidence with Politics," The Centre for Evidence-Based Medicine, July 23, 2020, https://www.cebm.net/covid-19/ masking-lack-of-evidence-with-politics/.

61.   T. Jefferson et al., "Do Physical Measures Such as Hand-Washing or Wearing Masks Stop or Slow Down the Spread of Respiratory Viruses?," Cochrane, November 20, 2020, https://www.cochrane.org/CD006207/ARI_do-physical-measures-such-hand -washing-or-wearing-masks-stop-or-slow-down-spread-respiratory-viruses.

62.   Lisa M. Brosseau and Margaret Sietsema, "Commentary: Masks-for-All for COVID-19 Not Based on Sound Data," Center for Infectious Disease Research and Policy, April

1, 2020, https://www.cidrap.umn.edu/news-perspective/2020/04/commentary-masks
-all-covid-19-not-based-sound-data.

63. C. Raina MacIntyre et al., "A Cluster Randomized Trial of Cloth Masks Compared
with Medical Masks in Healthcare Workers," *British Medical Journal Open* 5, no. 4
(April 22, 2015), https://pubmed.ncbi.nlm.nih.gov/25903751/.

64. Ines Kappstein, "Mund-Nasen-Schutz in der Öffentlichkeit: Keine Hinweise für eine
Wirksamkeit," *Krankenhaushygiene Up2date* 15, no. 3 (2020): 279–95, https://doi.org
/10.1055/a-1174-6591.

65. Thomas V. Inglesby et al., "Disease Mitigation Measures in the Control of Pandemic
Influenza," *Biosecurity and Bioterrorism: Biodefense Strategy, Practice, and Science*
4, no. 4 (2006): 366–75, http://citeseerx.ist.psu.edu/viewdoc/download?doi=10.1.1.552
.1109&rep=rep1&type=pdf.

66. Alex Berenson (@AlexBerenson), "1/ This is quite the paper on masks…," Twitter, July
8, 2020, 4:47 p.m., https://twitter.com/AlexBerenson/status/1280966807956992002
(Twitter has deleted Berenson's account has been deleted, but this tweet is available on
the Internet Archive's Wayback Machine: https://web.archive.org/web/20210324021
622/https://twitter.com/AlexBerenson/status/1280966807956992002); C. Raina
MacIntyre et al., "A Cluster Randomized Trial of Cloth Masks Compared with Medical
Masks in Healthcare Workers," *British Medical Journal Open* 5, no. 4 (April 22, 2015),
http://doi.org/10.1136/bmjopen-2014-006577.

67. Michael Klompas et al., "Universal Masking in the COVID-19 Era," *New England
Journal of Medicine* 383 (July 9, 2021), with an "Editor's Note" quoting a June 3, 2020,
letter to the editor from the authors, http://doi.org/10.1056/NEJMc2020836.

68. Jordan Boyd, "CDC Study Finds Overwhelming Majority of People Getting
Coronavirus Wore Masks," The Federalist, October 12, 2020, https://thefederalist.com
/2020/10/12/cdc-study-finds-overwhelming-majority-of-people-getting-coronavirus
-wore-masks/.

69. Eliza McGraw, "Everyone Wore Masks during the 1918 Flu Pandemic. They Were
Useless," *Washington Post*, April 2, 2020, https://www.washingtonpost.com/history
/2020/04/02/everyone-wore-masks-during-1918-flu-pandemic-they-were-useless/.

70. Becky Little, "'Mask Slackers' and 'Deadly' Spit: The 1918 Flu Campaigns to Shame
People into Following New Rules," History.com, July 16, 2020, https://www.history
.com/news/1918-pandemic-public-health-campaigns.

71. McGraw, "Everyone Wore Masks."

72. Becky Little, "When Mask-Wearing Rules in the 1918 Pandemic Faced Resistance,"
History.com, May 6, 2020, https://www.history.com/news/1918-spanish-flu-mask-we
aring-resistance.

73. E. Thomas Ewing, "Flu Masks Failed in 1918, but We Need Them Now," *Health
Affairs*, May 12, 2020, https://www.healthaffairs.org/do/10.1377/forefront.20200508
.769108/.

74. William M. Briggs, "Mask Madness—Our Latest Moral Panic," William M. Briggs:
Statistician to the Stars!, July 24, 2020,https://wmbriggs.com/post/31883/.

75. Vinay Prasad, MD MPH (@VPrasadMDMPH), "I keep seeing people telling
journalists…," Twitter, February 16, 2022, 7:36 p.m., https://twitter.com/VPrasadM
DMPH/status/1494108544173412352; "Short Biography," Vinay Prasad MD, MPH,
http://www.vinayakkprasad.com/bio.

76. Lisa Lerer, Luis Ferré-Sadurní, and Astead W. Herndon, "Dropping Indoor Mask
Mandate, New York Joins Blue States Easing Covid Rules," *New York Times*, February

8, 2022, https://www.nytimes.com/2022/02/08/us/politics/new-york-mask-mandate .html.

77. "CNN's Brian Stelter Mocks the CDC: 'It Is So Sad but It's True. The CDC Has Turned into a Punch Line,'" The Daily Wire, January 9, 2022, https://www.dailywire.com/ne ws/cnns-brian-stelter-mocks-the-cdc-it-is-so-sad-but-its-true-the-cdc-has-turned-into -a-punch-line.

78. Zoe Malin, "CDC Updates: Wear a Mask While Exercising Indoors at Gyms," NBC News, March 9, 2021, https://www.nbcnews.com/shopping/wellness/cdc-masks-dur ing-exercise-n1260261.

79. Fenit Nirappil, "Time to Double or Upgrade Masks as Coronavirus Variants Emerge, Experts Say," *Washington Post*, January 28, 2021, https://www.washingtonpost.com /health/2021/01/27/double-mask-variants-guidance/.

80. Jordan Schachtel, "The CDC's Double Mask Mannequin 'Study' is Lunacy Dressed Up as Science," The Dossier (Substack), February 10, 2021, https://dossier.substack .com/p/the-cdcs-double-mask-mannequin-study; Jordan Schachtel, "'Public Health Experts' Now Call for Three Masks to Slow the Spread," The Dossier (Substack), January 26, 2021, https://dossier.substack.com/p/public-health-experts-now-call-for.

81. "Is a Double Mask Really Better than a Single?," CNBC, January 25, 2021, https:// www.cnbc.com/video/2021/01/25/is-a-double-mask-really-better-than-a-single.html.

82. Erika Edwards, "What Do Coronavirus Variants Mean for Your Masks?," NBC News, January 26, 2021, https://www.nbcnews.com/health/health-news/what-do-coronavi rus-variants-mean-your-masks-n1255518; Schachtel, "'Public Health Experts' Now Call."

83. Jordan Schachtel @ dossier.substack.com (@JordanSchachtel), "Masks gave meaning to people with meaningless lives….," Twitter, May 14, 2021, https://twitter.com/Jord anSchachtel/status/1393293178636316674%5C (This tweet has been deleted, but it is available at the Internet Archive's Wayback Machine: https://web.archive.org/web/20 210514195344/https://twitter.com/JordanSchachtel/status/1393293178636316674).

84. Jeffrey H. Anderson, "The Masking of America," *Claremont Review of Books*, Summer 2021, https://claremontreviewofbooks.com/the-masking-of-america/.

85. "Fact Check: Outdated Video of Fauci Saying 'There's No Reason to Be Walking around with a Mask,'" Reuters, October 8, 2020, https://www.reuters.com/article/uk -factcheck-fauci-outdated-video-masks/fact-checkoutdated-video-of-fauci-saying-ther es-no-reason-to-be-walking-around-with-a-mask-idUSKBN26T2TR.

86. Jeffrey H. Anderson, "Do Masks Work?," *City Journal*, August 11, 2021, https://www .city-journal.org/do-masks-work-a-review-of-the-evidence?wallit_nosession=1%20 %0A.

87. Peter Hitchens, "Peter Hitchens: Face Masks Turn Us into Voiceless Submissives—and It's Not Science Forcing Us to Wear Them, It's Politics," *Daily Mail*, July 19, 2020, https://hitchensblog.mailonsunday.co.uk/2020/07/peter-hitchens-face-masks-turn-us -into-voiceless-submissives-and-its-not-science-forcing-us-to-wear-.html.

88. Greg Piper, "Noted COVID Expert Noam Chomsky Compares Anti-maskers to Mass Shooters," The College Fix, January 19, 2021, https://www.thecollegefix.com/noted -covid-expert-noam-chomsky-compares-anti-maskers-to-mass-shooters/.

89. Robert F. Kennedy Jr., "People in Authority Lie," Children's Health Defense, August 28, 2020, https://childrenshealthdefense.org/wp-content/uploads/08-31-20-RFK-Jr.-P ress-Conference-Transcript.pdf; OneSilentJoy, "Robert F Kennedy Jr in Berlin 28 Aug

2020," YouTube, August 28, 2020, https://www.youtube.com/watch?v=wM7NLlW ZD5I&t=4s.

90. Anderson, "The Masking of America."

91. John Tierney, "How Facebook Uses 'Fact-Checking' to Suppress Scientific Truth," *New York Post*, May 18, 2021, https://nypost.com/2021/05/18/how-facebook-uses-fact-ch ecking-to-suppress-scientific-truth/; Kirby Wilson and Allison Ross, "YouTube Removes Video of DeSantis Pandemic Roundtable with Atlas, Other Panelists," *Miami Herald*, April 12, 2021, https://www.miamiherald.com/news/politics-government/sta te-politics/article250611599.html.

92. Kathy Leonardo, "Paramount Drive In Theatres Continue to Offer Top-Notch Flicks," LA Art Party.com, https://www.laartparty.com/running-thru-march-4-2021-paramo unt-drive-in-theatres/.

93. Harry (@Harry_leb), "Science my a$$…," Twitter, June 1, 2021, 11:54 a.m., https:// twitter.com/Harry_leb/status/1399756318500548613.

94. Tom Woods, "This Is a Bit of Potpourri Issue," Mailchimp, https://mailchi.mp/tomw oods/goodnews?e=5c84172ffc.

95. Michael Fumento, "Covid Coverage Cherry-Picking," Michael Fumento, July 1, 2020, https://www.fumento.com/articles/covid-coverage-cherry-picking/.

96. Ibid.; Michael Fumento, "Media Enraged That More Swedes Aren't Dying," Michael Fumento, June 4, 2020, https://www.fumento.com/articles/media-enraged-that-more -swedes-aren-t-dying/.

97. Jordan Schachtel, "Freedom Prevails: COVID Data Shows 'Public Health' Mandates Only Harm People," The Dossier (Substack), September 25, 2021, https://dossier.subs tack.com/p/freedom-prevails-covid-data-shows.

98. Michael P. Senger (@MichaelPSenger), "40/ WHO cited the guidance by Chinese journal articles…," (thread) Twitter, January 10, 2021, 1:59 p.m., https://twitter.com /michaelpsenger/status/1348344410233131011 (Twitter has deleted Senger's account, but this thread is available at the Internet Archive's WayBack Machine: https://web.ar chive.org/web/20210406013250/https://twitter.com/MichaelPSenger/status/1348343 861618229248).

99. Michael P. Senger, "The Masked Ball of Cowardice," Tablet, August 29, 2021, https:// www.tabletmag.com/sections/news/articles/masked-ball-cowardice.

100. Michael P Senger (@MichaelPSenger), "41/ As Wall Street Journal Later Reported…," (thread) Twitter, January 10, 2021, 2:00 p.m., https://twitter.com/MichaelPSenger/st atus/1348343861618229248 (Twitter has deleted Senger's account, but this thread is available at the Internet Archive's WayBack Machine: https://web.archive.org/web/20 210406013250/https://twitter.com/MichaelPSenger/status/1348343861618229248); Melanie Evans, "Hospitals Retreat from Early Covid Treatment and Return to Basics," *Wall Street Journal*, December 20, 2020, https://www.wsj.com/articles/hospitals-retr eat-from-early-covid-treatment-and-return-to-basics-11608491436.

101. Anne McCloskey, "Rapid Response: Re: Covid-19: Social Murder, They Wrote— Elected, Unaccountable, and Unrepentant," *British Medical Journal*, March 4, 2021, https://www.bmj.com/content/372/bmj.n314/rr-33.

102. Alex Berenson, "New York Declares a Health-Care State of Emergency over a Covid Variant That Doesn't Exist in the State," Unreported Truths (Substack), November 27, 2021, https://alexberenson.substack.com/p/new-york-declares-a-health-care-state?s=r.

103. Marc Morano, "*BMJ* (*British Medical Journal*) COVID Editorial Seeks 'Social Murder' Charges against Anti-Lockdown Politicians Who 'Wilfully Neglect Scientific

Evidence...and Modeling,'" Climate Depot, February 13, 2021, https://www.climate depot.com/2021/02/13/bmj-british-medical-journal-editorial-seeks-social-murder-ch arges-against-anti-lockdown-politicians-who-wilfully-neglect-scientific-advice-and-mo deling/.

104. Marc Morano (@ClimateDepot), "Trump allowed the health bureaucracy and their failed models to dictate...," (thread) Twitter, May 29, 2020, 8:08 a.m., https://twitter .com/ClimateDepot/status/1266340712792154112.

105. Ari Natter, "Washington Reopens in a Win for Trump amid Nagging Safety Doubts," *Financial Post*, May 29, 2020, https://financialpost.com/pmn/business-pmn/washing ton-reopens-in-a-win-for-trump-amid-nagging-safety-doubts.

106. Geoffrey P. Hunt, "We've Been Had, and Trump Knows It," American Thinker, March 28, 2020, https://www.americanthinker.com/blog/2020/03/weve_been_had_and_tr ump_knows_it.html.

107. Ann Coulter, "How Do We Flatten the Curve on Panic?," Ann Coulter, March 25, 2020, https://anncoulter.com/2020/03/25/how-do-we-flatten-the-curve-on-panic/.

108. William M. Briggs, "The Burden of Proof on Climate Scientists—and Those Wishing for Its 'Solutions,'" William M. Briggs: Statistician to the Stars!, April 29, 2021, https:// wmbriggs.com/post/35462/.

109. Bill Barrow, "Biden Says He'd Shut Down Economy If Scientists Recommend," ABC News, August 23, 2020, https://abcnews.go.com/Politics/wireStory/biden-hed-shut-ec onomy-scientists-recommended-72559926.

110. Kate Yoder, "Why Is Science So Polarizing? Blame the Way We Talk about It," Grist, January 29, 2020, https://grist.org/politics/why-is-science-is-so-politicized-blame-the -way-we-talk-about-it/.

111. Pundit Class (@punditclass), "Those people at anti-mask protests...," Twitter, May 8, 2021, 6:25 p.m., https://twitter.com/punditclass/status/1391202519406170116 (Twitter has deleted Pundit Class's account, but this tweet is available at the Internet Archive's Wayback Machine: https://web.archive.org/web/20210509020851/https://twitter.com /punditclass/status/1391202519406170116).

112. Carlson, "Scientists Who No Longer Believe in Science."

113. Denis Rancourt (@denisrancourt), "Do not trust science....," Twitter, July 13, 2021, 3:30 p.m., https://twitter.com/denisrancourt/status/1415031014603304969.

114. Friends of Science, "Return to Eden: Online Premier," YouTube, September 17, 2020, https://www.youtube.com/watch?v=1s4vWrHw3WY.

115. Marc Morano, "Left-Wing Env. Scientist Bails Out of Global Warming Movement: Declares It a 'Corrupt Social Phenomenon...Strictly an Imaginary Problem of the 1st World MiddleClass,'" Climate Depot, July 26, 2010, https://www.climatedepot.com /2010/07/26/leftwing-env-scientist-bails-out-of-global-warming-movement-declares-it -a-corrupt-social-phenomenonstrictly-an-imaginary-problem-of-the-1st-world-middl eclass/.

116. Ioannidis, "How the Pandemic."

Chapter 7: Censorship and Tech Tyranny

1. Antony P. Mueller, "From Lockdowns to 'the Great Reset,'" Mises Wire, August 1, 2020, https://mises.org/wire/lockdowns-great-reset.

2. "Event 201: A Global Pandemic Exercise," Center for Health Security, https://www.ce nterforhealthsecurity.org/event201/.

3. "Event 201 Pandemic Exercise Segment 4, Communications Discussion," Children's Health Defense, September 23, 2020, https://childrenshealthdefense.org/wp-content /uploads/Event-201-Pandemic-Exercise-Segment-4-Communications-Discussion-and -Epilogue-Video-bill-gates.pdf; "Event 201 Videos," Center for Health Security, https:// www.centerforhealthsecurity.org/event201/videos.html.

4. "Event 201 Videos.

5. Ibid.

6. Jonathan Turley, "Twitter Suspends Science Writer after He Posts Results of Pfizer Clinical Trial," Jonathan Turley, July 31, 2021, https://jonathanturley.org/2021/07/31 /twitter-suspends-science-writer-after-he-posts-results-of-pfizer-clinical-test/.

7. John F. Kennedy, "Address on the 20th Anniversary of the Voice of America," American Rhetoric, February 26, 1962, https://www.americanrhetoric.com/speeches/jfkvoiceof america.htm.

8. Raelle Kaia, "Why Are They Doing This?" Medium, March 25, 2021, https://raellek aia.medium.com/why-are-they-doing-this-73963183a502 (Medium has deleted Kaia's account, but this article is available at Open Heart, Open Mind (Substack): https:// raellekaia.substack.com/p/why-are-they-doing-this-73963183a502?s=r).

9. guyjohn59, "John Denver at PMRC Hearings," YouTube, June 21, 2010, https://www .youtube.com/watch?v=VgSjjD6rRu4&t=1s.

10. Joe Rogan, "1757—Dr. Robert Malone, MD," *The Joe Rogan Experience*, December 31, 2021, https://joeroganpodcast.net/1757-dr-robert-malone/.

11. "Tucker: Academic Standards in America Are in Freefall," Fox News, August 21, 2021, https://www.foxnews.com/transcript/tucker-academic-standards-in-america-are-in-fr eefall.

12. Pedro Gonzalez, "'American Capitalism' Is the Enemy," *Chronicles*, February 3, 2021, https://chroniclesmagazine.org/web/american-capitalism-is-the-enemy/.

13. James Delingpole, "Nobel Winner Michael Levitt Cancelled for Coronavirus Wrongthink," Breitbart, October 20, 2020, https://www.breitbart.com/politics/2020 /10/20/delingpole-nobel-winner-michael-levitt-cancelled-for-coronavirus-wrongthink/; Michael Levitt (@MLevitt_NP2013), "My keynote uninvited from...," (thread) Twitter, Octover 18, 2020, 6:56 a.m., https://twitter.com/MLevitt_NP2013/status/131778154 8901363712.

14. Marc Morano, "'Dark Age Cometh': Nobel Winning Stanford U. Chemist Michael Levitt Cancelled for Coronavirus Wrongthink," Climate Depot, October 26, 2020, https://www.climatedepot.com/2020/10/26/dark-age-cometh-nobel-winning-stanfo rd-u-chemist-michael-levitt-cancelled-for-coronavirus-wrongthink/.

15. Delingpole, "Nobel Winner Michael Levitt."

16. David Marcus, "White House Expert Scott Atlas Censored by Twitter," The Federalist, October 18, 2020, https://thefederalist.com/2020/10/18/white-house-expert-scott-atl as-censored-by-twitter/.

17. Tom Jefferson and Carl Heneghan, "Masking Lack of Evidence with Politics," The Centre for Evidence-Based Medicine, July 23, 2020, https://www.cebm.net/covid-19/ masking-lack-of-evidence-with-politics/.

18. "Advice on the Use of Masks in the Context of Covid-19: Interim Guidance," World Health Organization, June 5, 2020, https://apps.who.int/iris/bitstream/handle/10665 /332293/WHO-2019-nCov-IPC_Masks-2020.4-eng.pdf?sequence=1&isAllowed=y.

19. Jingyi Xiao et al., "Nonpharmaceutical Measures for Pandemic Influenza in Nonhealthcare Settings—Personal Protective and Environmental Measures," *Emerging*

Infectious Diseases 26, no. 5 (May 2020), https://wwwnc.cdc.gov/eid/article/26/5/19 -0994_article.

20. Marcus, "White House Expert Scott Atlas Censored."

21. Alex Berenson (@AlexBerenson), "Does it seem like the entire elite media…," (thread) Twitter, May 30, 2021, 6:58 a.m., https://twitter.com/AlexBerenson/status/13990023 10693511169 (Twitter has deleted Berenson's account, but this tweet is available on the Internet Archive's WayBack Machine: https://web.archive.org/web/20210530135919 /https://twitter.com/AlexBerenson/status/1399002310693511169).

22. "Media and Tech Firms Join Forces to Tackle Harmful Covid Vaccine Myths," BBC News, December 10, 2020, https://www.bbc.com/news/entertainment-arts-55257814.

23. The BFD, "Jacinda Adern—'We Will Continue to Be Your Single Source of Truth,'" YouTube, May 15, 2020, https://www.youtube.com/watch?v=ENEUktOrQV8; "1. Question No. 1—Prime Minister," New Zealand Parliament, September 2, 2020, https://www.parliament.nz/en/pb/hansard-debates/rhr/document/HansS_20200902 _050580000/1-question-no-1-prime-minister.

24. Berenson (@AlexBerenson), "Does it seem like the entire elite media . . . " (thread).

25. "COVID-19 Medical Misinformation Policy," YouTube Help, https://support.google .com/youtube/answer/9891785?hl=en; "COVID-19 and Vaccine Policy Updates and Protections," Facebook Help Center, https://www.facebook.com/help/23076488149 4641; "Keeping People Informed, Safe, and Supported on Instagram," Instagram, March 24, 2020, https://about.instagram.com/blog/announcements/coronavirus-kee ping-people-safe-informed-and-supported-on-instagram; "COVID-19 Misleading Information Policy," Twitter Help Center, https://help.twitter.com/en/rules-and-polic ies/medical-misinformation-policy.

26. Victoria Knight, "Censorship or Misinformation? DeSantis and YouTube Spar Over Covid Roundtable Takedown," KHN, April 21, 2021, https://khn.org/news/article/ce nsorship-or-misinformation-desantis-and-youtube-spar-over-covid-roundtable-taked own/; Ashley Gold, "Exclusive: YouTube Removed 30,000 Videos with COVID Misinformation," Axios, March 11, 2021, https://www.axios.com/2021/03/11/youtu be-removed-30000-covid19-vaccine-videos-misinformation; Queenie Wong, "Facebook Removed More than 1 Million Posts for COVID-19 Information," CNET, February 11, 2021, https://www.cnet.com/news/facebook-removed-more-than-1-mill ion-posts-for-covid-19-misinformation/; Twitter Safety, "Updates to Our Work on COVID-19 Vaccine Misinformation," Twitter, March 1, 2021, https://blog.twitter.com /en_us/topics/company/2021/updates-to-our-work-on-covid-19-vaccine-misinformati on.html.

27. Fox Nation, "Big Tech's Big Threat on Democracy," Facebook, August 11, 2021, https:// ur-pk.facebook.com/TheFOXNation/videos/big-techs-big-threat-on-democracy/809 497016379743/.

28. Wikipedia, s.v., "Factcheck.org," https://en.wikipedia.org/wiki/FactCheck.org; Wikipedia, s.v. "Annenberg Foundation," https://en.wikipedia.org/wiki/Annenberg _Foundation; Katie Hafner, "Bill Gates and His Wife Give Away $3.3 Billion," *New York Times*, February 6, 1999, https://www.nytimes.com/1999/02/06/us/bill-gates -and-his-wife-give-away-3.3-billion.html; "UUSC Annenberg's Hollywood, Health, and Society Receives Grants to Launch New Initiatives," Bill & Melinda Gates Foundation, https://www.gatesfoundation.org/ideas/media-center/press-releases/2008 /04/usc-annenbergs-hollywood-health-and-society-receives-grants-to-launch-new-ini tiatives.

29. James Delingpole, "Big Tech Wants You to Stay Muzzled, Locked Down Forever," Breitbart, October 13, 2020, https://www.breitbart.com/europe/2020/10/13/big-tech-censors-the-great-barrington-declaration/.

30. William Sullivan, "The Fall of St. Fauci," American Thinker, June 6, 2021, https://www.americanthinker.com/articles/2021/06/the_fall_of_st_fauci.html.

31. Scott McKay, "Our Legacy Corporate Media Is Full of Liars and Propagandists," American Spectator, June 1, 2021, https://spectator.org/media-covid-19-lab-leak/.

32. Ron Wright, "The Unmasking of Dr. Anthony Fauci," American Thinker, June 5, 2021, https://www.americanthinker.com/articles/2021/06/the_unmasking_of_dr_anthony_fauci.html; Nicholas Wade, "Origin of Covid—Following the Clues," Medium, May 2, 2021, https://nicholaswade.medium.com/origin-of-covid-following-the-clues-6f03564c038; Wikipedia, s.v., "Bulletin of the Atomic Scientists," https://en.wikipedia.org/wiki/Bulletin_of_the_Atomic_Scientists; Ron Wright, "Secretary Hillary Clinton and the Deep State: A RICO Criminal Conspiracy," American Thinker, December 19, 2019, https://www.americanthinker.com/articles/2019/12/secretary_hillary_clinton_and_the_deep_state_a_rico_criminal_conspiracy.html.

33. Eric Weinstein (@EricRWeinstein), "Our fact-checkers have one job….," Twitter, May 23, 2021, 5:40 p.m., https://twitter.com/EricRWeinstein/status/1396581749665140738.

34. Anthony Watts, "Bombshell: In Court Filing: Facebook Admits Fact Checks Are Nothing More than Opinion," Watts Up With That?, December 9, 2021, https://wattsupwiththat.com/2021/12/09/bombshell-in-court-filing-facebook-admits-fact-checks-are-nothing-more-than-opinion/.

35. John Stossel, "Here's Where the 'Facts' about Me Lie: Facebook Bizarrely Claims Its 'Fact Checks' Are 'Opinion,'" New York Post, December 13, 2021, https://nypost.com/2021/12/13/facebook-bizarrely-claims-its-misquote-is-opinion/.

36. David Rutz, "Media Fact-Checkers, Facebook Cited Wuhan Lab-Linked Scientist to Knock Down Lab Leak Theory," Fox News, June 4, 2021, https://www.foxnews.com/media/daszak-fact-checks-coronavirus-wuhan-lab.

37. Melissa Chen (@MsMelChen), "Someone at @Facebook needs to explain why Peter Daszak…," Twitter, June 6, 2021, 3:06 p.m., https://twitter.com/MsMelChen/status/1401616401975025664.

38. Dr. Simone Gold (@drsimonegold), "When the media says 'listen to the science,' what they really mean is…," Twitter, October 15, 2020, 1:27 p.m., https://twitter.com/drsimonegold/status/1316792892485058560.

39. Bruce L. Miller, "Science Denial and COVID Conspiracy Theories," Journal of the American Medical Association 324, no. 22 (November 2, 2020): 225–56, https://doi.org/10.1001/jama.2020.21332.

40. Marc Morano, "No Dissent Allowed: COVID Debate Apes Climate Debate: Physician Compares People Who Disagree on COVID, Masks, Vaccines—to Patients with Severe Psychosis," Climate Depot, November 6, 2020, https://www.climatedepot.com/2020/11/06/no-dissent-allowed-covid-debate-apes-climate-debate-physician-compares-people-who-disagree-on-covid-masks-vaccines-to-patients-with-severe-psychosis/.

41. Jon Levine, "YouTube Censors Epidemiologist Knut Wittkowski for Opposing Lockdown," New York Post, May 16, 2020, https://nypost.com/2020/05/16/youtube-censors-epidemiologist-knut-wittkowski-for-opposing-lockdown/.

42. Sunetra Gupta, "A Contagion of Hatred and Hysteria: Oxford Epidemiologist Professor Sunetra Gupta Tells How She Has Been Intimidated and Shamed for Backing Shielding Instead of Lockdown," Daily Mail, October 30, 2020, https://www.dailymail.co.uk

/debate/article-8899277/Professor-Sunetra-Gupta-reveals-crisis-ruthlessly-weaponis ed.html.

43. Ethan Yang, "Reddit's Censorship of The Great Barrington Declaration," American Institute for Economic Research, October 8, 2020, https://www.aier.org/article/reddi ts-censorship-of-the-great-barrington-declaration/.

44. Gupta, "A Contagion of Hatred and Hysteria."

45. "How Fauci and Collins Shut Down Covid Debate" (editorial), *Wall Street Journal*, December 21, 2021, https://www.wsj.com/articles/fauci-collins-emails-great-barringt on-declaration-covid-pandemic-lockdown-11640129116.

46. John P. A. Ioannidis, "How the Pandemic Is Changing the Norms of Science," Tablet, September 8, 2021, https://www.tabletmag.com/sections/science/articles/pandemic-sc ience.

47. Neil Clark (@NeilClark66), "A lot of public figures have been intimidated…," Twitter, May 28, 2021, 3:43 p.m., https://twitter.com/NeilClark66/status/139836423844447 8473.

48. "Twitter Suspends Progressive Feminist Author Naomi Wolf after Slew of Tweets Opposing Covid-19 Vaccinations," RT, June 5, 2021, https://www.rt.com/usa/525782 -twitter-suspends-naomi-wolf/.

49. Sam Clark, "Twitter Bans *Beauty Myth* Author Naomi Wolf over Vaccine Misinformation," *i*, June 6, 2021, https://inews.co.uk/news/technology/naomi-wolf-ba nned-twitter-sharing-vaccine-falsehoods-1037608.

50. "Mary Beth Pfeiffer (@marybethpf), "How dare you, Twitter.…," Twitter, June 5, 2021, 5:00 a.m., screenshot in Lauren Lewis, "Twitter Suspends Feminist Author Naomi Wolf for Spreading Misinformation about Covid Vaccines," *Daily Mail*, June 6, 2021, https://www.dailymail.co.uk/news/article-9656953/Twitter-suspends-author -Naomi-Wolf-spreading-misinformation-Covid-vaccines.html.

51. Glenn Greenwald (@ggreenwald), "There's a virtual industry of operatives funded by the Atlantic Council…," Twitter, June 5, 2021, 9:14 a.m., https://twitter.com/ggreen wald/status/1401165640585580546.

52. Candace Owens (@RealCandaceO), "My post was removed because it made people think…," Twitter, March 27, 2021, 1:55 p.m., https://twitter.com/realcandaceo/status /1397974823205228554.

53. Gupta, "A Contagion of Hatred and Hysteria."

54. Jordan Schachtel @ dossier.substack.com (@JordanSchachtel), "YouTube has an official policy…," Twitter, May 24, 2021, 9:54 p.m., https://twitter.com/JordanSchachtel/sta tus/1397008203255255046.

55. Gupta, "A Contagion of Hatred and Hysteria."

56. Delingpole, "Nobel Winner Michael Levitt."

57. Marcus, "White House Expert Scott Atlas Censored."

58. Tom Elliott (@tomselliott), "@YouTube: Mothers having opinions about whether their children should be forced into masks…," (thread) Twitter, May 26, 2021, 7:13 a.m., https://twitter.com/tomselliott/status/1397511125651099649.

59. Tom Woods, "Guess What YouTube Thinks Is Dangerous Now," Mailchimp, May 26, 2021, https://mailchi.mp/tomwoods/masktube?e=5c84172ffc.

60. Bill D'Agostino, "NewsBusters Explainer Video: How Fact Checkers Abuse Their Role to Boost Democrat Causes," mrcNewsBusters, May 25, 2021, https://www.newsbust ers.org/blogs/nb/bill-dagostino/2021/05/25/newsbusters-explainer-video-how-fact-ch eckers-abuse-their-role.

61. D'Agostino, "NewsBusters Explainer Video."
62. Caleb Rossiter, "Statement for the Record U.S. Senate Committee on Commerce, Science, and Transportation Hearing on Does Section 230's Sweeping Immunity Enable Big Tech Bad Behavior? October 28, 2020," CO2 Coalition, October 28, 2020, https://co2coalition.org/news/statement-for-the-record-u-s-senate-committee-on-commerce-science-and-transportation-hearing-on-examining-section-230s-usefulness-has-the-digital-age-surpassed-it-october-28-2020/.
63. Chris Buskirk (@thechrisbuskirk), "Apple's action against Parler, like Google's, is a pay-off...," (thread) Twitter, January 9, 2021, 8:22 p.m., https://twitter.com/thechrisbuskirk/status/1348077722308734977.
64. Dan Kovalik, "The Progressive Case against Cancel Culture," Spiked, April 16, 2021, https://www.spiked-online.com/2021/04/16/the-progressive-case-against-cancel-culture/.
65. Jeffrey A Tucker (@jeffreyatucker), "The purpose of propaganda is not...," Twitter, February 7, 2022, 10:50 a.m., https://twitter.com/jeffreyatucker/status/1490714479306461186.
66. Anne Applebaum, "The New Puritans," The Atlantic, August 31, 2021, https://www.theatlantic.com/magazine/archive/2021/10/new-puritans-mob-justice-canceled/619818/.
67. Claire Simms, "GA House Committee Holds Hearing on Social Media Censorship," FOX 5 Atlanta, May 20, 2021, https://www.fox5atlanta.com/news/ga-house-committee-hearing-social-media-censorship.
68. Correspondence between James Taylor and Marc Morano.
69. Robert Knight, "Breaking Up Big Tech Hard to Do, but It Should Happen," Washington Times, May 14, 2021, https://www.washingtontimes.com/news/2021/may/14/breaking-up-big-tech-hard-to-do-but-it-should-happ/.
70. Marc Morano, "'Welcome to Neo-Stalinism': Google Promptly Vanishes Greenpeace Co-Founder Dr. Moore from Enviro Group's History after Trump Tweets His Skeptical Climate Views," Climate Depot, March 16, 2019, https://www.climatedepot.com/2019/03/16/tech-tyranny-google-promptly-vanishes-greenpeace-co-founder-dr-moore-from-enviro-groups-history-after-he-calls-climate-scare-fake-science/.
71. Dana Lee, "25 1984 Quotes That are Way Too Real," Book Riot, January 15, 2020, https://bookriot.com/1984-quotes/.
72. Robert F. Kennedy Jr., "People in Authority Lie," Children's Health Defense, August 28, 2020, https://childrenshealthdefense.org/wp-content/uploads/08-31-20-RFK-Jr.-Press-Conference-Transcript.pdf; OneSilentJoy, "Robert F Kennedy Jr in Berlin 28 Aug 2020," YouTube, August 28, 2020, https://www.youtube.com/watch?v=wM7NLlWZD5I&t=4s
73. "Robert F. Kennedy, Jr. Speaks at Berlin Rally for Freedom and Peace," Children's Health Defense, August 29, 2020, https://childrenshealthdefense.org/news/robert-f-kennedy-jr-speaks-at-berlin-rally-for-freedom-and-peace/; Natural Health Media Project, "Bobby Kennedy to Berlin Freedom Rally: Ich Bin Ein Berliner!...," Facebook, August 29, 2020, 6:57 p.m., https://www.facebook.com/NaturalHealthMediaProject/photos/a.751078158385449/1587913198035270/?type=3.
74. Kennedy, "People in Authority Lie"; OneSilentJoy, "Robert F Kennedy Jr in Berlin."
75. "Robert F. Kennedy, Jr. Speaks"; Natural Health Media Project, "Bobby Kennedy to Berlin."
76. Kennedy, "People in Authority Lie"; OneSilentJoy, "Robert F Kennedy Jr in Berlin."

77. Bill Chappell, "Instagram Bans Robert F. Kennedy Jr. for Spreading Vaccine Disinformation," NPR, February 11, 2021, https://www.npr.org/sections/coronavirus-live-updates/2021/02/11/966902737/instagram-bars-robert-f-kennedy-jr-for-spreading-vaccine-misinformation.

78. Anna Merlan, "Alec Baldwin Just Did an Hour-Long Instagram Chat with an Anti-vaccine Activist," Vice, August 6, 2020, https://www.vice.com/en/article/ep4q8e/alec-baldwin-just-did-an-hour-long-instagram-chat-with-an-anti-vaccine-activist.

79. Real Time with Bill Maher, "New Rule: Sex, Drugs & GOP | Real Time with Bill Maher (HBO)," YouTube, May 7, 2021, https://www.youtube.com/watch?v=DqSARDDdlsw.

80. Applebaum, "The New Puritans."

81. Knight, "Breaking Up Big Tech."

82. "Brent Bozell Letter to Facebook: We Must Reconsider Section 230 Protection," Newsbusters, May 18, 2021, https://www.newsbusters.org/blogs/free-speech/nb-staff/2021/05/18/brent-bozell-letter-facebook-we-must-reconsider-section-230.

83. Brent Bozell (@BrentBozell), "There are the consequences...," May 27, 2021, 10:27 a.m., https://twitter.com/BrentBozell/status/1397922391985037319.

84. "Brent Bozell Letter."

85. Knight, "Breaking Up Big Tech."

Chapter 8: The New Normal: Immunity Passports and Social-Credit Scores—You Will Exist to Serve the State's Interest

1. CBSMiami/CNN, "You May Need a COVID Vaccine Passport to Travel in 2021," 4CBS Miami, December 31, 2020, https://miami.cbslocal.com/2020/12/31/covid-vaccine-passport-travel/.

2. "Our Team," The Commons Project, https://thecommonsproject.org/assembly.

3. The Rockefeller Foundation and Global Business Network, Scenarios for the Future of Technology and International Development (New York: The Rockefeller Foundation, May 2010), http://www.nommeraadio.ee/meedia/pdf/RRS/Rockefeller Foundation.pdf.

4. David R. Baker, "Vaccine Requirements Spread in U.S., Sowing Concern on Overreach," Bloomberg, April 10, 2021, https://www.bloomberg.com/news/articles/2021-04-10/vaccine-requirements-spread-in-u-s-sowing-concern-on-overreach.

5. Christiaan Hetzner, "Europe Moves Closer to Adopting COVID Vaccine Passports. Here's Who Would Qualify," Fortune, May 21, 2021, https://fortune.com/2021/05/21/europe-moves-closer-to-adopting-covid-vaccine-passports-heres-who-would-qualify/.

6. Ibid.

7. World Health Organization, Digital Documentation of COVID-19 Certificates: Vaccination Status (Geneva, Switzerland: World Health Organization, August 27, 2021), https://apps.who.int/iris/bitstream/handle/10665/343361/WHO-2019-nCoV-Digital-certificates-vaccination-2021.1-eng.pdf?sequence=1&isAllowed=y.

8. Merriam-Webster, s.v. "Anti-vaxxer (n.)," https://www.merriam-webster.com/dictionary/anti-vaxxer; "Merriam-Webster's Update to 'Anti-vaxxer' Misrepresented Online," Associated Press, December 8, 2021, https://apnews.com/article/fact-checking-034481134066.

9. CBSMiami/CNN, "You May Need a COVID Vaccine Passport."

10. Ibid.

11. Breck Dumas, "CNN Analyst Urges Biden Administration to Tie Vaccinations to Americans' 'Freedoms,'" Blaze Media, April 1, 2021 https://www.theblaze.com/news/cnn-analyst-urges-biden-administration-to-tie-vaccinations-to-americans-freedoms.

12. Julie Mastrine, "Freedom Isn't a 'Carrot' to Force Us to Do What the Government Wants," Evie, April 8, 2021, https://www.eviemagazine.com/post/freedom-isnt-a-carrot-to-force-us-to-do-what-the-government-wants.

13. Tom Bartlett, "The Vaccine Scientist Spreading Vaccine Misinformation," *The Atlantic*, August 12, 2021, https://www.theatlantic.com/science/archive/2021/08/robert-malone-vaccine-inventor-vaccine-skeptic/619734/; "Dr. Robert Malone: Much-Anticipated Interview with Joe Rogan—Says Federal Government Is 'Lawless' and Actively 'Violating the Nuremberg Code,'" Deplorable Bloggers Alliance, January 1, 2022, http://ibloga.blogspot.com/2022/01/dr-robert-malone-much-anticipated.html.

14. Alex Berenson (@AlexBerenson), "1/ I'm watching baseball tonight…," (thread) Twitter, April 26, 2021, 8:22 p.m., https://twitter.com/AlexBerenson/status/1386838151327592450 (Twitter has permanently suspended Berenson, but this tweet is available at the Internet Archive's Wayback Machine: https://web.archive.org/web/20210616192901/https://twitter.com/AlexBerenson/status/1386838151327592450).

15. Douglas Broom, "Could This COVID-19 'Health Passport' Be the Future of Travel and Events?," World Economic Forum, July 30, 2020, https://www.weforum.org/agenda/2020/07/covid-19-passport-app-health-travel-covidpass-quarantine-event/.

16. CBSMiami/CNN, "You May Need a COVID Vaccine Passport."

17. Analisa Novak, "As COVID Restrictions Ease 'Vaccine Passport' Debate Intensifies," Yahoo News, May 23, 2021, https://news.yahoo.com/covid-restrictions-ease-vaccine-passport-155753710.html.

18. Italics in the original. "Denmark to Roll Out Coronavirus 'Vaccine Passport' for Travelers in Early 2021," RT, January 8, 2021, https://www.rt.com/news/511941-denmark-coronavirus-vaccine-passport/.

19. Yelena Dzhanova, "Democrats Are Asking Biden to Mandate That Airlines Require Passengers to Be Fully Vaxxed for COVID-19 before Flying," Business Insider, November 14, 2021, https://www.businessinsider.com/democrats-ask-biden-to-mandate-covid-vaccinations-for-airline-passengers-2021-11; "Letter to Joseph R. Biden," House.gov, November 11, 2021, https://beyer.house.gov/uploadedfiles/holiday_vax_flight_letter_11.12.21.pdf.

20. "Anthony Fauci: Covid-19 Vaccine Won't Be Mandatory in US, Says Anthony Fauci," *Times of India*, August 20, 2020, https://timesofindia.indiatimes.com/world/us/covid-19-vaccine-wont-be-mandatory-in-us-says-anthony-fauci/articleshow/77647138.cms.

21. Roadtoserfdom (@roadtoserfdom3), "They're not 'vaccine passports,' they're movement licenses…," Twitter, April 4, 2021, 10:12 p.m., https://twitter.com/roadtoserfdom3/status/1378893370421043204.

22. Yaron Steinbuch, "Anthony Fauci Says He Would Support Vaccination Requirement for Air Travel," *New York Post*, September 13, 2021, https://nypost.com/2021/09/13/fauci-says-he-would-support-vaccine-requirement-for-air-travel/.

23. "Dr. Leana Wen: It Is Not a Constitutional Right to Board a Plane So If You Want to Travel, You Better Go Get That Vaccine," Grabien, September 10, 2021, https://grabien.com/file.php?id=1324447.

24. Tucker Carlson, "The Degradation of Our People Is the Real American Crisis," Fox News, September 14, 2021, https://www.foxnews.com/opinion/tucker-carlson-degradation-people-american-crisis.

25. Stavroula Pabst and Max Blumenthal, "Flattening the Curve or Flattening the Global Poor? How Covid Lockdowns Obliterate Human Rights and Crush the Most Vulnerable," The Gray Zone, December 3, 2021, https://thegrayzone.com/2021/12/03/flattening-curve-global-poor-covid-lockdowns-human-rights-vulnerable/.

26. Rachel Bunyan, "Italy Begins Lockdown of the Unvaccinated: Only the Double Jabbed Will Be Able to Fully Participate in Public Life Using a 'Super Green Pass' from Today," Daily Mail, December 6, 2021, https://www.dailymail.co.uk/news/article-10279341/Italy-begins-lockdown-unvaccinated-double-jabbed-able-participate-public-life.html.

27. Jack Bingham, "Trudeau Scapegoats Those Who Refuse COVID-19 Jab: 'They Need to Get Vaccinated!,'" LifeSiteNews, August 20, 2021, https://www.lifesitenews.com/news/trudeau-scapegoats-those-who-refuse-covid-19-jab-they-need-to-get-vaccinated/.

28. Judy Kurtz, "Howard Stern Rips Vaccine Opponents: 'F—— Their Freedom, I Want My Freedom to Live,'" The Hill, September 8, 2021, https://thehill.com/blogs/in-the-know/in-the-know/571322-howard-stern-rips-vaccine-opponents-f-k-their-freedom-i-want-my.

29. John Ziegler (@Zigmanfreud), "It's truly amazing how many entertainers who made their careers…," Twitter, September 9, 2021, 10:36 a.m., https://twitter.com/Zigmanfreud/status/1435975524870807557.

30. Charles Walker, "To Understand the Dangers of Covid Passports, Simply Imagine an Obesity Equivalent," The Telegraph, April 18, 2021, https://www.telegraph.co.uk/politics/2021/04/18/understand-dangers-covid-passports-simply-imagine-obesity-equivalent/.

31. Italics in the original. Stacey Rudin, "First Comply, Then We'll Grant You Some Rights," Brownstone Institute, December 5, 2021, https://brownstone.org/articles/first-comply-then-well-grant-you-some-rights/.

32. Jan Jekielek, "Jeffrey Tucker: How the Working Class Was Betrayed by Lockdowns, Vaccine Mandates," Epoch Times, November 18, 2021, https://www.theepochtimes.com/jeffrey-tucker-how-the-working-class-was-betrayed-by-lockdowns-vaccine-mandates_4109859.html.

33. Matilda Boseley, "Sydney Police Fine Hundreds of Anti-lockdown Protesters for 'Filthy, Risky Behaviour,'" The Guardian, July 25, 2021, https://www.theguardian.com/world/2021/jul/25/covid-sydney-police-punish-anti-lockdown-protesters.

34. Timjbo (@Tim_jbo), "Wow, how embarrassing…, " Twitter, September 7, 2021, 11:05 a.m., https://twitter.com/Tim_jbo/status/1435257933000953857; Judd Boaz, "The Victorian Premier Says the State Is Heading for a 'Vaccine Economy': Here's What That Might Look Like," ABC News (Australia), September 5, 2021, https://www.abc.net.au/news/2021-09-06/daniel-andrews-vaccine-passport-double-vaccinated/100435606.

35. George Chistensen, "Rowan Dean of Sky News Australia's Outsiders is right…," Facebook, September 13, 2021, https://www.facebook.com/watch/?v=844529329580359.

36. Boseley, "Sydney Police Fine Hundreds."

37. "Teenagers from Remote NT Community Arrested after Escape from Howard Springs COIVD Quarantine Facility," ABC News (Australia), November 30, 2021, https://www.abc.net.au/news/2021-12-01/multiple-people-escape-howard-springs-quarantine-facility-darwin/100663994.

38. Caitlin Owens, "Vaccine Mandates Lose Steam in the U.S. while Europe Doubles Down," Axios, December 5, 2021, https://www.axios.com/america-europe-pandemic-coronavirus-vaccines-a41663cf-decf-4256-a739-898eb318edff.html.

39. Bob D'Angelo, "NY Hospital to Pause Baby Deliveries after Staffers Quit over Vaccine Mandate," KIRO 7, September 10, 2021, https://www.kiro7.com/news/trending/ny-ho spital-pause-baby-deliveries-after-staffers-quit-over-vaccine-mandate/NNMBMQ6V TFFT5DDAMXV46DQ5TQ/.

40. Tom Elliot, "Biden Admin: Don't Worry, We'd Never Impose a Vaccine Mandate!," GrabienNews, September 10, 2021, , https://news.grabien.com/story-biden-admin-do nt-worry-wed-never-impose-vaccine-mandate-supe.

41. "President Biden Outlines Plan on Delta Variant and Vaccinations," C-SPAN, September 9, 2021, https://www.c-span.org/video/?514532-1/president-biden-express es-frustration-pandemic-politics-mandates-vaccines-federal-workers; Roy Maurer, "Biden Orders Vaccination Mandates for Larger Employers, Federal Workforce," SHRM, September 9, 2021, https://www.shrm.org/resourcesandtools/hr-topics/talent -acquisition/pages/federal-vaccine-mandate.aspx.

42. Donald G. McNeil Jr., "Why Don't We Have Vaccines against Everything?," *New York Times*, November 19, 2018, https://www.nytimes.com/2018/11/19/health/vaccines-po verty.html.

43. Ed Yong, "Flu Survivors Still Immune after 90 Years," *National Geographic*, August 17, 2008, https://www.nationalgeographic.com/science/article/flu-survivors-still-imm une-after-90-years.

44. Laith J. Abu-Raddad et al., "SARS-CoV-2 Antibody-Positivity Protects against Reinfection for at Least Seven Months with 95% Efficacy," eClinicalMedicine 35 (2021): 100861, https://www.sciencedirect.com/science/article/pii/S258953702100 1413.

45. Jay Bhattacharya (@DrJBhattacharya), "My overall reaction to Pres. Biden's speech....," (thread) Twitter, December 21, 2021, 3:44 p.m., https://twitter.com/DrJBhattacharya /status/1473393921132613636.

46. Bannon's War Room, "A BioFascist Coup Was Declared Today," September 9, 2021, https://rumble.com/vmas3g-a-biofascist-coup-was-declared-today.html.

47. "Richard Wolff," Influence Watch, https://www.influencewatch.org/person/richard -wolff/; Richard D. Wolff (@prowolff), "It's NOT pro- vs anti-vaccine....," Twitter, October 29, 2021, 9:00 p.m., https://twitter.com/profwolff/status/145426681040097 2801.

48. Richard D. Wolff (@prowolff), "Anti-mandate movement is not all right=wing...," Twitter, November 1, 2021, 11:12 a.m., https://twitter.com/profwolff/status/1455206 129424867334.

49. The Jimmy Dore Show, "Workers Rebelling against Vaxx Mandates w/Professor Richard Wolff," YouTube, November 2, 2021, https://www.youtube.com/watch?v=Z 1S6KGzUX10&t=5s.

50. Robert Freudenthal, "The Medical Objectification of the Human Person," Brownstone Institute, December 3, 2021, https://brownstone.org/articles/the-medical-objectificati on-of-the-human-person/.

51. Günter Kampf, "COVID-19: Stigmatising the Unvaccinated Is Not Justified," *The Lancet* 398, no. 10314 (November 20, 2021), https://www.thelancet.com/action/showPdf?pi i=S0140-6736%2821%2902243-1.

52. Brendan O'Neill, "The Death of Europe: Mandatory Vaccination Spells the Violent End of European Liberalism," Spiked, December 6, 2021, https://www.spiked-online .com/2021/12/06/the-death-of-europe/.

53. Michael P. Senger, "The Masked Ball of Cowardice," Tablet, August 29, 2021, https://www.tabletmag.com/sections/news/articles/masked-ball-cowardice.
54. Alex Berenson, "If You Like Compulsory Vaccinations, You'll Love Child Labor and the Espionage Act," Unreported Truths (Substack), September 13, 2021, https://alexberenson.substack.com/p/if-you-like-compulsory-vaccinations?s=r.
55. Karen Weintraub, "Invisible Ink Could Reveal Whether Kids Have Been Vaccinated: The Technology Embeds Immunization Records into a Child's Skin," *Scientific American*, December 18, 2019, https://www.scientificamerican.com/article/invisible-ink-could-reveal-whether-kids-have-been-vaccinated/.
56. Anne Trafton, "Storing Medical Information below the Skin's Surface," MIT News, December 18, 2019, https://news.mit.edu/2019/storing-vaccine-history-skin-1218.
57. Weintraub, "Invisible Ink."
58. Trafton, "Storing Medical Information."
59. Mike Williams, "Quantum-Dot Tattoos Hold Vaccination Record," Rice University New and Media Relations, December 18, 2019, https://news.rice.edu/news/2019/quantum-dot-tattoos-hold-vaccination-record.
60. Hanna Ziady, "Covid Vaccine Profits Mint 9 New Pharma Billionaires," CNN Business, May 21, 2021, https://www.cnn.com/2021/05/21/business/covid-vaccine-billionaires/index.html.
61. "False Claim: Bill Gates Wants to Microchip People; Anthony Fauci Wants People to Carry Vaccination Certificates," Reuters, May 5, 2020, https://www.reuters.com/article/uk-factcheck-gates-fauci/false-claim-bill-gates-wants-to-microchip-people-anthony-fauci-wants-people-to-carry-vaccination-certificates-idUSKBN22H2JD.
62. Sam Dorman, "Andrew Yang Raises Eyebrows with Call for Proof-of-Vaccination Barcodes," Fox News, December 18, 2020, https://www.foxnews.com/politics/andrew-yang-vaccine-barcode.
63. Hannah Sparks, "'Daily Show' Host Trevor Noah Blasted for Knocking Moderna CEO's Vaccine Push," *New York Post*, December 3, 2021, https://nypost.com/2021/12/03/trevor-noah-criticized-for-blasting-moderna-ceos-vaccine-push/.
64. Meghan Roos, "People Get Microchips Implanted That Include Vaccine Records amid New COVID Restrictions," *Newsweek*, December 3, 2021, https://www.newsweek.com/people-get-microchips-implanted-that-include-vaccine-records-amid-new-covid-restrictions-1655916.
65. Bruce Walker, "Michigan House Oversight Committee Considers Legislation to Ban Vaccine Passports," The Center Square, May 6, 2021, https://www.thecentersquare.com/michigan/michigan-house-oversight-committee-considers-legislation-to-ban-vaccine-passports/article_221e7270-aea0-11eb-954f-1f8d8bbd8713.html.
66. Fox 17, "Michigan House Oversight Committee Vaccine Passport Hearing," Facebook, May 6, 2021, https://www.facebook.com/watch/live/?v=753401042043912&ref=watch_permalink.
67. J. D. Rucker, "Naomi Wolf: 'Fascistic Atmosphere' from Oregon's Vaccine Passport Mandate Has Created 'Jim Crow' Two-Tier Society," NOQ Report, May 23, 2021, https://noqreport.com/2021/05/23/naomi-wolf-fascistic-atmosphere-from-oregons-vaccine-passport-mandate-has-created-jim-crow-two-tier-society/.
68. Walker, "Michigan House Oversight Committee."
69. Fox 17, "Michigan House Oversight Committee Vaccine Passport Hearing."

70. Molly Ball, Jeffrey Kluger, and Alejandro de la Garza, "*Time* 2021 Person of the Year: Elon Musk," *Time*, December 13, 2021, https://time.com/person-of-the-year-2021-el on-musk/.

71. Esha Bhandari and ReNika Moore, "Coronavirus 'Immunity Passports' Are Not the Answer," ACLU, May 18, 2020, https://www.aclu.org/news/privacy-technology/coro navirus-immunity-passports-are-not-the-answer/.

72. Joseph Vazquez, "Soros-Funded ACLU to Americans: Want to Enhance Civil Liberties? Embrace Vax Mandates," mrcBusiness, September 7, 2021, https://www.newsbusters .org/blogs/business/joseph-vazquez/2021/09/07/soros-funded-aclu-americans-want-en hance-civil-liberties.

73. David Cole and Daniel Mach, "Want to Enhance Civil Liberties? Embrace Vaccine Mandates," *New York Times*, September 2, 2021, https://web.archive.org/web/2021 0902091819/https://www.nytimes.com/2021/09/02/opinion/covid-vaccine-mandates -civil-liberties.html.

74. Vazquez, "Soros-Funded ACLU to Americans."

75. Glenn Greenwald, "The ACLU, Prior to COVID, Denounced Mandates and Coercive Measures to Fight Pandemics," Glenn Greenwald (Substack), September 7, 2021, https://greenwald.substack.com/p/the-aclu-prior-to-covid-denounced?r=j05m&utm _campaign=post&utm_medium=web&utm_source=&s=r; see also George J. Annas, Wendy K. Mariner, and Wendy E. Parmet, *Pandemic Preparedness: The Need for a Public Health—Not a Law Enforcement/National Security—Approach* (New York: ACLU, 2008), https://www.aclu.org/sites/default/files/pdfs/privacy/pemic_report.pdf.

76. Jordan Schachtel, "Welcome to Dystopia: Get Your COVID-19 'Health Pass' Today!," The Dossier (Substack), August 3, 2020, https://dossier.substack.com/p/welc ome-to-dystopia-get-your-covid.

77. Antony P. Mueller, "From Lockdowns to 'The Great Reset,'" Mises Institute, August 1, 2020, https://mises.org/wire/lockdowns-great-reset/page/88.

78. Marc Morano, "'Raw Authoritarian Power': Morano on Newsmax TV—Covid Lockdowns & Vaccine Passports Are Transforming USA into Chinese-Style One-Party State," September 10, 2021, https://www.climatedepot.com/2021/09/10/raw-authorit arian-power-morano-on-newsmax-tv-covid-lockdowns-vaccine-passports-are-transf orming-usa-into-chinese-style-one-party-state/.

79. Nicole Kobie, "The Complicated Truth about China's Social Credit System," *Wired*, June 7, 2019, https://www.wired.co.uk/article/china-social-credit-system-explained.

80. Nathan Vanderklippe, "Chinese Blacklist an Early Glimpse of Sweeping New Social-Credit Control," *Globe and Mail*, January 3, 2018, https://www.theglobeandmail.com /news/world/chinese-blacklist-an-early-glimpse-of-sweeping-new-social-credit-contr ol/article37493300/.

81. Kobie, "The Complicated Truth."

82. Mark Green, "Rep. Mark Green: Cancel Culture Eerily Similar to Communist China Playbook to Control Its People," Fox News, February 9, 2021, https://www.foxnews .com/opinion/cancel-culture-similar-communist-china-playbook-rep-mark-green.

83. Kobie, "The Complicated Truth."

84. Ibid.

85. Christian Britschgi, "Los Angeles Will Shut Off People's Utilities for Hosting Parties, Not for Failing to Pay Their Utility Bills," *Reason*, August 6, 2020, https://reason.com /2020/08/06/los-angeles-will-shut-off-peoples-utilities-for-hosting-parties-not-for-fail ing-to-pay-their-utility-bills/.

86. Celeste McGovern, "Only the Vaccinated Can Escape St. Vincent's Volcano via Rescue Cruise Ships, Says Island PM," LifeSiteNews, April 13, 2021, https://www.lifesitenews .com/news/only-the-vaccinated-can-escape-st-vincents-volcano-via-rescue-cruise-shi ps-says-island-pm/.

87. CBS Evening News (@CBSEveningNews), "Nearly 20,000 people have been forced out of their homes on the Caribbean island of St. Vincent...," Twitter, April 9, 2021, 6:54 p.m., https://twitter.com/cbseveningnews/status/1380655503693520898.

88. McGovern, "Only the Vaccinated."

89. PA State Rep. Andrew Lewis, "Whoa. 'Cruise ships are evacuating people from the island...,'" Facebook, April 11, 2021, https://www.facebook.com/RepAndrewLewis /photos/a.2657125641179743/3472115829680716/.

90. Tom Elliot (@tomselliott), "CNN's @DonLemon: We need to 'start telling people...,'" Twitter, July 29, 2021, 11:06 p.m., https://twitter.com/tomselliott/status/1420946019 488043011.

91. Geoff Herbert, "NY Lawmaker Proposes Bill Denying Coverage for Those Who Refuse to Get Vaccinated," Syracuse.com, November 24, 2021, https://www.syracuse.com/co ronavirus/2021/11/ny-lawmaker-proposes-bill-denying-coverage-for-those-who-refu se-to-get-vaccinated.html.

92. David Frum (@davidfrum), "Seems the best option is...," Twitter, December 12, 2021, 9:02 a.m., https://twitter.com/davidfrum/status/1470031425684582406.

93. Maria Usman, "Millions of Pakistanis Threatened with Cell Phone Cut-Off If They Don't Get a COVID Vaccine," CBS News, June 14, 2021, https://www.cbsnews.com /amp/news/pakistan-covid-vaccine-punjab-threat-cell-phone-cut-off-no-vaccination/ #app.

94. "Nigeria: Covid 'Health Pass' May Soon Be Imposed in Two States," AfricaNews, January 9, 2021, https://www.africanews.com/2021/09/01/nigeria-covid-health-pass -may-soon-be-imposed-in-two-states/.

95. Thomas Sowell, "Freedom, as Understood by the Far Left, Is Oppression," *Naples Daily News*, December 2, 2008, https://archive.naplesnews.com/columnists/opinion /thomas-sowell-freedom-as-understood-by-the-far-left-is-oppression-ep-400721367 -344287142.html.

96. Natalie Prieb, "Candace Owens Says COVID-19 Testing Lab Denied Her Service," *The Hill*, September 9, 2021, https://thehill.com/homenews/media/570613-candace -owens-says-covid-19-testing-lab-denied-her-service.

97. Pat Condell (@patcondell), "Vaccine passports were the plan from the start....," Gab, December 8, 2021, https://gab.com/patcondell/posts/107411747451955491.

98. Tim Wallace, "Bank of England Tells Ministers to Intervene on Digital Currency 'Programming,'" *The Telegraph*, June 21, 2021, https://www.msn.com/en-gb/money /other/bank-of-england-tells-ministers-to-intervene-on-digital-currency-programming /ar-AALhtDP.

99. Jennifer Smith, "Chase Sends Letter to General Flynn's Wife Telling Her They're Cancelling Her Card Because She's a 'Reputational Risk' to the Bank—Then Backtracks and Claims It Was an 'Error,'" *Daily Mail*, August 31, 2021, https://www.dailymail .co.uk/news/article-9944457/Chase-tells-General-Flynns-wife-theyre-cancelling-card .html; Tyler Durden, "Chase Bank Cancels General Mike Flynn's Credit Cards," ZeroHedge, August 31, 2021, https://www.zerohedge.com/political/chase-bank-canc els-general-mike-flynns-credit-cards.

100. Jason Abbruzzese and Kevin Collier, "Biden Takes Big Step toward Government-Backed Digital Currency," March 9, 2022, NBC News, https://www.nbcnews.com/te ch/crypto/us-government-digital-currency-rcna19248.

101. Jack Bingham, "2018 Video of Top Canadian Banker Pushing Digital IDs Goes Viral after Trudeau Freezes Bank Accounts," LifeSiteNews, March 3, 2022, https://www.li fesitenews.com/news/canadian-banks-and-world-economic-forum-pushing-national -digital-id/; Cecil Charles (@thececilcharles), "Canada's banks are perfectly situated...," Twitter, February 23, 2022, 7:18 a.m.,https://twitter.com/thececilcharles/status/1496 459393604460544.

102. Annelise Butler, "Bank Account Deplatforming Is Cancel Culture's New Weapon," The Daily Signal, February 25, 2022, https://www.dailysignal.com/2022/02/25/bank -account-deplatforming-is-cancel-cultures-new-weapon/.

103. Aaron McDade, "GiveSendGo Says It Will Refund Remaining Donations to Truckers Convoy," *Newsweek*, March 10, 2022, https://www.newsweek.com/givesendgo-says -it-will-refund-remaining-donations-truckers-convoy-1686992.

104. CNN, "Canadian Prime Minister Trudeau to Protesters: 'It Has to Stop,'" KITV4 ABC Island Television, February 7, 2022, https://www.kitv.com/news/local/canadian-prime -minister-trudeau-to-protesters-it-has-to-stop/article_959aa49e-88a2-11ec-9d00-8bd 1d157d37b.html.

105. Butler, "Bank Account Deplatforming."

106. Kobie, "The Complicated Truth."

107. Bob Moran (@bobscartoons), "Health Passport...," Twitter, January 10, 2021, 4:08 a.m., https://twitter.com/bobscartoons/status/1348194951700639744.

108. Fox 17, "Michigan House Oversight Committee Vaccine Passport Hearing."

109. "Health First, Freedom Second? How Covid Is Changing Democracies," France24, January 6, 2022, https://www.france24.com/en/live-news/20220106-health-first-free dom-second-how-covid-is-changing-democracies.

110. Eli Rabett (@EthonRaptor), "s'ok, Traitors like you...," Twitter, January 10, 2021, 3:36 p.m., https://twitter.com/EthonRaptor/status/1348368073800228864.

111. Marc Morano, "New Normal: Warmist Howard University Professor Hopes Morano & Other Trump Supporters Will Be 'Going on the No-Fly List' for Being 'Traitors,'" Climate Depot, January 10, 2021, https://www.climatedepot.com/2021/01/10/new-no rmal-warmist-howard-university-professor-hopes-morano-other-trump-supporters-wi ll-be-going-on-the-no-fly-list-for-being-traitors/.

112. Gareth Dale, "Absolute Zero," *The Ecologist*, March 24, 2020, https://theecologist .org/2020/mar/24/absolute-zero.

113. Carl Bennett, "Covid: Hardcore Vaccine Refuseniks Could Need Deradicalizing like Terrorits, Says Expert," GB News, December 8, 2021, https://www.gbnews.uk/news /covid-hardcore-vaccine-refuseniks-could-need-deradicalising-like-terrorists-says-exp ert/175040.

114. Whitney Webb, "Cyber War Declared in U.S. and UK to Quash Vaccine Hesitancy as Nations Prepare for Mass Inoculations," The Defender, November 16, 2020, https:// childrenshealthdefense.org/defender/cyber-war-declared-u-s-u-k-vaccine-hesitancy-pr epare-mass-inoculations/; see also Whitney Webb, "Google and Oracle to Monitor Americans Who Get Warp Speed's Covid-19 Vaccine for up to Two Years," The Last American Vagabond, October 15, 2020, https://www.thelastamericanvagabond.com /google-oracle-monitor-americans-who-get-warp-speeds-covid-19-vaccine-for-two-ye ars/; Peter Loftus and Rolfe Winkler, "Palantir to Help U.S. Track Covid-19 Vaccines,"

Wall Street Journal, October 22, 2020, https://www.wsj.com/articles/palantir-to-help
-u-s-track-covid-19-vaccines-11603367276.

115. Wittgenstein (@Kukicat7), "Robert Kennedy Jr. nails it...," Twitter, November 13,
2021, 8:46 a.m., https://twitter.com/Kukicat7/status/1459563355803377667 (Twitter
has deleted this account, but this tweet is available at the Internet Archive's Wayback
Machine: https://web.archive.org/web/20211115034143/https://twitter.com/Kukicat7
/status/1459563355803377667; this video can also be viewed at NO Suger Added,
"Robert F Kennedy Jr. Speaks to Switzerland—Press Conference—12th Nov 2021,"
BitChute, November 14, 2021, https://www.bitchute.com/video/5cgQUzOLPW4D/;
and at Tony Heller, "The Biggest Transfer of Wealth in World History," YouTube,
November 14, 2021, https://www.youtube.com/watch?v=gjhkaEsTllM).

116. Teny Sahakian, "Political Class Is a 'Machine That's Just Devouring the City,'
Economist Says of NYC's COVID-19 Mandates," Fox News, December 29, 2021,
https://www.foxnews.com/us/political-class-is-a-machine-thats-just-devouring-the-ci
ty-economist-says-of-nycs-covid-19-mandates.

117. "Transcript: Mayor de Blasio Appears Live on CNN with Michael Smerconish," City
of New York, December 16, 2021, https://www1.nyc.gov/office-of-the-mayor/news
/837-21/transcript-mayor-de-blasio-appears-live-cnn-michael-smerconish.

118. Sahakian, "Political Class Is a 'Machine.'"

Chapter 9: "One of the Greatest Transfers of Wealth in History"

1. James Glanz and Campbell Robertson, "Lockdown Delays Cost at Least 36,000 Lives,
Data Show," *New York Times*, May 20, 2020, https://www.nytimes.com/2020/05/20
/us/coronavirus-distancing-deaths.html.

2. "Billionaire Wealth Reaches New High during COVID-19 Pandemic—UBS," Reuters,
October 7, 2020, https://news.trust.org/item/20201007000753-x4yv2.

3. Tyler Clifford, "Jim Cramer: The Pandemic Led to 'One of the Greatest Wealth
Transfers in History,'" CNBC, June 4, 2020, https://www.cnbc.com/2020/06/04/cra
mer-the-pandemic-led-to-a-great-wealth-transfer.html.

4. World Economic Forum, "COVID-19: The Great Reset," YouTube, July 14, 2020,
https://www.youtube.com/watch?v=VHRkkeecg7c.

5. "Great Reset Hints at New Digital, International Currency," Glenn, January 4, 2022,
https://www.glennbeck.com/radio/great-reset-hints-at-new-digital-international-curr
ency.

6. Jay Lehr, "Don't Despair: The Great Reset Will Lose (Part Two of a Periodic Series on
Optimism)," CFACT, February 7, 2022, https://www.cfact.org/2022/02/07/dont-des
pair-the-great-reset-will-lose-part-two-of-a-periodic-series-on-optimism/.

7. Sanjeev Sabhlok, Pope @Church of Reason & Liberty (@sabhlok), "Absolutely. Small
retailers and hospitality establishments, gyms....," Twitter, August 2, 2020, 7:04 a.m.,
https://twitter.com/sabhlok/status/1289879789830983682; (Twitter has deleted
Sabhlok's account, but this tweet is available at the Internet Archive's Wayback
Machine, https://web.archive.org/web/20200802110452/https://twitter.com/sabhlok
/status/1289879789830983682.

8. Scott Santens, "The Story of George McGovern's Failure to Guarantee Every American
$1,000," ScottSantens.com, July 31, 2019, https://www.scottsantens.com/george-mc
govern-failure-guarantee-every-american-1000-demogrant-basic-income-ubi.

9. Blaire Bryant, "HHS Renews Public Health Emergency Declaration through January
2022," National Association of Counties, October 21, 2021, https://www.naco.org/bl

og/hhs-renews-public-health-emergency-declaration-through-january-2022; "Eligible Emergency Protective Measures," FEMA, https://www.fema.gov/fact-sheet/eligible-em ergency-protective-measures.

10. David Aaro, "Los Angeles' Garcetti 'Ecstatic' as City Expects to Receive $1.35B from COVID Relief Bill," Fox News, March 11, 2021, https://www.foxnews.com/us/garce tti-ecstatic-as-la-expects-to-get-1-35b-from-covid-relief-bill.

11. Fox News, "This is how the Democratic LA Mayor is Spending COVID Relief," YouTube, March 13, 2021, https://youtu.be/sM9FcC0OkUI.

12. Aaro, "Los Angeles' Garcetti 'Ecstatic.'"

13. Tom Tapp, "Los Angeles Mayor Eric Garcetti Issues Copycat Safer-at-Home Order: 'It's Time to Cancel Everything'—Updated," Deadline, December 2, 2020, https://de adline.com/2020/12/los-angeles-mayor-eric-garcetti-sounds-urgent-covid-19-alert-its -time-to-cancel-everything-1234636955/.

14. Brianna Lyman, "LA Mayor Bans Unnecessary Walking as Part of New COVID-19 Restrictions," The Daily Caller, December 3, 2020, https://dailycaller.com/2020/12 /03/los-angeles-mayor-eric-garcetti-covid-restrictions-ban-walking-traveling/.

15. Alina Selyukh, "Amazon Doubles Profit to $5.2 Billion as Online Shopping Spikes," NPR, July 30, 2020, https://www.npr.org/sections/coronavirus-live-updates/2020/07 /30/897271729/amazon-doubles-profit-to-5-8-billion-as-online-shopping-spikes.

16. Jeremy Bowman, "4 Takeaways from Jeff Bezos' Annual Shareholder Letter," The Motley Fool, April 19, 2020, https://www.fool.com/investing/2020/04/19/4-takeawa ys-from-jeff-bezos-shareholder-letter.aspx.

17. Marc Morano (@ClimateDepot), "So Amazon CEO Jeff Bezos says more testing is necessary…," Twitter, April 19, 2020, 1:41 p.m., https://twitter.com/ClimateDepot/st atus/1251928855318802432?ref_src=twsrc%5Etfw.

18. Kari Paul and Dominic Rushe, "Tech Giants' Shares Soar as Companies Benefit from Covid-19 Pandemic," The Guardian, July 30, 2020, https://www.theguardian.com/bu siness/2020/jul/30/amazon-apple-facebook-google-profits-earnings.

19. "Robert F. Kennedy, Jr. Speaks at Berlin Rally for Freedom and Peace," Children's Health Defense, August 29, 2020, https://childrenshealthdefense.org/news/robert-f-k ennedy-jr-speaks-at-berlin-rally-for-freedom-and-peace/; Natural Health Media Project, "Bobby Kennedy to Berlin Freedom Rally: Ich Bin Ein Berliner!…," Facebook, August 29, 2020, 6:57 p.m., https://www.facebook.com/NaturalHealthMediaProject /photos/a.751078158385449/1587913198035270/?type=3.

20. "'Great Polarization' May Be Next for World's Richest, UBS Says," Mint, October 7, 2020, https://www.livemint.com/news/world/-great-polarization-may-be-next-for-wo rld-s-richest-ubs-says-11602031975218.html.

21. James Altucher, "New York City Is Dead Forever," New York Post, August 17, 2020, https://nypost.com/2020/08/17/nyc-is-dead-forever-heres-why-james-altucher/.

22. "Tucker: This Is 'the Single Most Successful Human Rights Protest in a Generation,'" Fox News, February 11, 2022, https://www.foxnews.com/transcript/tucker-this-is-the -single-most-successful-human-rights-protest-in-a-generation.

23. Vivek Ramaswamy, "China Is Playing Us with Vivek Ramaswamy," YouTube, August 13, 2021, https://www.youtube.com/watch?v=1FhK9qz6zak.

24. The Spectator, "The Week in 60 Minutes #6—With Andrew Neil and WHO Covid-19 Envoy David Nabarro | SpectatorTV," YouTube, October 8, 2020, https://www.youtu be.com/watch?v=x8oH7cBxgwE&t=915s.

25. Sarah Newey, "Unicef Warns Lockdown Could Kill More Than Covid-19 as Model Predicts 1.2 Million Child Deaths," *The Telegraph*, May 13, 2020, https://www.teleg raph.co.uk/global-health/science-and-disease/unicef-warns-lockdown-could-kill-cov id-19-model-predicts-12/.

26. "COVID-19 Has Reversed Years in Gains in the War on Poverty," *The Economist*, September 26, 2020, https://www.economist.com/leaders/2020/09/26/covid-19-has -reversed-years-of-gains-in-the-war-on-poverty.

27. Stavroula Pabst and Max Blumenthal, "Flattening the Curve or Flattening the Global Poor? How Covid Lockdowns Obliterate Human Rights and Crush the Most Vulnerable," The Grayzone, December 3, 2021, https://thegrayzone.com/2021/12/03 /flattening-curve-global-poor-covid-lockdowns-human-rights-vulnerable/.

28. Susan Jones, "Record 157,878,000 Employed in August: Record Low Unemployment Rate for Blacks," CNS News, September 6, 2019, https://www.cnsnews.com/news/ar ticle/susan-jones/record-157878000-employed-august-21st-record-under-trump.

29. Marc Morano (@ClimateDepot), "My take: In the end…," Twitter, November 6, 2020, 10:40 a.m., https://twitter.com/ClimateDepot/status/1324738379037220866.

30. Jim Tankersley, Matthew Goldstein, and Glenn Thrush, "As Government Shutdown Persists, Americans Feel the Bite, *New York Times*, January 7, 2019, https://www.nyt imes.com/2019/01/07/us/politics/govenment-shutdown-impact-effects.html.

31. "Billionaire Wealth Reaches New High During COVID-19 Pandemic—UBS," Reuters, October 7, 2020, https://news.trust.org/item/20201007000753-x4yv2.

32. Davide Scigliuzzo, "Charging 589% Interest in the Pandemic Is a Booming Business," Bloomberg, May 17, 2021, https://www.bloomberg.com/graphics/2021-payday-loan -lenders/.

33. Niall McCarthy, "U.S. Billionaires Added $1 Trillion to Their Collective Wealth Since the Start of the Pandemic," *Forbes*, November 27, 2020, https://www.statista.com/ch art/22068/change-in-wealth-of-billionaires-during-pandemic/.

34. NBC Los Angeles (@NBCLA), "Gov. Gavin Newsom forcefully pushed back on criticisms that California is becoming unfriendly for business…," Twitter, January 10, 2021, 3:01 p.m., https://twitter.com/NBCLA/status/1348359224674365447.

35. "McDonald's French Fries, Carrots, Onions: All of the Foods That Come from Bill Gates Farmland," NBC News, https://www.nbcnews.com/tech/tech-news/mcdonald -s-french-fries-carrots-onions-all-foods-come-bill-n1270033.

36. Tom Elliott (@tomselliott), ".@BillGates on Covid…," Twitter, December 13, 2020, 1:59 p.m., https://twitter.com/tomselliott/status/1338196775564435459.

37. David Leonhardt, "Do Covid Precautions Work?," *New York Times*, March 9, 2022, https://www.nytimes.com/2022/03/09/briefing/covid-precautions-red-blue-states.html (this article is also available here: https://milled.com/nytimes/the-morning-do-covid-pr ecautions-work-Gh4T0il0_AUg1W_g).

38. Alex Berenson (@AlexBerenson), "Who loves lockdowns? Who makes more money in lockdowns than anyone else?…," Twitter, October 28, 2020, 9:58 a.m., https://twitter .com/AlexBerenson/status/1321451355337347074 (Twitter has deleted Berenson's account, but this tweet is available at the Internet Archive's Wayback Machine: https:// web.archive.org/web/20210408033234/https://twitter.com/AlexBerenson/status/132 1451355337347074).

39. Alex Berenson (@AlexBerenson), "So at what point are the rest of us…," Twitter, December 13, 2020, 6:46 p.m., https://twitter.com/AlexBerenson/status/1338269173 458362368 (Twitter has deleted Berenson's account, but this tweet is available at the

Internet Archive's Wayback Machine: https://web.archive.org/web/20201214000138 /https://twitter.com/AlexBerenson/status/1338269173458362368).

40. Nick Reisman, "Wall Street Profits Up 82% in First Half of 2020," Spectrum News 1, October 22, 2020, https://spectrumlocalnews.com/nys/buffalo/ny-state-of-politics/20 20/10/22/wall-street-profits-up-82—in-first-half-of-2020.

41. Paul Bois, "Joe Rogan: COVID Lockdowns 'Irreversibly F***ed' New York, Parts of Los Angeles," The Daily Wire, May 11, 2021, https://www.dailywire.com/news/joe -rogan-covid-lockdowns-irreversibly-fed-new-york-parts-of-los-angeles.

42. Nicholas Ballasy, "Restaurants Struggle to Rehire Workers Due to Unprecedented Pandemic Jobless Payments," Just the News, April 27, 2021, https://justthenews.com /government/congress/restaurants-around-nation-struggle-rehire-workers-due-federal -pandemic-jobless.

43. Juliana Kaplan, "Workers Lost $3.7 Trillion in Earnings During the Pandemic. Women and Gen Z Saw the Biggest Loses," Business Insider, January 25, 2021, https://www .businessinsider.com/workers-lost-37-trillion-in-earnings-during-the-pandemic-2021 -1.

44. Juliana Kaplan, "Billionaires Made $3.9 Trillion during the Pandemic—Enough to Pay for Everyone's Vaccine," Business Insider, January 26, 2021, https://www.businessins ider.com/billionaires-made-39-trillion-during-the-pandemic-coronavirus-vaccines-20 21-1?op=1.

45. "Mega-Rich Recoup COVID-Losses in Record-Time Yet Billions Will Live in Poverty for at Least a Decade," Oxfam, January 24, 2021, https://www.oxfamamerica.org/pr ess/mega-rich-recoup-covid-losses-record-time-yet-billions-will-live-poverty-least-dec ade/.

46. Joel Kotkin, "Welcome to the End of Democracy," The Spectator, January 8, 2022, https://www.spectator.co.uk/article/welcome-to-the-end-of-democracy.

47. Marc Morano, "Watch: Morano on Fox and Friends on Bill Gates Private Jet & COVID Lockdown Hypocrisy—'Gates is #1 Carbon Footprint of All Celebrity Climate Activists'—$30K a Month Electricity Bill at His Home," Climate Depot, January 10, 2021, https://www.climatedepot.com/2021/01/10/watch-morano-on-fox-and-friends -on-bill-gates-private-jet-covid-lockdown-hypocrisy-gates-is-1-carbon-footprint-of-all -celebrity-climate-activists-30k-a-month-electricity-bill-at-his-home/.

48. Bryan Walsh, "How Stalling Growth Hurts the Planet," Axios, March 20, 2021, https://www.axios.com/2021/03/20/degrowth-economic-growth-climate-change-pa ndemic.

49. Willis Eschenbach, "The Real Cost of Lockdowns," Watts Up With That?, September 1, 2020, https://wattsupwiththat.com/2020/09/01/the-real-cost-of-lockdowns/?utm _source=whatfinger.

50. Marc Morano, Green Fraud: Why the Green New Deal Is Even Worse Than You Think (Washington, D.C.: Regnery, 2021).

51. Willis Eschenbach (@WEschenbach), "Show us a scientific study showing lockdowns saved the health system....," Twitter, June 3, 2021, 6:56 p.m., https://twitter.com/WE schenbach/status/1400587241005535234.

52. Tom DeWeese, "Green New Deal Reveals the Naked Truth of Agenda 21," American Policy Center, February 25, 2019, https://americanpolicy.org/2019/02/25/green-new -deal-reveals-the-naked-truth-of-agenda-21/.

53. Ibid.; see also "Resolution Adopted by the General Assembly on 25 September 2015," United Nations General Assembly, September 25, 2015, https://www.un.org/ga/search /viewm_doc.asp?symbol=A/RES/70/1.

54. DeWeese, "Green New Deal Reveals."

55. "User Clip: Agenda 21—1992 Nancy Pelosi,"C-SPAN, October 2, 1992, https://www .c-span.org/video/?c4863326/user-clip-agenda-21-1992-nancy-pelosi.

56. DeWeese, "Green New Deal Reveals."

57. James Glanz and Campbell Robertson, "Lockdown Delays Cost at Least 36,000 Lives, Data Show," *New York Times,* May 20, 2020, https://www.nytimes.com/2020/05/20 /us/coronavirus-distancing-deaths.html.

Chapter 10: Prominent Left-Wing Figures Dissent from the Great Reset

1. Marc Morano, "Update: Video: Robert F. Kennedy Jr. Wants to Jail His Political Opponents—Accuses Koch Brothers of 'Treason'—'They Ought to Be Serving Time for It,'" September 21, 2014, https://www.climatedepot.com/2014/09/21/robert-f-ken nedy-jr-wants-to-jail-his-political-opponents-accuses-koch-brothers-of-treason-they -ought-to-be-serving-time-for-it/; Marc Morano, (@ClimateDepot), "My New Hero?!...," (thread) Twitter, August 30, 2020, 10:18 a.m., https://twitter.com/Climat eDepot/status/1300075459976323073.

2. "Robert F. Kennedy, Jr. Speaks at Berlin Rally for Freedom and Peace," Children's Health Defense, August 29, 2020, https://childrenshealthdefense.org/news/robert-f-k ennedy-jr-speaks-at-berlin-rally-for-freedom-and-peace/; Natural Health Media Project, "Bobby Kennedy to Berlin Freedom Rally: Ich bin ein Berliner!" Facebook, August 29, 2020, https://www.facebook.com/NaturalHealthMediaProject/photos/a.75 1078158385449/1587913198035270/?type=.

3. "Brave Vandana Shiva Speaks Out against the Great Reset," Transcend Media Service, November 30, 2020, https://www.transcend.org/tms/2020/11/brave-vandana-shiva -speaks-out-against-the-great-reset/; Jeremy Loffredo, "World Economic Forum's 'Great Reset' Plan for Big Foods Benefits Industry, Not People," Navdanya International, November 10, 2020, https://navdanyainternational.org/world-economic-forums-gre at-reset-plan-for-big-food-benefits-industry-not-people/.

4. Russell Brand, "The Great Reset: Bill Gates & Farming—What's Going On?," YouTube, February 19, 2021, https://www.youtube.com/watch?v=fg0c2x74mgU& t=1s.

5. Marc Morano (@ClimateDepot), "Not Naomi Klein, Naomi Wolf. & yes, I prefer...," Twitter, December 9, 2021, 8:08 p.m., https://twitter.com/ClimateDepot/status/1469 111769784279041.

6. The Jimmy Dore Show, "Fauci Squirms over Lab Leak Questions," YouTube, May 13, 2021, https://www.youtube.com/watch?v=8Cxm4g_cKrY&t=1531s.

7. Jeremy Loffredo, "World Economic Forum's 'Great Reset' Plan for Big Food Benefits Industry, Not People," The Defender, November 11, 2020, https://childrenshealthdef ense.org/defender/world-economic-forums-great-reset-plan-for-big-food-benefits-ind ustry-not-people/.

8. "The Big Tech Takeover of Agriculture Is Dangerous," Grain, February 5, 2021, https:// grain.org/en/article/6613-the-big-tech-takeover-of-agriculture-is-dangerous.

9. Dr Naomi Wolf (@NaomiWolf), "If I'd known Biden was open to 'lockdowns'. . . ," Twitter, November 8, 2020, 5:03 p.m., https://twitter.com/naomirwolf/status/132560

4856283869189?ref_src=twsrc%5Etfw (Twitter has deleted Wolf's account, but this tweet is available at the Internet Archive's Wayback Machine: https://web.archive.org /web/20210313003057/https://twitter.com/naomirwolf/status/13256048562838691 89?ref_src=twsrc%5Etfw).

10. Naomi Wolf, "Fascism's Step Ten: 'Lockdown' Is Not a 'Quarantine,'" Wolf: Author and Journalist, October 3, 2020, https://web.archive.org/web/20210506060133/http s://drnaomiwolf.com/lockdown-is-not-a-quarantine/.

11. Dr Naomi Wolf (@naomiwolf), "Of course. We all need to...," (thread) Twitter, March 3, 2020, 7:23 a.m., https://twitter.com/naomirwolf/status/1334518585520254976 (Twitter has deleted Wolf's account, but this thread is available at the Internet Archive's Wayback Machine, https://web.archive.org/web/20210227105419/https://twitter.com /naomirwolf/status/1334518585520254976).

12. Naomi Wolf, "What Are the Ten Steps to Fascism? How Did We Get Here?," Wolf: Author and Journalist, September 22, 2020, https://web.archive.org/web/202203031 73320/https://drnaomiwolf.com/ten-steps-to-fascism-updated/.

13. Daily Clout, "Are We at Step Ten of Dr Naomi Wolf's Well-Known 'Ten Steps' to Fascism—Part 1," YouTube, September 5, 2020, https://www.youtube.com/watch?v= 9faeUObJwj4.

14. Virginia Kruta, "'It Pains Me to Say This': CNN's Dr. Sanjay Gupta Says Sen. Susan Collins Might Be Right to Question CDC," The Daily Caller, May 12, 2021, https:// dailycaller.com/2021/05/12/keilar-berman-cnn-dr-sanjay-gupta-susan-collins-cdc-ma sks-indoors-vaccinated-people/.

15. Matthew Dimitri (@themattdimitri), "Beck: Are you looking into... ," Twitter, April 23, 2020, 3:00 a.m., https://twitter.com/themattdimitri/status/1385488704941088774.

16. Roy Greenslade, "How Edward Snowden Led Journalist and Film-maker to Reveal NSA Secrets," The Guardian, August 19, 2013, https://www.theguardian.com/world /2013/aug/19/edward-snowden-nsa-secrets-glenn-greenwald-laura-poitras.

17. Glenn Greenwald, "My Resignation from the Intercept," Glenn Greenwald (Substack), October 29, 2020, https://greenwald.substack.com/p/my-resignation-from-the-interc ept?s=r.

18. Ian Schwartz, "Glenn Greenwald: There Is an Addiction to Being Protected by the State, to Not Having a Return to Normal Life," RealClear Politics, January 3, 2022, https://www.realclearpolitics.com/video/2022/01/03/glenn_greenwald_there_is_an _addiction_to_being_protected_by_the_state_to_not_having_a_return_to_normal _life.html.

19. Blake Montgomery, "Van Morrison Is Releasing Songs Railing against COVID-19 Lockdowns," The Daily Beast, September 18, 2020, https://www.thedailybeast.com/ van-morrison-is-releasing-songs-railing-against-covid-19-lockdowns.

20. Jeremy Fuster, "Eric Clapton Sparks Backlash for New Anti-Lockdown Song with Van Morrison," The Wrap, November 27, 2020, https://www.thewrap.com/eric-clapton-sp arks-backlash-for-new-anti-lockdown-song-with-van-morrison/.

21. Mary Papenfuss, "'This Has Gotta Stop': Eric Clapton Releases Apparent Anti-Vax Anthem," HuffPost, August 28, 2021, https://www.huffpost.com/entry/eric-clapton -gotta-stop-anti-vaccination-anthem_n_612aa8cae4b0231e369c78d1.

22. Scarlett Howes, "Lockdown-Sceptic Rockstar Eric Clapton Blasts Vaccine Safety 'Propaganda' and Claims He Had a 'Disastrous Reaction' to AstraZeneca Covid Jab Which Made Him Fear He'd Never Play Again," Daily Mail, May 15, 2021, https://

www.dailymail.co.uk/news/article-9583109/Eric-Clapton-hits-propaganda-vaccine-sa fety.html.

23. Joshua Q. Nelson, "Former Democrat Rubin on Why He Is Voting for Trump: 'No Feeling of Patriotism' on the Left Anymore," Fox News, October 29, 2020, https:// www.foxnews.com/politics/dave-rubin-why-voting-trump-no-feeling-patriotism-left -biden.

24. Glenn Beck, "How COVID Masks Created a 'Psychological Condition' to Fear Others," YouTube, May 14, 2021, https://www.youtube.com/watch?v=mON0CvD m0W8.

25. Claudia Assis, "Elon Musk on Donald Trump: 'Just No,'" Market Watch, November 4, 2016, https://www.marketwatch.com/story/elon-musk-on-donald-trump-just-no-20 16-11-04; Kevin Webb, "Tesla CEO Elon Musk Says He Supports Democratic Presidential Candidate Andrew Yang, Calling Universal Basic Income 'Obviously Needed,'" Business Insider, August 10, 2019, https://www.businessinsider.com/tesla -ceo-elon-musk-2020-election-endorsement-andrew-yang-president-2019-8.

26. Andrea Widburg, "Elon Musk, Having Taken the 'Red Pill,' Now Urges Others to Join Him," American Thinker, May 18, 2020, https://www.americanthinker.com/blog/20 20/05/elon_musk_having_taken_the_red_pill_now_urges_others_to_join_him.html; Kari Paul, "Elon Musk Rails against 'Facist' Shelter-in-Place Orders in Tesla Earnings Call," *The Guardian*, April 29, 2020, https://www.theguardian.com/technology/2020 /apr/29/tesla-quarterly-earnings-coronavirus-shares.

27. Bill Bostock, "Elon Musk Called One of the World's Top Lockdown Advocates an 'Utter Tool' Who Does 'Absurdly Fake Science' after He Was Caught Breaking His Own Rules to Meet His Lover," Business Insider, May 6, 2020, https://www.business insider.com/elon-musk-prof-neil-ferguson-resigned-moron-absurdly-fake-science-20 20-5.

28. Joseph Curl, "Elon Musk: What I Find Most Surprising Is That CNN Still Exists," The Daily Wire, April 17, 2020, https://www.dailywire.com/news/elon-musk-what-i-find -most-surprising-is-that-cnn-still-exists.

29. Grace Kay, "Elon Musk and Trump Praised the Canadian Vaccine Protest That the Police Say Spurred Investigations into 'Threatening' and 'Illegal' Behavior," Business Insider, January 31, 2022, https://www.businessinsider.com/elon-musk-donald-trump -praised-canadian-trucker-vaccine-mandate-protest-2022-1.

30. Widburg, "Elon Musk."

31. JRE Clips, "Joe Rogan: I've Been Liberal My Whole Life," YouTube, January 16, 2020, https://www.youtube.com/watch?v=9ctTmQn8w7A.

32. Bernie Sanders (@BernieSanders), "I think I'll probably vote for Bernie… ," Twitter, January 23, 2020, 3:38 p.m., https://twitter.com/BernieSanders/status/12204458205 05546755.

33. Tyler Durden, "WEF 'Infiltration'; Rogan Red-Pilled, Canadian MP Cut Off for Asking—Accused of Spreading 'Disinformation,'" ZeroHedge, February 20, 2022, https://www.zerohedge.com/covid-19/wef-infiltration-rogan-redpilled-canadian-mp -cut-asking-accused-spreading-disinformation.

34. The Jimmy Dore Show, "Video: Trudeau & Cabinet Trained by Global Economic Cabal—Admits WEF Chairman," YouTube, February 19, 2022, https://www.youtu be.com/watch?v=WJdHF7J_ZZM.

35. Fox News, "Comedian Tells Tucker Carlson His Take on Identity Politics," YouTube, July 22, 2022, https://www.youtube.com/watch?v=iR7nJutI5iI&t=65s.

36. Jenin Younes (@Leftylockdowns1), "Civil liberties attorney…," (profile) Twitter, https://twitter.com/Leftylockdowns1 (Younes has updated her profile, but a screenshot is available on the Internet Archive's Wayback Machine: https://webcache.googleuser content.com/search?q=cache:Q9A1uziusgAJ:https://twitter.com/Leftylockdowns1%3F ref_src%3Dtwsrc%255Etfw%257Ctwcamp%255Etweetembed%257Ctwterm%25 5E1472239256382885891%257Ctwgr%255E%257Ctwcon%255Es1_%26ref_url %3D+&cd=2&hl=en&ct=clnk&gl=us).

37. Jenin Younes (@Leftylockdowns1), "How do people not see the dangers…," Twitter, November 27, 2021, 9:58 p.m., https://twitter.com/Leftylockdowns1/status/1464790 666525949957.

38. Jenin Younes (@Leftylockdowns1), "Yesterday someone I went to college with…," Twitter, February 6, 2022, 2:00 p.m., https://twitter.com/Leftylockdowns1/status/14 90400078846119939.

39. Russell Brand, "Russell Brand on Revolution: 'We No Longer Have the Luxury of Tradition,'" *New Statesman*, October 24, 2013, https://www.newstatesman.com/unc ategorized/2013/10/russell-brand-on-revolution.

40. Brackets in the original. "Russell Brand Attacks Capitalism," The Socialist Party of Great Britain, December 2013, https://www.worldsocialism.org/spgb/socialist-standa rd/2010s/2013/no-1312-december-2013/russell-brand-attacks-capitalism/.

41. Russell Brand, "You Will Own Nothing & Be Happy," YouTube, January 24, 2022, https://www.youtube.com/watch?v=QOrS6buynAk&list=WL&index=9&t=1.

42. Russell Brand, "So, I'm Right-Wing Now?," YouTube, February 8, 2022, https://www .youtube.com/watch?v=h4e8lSQy64c.

43. Russell Brand, "WHAT?! The Great Reset Is NOT a Conspiracy!," YouTube, January 30, 2022, https://www.youtube.com/watch?v=BXTPzFSx6oI.

44. Cynthia McKinney (@cynthiamckinney), "WEF Puppets and Core Members are kooks…," Twitter, February 21, 2022, 12:29 a.m., https://twitter.com/cynthiamckin ney/status/1495631635819208712.

45. Cynthia McKinney (@cynthiamckinney), "Imagine you have an idea…," Twitter, January 26, 2022, 10:27 a.m., https://twitter.com/cynthiamckinney/status/14863601 86314969096.

46. Cynthia McKinney (@cynthiamckinney), "Weekend Watching: Aldous Huxley's…," Twitter, August 20, 2021, 7:01 p.m., https://twitter.com/cynthiamckinney/status/142 8854707175428100.

47. The Hill, "Kim Iversen: 'Leftugees' Fly Blue States amid HORRIBLE Dem Policies, DIRE Need for Self-Reflection," YouTube, December 14, 2021, https://www.youtube .com/watch?v=3R9rbm6S0mQ&t=266s.

48. Max Blumenthal (@MaxBlumenthal), "Here is the Lockdown Left closing ranks with the imperial Trudeau regime…," Twitter, February 14, 2022, 12:53 a.m., https://twit ter.com/MaxBlumenthal/status/1493463361148923910.

49. The Jimmy Dore Show, "How Lockdowns Devastate You While Boosting Billionaires," YouTube, December 5, 2021, https://www.youtube.com/watch?v=aGdxfQe1yNM& t=3176s.

50. Stavroula Pabst and Max Blumenthal, "Flattening the Curve or Flattening the Global Poor? How Covid Lockdowns Obliterate Human Rights and Crush the Most Vulnerable," The Grayzone, December 3, 2021, https://thegrayzone.com/2021/12/03 /flattening-curve-global-poor-covid-lockdowns-human-rights-vulnerable/.

51. The Jimmy Dore Show, "How Lockdowns Devastate You."

52. Tims Hains, "Joe Rogan to Bill Gates: 'How Are You Giving Any Health Advice When You Look like That?,'" RealClear Politics, March 7, 2022, https://www.realclearpolit ics.com/video/2022/03/07/joe_rogan_to_bill_gates_how_are_you_giving_any_heal th_afvice_when_you_look_like_.html.

53. Timothy P. Carney, "Disparate Impact: Bill de Blasio's Vaccine Passport Rule Is Racist according to the Left's Definition," *Washington Examiner*, August 3, 2021, https://www.msn.com/en-us/news/us/disparate-impact-bill-de-blasio-s-vaccine-passport-rule -is-racist-according-to-the-left-s-definition/ar-AAMTHNV.

54. Caroline Downey, "After Altercation at Restaurant, Black Lives Matter Claims NYC Vaccine Mandate Is Being Weaponized," *National Review*, September 20, 2021, https://www.nationalreview.com/news/after-altercation-at-restaurant-black-lives-matter-clai ms-nyc-vaccine-mandate-is-being-weaponized/.

55. Brigid Delaney, "The Pandemic Has Forced 'Safe, Comfortable' Australians to Confront Human Rights. So What's Next?," *The Guardian*, December 3, 2021, https://www.theguardian.com/commentisfree/2021/dec/03/the-pandemic-has-forced-safe-co mfortable-australians-to-confront-human-rights-so-whats-next.

56. Ibid.

57. Naomi Klein, "The Great Reset Conspiracy Smoothie," The Intercept, December 8, 2020, https://theintercept.com/2020/12/08/great-reset-conspiracy/?utm_medium=so cial&utm_source=facebook&utm_campaign=theintercept&fbclid=IwAR1v5OgWo7 Xg620Y2dl669bn6rm8-Q5Nsd-9IImDqYJ5oBo7oSNTBmqq0as.

58. "'The Great Reset' Conspiracy Flourishes amid Continued Pandemic," Anti-Defamation League, December 29, 2020, https://www.adl.org/blog/the-great-reset-co nspiracy-flourishes-amid-continued-pandemic.

59. "What Is the Great Reset—and How Did It Get Hijacked by Conspiracy Theories?," BBC News, June 24, 2021, https://www.bbc.com/news/blogs-trending-57532368.

60. Ibid.

61. World Economic Forum, "What is the Great Reset? | Davos Agenda 2021," YouTube, January 25, 2021, https://www.youtube.com/watch?v=uPYx12xJFUQ&t=44s.

62. Real Time with Bill Maher, "New Rule: Give It to Me Straight, Doc | Real Time with Bill Maher (HBO)," YouTube, April 16, 2021, https://www.youtube.com/watch?v=Q p3gy_CLXho.

63. Ibid.; "Bill Maher's Insightful and Funny Covid Monologue," American Institute for Economic Research, April 17, 2021, https://www.aier.org/article/bill-mahers-insightf ul-and-funny-covid-monologue/.

64. Ross A. Lincoln and Phil Owen, "Bill Maher Rips Media's 'Panic Porn': 'Calm Down and Treat Us like Adults,'" The Wrap, April 17, 2020, https://www.thewrap.com/bill -maher-panic-porn-coronavirus/.

65. Real Time with Bill Maher, "New Rule: Give It to Me Straight"; Bruce Y. Lee, "Bill Maher Rants About Covid-19 Coronavirus, Here Is What He Got Wrong," *Forbes*, April 17, 2021, https://www.forbes.com/sites/brucelee/2021/04/17/bill-maher-rants-ab out-covid-19-coronavirus-here-are-the-issues-with-what-he-said/?sh=4e7d567d38ab.

66. Jill Goldsmith, "Bill Maher Begs Millennials to Storm Beaches and Malls, Buy Pants," Deadline, June 19, 2020, https://deadline.com/2020/06/bill-maher-millennials-beach es-malls-pants-1202964669/.

67. Real Time with Bill Maher, "New Rule: America Out of Order | Real Time with Bill Maher (HBO)," YouTube, June 9, 2020, https://www.youtube.com/watch?v=DqSAR DDdlsw.

68. Real Time with Bill Maher, "New Rule: Give It to Me Straight."
69. Bill Maher (@billmaher), "It's not my fault that the party of FDR...," Twitter, January 29, 2022, 12:02 a.m., https://twitter.com/billmaher/status/1487290045828501506; Bruce Haring, "Bill Maher Fires Back at Those Who Say His Politics Have Changed, Blames Loony Left Policies," Yahoo!News, January 28, 2022, https://news.yahoo.com /bill-maher-fires-back-those-050537569.html; Real Time with Bill Maher, "New Rule: How the Left Was Lost | Real Time (HBO), YouTube, January 28, 2022, https://www .youtube.com/watch?v=OdJOLMgY4p0.
70. Real Time with Bill Maher, "Give It to Me Straight."

Chapter 11: The COVID-Climate–Reset Connection

1. "Transcript of Interview by James Corbett of Professor Richard Lindzen," English Lab, November 22, 2010, http://ielts-yasi.englishlab.net/TRANSCRIPT_LINDZEN_NO V22_INTERVIEW.htm.
2. "CO2 for Different People Has Different Attractions," Not PC, November 13, 2019, http://pc.blogspot.com/2019/11/co2-for-different-people-has-different.html.
3. Peter Barry Chowka, "Will the Covid-19 PsyOp Succeed?," American Thinker, April 19, 2020, https://www.americanthinker.com/blog/2020/04/will_the_covid19_psyop _succeed.html.
4. Joel Kotkin, "How the Democrats Fell for Mussolini," UnHerd, July 5, 2021, https:// unherd.com/2021/07/how-the-democrats-fell-for-mussolini/.
5. Jordan Schachtel, "At the G7, Global Elite Clown Show Pivots from COVID Crisis to Climate Crisis," The Dossier (Substack), June 13, 2021, https://dossier.substack.com /p/at-the-g7-global-elite-clown-show?s=r.
6. Klaus Schwab, "Now Is the Time for a 'Great Reset,'" World Economic Forum, June 3, 2020, https://www.weforum.org/agenda/2020/06/now-is-the-time-for-a-great-re set/.
7. Thomas Schomerus, "Corona und Klima—Krise als Chance," Verfassungsblog, March 24, 2020, https://verfassungsblog.de/corona-und-klima-krise-als-chance/. See English translation at Pierre Gosselin, "German Public Law Professor, High Court Judge: Climate Crisis 'Requires Freedom-Limiting Measures,'" NoTricksZone, April 4, 2020, https://notrickszone.com/2020/04/04/german-public-law-professor-judge-climate-cri sis-requires-freedom-limiting-measures/.
8. World Health Organization, COP24 Special Report: Health and Climate Change (Geneva, Switzerland: World Health Organization, 2018), 10, https://apps.who.int/ir is/bitstream/handle/10665/276405/9789241514972-eng.pdf?sequence=1&isAllow ed=y.
9. Cory Morningstar and Paul Cudenec, "Klaus Schwab and His Great Fascist Reset—an Overview," Wrong Kind of Green, October 14, 2020, https://www.wrongkindofgreen .org/2020/10/14/klaus-schwab-and-his-great-fascist-reset-an-overview/; Paul Cudenec, "Klaus Schwab and His Great Fascist Reset," Winter Oak, October 5, 2020, https:// winteroak.org.uk/2020/10/05/klaus-schwab-and-his-great-fascist-reset/.
10. David Williamson, "'Dream On!' Speaker Lindsay Hoyle Slapped Down for Lockdown-Style Climate Change Rules," The Express, https://www.express.co.uk/news/politics /1334816/climate-change-rules-lindsay-hoyle-G7.
11. "Al Gore Talks Climate Crisis: 'This Is the Time for a Great Reset,'" Today, June 19, 2020, https://www.today.com/video/al-gore-talks-climate-crisis-this-is-the-time-for -a-great-reset-85439045592.

12. Sean Fleming, "Good Grub: Why We Might Be Eating Insects Soon," World Economic Forum, July 16, 2018, https://www.weforum.org/agenda/2018/07/good-grub-why-we-might-be-eating-insects-soon.

13. Marc Morano, "Canadian PM Trudeau Confirms Great Reset: 'This Pandemic Has Provided an Opportunity for a Reset'—We Need 'To Re-imagine Economic Systems' by 'Building Back Better,'" Climate Depot, November 16, 2020, https://www.climate depot.com/2020/11/16/canadian-pm-trudeau-confirms-covids-great-reset-this-pande mic-has-provided-an-opportunity-for-a-reset-we-need-to-re-imagine-economic-syste ms-by-building-back-better/.

14. Rachel Koning Beals, "COVID-19 and Climate Change: 'The Parallels Are Screaming at Us,' Says John Kerry," MarketWatch, April 22, 2020, https://www.marketwatch .com/story/covid-19-and-climate-change-the-parallels-are-screaming-at-us-says-john -kerry-2020-04-22.

15. John F. Kerry, "The Parallels between the Coronavirus and the Climate Crisis," *Boston Globe*, April 21, 2020, https://www.bostonglobe.com/2020/04/21/opinion/parallels -between-coronavirus-climate-crisis/.

16. Brian C. Joondeph, "COVID and Climate Policy Following the Same Playbook," American Thinker, August 17, 2020, https://www.climatedepot.com/2020/08/18/cov id-and-climate-policy-following-the-same-playbook-benevolent-government-seeks-to -control-all-aspects-of-our-lives/.

17. Tony Heller (@Tony_Heller), "We have arrived at the end game....," Twitter, March 18, 2020, 12:27 a.m., https://twitter.com/Tony__Heller/status/1240132755574394880 (Twitter has deleted Heller's account, but this tweet is available at the Internet Archive's WayBack Machine: https://web.archive.org/web/20200318050317/https://twitter.com /Tony__Heller/status/1240132755574394880).

18. Tony Heller (@Tony_Heller), "I've been saying this for the past four months....," Twitter, July 29, 2020, 8:22a.m., https://twitter.com/Tony__Heller/status/128844986 7455504387 (Twitter has deleted Heller's account, but this tweet is available at the Internet Archive's WayBack Machine: https://web.archive.org/web/20200729122305 /https://twitter.com/Tony__Heller/status/1288449867455504387).

19. Martín López Corredoira, "The Benefits of Coronavirus for the Health of the Planet," Science 2.0, March 4, 2020, https://www.science20.com/martin_lopez_corredoira/the _benefits_of_coronavirus_for_the_health_of_the_planet-245939.

20. Ed Dawson, "Gov Inslee Calls Covid Crisis 'an Opportunity' to Move State to More 'Green' Economy," 610Kona News Radio, May 20, 2020, https://www.610kona.com /gov-inslee-calls-covid-crisis-an-opportunity-to-move-state-to-more-green-economy/.

21. John Schwartz, "Social Distancing? You Might Be Fighting Climate Change, Too," *New York Times*, March 13, 2020, https://www.nytimes.com/2020/03/13/climate/co ronavirus-habits-carbon-footprint.html.

22. Mark Hertsgaard and Kyle Pope, "The Coronavirus Has Lessons for Journalists Covering the Climate Crisis," *The Nation*, April 20, 2020, https://www.thenation.com /article/environment/coronavirus-climate-crisis-journalism/.

23. Real Time with Bill Maher, "Al Gore: The Climate Connection | Real Time with Bill Maher (HBO)," YouTube, April 10, 2020, https://youtu.be/2IbdTnID7sU.

24. Martin Durkin (@Martin_Durkin), "Lockdown feels like the new Climate Change....," Twitter, June 17, 2020, 1:27 p.m., https://twitter.com/Martin_Durkin/status/127330 6347627589633.

25. Michael Segalov, "The Parallels between Coronavirus and Climate Crisis Are Obvious," *The Guardian*, May 4, 2020, https://www.theguardian.com/environment/2020/may/04/parallels-climate-coronavirus-obvious-emily-atkin-pandemic.

26. John Bickley, "Hollywood Stars Demand 'Radical Transformation' of World, No 'Return to Normal' after Covid Crisis," The Daily Wire, May 6, 2020, https://www.dailywire.com/news/read-it-hollywood-stars-demand-radical-transformation-of-world-no-return-to-normal-after-covid-crisis.

27. PlanB Earth, "3. Economic Policy, Covid-19 and the Climate Crisis," April 3, 2020, https://www.youtube.com/watch?v=vkT-HKAx7RU.

28. James Delingpole, "'Build Back Better'—The Latest Code Phrase for Green Global Tyranny," Breitbart, May 31, 2020, https://www.breitbart.com/europe/2020/05/31/delingpole-build-back-better-the-latest-code-phrase-for-green-global-tyranny/.

29. James P. Tucker Jr., "Global Elite Wants U.S. to Sign Treaty," AmericanFreePress.net, July 14, 2005, https://www.americanfreepress.net/html/kyoto.html.

30. Larry Elliott, "Gordon Brown Calls for Global Government to Tackle Coronavirus," *The Guardian*, March 26, 2020, https://www.theguardian.com/politics/2020/mar/26/gordon-brown-calls-for-global-government-to-tackle-coronavirus.

31. Jack Montgomery, "Boris to G7: We Must 'Build Back Better' in a 'More Gender-Neutral, More Feminine Way,'" Breitbart, June 12, 2021, https://www.breitbart.com/europe/2021/06/12/boris-g7-we-must-build-back-better-in-a-more-gender-neutral-feminine-way/.

32. "Kudlow Predicts the Unemployment Numbers 'Will Continue to Be Poor' in Weeks Ahead," Fox News, April 3, 2020, https://video.foxnews.com/v/6146876412001#sp=show-clips.

33. Sean Fleming, "This 3D-printed Steak Could Help Us Reduce Meat Consumption," World Economic Forum, July 8, 2020, https://www.weforum.org/agenda/2020/07/3d-printed-steak-cut-meat-consumption.

34. Beals, "COVID-19 and Climate Change."

35. Sarah Kaplan, "Climate Change Affects Everything—Even the Coronavirus," *Washington Post*, April 15, 2020, https://www.washingtonpost.com/climate-solutions/2020/04/15/climate-change-affects-everything-even-coronavirus/.

36. Jordan Schachtel, "Fauci Draws Full Pseudoscience: COVID-19 Is Due to 'Extreme Backlashes from Nature,'" The Dossier (Substack), September 4, 2020, https://dossier.substack.com/p/fauci-goes-full-pseudoscience-covid.

37. Jane Fonda, "COVID-19 Has Created a Pivotal Time When the Future May Be Decided," Jane Fonda, March 31, 2020, https://www.janefonda.com/2020/03/covid-19-has-created-a-pivotal-time-when-the-future-may-be-decided/.

38. Laurie Macfarlane, "Governments Must Act to Stop the Coronavirus—but We Can't Return to Business as Usual," openDemocracy, March 12, 2020, https://www.opendemocracy.net/en/oureconomy/we-must-act-to-contain-the-coronavirus-but-we-cant-return-to-business-as-usual/.

39. H. Sterling Burnett, "Science Crushes *Rolling Stone*'s Claimed Linked Between COVID and Climate," Climate Realism, December 11, 2020, https://climaterealism.com/2020/12/science-crushes-rolling-stones-claimed-link-between-covid-and-climate/.

40. Alex Morales, "Kyoto Veterans Say Global Warming Goal Slipping Away," Bloomberg, November 4, 2013, https://www.bloomberg.com/news/articles/2013-11-04/kyoto-veterans-say-global-warming-goal-slipping-away.

41. Eric Holthaus (@EricHolthaus), "This is roughly the pace…," Twitter, April 22, 2020, 9:27 a.m., https://twitter.com/EricHolthaus/status/1252952128131342336.
42. Joel Kotkin, "Welcome to the End of Democracy," *The Spectator*, January 8, 2022, https://www.spectator.co.uk/article/welcome-to-the-end-of-democracy.
43. Roy Spencer, "Why the Current Economic Slowdown Won't Show Up in the Atmospheric CO2 Record," Roy Spencer, Ph.D., May 15, 2020, https://www.drroysp encer.com/2020/05/why-the-current-economic-slowdown-wont-show-up-in-the-atm ospheric-co2-record/.
44. DSA (@DemSocialists), "The coronavirus pandemic…," Twitter, March 18, 2020, 9:05 a.m., https://twitter.com/DemSocialists/status/1240262981973422080.
45. Eric Holthaus (@EricHolthaus), "This is a really heartening trend….," Twitter, April 21, 2020, 12:36 p.m., https://twitter.com/EricHolthaus/status/1252637224413339655.
46. Adam Taylor, "As Omicron Variant Alarm Spreads, Countries Mull a Radical 'Pandemic Treaty,'" *Washington Post*, November 30, 2021, https://www.washington post.com/world/2021/11/30/omicron-pandemic-treaty-who/; Adam Taylor and Adela Suliman, "World Agrees to Negotiate a Global 'Pandemic Treaty' to Fight the Next Outbreak," *Washington Post*, December 1, 2021, https://www.washingtonpost.com /world/2021/12/01/who-coronavirus-pandemic-agreement-treaty/.
47. Taylor and Suliman, "World Agrees to Negotiate a Global 'Pandemic Treaty.'"
48. Marc Morano, "A 'Radical' UN Climate Style 'Pandemic Treaty' for Viruses!? World Health Organization Agrees to Negotiate 'Pandemic Treaty' to Prevent Next Outbreak," Climate Depot, December 1, 2021, https://www.climatedepot.com/2021/12/01/a-rad ical-un-climate-style-pandemic-treaty-for-viruses-world-health-organizations-agrees -to-negotiate-a-pandemic-treaty-to-prevent-next-outbreak/.
49. Stefan Labbé, "B.C. Doctor Clinically Diagnoses Patient as Suffering from 'Climate Change,'" *Times Colonist*, November 4, 2021, https://www.timescolonist.com/bc-ne ws/bc-doctor-clinically-diagnoses-patient-as-suffering-from-climate-change-4723540 ?utm_source=dlvr.it&utm_medium=twitter.
50. Anthony Watts, "Rebuttal to Doctor Merritt: 'Climate Change' Does Not Affect Human Health, Weather Does," Watts Up with That?, November 8, 2021, https://wa ttsupwiththat.com/2021/11/08/rebuttal-to-doctor-merritt-climate-change-does-not-af fect-human-health-weather-does/.
51. "Calls to Add 'Climate Change' to Death Certificates," Australian National University, May 21, 2020, https://www.anu.edu.au/news/all-news/calls-to-add-%E2%80%98cli mate-change%E2%80%99-to-death-certificates; Thomas Longden et al., "Heat-Related Mortality: An Urgent Need to Recognise and Record," *Lancet Planetary Health* 4, no. 5 (May 2020): e171, https://doi.org/10.1016/S2542-5196(20)30100-5.
52. NowThis (@nowthisnews), "Former Irish President Mary Robinson says…," Twitter, June 23, 2020, 11:13 a.m., https://twitter.com/nowthisnews/status/12754467661968 09728.
53. "Climate Change Is a Bigger Disaster Than Coronavirus: Bill Gates," Bloomberg, August 6, 2020, https://www.bloomberg.com/news/videos/2020-08-06/climate-chan ge-is-a-bigger-disaster-than-coronavirus-bill-gates-video.
54. Ron Clutz, "The Push for Climate Death Certificates," Science Matters, May 23, 2020, https://rclutz.com/2020/05/23/the-push-for-climate-death-certificates/.
55. Marc Morano, "Calls to Add 'Climate Change' to Death Certificates," Principia Scientific International, May 22, 2020, https://principia-scientific.com/calls-to-add-cl imate-change-to-death-certificates/.

56. D. J. Patil and Mark Rosekind, "2015 Traffic Fatalities Data Has Just Been Released: A Call to Action to Download and Analyze," The White House: President Barack Obama, August 29, 2016, https://obamawhitehouse.archives.gov/blog/2016/08/29/20 15-traffic-fatalities-data-has-just-been-released-call-action-download-and-analyze.

57. Leticia M. Nogueira, K. Robin Yabroff, and Aaron Bernstein, "Climate Change and Cancer," CA: A Cancer Journal for Clinicians 70, no. 4 (July/August 2020): 239–44, https://doi.org/10.3322/caac.21610.

58. Al Gore, An Inconvenient Sequel: Truth to Power (New York: Rodale, 2017), 110.

59. Christopher Monckton, "Monckton Letter to The Lancet on the 'Climate Crisis,'" The Heartland Institute, December 4, 2020, https://www.heartland.org/news-opinion/ne ws/monckton-letter-to-the-lancet-on-the-climate-crisis—-december-2020.

60. Thomas Lifson, "Latest Warmist Scheme: Record 'Climate Change' as Cause of Death on Death Certificates," American Thinker, May 23, 2020, https://www.americanthin ker.com/blog/2020/05/latest_warmist_scheme_record_climate_change_as_cause_of _death_on_death_certificates_.html.

61. Anthony Watts, "After 100 Years of Climate Change, 'Climate Related Deaths' Approach Zero," Climate Realism, January 2, 2021, https://climaterealism.com/2021 /01/after-100-years-of-climate-change-climate-related-deaths-approach-zero/.

62. Brackets in the original. "CNN Exposed," Project Veritas, April 13, 2021, https://www .projectveritas.com/news/part-1-cnn-director-admits-network-engaged-in-propagan da-to-remove-trump/.

63. Marc Morano, "1941 Theory Linking Warmer Temps to Rise of Hitler & Mussolini Could Explain Public's Acceptance of COVID Lockdowns—'People Are More Docile & Easily Led in Warm Weather,'" Climate Depot, December 8, 2021, https://www.cl imatedepot.com/2021/12/08/professors-1941-theory-linking-global-warming-to-rise -of-hitler-mussolini-could-explain-why-citizens-surrendered-so-easily-to-covid-lockd owns-people-are-more-docile-easily-led-in-warm-weathe/.

64. Christopher Anstey, "Summers Blasts Gas-Tax Holiday as 'Plumbing Depths' of Bad Ideas," BNN Bloomberg, February 18, 2022, https://www.bnnbloomberg.ca/summe rs-blasts-gas-tax-holiday-as-plumbing-depths-of-bad-ideas-1.1725740.

65. Kotkin, "Welcome to the End."

Chapter 12: COVID Lockdowns Morph to Climate Lockdowns

Epigraph: World Economic Forum, "COVID-19: The Great Reset," YouTube, July 14, 2020, https://www.youtube.com/watch?v=VHRkkeecg7c; Kyle Kashuv (@KyleKashuv), "Twitter pulled down this video....," Twitter, February 22, 2022, 6:17 p.m., https:// twitter.com/KyleKashuv/status/1496262915367870465; Christopher Nunn, "Great Reset Timeline," Christopher Nunn: Understanding the World, December 18, 2021, https://www.christophernunn.net/post/great-reset-timeline.

1. "What Is the Great Reset—and How Did It Get Hijacked by Conspiracy Theorists?," BBC News, June 24, 2021, https://www.bbc.com/news/blogs-trending-57532368.

2. Fiona Harvey, "Equivalent of Covid Emissions Drop Needed Every Two Years—Study," The Guardian, March 3, 2021, https://www.theguardian.com/environment /2021/mar/03/global-lockdown-every-two-years-needed-to-meet-paris-co2-goals-study (This headline has since been changed, but the original title can be found at the Internet Archive's WayBack Machine: https://web.archive.org/web/20210303160620/https:// www.theguardian.com/environment/2021/mar/03/global-lockdown-every-two-years -needed-to-meet-paris-co2-goals-study); Marc Morano, "UK Guardian: 'Global

Lockdown Every Two Years Needed to Meet Paris CO2 Goals—Study'—CO2
Emissions Must Fall by Equivalent [of] COVID Global Lockdown Every Two Years
for Next Decade to Combat Global Warming," Climate Depot, March 4, 2021, https://
www.climatedepot.com/2021/03/04/study-co2-emissions-must-fall-by-equivalent-co
vid-global-lockdown-every-two-years-for-next-decade-to-combat-global-warming/.

3. J. M. Allwood et al., *Absolute Zero* (Cambridge: UK Fires, November 29, 2019), http://
www.ukfires.org/wp-content/uploads/2019/11/Absolute-Zero-online.pdf, 1–3, 15, 39.

4. Gareth Dale, "Absolute Zero," *The Ecologist*, March 24, 2020, https://theecologist
.org/2020/mar/24/absolute-zero.

5. Eric Holthaus (@EricHolthaus), "If you are wondering...," Twitter, October 8, 2018,
12:45 p.m., https://twitter.com/EricHolthaus/status/1049339997827084295.

6. "Climate Change," UK Parliament, February 6, 2020, https://hansard.parliament.uk
/lords/2020-02-06/debates/22BE288A-6BCF-4D5A-BE0E-F3EFAB702D4A/Climat
eChange.

7. Peter Foster, "Peter Foster: Mark Carney, Man of Destiny, Arises to Revolutionize
Society. It Won't Be Pleasant," *National Post*, June 5, 2021, https://nationalpost.com
/opinion/peter-foster-mark-carney-man-of-destiny-arises-to-revolutionize-society-it
-wont-be-pleasant.

8. Valerie Richardson, "Professor Floats Idea of 'Climate Lockdown' with Bans on Red
Meat, 'Extreme' Energy Limits," *Washington Times*, September 28, 2020, https://www
.washingtontimes.com/news/2020/sep/28/professor-floats-idea-climate-lockdown-ba
ns-red-me/; Marc Morano, "Gates/Soros/Ford Foundation-Funded Professor Floats
Idea of 'Climate Lockdown' with Bans on Red Meat, 'Extreme' Energy Limits,"
Climate Depot, September 28, 2020, https://www.climatedepot.com/2020/09/28/gat
es-soros-ford-foundation-funded-professor-floats-idea-of-climate-lockdown-with-ba
ns-on-red-meat-extreme-energy-limits/.

9. Mariana Mazzucato, "Avoiding a Climate Lockdown," Project Syndicate, September
22, 2020, https://www.project-syndicate.org/commentary/radical-green-overhaul-to
-avoid-climate-lockdown-by-mariana-mazzucato-2020-09.

10. Richardson, "Professor Floats Idea of 'Climate Lockdown.'"

11. Mariana Mazzucato, "The Covid-19 Crisis Is a Chance to Do Capitalism Differently,"
The Guardian, March 18, 2020, https://www.theguardian.com/commentisfree/2020
/mar/18/the-covid-19-crisis-is-a-chance-to-do-capitalism-differently.

12. "WHO Establishes Council on the Economics of Health for All," World Health
Organization, November 13, 2020, https://www.who.int/news/item/13-11-2020-who
-establishes-council-on-the-economics-of-health-for-all.

13. "Professor Mariana Mazzucato," Mariana Mazzucato, December 2021, https://cms
.marianamazzucato.com/wp-content/uploads/2022/01/CV-Mazzucato-2021-Decem
ber.pdf.

14. Kit Knightly, "Is a 'Climate Lockdown' on the Horizon?," OffGuardian, June 10, 2021,
https://off-guardian.org/2021/06/10/is-a-climate-lockdown-on-the-horizon/.

15. Kevin A. Hassett, "Death by 1,000 Climate Faucis," *National Review*, December 1,
2021, https://www.nationalreview.com/2021/12/death-by-1000-climate-faucis/?utm
_source=recirc-desktop&utm_medium=blog-post&utm_campaign=river&utm_con
tent=more-in&utm_term=first.

16. International Energy Agency (IEA), *Net Zero by 2050: A Roadmap for the Global
Energy Sector* (Paris: IEA Publications, October 2021), https://www.iea.org/reports
/net-zero-by-2050, 85–87, 142, 173.

17. Ellipses in the original. Marc Morano, "Intl Energy Agency Report Urges ENERGY LOCKDOWNS: 'Banning Use of Private Cars on Sundays… Reducing Highway Speed Limits…More Working from Home…Cutting Business Air Travel' & SUV 'Tax,'" Climate Depot, March 18, 2022, https://www.climatedepot.com/2022/03/18/interna tional-energy-agency-report-urges-energy-lockdowns-due-to-russian-war-banning-use -of-private-cars-on-sundays-reducing-highway-speed-limits-more-working-from-ho me-cutting-business-air-t/.

18. Justin Worland, "The Pandemic Remade Every Corner of Society. Now It's the Climate's Turn," *Time*, April 15, 2021, https://time.com/5953374/climate-is-everything/.

19. Alice Bows-Larkin, "Climate Change Is Happening. Here's How We Adapt," TED, June 2015, https://www.ted.com/talks/alice_bows_larkin_climate_change_is_happe ning_here_s_how_we_adapt/details?.

20. Dominic Mealy, "'To Halt Climate Change, We Need an Ecological Leninism': An Interview with Andreas Malm," *Jacobin*, June 15, 2020, https://jacobin.com/2020/06 /andreas-malm-coronavirus-covid-climate-change?mc_cid=9aab712a86&mc_eid=58 1c6ff5ff.

21. Ben Pile (@clim8resistance), "The green blob and its 'High Level Climate Action Champions' have wet dreams about Lockdown….," Twitter, July 9, 2020, 8:07 a.m., https://twitter.com/clim8resistance/status/1281198376579719170.

22. Bryan Walsh, "How Stalling Growth Hurts the Planet," Axios, March 20, 2021, https://www.axios.com/degrowth-economic-growth-climate-change-pandemic-7749 33af-9209-4b74-89fb-b4a783a87305.html.

23. "Biden, in Pennsylvania, Details $2 Trillion Infrastructure Plan," *New York Times*, March 31, 2021, https://www.nytimes.com/live/2021/03/31/us/biden-news-today.

24. Ari Natter, "Climate Groups Prod Biden to Bolster Kerry by Declaring Crisis," Bloomberg, November 25, 2020, https://www.bloomberg.com/news/articles/2020-11 -25/climate-groups-prod-biden-to-bolster-kerry-by-declaring-crisis.

25. Marc Morano, "Climate Lockdowns Coming Soon: Dem Sen Merkley Urges Biden 'To Declare a National Climate Emergency'—'Using Every Tool Available to Him'— 'Treat this Crisis Like the Emergency It Is,'" Climate Depot, December 21, 2020, https:// www.climatedepot.com/2020/12/21/climate-lockdowns-coming-soon-dem-sen-merk ley-urges-biden-to-declare-a-national-climate-emergency-using-every-tool-available-to -him-treat-this-crisis-like-the-emergency-it-is/.

26. Adam Aton, "Schumer Urges Biden to Declare Climate Emergency," ClimateWire, January 26, 2021, https://subscriber.politicopro.com/article/eenews/1063723529.

27. Andrew Mark Miller, "House Dems Want Biden to Declare National 'Climate Emergency' and Ban Oil Drilling on Federal Lands," Fox News, March 15, 2022, https://www.foxnews.com/politics/house-democrats-biden-declare-climate-emergen cy-ban-oil-drilling-federal-lands.

28. Jean Su and Maya Golden-Krasner, "The Case for Declaring a National Climate Emergency," *The Nation*, March 11, 2022, https://www.thenation.com/article/enviro nment/biden-climate-emergency-dpa/.

29. Steve Milloy (@JunkScience), "This is true. … ," Twitter, April 18, 2020, 11:38 a.m., https://twitter.com/JunkScience/status/1251535611976126468.

30. Luke Kemp, "The 'Stomp Relflex': When Governments Abuse Emergency Powers," BBC News, April 28, 2021, https://www.bbc.com/future/article/20210427-the-stomp -reflex-when-governments-abuse-emergency-powers.

31. "People Must Explain Travel Reasons under New British Border Measures," Reuters, January 27, 2021, https://news.trust.org/item/20210127135918-tptoe.

32. Eric Holthaus (@EricHolthaus), "More than half of Americans...," Twitter, November 18, 2020, 11:27 a.m., https://twitter.com/EricHolthaus/status/1329098925446492165; Eric Holthaus (@EricHolthaus), "1% of people cause half...," Twitter, November 18, 2020, 11:18 a.m., https://twitter.com/EricHolthaus/status/1329096682932461574.

33. Pierre L. Gosselin (@NoTricksZone), "USA morphing into communist...," Twitter, January 27, 2021, 2:41 p.m., https://twitter.com/NoTricksZone/status/13545148560 37244932 (Twitter has deleted Gosselin's account, but this tweet is available at the Internet Archive's WayBack Machine: https://web.archive.org/web/20210428115657 /https://twitter.com/NoTricksZone/status/1354514856037244932).

34. Damian Carrington, "1% of People Cause Half of Global Aviation Emissions—Study," *The Guardian*, November 17, 2020, https://www.theguardian.com/business/2020/nov /17/people-cause-global-aviation-emissions-study-covid-19.

35. Christopher Ketcham, "Op-Ed: Coronavirus Has Something to Teach Us about How to Save the Planet—by Staying Put," *Los Angeles Times*, March 14, 2020, https://www .latimes.com/opinion/story/2020-03-14/coronavirus-travel-ban-air-travel-climate-ch ange-carbon-emissions.

36. Marc Morano, "Watch: Morano on *Fox and Friends* on Bill Gates Private Jet & COVID Lockdown Hypocrisy—'Gates is the #1 Carbon Footprint of All Celebrity Climate Activists'—$30K a Month Electricity Bill at His Home," Climate Depot, January 10, 2021, https://www.climatedepot.com/2021/01/10/watch-morano-on-fox -and-friends-on-bill-gates-private-jet-covid-lockdown-hypocrisy-gates-is-1-carbon-fo otprint-of-all-celebrity-climate-activists-30k-a-month-electricity-bill-at-his-home/.

37. Rob Picheta and Barbara Wojazer, "France to Ban Domestic Flights Where Trains Are Available, in Move to Cut Emissions," CNN, April 12, 2021, https://www.cnn.com/tr avel/article/france-domestic-flight-ban-emissions-scli-intl/index.html.

38. Graham Piro, "Yang: Climate Change May Require Elimination of Car Ownership," Washington Free Beacon, September 19, 2019, https://freebeacon.com/politics/yang -well-eliminate-car-ownership-to-fight-climate-change/.

39. Fox News, "Tucker: Brace Yourselves, Climate Lockdowns Are Coming," YouTube, June 22, 2021, https://www.youtube.com/watch?v=gD9JulHePh8.

40. Craig Rucker (@CJRucker), "Social planners, ecologists look to exploit pandemic...," Twitter, April 15, 2020, 4:00 p.m., https://twitter.com/CJRucker/status/12505143671 89311489; Alex Davies, "The Pandemic Could Be an Opportunity to Remake Cities," *Wired*, April 13, 2020, https://www.wired.com/story/pandemic-opportunity-remake -cities/.

41. "Flashback 1975: Holdren Says Real Threat to USA Is Cheap Energy," hauntingthelibrary, January 31, 2011, https://hauntingthelibrary.wordpress.com/2011 /01/31/flashback-1975-holdren-says-real-threat-to-usa-is-cheap-energy/.

42. Brittany Bernstein, "Australian State Limits Residents of COVID-19 Lockdown Apartments to Six Beers per Day: Report," *National Review*, September 8, 2021, https://www.nationalreview.com/news/australian-state-limits-residents-of-covid-19-lo ckdown-apartments-to-six-beers-per-day-report/.

43. "*The Guardian* View on the Climate and Coronavirus: Global Warnings" (editorial), *The Guardian*, April 12, 2020, https://www.theguardian.com/commentisfree/2020 /apr/12/the-guardian-view-on-the-climate-and-coronavirus-global-warnings.

44. Svein Tveitdal (@tveitdal), "If we can put the whole world on pause...," Twitter, March 17, 2020, 6:33 a.m., https://twitter.com/tveitdal/status/1239862376310222848.

45. Jamie Margolin, "Coronavirus Response Should Be a Model for How We Address Climate Change," *Teen Vogue*, March 18, 2020, https://www.teenvogue.com/story/co ronavirus-response-climate-crisis (The article title has since been changed to "Coronavirus Shows Us Rapid Global Response to Climate Change Is Possible," but a screenshot of the original title is available at Climate Depot: https://www.climatedep ot.com/2020/03/17/teen-vogue-op-ed-coronavirus-response-should-be-a-model-for -how-we-address-climate-change/).

46. Valerie Richardson, "'Earth Day Climate Activists: Treat Climate like Coronavirus Crisis," *Washington Times*, April 22, 2020, https://www.washingtontimes.com/news /2020/apr/22/earth-day-climate-activists-treat-climate-coronavi/.

47. Benjamin Zycher, "Statement Submitted for the Record, Subcommittee on Investor Protection, Entrepreneurship and Capital Markets, Committee on Financial Services, U.S. House of Representatives," JunkScience.com, March 3, 2021, https://junkscience .com/wp-content/uploads/2021/03/ESG-House-Finance-K-Mkts-sub-Zycher-March -2021.pdf.

48. The Heartland Institute, "Glenn Beck and Justin Haskins Discuss America's Newest Threat to Freedom," YouTube, March 8, 2021, https://www.youtube.com/watch?v=r NHgk0XLLTw.

49. Alex Epstein (@AlexEpstein), "The ESG divestment movement...," (thread) Twitter, June 10, 2021, 8:54: a.m., https://twitter.com/AlexEpstein/status/140297244049017 6519.

50. Fiona Harvey, "Tackle Climate Crisis and Poverty with Zeal of Covid-19 Fight, Scientists Urge," *The Guardian*, March 28, 2020, https://www.theguardian.com/wor ld/2020/mar/28/coronavirus-tackle-climate-crisis-and-poverty-with-zeal-of-covid-19 -fight-scientists-urge.

51. Ed Conway, "Coronavirus Can Trigger a New Industrial Revolution," *The Times*, March 5, 2020, https://www.thetimes.co.uk/article/coronavirus-has-a-silver-lining-cz 8wpc6xj.

52. Pete Schroeder, "U.S. Regulator Proposes Sweeping Climate Risk Guidance for Banks," *U.S. News & World Report*, December 16, 2021, https://money.usnews.com/investi ng/news/articles/2021-12-16/u-s-banking-regulator-solicits-feedback-on-monitoring -climate-change-risk.

53. "Executive Order on Ensuring Responsible Development of Digital Assets," The White House, March 9, 2022, https://www.whitehouse.gov/briefing-room/presidential-actio ns/2022/03/09/executive-order-on-ensuring-responsible-development-of-digital-ass ets/.

54. Glenn Beck, "Proof a Government-Controlled Dollar Is Coming," YouTube, March 23, 2022, https://www.youtube.com/watch?v=0DWv9CZH860.

55. "Tucker: This Is 'the Single Most Successful Human Rights Protest in a Generation,'" Fox News, February 10, 2022, https://www.foxnews.com/transcript/tucker-this-is-the -single-most-successful-human-rights-protest-in-a-generation.

56. New York Times Events, "DealBook 2017: The Economy, Consumers and Redefining Long Term," YouTube, November 9, 2017, https://www.youtube.com/watch?v=-cCs 9Kh2Q08; NewsTime, "BlackRock CEO Larry Fink Says He Believes in 'Forcing Behaviors,'" YouTube, March 31, 2022, https://www.youtube.com/watch?v=1mfEln S0EOg..

57. "Tucker: This Is 'the Single Most Successful Human Rights Protest.'"

58. Class Redux Killa (@BLCKD_COM_PlLLD), "You're watching a master level ponzi scheme…," Twitter, March 19, 2022, 5:32 p.m., https://twitter.com/BLCKD_COM _PlLLD/status/1505296205538070536.

59. Marc Morano, "Listen: Vivek Ramaswamy Gives Best Explanation of ESG: 'The Defining Scam of Our Time'—'Agendas That Would Make the Blood of Those Retirees Boil If They Knew,'" Climate Depot, March 23, 2022, https://www.climatedepot.com /2022/03/23/listen-vivik-ramaswamy-gives-best-explanation-of-esgr-the-defining-sc am-of-our-time-agendas-that-would-make-the-blood-of-those-retirees-boil-if-they -knew/.

60. "Tucker: This Is 'the Single Most Successful Human Rights Protest.'"

61. Sebastian Tong, "Musk Says ESG 'an Outrageous Scam' after Tesla Index Exclusion," Bloomberg, May 18, 2022, https://www.bloomberg.com/news/articles/2022-05-18/mu sk-says-esg-an-outrageous-scam-after-tesla-index-exclusion.

62. Ron Paul, "End the Fed and Get More Doritos," Ron Paul Institute, March 21, 2022, http://ronpaulinstitute.org/archives/featured-articles/2022/march/21/end-the-fed-and -get-more-doritos/.

63. Marc Morano, "Climate Lockdowns: New CO_2 Monitoring Credit Card Enables Tracking of 'Carbon Footprint on Every Purchase'—'Monitors & Cuts Off Spending When We Hit Our Carbon Max'—Mastercard & UN Join Forces," Climate Depot, September 13, 2021, https://www.climatedepot.com/2021/09/13/new-co2-monitoring -credit-card-enables-tracking-of-carbon-footprint-on-every-purchase-monitors-cuts -off-spending-when-we-hit-our-carbon-max-mastercard-un-join-forces/.

64. Marc Morano, "'Fight Climate Change with Every Swipe': New Climate Change Debit Card Debuting: Monitors Your 'Personal Sustainability Score'—'Plant a Tree Every Time You Make a Purchase,'" Climate Depot, September 24, 2021, https://www.clim atedepot.com/2021/09/24/fight-climate-change-with-every-swipe-new-climate-chan ge-debt-card-debuting-monitors-your-personal-sustainability-score-plant-a-tree-every -time-you-make-a-purchase/.

65. Francesco Fuso Nerini et al., "Personal Carbon Allowances Revisited," Nature Sustainability 4 (2021): 102–31, https://doi.org/10.1038/s41893-021-00756-w.

66. Colin Drury, "Should Everyone Have Their Own Personal Carbon Quota? Calls Grow for Emission Allowances," The Independent, November 13, 2021, https://www.inde pendent.co.uk/climate-change/news/personal-carbon-allowance-trading-climate-cris is-b1956705.html.

67. Ron Clutz, "Covid/Climate Prigs Are Out to Spoil Your Day," Climate Matters, December 1, 2021, https://rclutz.com/2021/12/01/covid-climate-prigs-are-out-to-spo il-your-days/.

68. Ross Mittiga, "Political Legitimacy, Authoritarianism, and Climate Change," American Political Science Review (2021): 1–14, https://doi.org/10.1017/S0003055421001301.

69. Ronald Bailey, "To Stop Climate Change Americans Must Cut Energy Use by 90 Percent, Live in 640 Square Feet, and Fly Only Once Every 3 Years, Says Study," Reason, July 2, 2021, https://reason.com/2021/07/02/to-stop-climate-change-americ ans-must-cut-energy-use-by-90-percent-live-in-640-square-feet-and-fly-only-once-ev ery-3-years-says-study/.

70. Jefim Vogel et al., "Socio-Economic Conditions for Satisfying Human Needs at Low Energy Use: An International Analysis of Social Provisioning," Global Environmental Change 69 (July 2021), https://doi.org/10.1016/j.gloenvcha.2021.102287.

71. 1News, "Trio of Covid Scientists Chuffed after Winning Prizes at PM's Awards," YouTube, April 13, 2021, https://www.youtube.com/watch?v=T7XjO-57F4Q.

72. A. R. Ravishankara and Mary M. Glackin, "We're Flattening the Coronavirus Curve. We Can Flatten the Climate Curve, Too.," *Washington Post,* May 19, 2020, https://www.washingtonpost.com/outlook/2020/05/19/coronavirus-action-climate-change/.

73. Marc Morano, "Climate Lockdowns?! Climate Is 'Greatest Threat' to Global Public Health, Say 230 Medical Journals: Declare COVID-19 'Response' Be 'Template' for Climate Response," Climate Depot, September 6, 2021, https://www.climatedepot.com/2021/09/06/further-corruption-of-public-health-orgs-more-than-230-medical-journals-warn-made-up-number-of-1-5c-of-global-warming-could-be-catastrophic-for-health-despite-99-drop-in-climate-rel/.

74. Marc Morano, "Climate Lockdown: 'It's Time to Ban the Sale of Pickup Trucks'— 'Shift Away from Relying on Private Vehicles Entirely,'" Climate Depot, July 16, 2021, https://www.climatedepot.com/2021/07/16/climate-lockdown-its-time-to-ban-the-sale-of-pickup-trucks-shift-away-from-relying-on-private-vehicles-entirely/.

75. Marc Morano, "Climate Lockdowns: *British Medical Journal* Study Calls for Meat & Dairy Price Hikes to Fight 'Climate Change'—Meat Consumption in N. America Must Fall 79%—'Substantially Fewer Journeys by Car,'" Climate Depot, October 9, 2021, https://www.climatedepot.com/2021/10/09/climate-lockdowns-british-medical-journal-study-calls-for-meat-dairy-price-hikes-to-fight-climate-change-meat-consumption-in-n-america-must-fall-79-substantially-fewer-journeys-by-car/.

76. Marc Morano, "*Foreign Policy* Mag: 'What if Democracy & Climate Mitigation Are Incompatible?'—Democracy 'Is Not Necessarily the Path to a Solution. I Might, Instead, Be Part of the Problem,'" Climate Depot, January 11, 2022, https://www.climatedepot.com/2022/01/11/foreign-policy-mag-what-if-democracy-climate-mitigation-are-incompatible-democracy-is-not-necessarily-the-path-to-a-solution-it-might-instead-be-part-of-the-problem/.

77. Marc Morano, "Business Insider Mag: 'Electric Vehicles Won't Save Us—We Need to Get Rid of Cars Completely,'" Climate Depot, November 24, 2021, https://www.climatedepot.com/2021/11/24/business-insider-mag-electric-vehicles-wont-save-us-we-need-to-get-rid-of-cars-completely/.

78. Marc Morano, "Owning a Car Is Outdated '20th Century Thinking' & We Must Move to 'Shared Mobility' to Cut Carbon Emissions," Climate Depot, December 11, 2021, https://www.climatedepot.com/2021/12/11/owning-a-car-is-outdated-20th-century-thinking-we-must-move-to-shared-mobility-to-cut-carbon-emissions-uk-transport-minister-says/.

79. Marc Morano, "First, They Came for Energy, Then Your SUV—& Now: 'Houses Pose More Danger to Climate Than Vehicles,'" August 30, 2021, https://www.climatedepot.com/2021/08/30/first-they-came-for-energy-then-your-suv-now-houses-pose-more-danger-to-climate-than-vehicles/.

80. Marc Morano, "*Vogue* Article Asks, 'Is Having A Baby in 2021 Pure Environmental Vandalism?,'" Climate Depot, May 11, 2021, https://www.climatedepot.com/2021/05/11/vogue-article-asks-is-having-a-baby-in-2021-pure-environmental-vandalism/.

81. Jamie Burton, "Russia's Top YouTubers Set to Lose Millions as Platform Suspends Monetization," *Newsweek,* March 10, 2022, https://www.newsweek.com/russia-youtube-influencers-suspends-monetization-1686690.

82. Marc Morano, "Google & Big Tech Now Treating Russia like Climate Skeptics: 'Google Has Now Suspended Monetization on YouTube for All Users in Russia,'"

Climate Depot, March 11, 2022, https://www.climatedepot.com/2022/03/11/google
-now-treating-russia-like-climate-skeptics-google-has-now-suspended-monetization
-on-youtube-for-all-users-in-russia/.

83. Tom Steyer (@TomSteyer), "To get climate right, let's start with listening to communities of color....," Twitter, February 24, 2020, 11:44 p.m., https://twitter.com/TomSteyer /status/1232164461613465600.

84. Farz Edraki and Ann Arnold, "Could Climate Change Become a Security Issue—and Threaten Democracy?," ABC News (Australia), December 2, 2019, https://www.abc .net.au/news/2019-12-03/climate-change-international-security-risk/11714284.

85. Mark P. Mills, "The Green New Deal Can't Break the Laws of Physics," The Daily Caller, October 27, 2020, https://dailycaller.com/2020/10/27/green-new-deal-laws-of -physics/.

86. Stan Cox, "If There's a World War II–Style Climate Mobilization, It Has to Go All the Way—and Then Some," CounterPunch, September 22, 2016, https://www.counterp unch.org/2016/09/22/if-theres-a-world-war-ii-style-climate-mobilization-it-has-to-go -all-the-way-and-then-some/.

87. Marc Morano, "'Puritans of the Green Deal' Promote 'Unworkable Utopia'—'For the First Time Since It Began, the EU's Agenda Is to Impoverish Europeans,'" Climate Depot, July 27, 2021, https://www.climatedepot.com/2021/07/27/puritans-of-the-gre en-deal-promote-unworkable-utopia-for-the-first-time-since-it-began-the-eus-agenda -is-to-impoverish-europeans/.

88. Christopher Bedford, "How COVID Lockdowns Handed Global Warming Extremists the Tools to Crush Freedom," The Federalist, November 15, 2021, https://thefederali st.com/2021/11/12/how-covid-lockdowns-handed-global-warming-extremists-the-to ols-to-crush-freedom/.

Chapter 13: The Great Reject—Mass Defiance Can Defeat the Great Reset

Epigraph: Carlo Viganò, "Open Letter to President Donald Trump," Catholic Family News, October 30, 2020, https://catholicfamilynews.com/blog/2020/10/30/open-letter-to-pr esident-donald-trump/

1. planetlockdown, "Planet Lockdown: A Documentary," Rumble, January 19, 2022, https://rumble.com/vsw5gf-planet-lockdown-a-documentary.html.

2. C. Douglas Golden, "Warren Says She's Willing to Ban Construction of New Homes in America," Western Journal, January 12, 2020, https://www.westernjournal.com/ warren-says-willing-ban-construction-new-homes-america/.

3. Marc Morano, Green Fraud: Why the Green New Deal Is Even Worse Than You Think (Washington, D.C.: Regnery, 2021), 78, citing Kian Goh, "California's Fires Prove the American Dream Is Flammable," The Nation, December 23, 2019, https:// www.thenation.com/article/archive/california-fires-urban-planning/.

4. Fola Akinnibi, "Biden Scorns 'Defund the Police' as Cities Rush to Spend on Cops," Bloomberg, March 2, 2022, https://www.bloomberg.com/news/articles/2022-03-02/ biden-calls-to-fund-the-police-in-state-of-the-union.

5. County of Butler v. Wolf, 486 F. Supp. 3d 883, 926 (W.D. Pa. 2020), https://casetext .com/case/cnty-of-butler-v-wolf-1.

6. Shawn Langlois, "Carl Sagan Saw Today's 'Demon-Haunted' America Coming over 20 Years Ago," MarketWatch, August 13, 2017, https://www.marketwatch.com/story

/carl-sagan-saw-todays-demon-haunted-america-coming-over-thirty-years-ago-2017
-08-10.

7. Cosmin Dzsurdzsa, "Clip Resurfaces of Trudeau Calling Unvaccinated 'Extremists,
    Misogynists, Racists,'" True North, January 4, 2022, https://tnc.news/2022/01/04/cl
    ip-resurfaces-of-trudeau-calling-unvaccinated-extremists-misogynists-racists/.

8. Alyssa Guzman, "Bill Maher Says Freedom Convoy Truckers Have a Right to Be 'Pissed
    Off' at Elitists Who 'Sit at Home in Their Lululemons' before Comparing Canadian
    PM Justin Trudeau to Hitler for Questioning If the Unvaccinated Should Be 'Tolerated,'"
    Daily Mail, February 12, 2022,https://www.dailymail.co.uk/news/article-10505489
    /Bill-Maher-says-Freedom-Convoy-truckers-right-pissed-elitists.html.

9. Disclose.tv (@disclose.tv), "NOW—Canada's PM Trudeau…," Twitter, February 8,
    2022, 2:48 p.m., https://twitter.com/disclosetv/status/1491136812412436481.

10. Jon Henley, "Macron Declares His Covid Strategy Is to 'Piss Off' the Unvaccinated,"
    The Guardian, January 4, 2022, https://www.theguardian.com/world/2022/jan/04/
    macron-declares-his-covid-strategy-is-to-piss-off-the-unvaccinated.

11. "Ottawa Police Chief: Protesters to Get 'Financial Sanctions,' 'Criminal Charges' Even
    After Event Ends," Conservative News Daily, February 20, 2022, https://www.conse
    rvativenewsdaily.net/breaking-news/ottawa-police-chief-protesters-to-get-financial-sa
    nctions-criminal-charges-even-after-event-ends/.

12. Mackenzie Gray (@Gray_Mackenzie), "A senior police sources [sic] tells us…," Twitter,
    February 19, 2022, 7:50 a.m., https://twitter.com/Gray_Mackenzie/status/149501788
    8486506500.

13. Balaji Srinivasan (@balajis), "'The Soviet security police…," Twitter, February 19, 2022,
    3:16 p.m., https://twitter.com/balajis/status/1495130264166895618.

14. Golfo Alexopoulos, "Stalin and the Politics of Kinship: Practices of Collective
    Punishment, 1920s–1940s," Comparative Studies in Society and History 50, no. 1
    (January 14, 2008): 91–117, https://doi.org/10.1017/S0010417508000066. ; Balaji
    Srinivasan (@balajis), "The Soviet security police."

15. Valerie Volcovici, "Explainer: How Biden Could Use His Whole Government to Take
    on Climate Change," Reuters, January 19, 2021, https://www.reuters.com/article/us
    -usa-biden-climate-policy-explainer-idUSKBN29O260.

16. Tyler O'Neill, "Breaking: Andrew Cuomo Seizes Emergency Powers to Fight Gun
    Violence 'Public Health' Emergency," PJ Media, July 6, 2021, https://pjmedia.com/ne
    ws-and-politics/tyler-o-neil/2021/07/06/breaking-andrew-cuomo-seizes-emergency
    -powers-to-fight-gun-violence-public-health-emergency-n1459811.

17. Patricia McCarthy, "'People Are Dying,' Say Biden and Psaki," American Thinker, July
    17, 2021, https://www.americanthinker.com/blog/2021/07/people_are_dying_say_bi
    den_and_psaki.html; Richard Davis, "'Physician, Cancel Thyself…' Dr. Mercola, One
    of Biden's 'Disinformation Dozen' Removes 25 Years of Content," Chicago Now,
    August 4, 2021, https://www.chicagonow.com/life-tv-dinner/2021/08/doctor-cancel
    -thyself-dr-mercola-one-of-bidens-disinformation-dozen-removes-25-years-of-content/.

18. William M. Briggs, "Capitalism Is Dead: Long Live the Expertocracy. Burnham's The
    Managerial Revolution at 80," William M. Briggs: Statistician to the Stars!, September
    9, 2021, https://wmbriggs.com/post/37075/.

19. Dr Naomi Wolf (@naomirwolf), "'The Great Reject': everyone needs to…," Twitter,
    March 26, 2021, 10:59 a.m., https://twitter.com/naomirwolf/status/13755078370701

39397 (Twitter has deleted Wolf's account, but this tweet is available at the Internet Archive's Wayback Machine: https://web.archive.org/web/20210326181728/https://twitter.com/naomirwolf/status/1375507837070139397).

20. Rooted.wings (@BrittRooted), "ENOUGH IS ENOUGH….," Twitter, August 18, 2021, 12:26 a.m., https://twitter.com/BrittRooted/status/1427849481551106056.

21. Paul Cudenec, "Klaus Schwab and His Great Fascist Reset," Winter Oak, October 5, 2020, https://winteroak.org.uk/2020/10/05/klaus-schwab-and-his-great-fascist-reset/.

22. Glenn Beck, "Letter to Congress: How You Can Fight Back against the Great Reset," Glenn, June 8, 2021, https://www.glennbeck.com/glenn-beck/how-you-can-fight-back-against-the-great-reset.

23. Thomas Sowell, *The Thomas Sowell Reader* (New York: Basic Books, 2011), Google Play Books.

24. Joel Kotkin, "Welcome to the End of Democracy," *The Spectator*, January 8, 2022, https://www.spectator.co.uk/article/welcome-to-the-end-of-democracy.

25. Peter Hitchens (@ClarkeMicah), "If you have at any time…," Twitter, August 15, 2020, 2:16 p.m., https://twitter.com/ClarkeMicah/status/1294699383745916928.

26. Robert F. Kennedy Jr., "People in Authority Lie," Children's Health Defense, August 28, 2020, https://childrenshealthdefense.org/wp-content/uploads/08-31-20-RFK-Jr.-Press-Conference-Transcript.pdf; OneSilentJoy, "Robert F Kennedy Jr in Berlin 28 Aug 2020," YouTube, August 28, 2020, https://www.youtube.com/watch?v=wM7NLlWZD5I&t=4s.

27. Jesse Berger, "Risk It for the Brisket," Medium, March 26, 2021, https://jesse-b-berger.medium.com/risk-it-for-the-brisket-edb282b1e245.

28. Berkeley Lovelace Jr., "WHO Says Pandemic Is Far from Over despite High Vaccination Rates in Some Countries," CNBC, May 17, 2021, https://www.cnbc.com/2021/05/17/who-says-pandemic-is-far-from-over-despite-high-vaccination-rates-in-some-countries.html.

29. William M. Briggs, "The Great Reset and Our Inevitable Expertocracy," William M. Briggs: Statistician to the Stars!, August 26, 2021, https://wmbriggs.com/post/37134/.

30. Jordan Schachtel, "How Ron DeSantis Saved America from COVID Tyranny," The Dossier (Substack), June 1, 2021, https://dossier.substack.com/p/how-ron-desantis-saved-america-from.

31. Jay Bhattacharya (@DrJBhattacharya), "A reckoning on the catastrophe…," Twitter, January 15, 2022, 3:01 p.m., https://twitter.com/DrJBhattacharya/status/1482442714759106564.

32. Tim Hinchliffe, "Brazil Says 'No' to Great Reset: 'Totalitarian Social Control Is Not the Remedy for Any Crisis,'" The Sociable, December 8, 2020, https://sociable.co/government-and-policy/brazil-says-no-great-reset-totalitarian-social-control-not-remedy-crisis/.

33. C. J. Hopkins, "The Last Days of the Covidian Cult," OffGuardian, January 18, 2022, https://off-guardian.org/2022/01/18/the-last-days-of-the-covidian-cult/.

34. Healthful Heart, "Dr. Anne McCloskey of Ireland…," Facebook, March 14, 2021, https://www.facebook.com/watch/?v=126163972783869.

35. Anne McCloskey, "Rapid Response: Re: Covid-19: Social Murder, They Wrote—Elected, Unaccountable, and Unrepentant," *British Medical Journal* 372, no. 314 (March 4, 2021), https://www.bmj.com/content/372/bmj.n314/rr-33.

36. Paul Cudenec, "Klaus Schwab and His Great Fascist Reset," Winter Oak, October 5, 2020, https://winteroak.org.uk/2020/10/05/klaus-schwab-and-his-great-fascist-reset/.

37. Ibid.

INDEX

A

Abbott, Greg, 334
Abbott, Tony, 2, 37
abuses, 92, 94
　of children, 107, 249
　of human rights, 241
　mental, 15
　of emergency powers, 9,
　　11–12, 102, 187
　substance, 120–21, 141, 306
academia, 16, 25, 62, 70, 169–70,
　241, 335
accountability, xvii, 3, 13, 51, 77,
　107, 165, 315, 322
ACLU (American Civil Liberties
　Union), 220–21, 257
activists, 13, 25, 33, 68, 76–77, 79,
　105, 131, 178, 194, 205, 222,
　239, 241, 248, 250–54, 260,
　262, 266, 273–77, 280–85, 288,
　291–92, 295, 297, 302–3, 306,
　308–11, 317, 319, 322
Adams, Jerome, 144, 159
addiction, 7, 105, 120, 264
Adhanom, Tedros. *See*
　Ghebreyesus, Tedros Adhanom
administrative state, 3, 35, 133,
　273, 276, 308, 311, 322, 327
Afghanistan, 37, 100
Africa, 12, 44–45, 112–13, 138,
　263
Agenda 21, 14, 249–50
Ahlander, Johan, 109–10

AIDS, 16, 46, 48–49, 53–55, 275
AIM (Aspiration Impact
　Measurement), 315
Alonso, Pedro L., 128
Amazon, 7, 25, 108, 122, 200,
　222, 239, 244, 248
American Academy of Pediatrics,
　162
American Civil Liberties Union,
　220–21, 257
American Institute for Economic
　Research, 30, 45, 75, 139, 188
Anderson, Jeffrey H., 75, 158, 161
anthrax, 117
antidepressants, 120–21
anti-vaxxer, 203
app
　CommonPass, 203
　Digital Health Pass, 205
Apple, 25, 193–94, 230, 239
Araújo, Ernesto, 335
Ardern, Jacinda, 146, 181
Argentina, 41
Article 48 of the Weimar
　Republic, 12
Asia, 44, 116
Asian flu, 54, 130, 139–41
Aspiration Impact Measurement
　(AIM), 315
Atlas, Scott, 106–7, 162, 179–80
Australia, 37, 42, 58, 88, 101,
　103, 128, 209–11, 266, 288,
　309